FIELDWORK

9/02

UNIVERSITY OF
WOLVERHAMPTON
ENTERPRISE LTD.

LR/LEND/001

SAGE Benchmarks in Social Research Methods

FIELDWORK

VOLUME II

The Fieldwork Experience
Methods and Methodology

EDITED BY
CHRISTOPHER POLE

SAGE Publications
London • Thousand Oaks • New Delhi

SAGE Publications Ltd
1 Oliver's Yard
55 City Road
London EC1Y 1SP

SAGE Publications Inc.
2455 Teller Road
Thousand Oaks, California 91320

SAGE Publications India Pvt Ltd
B-42, Panchsheel Enclave
Post Box 4109
New Delhi 110 017

British Library Cataloguing in Publication data

A catalogue record for this book is available from the British Library

ISBN 1-4129-0030-1 (set of four volumes)

Library of Congress Control Number: 2004096709

Typeset by Kestrel Data, Exeter, Devon
Printed and bound in Great Britain by TJ International Ltd, Padstow, Cornwall

CONTENTS

VOLUME 2:
THE FIELDWORK EXPERIENCE. METHODS AND METHODOLOGY

Section One
Early Days in the Field

Section Two
Sampling in the Field

Section Three
Observing in the Field

Section Four
Field Talk: Interviews and Conversations

Section Five
Documents and The Field

Section Six
Viewing the Field: Visual Methods

Section Seven
Reflecting on Fieldwork Experience

Section One
Early Days in the Field

21

First Days in the Field*

Blanche Geer

Participant-observation studies, as we have been doing them,[1] follow a pattern of several years in the field, a period of analytic model-building, outlining, and drafting, and the final assembly of data in the form of description, evidence, and argument for the monograph. The beginning of the final stage, when we go back to the field notes to see if there is evidence for what we want to say, is a time of suspense and self-questioning. It brings up a point seldom mentioned, in monographs but frequently discussed by field workers among themselves: the relationship of initial field experiences to our thinking before entering the field and after the field work has been completed. There is so much reiteration of findings in our work that we sometimes think we have always known what we find (everybody knows it; why bother to write a book?) and at other times that it all became clear in some magical way on the very first day in the field.

Most field workers include in their notes material which is not narration, quotation, or description, but comment. It occurred to me that I might use, as a partial answer to questions about what happens in initial field work, the comments recorded during my first days in the field on our current research. Do strategies and concepts change? By what mechanisms? How is subsequent field work affected, and how much of the first experience gets into a final monograph?

Method

Field work on our present study of undergraduates at the University of Kansas began during the summer orientation period for prospective freshmen in

Source: *Sociologists at Work*, 1964, Basic Books, pp. 322-344.
*A chronicle of research in progress.

1959.[2] At the end of a six-hour day in the field, I dictated an account of what I had seen and heard, occasionally inserting comments on the material or appending an interpretive summary. In this report, I shall use the thirty-four comments in the first eight days of field notes. They have been edited when in need of grammatical correction, and names have been changed. When comments duplicate each other, I use one but tabulate all of them as a rough measure of my initial interests.

In addition to the comments, I shall draw on letters and memoranda exchanged by project members before entering the field and the original proposal for a one-year pilot study. The full proposal and a memorandum written after the summer field work complete the documentation.

Beginnings of the Undergraduate Study – The Previews

Tentative arrangements for a study of undergraduates were made with the University of Kansas while we were still engaged on a study of the University's medical school. During the academic year 1958-1959, we met with members of the administration interested in the project. They provided a gradual introduction to the University and indicated what they wished it to become.

In November of 1958, we submitted a proposal to investigate the following question: What are the differing perspectives on academic work characteristic of an undergraduate college, and how are these influenced by participation in student groups characterized by the possession of a student culture? Our method would be participant observation and interviews of a random sample of one or more subgroups of the student body, beginning with premedical students.

On January 22, 1959, at a lunch meeting with members of the administration, the dean[3] mentioned that the University conducted summer orientation sessions, or previews, for prospective freshmen. In notes on the conversation I summarized what he said as follows:

> Throughout the month of July, groups of prefreshmen come to the University for talks by administrators and for a session of filling out forms. ... Approximately half the prospective freshman class is processed in July to relieve the pressure at fall orientation time. Each preview group contains about two hundred students with an approximately equal number of boys and girls. The selection is first-come first-served, so that the groups are mixed in respect to the schools of the University (engineering, fine arts, liberal arts, and so forth) they plan to enter and the region from which they come. There is, however, some tendency for students in the same high school to send in their applications together so that sometimes there are groups that know each other at a preview, particularly from the larger high schools in the state.

In June, I talked to the director of the previews, who agreed to supply me with the names and home towns of students attending, banquet tickets, and a schedule of events. There would be two previews a week—the first on Monday and Tuesday, the second on Thursday and Friday—for the first three weeks of July.

I arrived on campus on the morning of the first preview (July 6) and picked up the list of names from the director's office. At the Union, where orientation sessions were being held, I introduced myself to previewers and attended meetings with them to get their comments and make appointments to meet later on. In the afternoon, many students had free time which gave me a chance to talk to them at length in the Union or dormitories or to explore the campus with them. At six o'clock, everybody went to a social hour and banquet, and I received a name tag and table assignment along with the previewers. After dinner, the previewers again had free time (at some previews there was a dance) until the house meeting held after closing hours at ten thirty.

The second morning was taken up for most students by placement and physical examinations, which left me little time for interviewing. My best opportunities were during the afternoon free time, at dinner, and the dance.

This pattern of going to formal sessions and interviewing during free time followed our plans for the field work. It produced enough data on the previewers' backgrounds and their expectations of what college would be like to orient us. We did not anticipate one feature of the previews which materially changed our plans. No one had told us, thinking it unimportant perhaps, that college seniors acted as speakers, entertainers, and hosts at the dinner table. They were also dormitory counselors.

Analysis of Field Comments

Data, no matter how you collect them, are recalcitrant. They will not always answer the questions you put to them. In this report, since I am dealing with my own work, I want to be particularly careful to stick to the data, to avoid reading more into the comments than is in them by interpreting them in the light of our subsequent findings. I have, therefore, subjected the comments, somewhat grandiosely, to the kind of analysis we use in regular studies, collecting all data in the notes that bear on a topic (in this case all comments), grouping them by subtopic, and then looking to see what I have. The thirty-four comments fall into five categories: the field worker's role, the problem of empathy, the solution of anticipated problems, the nature of working hypotheses, and the recognition of a major theme. I shall consider the categories in order, noting for each of them the number of comments included. Discussion of the relationship of the comments to our original planning of the study and the monograph we are now writing follows the analysis.

The Field Workers Role

To those who have not done field work, the adoption of a role with informants presents a difficult problem. There is a large literature on the pitfalls of role and failures of rapport, but it is usually written with the interviewer rather than the observer in mind. The interviewer starts from scratch with an informant. He must rapidly establish himself securely enough in a relationship with another person to permit intimate questioning. The participant-observer establishes a relationship with a group. To a single informant, he is much less of a stranger because he moves freely in the informant's own setting and can be seen interacting with other members of the informant's group.

If the setting and the group are reasonably familiar to the observer, his problem in initiating a role is a matter of judicious negatives. He should not have the manner or appearance of any group which his informant group distinguishes sharply from itself. This does not mean forcing identity with the informant group; it does mean that the observer of students, if he wishes a good understanding with them, will avoid the manner of teacher and authoritative adult. Selecting a neutral, approachable role in the sense of acting and speaking in ways which are not threatening to informants smooths the first days of participant observation. But the field worker must soon become aware of the role he plays in more detail to assess its effect. The first comment in my field notes on role deals with this problem.

> 7/9/59: I am conscious that part of my role for [the previewers] is an educational one. I am somebody in a profession that they have not run up against before, and I have a lot of knowledge about universities that they could use. This is quite different from the role you play with medical students who are tolerant of you but not seeking anything.

Occasioned by a previewer who wanted me to tell him whether he must study medicine to be a psychologist, the comment is a warning to myself: Don't wise up your informant! More subtly, the comment suggests the field worker's effort to uncover informants' concepts of who he is and what he wants to know, since such definitions govern what people tell him and how they say it, whether they will volunteer or must be questioned.

After this warning, role in the sense of presentation of self does not turn up in the confessional of the comments, but I become conscious of doing a number of things in the field not planned in our proposal or memoranda and of leaving other things undone. I am concerned about role in the sense of my function as coworker on the larger study of which the previews are a small part. After five days in the field, I evaluate this role as follows.

> 7/13/59: I want briefly to take a look at the kind of questions I have been asking and my general goals during this period of field work. First of all, I've been getting background data [on previewers]; this is necessary if we are to

understand the types of students we are dealing with. Second, I've been trying, evidently, to pick up a tremendous body of facts and names, about campus organizations, slang, and customs. This is a natural thing for any field worker, trying to orient himself, to do, and I think it is particularly important in our study if we are to identify groups, as it is by these means that we are able to separate students from each other and recognize them easily and quickly. In other words, if we get all this stuff down we may be able to sort them out without going to such lengthy interviews as this [a three-hour talk with a senior].

I seem to have the feeling that information of this kind is necessary in order to be able to find [the boundaries of] groups. I also seem to be developing a technique for next fall in which I talk with a student long enough to get his confidence thoroughly and make plans to meet him next fall and attend some class or activity and get to know his friends. This, I think, will be quite a reasonable way of bounding groups, at the same time learning more about the actual activity.

I think I have developed an impatience as a result of our various theoretical and methodological innovations of last year. I apparently want to go right out and put data into perspectives and tables.[4] I am impatient with the mountain of background information that I must first learn before I can interpret any of this. ... Of course, there are repeats and reiterations coming already, and these are the material of perspectives. At the same time, an outline of the place is forming in my mind, a kind of topographical map in which it becomes more and more easy to locate what the various students say to me.

As I begin to see what we need to learn and ways of learning it, my conception of my role in the study rapidly expands from that of interviewer of prefreshmen to general spadeworker. I do not want to lose the opportunity presented by the previews of laying the groundwork for what we will do in the fall. Getting campus background, learning the lingo, and setting up future meetings with informants are important. Almost in spite of myself, I have embarked on an attempt to apprehend undergraduate culture as a whole.

Our proposal seems forgotten. Of course, there were not enough pre-medical students at the previews for me to concentrate on them. To limit myself to our broader objective, the liberal-arts college student, was difficult. The previewers did not group themselves according to the school or college of the University they planned to enter. Out of ordinary politeness (at the dinner table, for instance), I found myself talking to prefreshmen planning careers in engineering, pharmacy, business, and fine arts, as well as the liberal arts. Perhaps it is impossible to stick to a narrow objective in the field. If, as will nearly always be the case, there are unanticipated data at hand, the field worker will broaden his operations to get them. Perhaps he includes such data because they will help him to understand his planned objectives, but he may very well go after them simply because, like the mountain, they are there.[5]

Three comments in the field notes deal with role. I have quoted the one dealing with role as presentation of self and one of two extended discussions of my role as coworker in the undergraduate study.

The Problem of Empathy

Developing empathy with informants as a group often presents more of a problem to field workers planning a study, at least in anticipation, than the adoption of an interaction-facilitating role. Role in this sense is a public stance which all of us practice, but empathy is personal. Field workers are not free of prejudice, stereotypes, or other impediments to the understanding of out-groups. But to study, as we proposed to do, the experience of going to college from the point of view of the student necessarily entails at least reconition of personal bias in order to achieve empathy with the informant group.

Throughout the time the undergraduate study was being planned, I was bored by the thought of studying undergraduates. They looked painfully young to me. I considered their concerns childish and unformed. I could not imagine becoming interested in their daily affairs – in classes, study, dating, and bull sessions. I had memories of my own college days in which I appeared as a child: overemotional, limited in understanding, with an incomprehensible taste for milk shakes and convertibles.

Remembering my attitude as I began to sort out the thirty-four comments in the field notes on the prefreshmen, I expected to find evidence of this unfavorable adult bias toward adolescents. But on the third day in the field I am already taking the students' side.

> 7/9/59: Some of these statements by boys like Joe Ropes may sound overdramatic, or self-conscious, or just plain foolish to an adult, and yet … when [you] see their serious and tlhoughtful faces you realize you [are] getting the best fruit of their experience and thoughts and you take them very seriously when they make statements like this.

Humorless seriousness evidently does not fit the stereotype of college students I took with me into the field. In my own person, I might have kidded the students out of it, but as a field worker I must listen and record. My disbelief is reserved for the comment:

> 7/9/59: Here, again, this sounds just too fatuous but I can not do anything but repeat that these kids are speaking seriously from their hearts. They're not trying to be humorous, and they're really not trying to brag. They're explaining the world as they see it to me in [a] kind of man-to-man fashion, and they're not trying to be overearnest about it or anything. It's just apparently a normal conversation with a kid of this age, at least on such an important day in his life as his first day of a college preview. [This observer's comment comes after a student said, "I think getting into student politics here would be a good thing. You get to be well known and people get to like you. I guess that's an important thing if you want to have your place in the sun."]

I have lost the adult tendency to laugh at such statements, but I think my colleagues will. (They are reading the field notes but are not yet on the scene.) To read what the students say is not as compelling as experiencing it in the flesh, hearing the voices, seeing the gesture and expression. Responding to the students with a solemnity equal to their own, I have fallen into empathy by acting it out.

Later in the field work, I attend a dance in the Trail Room of the Student Union and comment as follows.

> 7/16/59: I am amazed again, in starting the field work, at how quickly ... you respond in quite other ways than you ordinarily would. I now react with a startled reaction when some dean or other says, as Dean Brown did the other day, "Isn't it boring, talking to all these children?" No, it is not boring when you are doing it, nor is the behavior odd. It has a great deal of inevitability. [What I am referring to here as not being odd is the shyness of the boys at the dance; great numbers of boys walking up and down and standing in groups and some sitting with their heads in their hands, looking at the girls and presumably wondering if they want to dance with them. One or two Romeos leaned nonchalantly against a pillar or two and surveyed the scene without becoming a part of it.]

This comment is part of the notes for the last day of field work on the previews. My reaction to the dean's question suggests not only anger at his failure to understand my job (whatever field work is, it is not boring) but also anger on the student's behalf: why call them children? I am taking up cudgels on their side. Perhaps the rapid development of empathy for a disliked group does not surprise old hands at field work, since it seems to happen again and again. But it surprised me; I comment on it seven times in eight days. Three of the comments have been quoted here.

The Solution of Anticipated Problems

The development of empathy in the field is not the only surprise an observer experiences. Theory, other studies, and common sense make one anticipate difficulties which do not materialize. People one expects to be hostile are not; situations one expects to be incoherent reveal themselves as relatively easily grasped when one is in the midst of them; apparently difficult problems of finding subjects or grouping them in manageable categories are easier in the doing than in theoretical discussion. There are only three comments in the field notes on anticipated problems. One deals with the kind of continuing concern one seldom puts down on paper.

> 7/8/59: Throughout my contacts with administrative officials on this day I express surprise at their friendliness and my ease of access to them. I evidently expect them to ask me personal questions about students.

Absence of one problem provokes anticipation of another. Friendly administrators may expect information about students it would be impossible for us to give while keeping students' confidence. To deal with this problem, we later began efforts to educate members of the administration in field workers' ethics.

In the medical-school study, student fraternity groups were a major variable, meaningfully related to academic perspectives in the freshmen year.[6] But we anticipated serious problems in identifying similar groups among nine thousand undergraduates. We thought and wrote on the formation of groups and the technical problems of observing them. Here is a comment intended to allay some of our fears.

> 7/6/59: I think that this one afternoon and evening has given us some idea of the friend-making process at the beginning of college. When you see it happening under your nose this way, it seems so natural that I wonder why we ever had any questions about it. I think you could make a typology somewhat as follows: There are the students who come from the same high schools or nearby towns and have some acquaintance with each other, and if there is a small number of these they get together and stay together, at least at the beginning of school. It is probable, for instance, that Tom, Dick, Harry ... from [a small town] will room together in some combination. Those students who come from Kansas City can get together rather easily, although they have come from different schools, by placing each other by means of country clubs, addresses, and boys they have dated. All of these [cues], of course, [are] in addition to the obvious, immediately grasped detail of hair, manner, and clothing. Isolated students from different towns pair up with their assigned roommates for the preview, and they perhaps make a friend to room with the rest of the year or may simply take their chances on being assigned a good person.

Watching people initiate friendships lessens the mystery. Seeing ten students choose a roommate is to begin to structure the activity. The observer now has a list of commonalities to look for: home town, country club, dress, and temporary propinquity.

Getting into the field disposed of another problem.

> 7/16/59: This is really a summary comment. I had the idea before I started this field work that because of the complete turnover in students each time it would be a rather disjointed affair in which the observer did not get a cumulative and continuing sense of growing knowledge of what college is all about. I find that I was quite mistaken in this and that this feeling is going on at a great rate and that I am already at the stage in which I quite falsely pretend to ignorance to get somebody's viewpoint on such things as the fraternity.

Why do field workers so frequently anticipate problems that do not materialize? We do it on each new study. We underestimate people's trust in our neutrality, their lack of interest, perhaps, if we seem to be doing no harm. And we project the theoretical problems into the field. Because the process of group formation is difficult to conceptualize, we suppose it will be difficult to observe. We expect ephemeral, unstructured situations like the previews to appear incoherent. Perhaps such mistakes are a necessary part of our efforts to design the study in advance.

The Nature of Working Hypotheses

Although the term *observer* suggests passivity, a participant-observer in the field is at once reporter, interviewer, and scientist. On the scene, he gets the story of an event by questioning participants about what is happening and why. He fills out the story by asking people about their relation to the event, their reactions, opinions, and evaluation of its significance. As interviewer, he encourages an informant to tell his story or supply an expert account of an organization or group. As scientist, he seeks answers to questions, setting up hypotheses and collecting the data with which to test them.

One type of hypothesis is drawn up before entering the field. Essentially a list of variables which theory or common sense suggests may be relevant to what the investigator wishes to study, the hypothesis, for the field worker, takes the practical form of kinds of people to see, places to go, and questions to ask. Although he spends a good part of his time just listening to informants or drifting along with a group to see what will happen, the observer also forms hypotheses during the field-work period. These are called working hypotheses. Some of them are so simple they can be tested immediately by having a look at a group or asking questions of informants. Others, usually based on an accumulation of data, predict an event or state that will behave in specified ways under certain conditions. These undergo a prolonged process of testing and retesting, preferably by more than one field worker, over a period of months and years. There is no finality about them. They must be refined, expanded, and developed. Checking out may depend on the return of the organizational calendar to its beginning point or the election of a fresh group of officials.

The concept of working hypothesis is not difficult, but field workers often have trouble explaining it to others and sometimes to themselves. The concept is clear as a generality, but its mechanics, the doing of it, smacks of magic. Untrained observers, for instance, can spend a day in a hospital and come back with one page of notes and no hypotheses. It was a hospital, they say; everyone knows what hospitals are like. My comments in the field notes suggest that working hypotheses are a product of the field data itself and of whatever ideas the fieldworker can summon. The initial stimulus may come from repetition or anomalies in the data which catch the observer's attention so that he searches his mind for explanations. Or he may start from the opposite end – what is in his head – and search the data for evidence of stereotypes from the general culture or notions derived from discussions with colleagues, previous research, and reading.

I do not wish to dignify an impromptu process by formal discussion. My field-note comments are not technical. They are summaries, not of an entire day's work, but of parts of it drawn together into tentative statements of findings, often in quasi-quantitative language. A comment at the end of the first day's field work shows I have been using the general hypothesis: previewers will have concrete knowledge of academic arrangements in college. (We had drawn up a list of questions to test this proposition before I went into the field.) But:

> 7/6/59: The tremendous ignorance of the prefreshmen of college is somewhat startling. They don't know how many hours of classes there will be. I think they are going to get a big surprise when they find that they may have only one class in the morning and another late in the afternoon on a given day. They have many different notions of how many hours of study they are going to get in.

One day's observation has shaken the prefield hypothesis – students have specific knowledge of the academic side of college before entrance – and substituted the hypothesis that they do not.

The comment continues with a statement about an area of college life we did not plan to study. We had no hypotheses about it, no list of questions prepared.

> 7/6/59 (continued): [The previewers] have very little notion of the tremendous numbers of organizations and activities open to them on the campus. Their ideas are rather limited to the advantages of learning manners, meeting girls, singing or other musical activities, and occasionally sports.

It is not clear why I was struck by the fact that previewers do not talk about college activities. We had on hand University bulletins listing hundreds of organizations. I may have picked up the notion that activities were important from conversation with seniors even on this first day.

It is clear, however, that in the concluding portion of the comment I am drawing on stereotypes in the general culture.

> 7/6/59 (continued): Sports seem, so far, with this group to be a pretty minor undertaking. I wonder if by any chance there is some selective factor acting here and the athletes or even those interested in athletics do not even show up at previews? No freshman has mentioned big football week ends or college rah-rah shindigs in any connection.

Athletes turned up at subsequent previews to lay my sampling doubt at rest, but at the time the hold on me of the tradition of collegiate sports and big week ends was strong. I very tentatively state the working hypothesis that they are not interested.

The first day in the field leaves me with three working hypotheses, each expressed, interestingly enough, in negative form. If I did my work well on subsequent days in the field, I was on the lookout for data to substantiate or disprove these propositions. Reading the educational literature, as we continued to do in the field, probably supplied me with another working hypothesis: college students are not interested in "culture" or religion. There is no comment on these points until July 16, perhaps because I was not getting much data.

> 7/16/59: They had no notion of "cultural advantages" in the way of concerts, lectures, and so on. I noticed again at the dinner the very solemn and attentive faces that watched the students playing the violin and piano. The faces of the dean's staff and the senior students wore that half-smile of gracious appreciation which particularly in the Middle West, I think, accompanies or encourages a performer – or perhaps what I'm describing is a middle-class phenomenon. All the faces of the freshmen that I could see as I ranged around the room with my eyes, however, were quite unsmiling. It was impossible to tell whether they liked it or didn't like it, but it was clear that they had no social conventions of the proper listener's face.
>
> I haven't heard anybody talk down culture nor have I heard anybody talk it up. It is the same with religion. Those who are religious reveal it by their conversation about something else as very much a part of their lives and connected with their choice of a fraternity or a profession.

The working hypothesis proposed is again negative but more complex than those about sports and knowledge of academic matters, which were relatively simple to test. In a group of x previewers, so many express interest in college sports; so many do not. It is a matter of asking the question and counting. The comment above suggests that previewers use their religion when making important decisions. This is a two-step hypothesis. It directs me to look for religious influences only under certain conditons. It is a statement of the logical type: if this, then that.

If some working hypotheses mercifully narrow the area the field workers must observe by specifying a relationship between variables, others ask him to broaden his perspective, to look at something small and apparently unimportant as a matter of regional history.

> 7/13/59: I had a conversation the other night with Mary and Dave Newell [sociologists], in which they asked me about the new field work, and I told them as an amusing anecdote about the stress in the fraternities on the teaching of manners. Mary was appalled and said she thought she should immediately leave the Middle West, at least before the great quantities of KU freshmen began to spread finger bowls on the streets of the Plaza. She seemed extremely upset [she is an English girl who has been over here about three years] and seemed to think that this sort of thing was the downfall of education and of America. David said that, on the contrary, he found it very heartening as it was clear the future generations of Kansas Citians would already know what to do with their finger bowls because their fathers, who had been to KU, would be able to teach them as children. And in this way the progress of the race would go on. I concurred in this.
>
> The image of KU as a civilizer taking the grandchildren of the frontier at least one step along the path to a world comparable, at least at the dinner table, all over the world for "educated people," is a good perspective, I think, and one that we must not forget. In this way, it looks quite reasonable for a student

whose parents have a grocery store in that distant Kansas town to spend four
years acquiring the rudiments of manners that he was not taught at home, and
with these he can go on to the real business of life and study in graduate school.

Perhaps because my friends were not midwesterners, they suggested an
important relationship to me, putting manners in a historical perspective. My
working hypothesis expanded: look for evidence that training in the social
graces is a major function of the University.

Inclusive hypotheses, of course, cannot be immediately tested in the field.
If something is really important, we should expect to find it cropping out in
many sectors of college life. Evidence for and against must be accumulated
throughout the study; we must look for it in classes, living groups, and
everyday activities. Detailed hypotheses derived from one's own or other
people's work on similar institutions may also be useful models for the field
worker, whether or not they can be immediately checked. In a long postscript
to the summer field notes, I try to relate data on the previewers to a complex
model of student development over time which we used for the medical
school.[7]

> 7/16/59: No one so far has made any distinction between practical and
> impractical learning in the fashion of the medical students. I used this as a
> probe a couple of times and got uncomprehending looks. What there is in
> college is something to learn, and then in another compartment are their
> aspirations toward various positions and professions ...
>
>   Again, [the previewers] have no smartalecky knowledgeableness about rules
> and regulations of how to beat the dean or the test or anything else. College is a
> very serious place, and at least at a preview you don't think about these things
> in connection with it. In this way, they are very similar to the medical-school
> freshmen, and it will be interesting to see if the conflict between learning for
> the professor and learning for yourself develops in these students. I know I
> certainly had an extremely acute case of it as a college student, to the point of
> wondering whether I should go on.

Working with the hypothesis that previewers may have attitudes toward
studying similar to those of medical-school upperclassmen, I find they have
instead the idealistic acceptance of college of medical-school freshmen at
entrance. Since the latter rapidly become test-wise, I tentatively advance the
hypothesis that previewers will also, when they get into college. The basic
hypothesis – attitudes toward academic work arise in response to some facet
of college experience – is in two steps with a specific time condition. It can be
tested only in the fall. Although our plan was to talk to prefreshmen, I
increasingly found myself with older students, present to direct the previews,
who told me about the college in great detail. I was acquiring, as I continued
to interview freshmen, an idea of what was ahead of them and the contrast in
knowledge, interests, and manner between prefreshmen and upperclassmen.
The seniors spoke frequently about activities and cultural-advantages; previewers did not. The sense of contrast was an unanticipated consequence of

what I regarded as a mistake in my field behavior. The next comment reflects information picked up from seniors and staff.

> 7/16/59: Here is an addition to the conversation with Betty Jones [Student Union staff]. She said, "There are some students here who spend practically all their time on activities. I don't know when they do any studying. And really I don't know sometimes what things are coming to. On Monday night they have house meetings in the dorms, and that takes two hours. On Wednesday night there's a dance, and on Thursday night there are all kinds of other meetings."
>
> It is quite clear that the [preview] students are unprepared for this wealth of competition for their time, this wealth of choice, and I would say that probably only the ones with something very specific in mind are going to get over the realization of this variety as a painful and difficult thing when it comes to them after they arrive. This is really a prediction, I suppose, and I feel that it is reinforced by their earnestness and wanting to do well in their studying and have their family be proud of them, which is going to set up a conflict between all these fascinating things and their rather weak direction in themselves. They want to study, but they don't know what and they don't know how much. They are earnest and sincere, but they have no guideposts. They look to me at the moment like ... a bunch of very sweet lambs being led into a slaughter of decisions to make, pressures to withstand, and moral fiber to reinforce. And yet many of them speak regretfully of their casual high-school years, and you get the strong flavor of missed opportunities and lack of foresight.
>
> This is not true of all students, and I think I am right in saying that the ones from the small schools far out in the state are more apt to have experienced a studious atmosphere in high school.

Provided by seniors with a view of college as full of decisions, pressures, and demands in addition to the academic (to be checked out later) and sufficient acquaintance with previewers to suggest that they do not see it this way, I am possessed of an elaborated hypothesis about change and major learning areas in college.

The five comments quoted in this section (four additional examples are omitted) suggest that the field worker makes constant use of working hypotheses from many sources. My use of hypotheses falls roughly into three sequential types. The first operation consisted of testing a crude yes-or-no proposition. By asking informants or thinking back over volunteered information in the data ("nearly all students today" or "no student"), I stated a working hypothesis in the comments and began the second operation of the sequence: looking for negative cases or setting out deliberately to accumulate positive ones. At the second stage, working with negatively expressed hypotheses gave me a specific goal. One instance that contradicts what I say is enough to force modification of the hypothesis. It is a process of elimination in which I try to build understanding of *what is* by pinning down *what is not*.

The third stage of operating with hypotheses in the field involves two-step formulations and eventually rough models. Hypotheses take the form of predictions about future events which may take place under specific conditions or changes in informants over time in conjunction with events. Needless to say, particularly in the first days in the field, the worker is never at the same stage with all his data; he may be operating at the yes-or-no level in one area and advancing to the model stage with another at any given time.

Recognition of a Major Theme

Participant-observers sometimes say that the major themes of a study appeared very early in the field of work, although they may have been unrecognized. The field comments present an opportunity to investigate the phenomenon – one case in what should be a larger study.

Is there early and sudden insight? If so, what brings it about? On what grounds can an observer predict that a major theme will be central to the study? To get at my reasoning retrospectively, I take the comments related to recognition of a possible major theme in chronological order. After the first day in the field, I tentatively suggest a relationship between two reiterated findings.

> 7/6/59: I had been probing very gently all day when I asked students about KU as to whether their image of it was a place where you did not study but just had a good time, but I had gotten no flavor of this from any of the students I've talked to. They seem to be very serious about college and, if they were not, were pretending to it or were simply overawed by its social challenge. I think this is part of their saying it is such a big place, certainly a place where you come with some trepidation and with respect.

Since I talked to as many visibly different types of previewers as possible, I was interested that, even after probing, no student provided expected data. As statements on "bigness" were volunteered, I regarded them with added confidence.[8] Considering the comment now, we can say that my tentative statement of the relationship between the academic seriousness of the previewers and their notion that KU is a big place takes the form (following Polya) that A is made somewhat more plausible by B.[9]

The next day I comment on another form of seriousness.

> 7/7/59: Throughout this day there are small indirect references to the fact that I have found students more serious about academic affairs than I expected. From Dean Brown's conversation, I get the notion that the administration is just as serious about educating them in the social realm as are the students themselves. This is evidently a major change in my orientation to the college.

While the increment is not great, if previewers are serious about social matters (C) as well as academic (A), A becomes more plausible. The dean's concern about the social realm helps still more.

On July 8, I announce "bigness" as a major theme because it is frequent and widespread.[10]

7/8/59: One major theme is evidently already coming out in today's field notes: KU is a very big place. I am already comparing coming to KU as similar to going to New York City [to Eastern kids].

If I think there is a relationship between academic seriousness (*A*) and "bigness" (*B*), to feel certain about *B*, in the primitive analysis I am conducting in the field, increases my confidence in A once more.

Later in the same day's notes, I speculate about the origins of seriousness.

7/8/59: In summary of these two days of field work, I feel frustrated at having talked to a very few students, and yet at the same time I feel that I have the beginning of some sound knowledge of how things are up here and that this will increase if I attend more previews. There already seems to be some repetition in the students' reasons for coming to KU, the amount they expect to study, and the general serious academic outlook that they have. They are more focused on academic matters here at the beginning than you would expect, but I have an idea this may be because these things appear manageable or more manageable to them than the great unspoken questions about whether they will make it socially. They have real fears about this last and very much of a do-or-die attitude, I think, although they did not express this to me directly. Real life has begun, and if you don't make it now perhaps you never will.

The existence of seriousness about academic and social aspects of college (*A* and *C*) is made more understandable, hence plausible, if there is evidence of common cause: previewers think college is "real life" (*D*). We have an explanatory proposition: *D* leads to A + C.

On the third day in the field, taking a subgroup of the preview population – prospective graduate students – I explain their seriousness by the fact that for them college is a step in an irreversible career sequence.

7/9/59: Apparently the recent introduction of psychology into the high schools has had a great effect, and that, plus nuclear physics, is leading many students, who probably would have before been at a loss if they did not want to be doctors, to think of graduate work and academic research careers. These kids are taking a really big jump in coming to college because they have no intention of going back to the small town which they came from, and they are aware that there would be no place for their knowledge there.

Since an irreversible career sequence (D_1) is certainly "real life," we now have a proposition of the form $D_1 = A$. Plausible explanation of seriousness in a subgroup lends greater strength to the proposition $D \rightarrow A + C$ for the population as a whole.[11]

At the time of the fourth preview, although I do not use the phrase "major theme," I make a last statement associating the "bigness" of the University, academic seriousness, and seriousness about social life.

7/16/59: I have so far found absolutely nothing to contradict the image of KU students, prefreshmen that is, as very serious and in many cases academic-minded. Their fears are of its bigness, possible unfriendliness, and snobbishness and how hard the work will be.

In the primitive analysis carried on during field work, I now seem to take it for granted that previewers define college as real life and that their seriousness toward it and reference to it as big express this definition $(A + B + C = D)$.

In what sense can we say that I recognized a major theme in the eight days of field work? Certainly there is no flash of insight, no sudden revelation. The formulation proceeds slowly along lines of other working-hypothesis sequences, but the data bear up under elaboration. Unlike some of the working hypotheses mentioned earlier, the "seriousness" theme does not peter out. According to the comments, the field notes are full of it. I cannot turn up a negative case. As at least part of the data is volunteered, I am not afraid that my questioning has put it in my informants' heads. Insofar as I was able to identify visible groups or types of previewers, I found seriousness present in each. It characterized both of the two dimensions of college, academic and social, that previewers perceived.

Equally important in suggesting status as a major theme, seriousness has no rivals. It is easy to elaborate[12] and not trivial; if we find in subsequent field work that students consider college real life, it should prove important for understanding their behavior.

Discussion

The comments make clear that the answer to the question "Do strategies and concepts change in the first days of field work?" is emphatically *yes*. Furthermore, many of the changes are of such a nature as to affect subsequent field work radically. Table I summarizes the discussion.

Perhaps because of our experience with medical students of the same University, role as presentation of self to informants changes least. My role as coworker on the larger study changed rapidly from interviewer of prefreshmen to general ground-breaker. Largely because of the unanticipated presence of college seniors, several of whom I interviewed at length, I became aware of students' interests in prestige rankings among living groups, extracurricular activities, and politics. In the fall, we dropped our plan to interview students in order to map out important areas of interest to them and proceeded on the preview leads.

Three days of field work were enough to change my concept of college students dramatically. Before entering the field, I thought of them as irresponsible children. But as I listened to their voices, learned their language, witnessed gesture and expression, and accumulated the bits of information about them which bring people alive and make their problems real, I achieved a form of empathy with them and became their advocate. The

Concept before Previews	Comments showing		Total
	Change	No Change	
Role	2	1	3
Empathy	7	0	7
Anticipated problems	3	0	3
Hypotheses	9	0	9
Major themes	9	0	9
Miscellaneous	3	0	3
Total	33	1	34

Table 1. Changes in Concepts during Early Field Work

observers who began work in the fall experienced the same change, but not until they got into the field. Reading my field notes did not help.

Parenthetically, one might suppose that empathy for informants, once developed, would become a problem in itself. It often feels like one in the field but drops sharply on leaving it. After a few weeks on analysis, I wondered how I could stand those silly kids. Discussion with coworkers and getting the faculty perspective later in the study also helped to restore a balance.

The problems we anticipated with the administration remained as illusory in the fall as they were during the previews. Identifying student groups, which we thought would be difficult, did not turn out to be a problem in the fall. As at the previews, it was easy to meet individuals who then told us about friends or fellow group-members; we could, over time, get at more of the variables related to formation and maintenance.

Many of the hypotheses I took into the field at the previews did not check out. Prefreshmen did not have concrete enough information about what college would be like to answer our questions about studying, using time, choosing courses or activities. Making the hypotheses and asking questions, however, served to structure initial contacts and produced negative findings which changed our concept of what previewers were like and what they would experience as freshmen. The working hypotheses I used provided a similar entree for work in the fall. The major theme I began to elaborate during the previews– students take college very seriously as part of real life–was a change, not so much from our prefield-work concepts as from the stereotype in the general culture (which the comments suggest I shared) that finds college students, particularly at large state universities, frivolous and sports-minded. This is the way they are in fiction and much of the literature. My efforts to uncover frivolity in the previewers failed. Seniors swamped me with complicated accounts of their activities. In the fall, we started out looking for negative cases and continued to look throughout the field work without much result. The theme should have a place in the monograph in a more differentiated form, along with others we developed later.

Conclusions

If early field work reaches few conclusions, it may nevertheless have far-reaching effects on the rest of the study. Memoranda written after the previews indicate that the idea of dealing only with premedical students in the fall has gone by the board. We are aware that students in the different schools of the University are so intermingled in living groups and activities that we must deal with all of them. Our proposal to investigate only the academic aspects of college no longer seems feasible. The academic is too closely tied to other aspects of students' lives.

Evidently the preview data – particularly those from the senior leaders – went beyond my comments in giving us a picture of the campus as we might expect to find it in the fall. In a memorandum based on discussion of the summer field notes written before entering the field in September, Becker states:

> The major units of the college in which students belong are based on residence and are contained in the following list: large fraternities, small fraternities, ... scholarship halls, other dormitories, married students' residences, and rooms in town ... each of these groups can be thought as a network of interconnected cliques ..., essentially similar in their views of academic effort.[13]

Becker goes on to hypothesize several student cultures on campus. He later wonders if all may not have the same general goals, but, à la Cohen, differential access to success.[14]

It is clear that while one may reasonably expect initial field work to settle questions of role, empathy, and anticipated problems and to lay the grounds of later work by developing hypotheses and beginning the elaboration of a major theme, the observer may fail to comment on important things. My comments were concerned almost entirely with the previewers. I let the long interviews with seniors speak for themselves. Having more than one person on a study lessens the danger that such leads will be missed. Practically, the early field work provided us with informants to follow up and previewers as foils for college students when we met them. Its most far-reaching result was our broadened objective. We would study all the students, abandon interviews in the formal sense, and take our chances in the field, trusting the students to be as articulate and helpful as previewers.

One must conclude that the first days of field work may transform a study, rightly or wrongly, almost out of recognition.

Notes

1. See Howard S. Becker *et al., Boys in White* (Chicago, Ill.: The University of Chicago Press, 1961).
2. The study is financed by the Carnegie Corporation and directed by Everett C. Hughes. The field workers were Howard S. Becker (director), Blanche Geer, and Marsh Ray, then of Community Studies, Inc., Kansas City, Missouri.
3. The "dean" mentioned here and in subsequent comments is a general term for all administrators. There are so few that to give anyone a more precise title might identify him.
4. For a discussion of our use of the term *perspective* and the type of tables we used, see Becker, *op. cit.,* pp. 33-45.
5. I have been accustomed to think of the field worker's tendency to look at wholes as an important theoretical principle, maintaining that those who look at limited portions of a community or institution leave themselves open to serious misapprehension. On reflection, the interpretation offered here seems more likely. Compulsive or inelegant origins, however, do not make the "whole" any less necessary and important to understand.
6. There is extended discussion of friendship groups in relation to academic perspectives in Becker, op. *cit.,* chap. 9.
7. *Ibid.,* especially chaps. 8 and 10. Medical-school freshmen often thought they knew better than their teachers what they needed to know to practice medicine.
8. See Howard S. Becker, "Problems of Inference and Proof in Participant Observation," *American Sociological Review,* XXIII (1958) 655-856.
9. George Polya, *Mathematics and Plausible Reasoning* (2 vols.; Princeton, N. J.: Princeton University Press, 1954), vol. 2. *Patterns of Plausible Inference.* On pages 18-54 and 109-141, he discusses a "calculus of plausibility" based on everyday reasoning.
10. See Howard S. Becker and Blanche Geer, "Participant Observation: The Analysis of Qualitative Field Data," in Richard N. Adams and Jack J. Preiss, eds., *Human Organization Research* (Homewood, Ill.: The Dorsey Press, Inc., 1960), pp. 283-285.
11. Hanan Selvin has called similar reasoning "internal replication." See his discussion in "Durkheim's *Suicide* and Problems of Empirical Research," *American Journal of Sociology,* LXIII (1958), 613-618.
12. The term *elaborate* is used to suggest the general similarity of the reasoning process with that described in Paul F. Lazarsfeld and Morris Rosenberg, eds., *The Language of Social Research* (Glencoe, Ill.: The Free Press, 1955), pp. 121-124.
13. Memorandum entitled "Comments on Theory and Techniques for the Undergraduate Study," September 9, 1959. It begins, "This is written on the eve of going into the field. I am simply recording the more or less tentative conclusions that Ray, Geer, and I arrived at in discussing our preliminary strategy."
14. Albert E. Cohen, *Delinquent Boys* (Glencoe, Ill.: The Free Press, 1955).

22

Managing a Convincing Self-Presentation: Some Personal Reflections on Entering the Field

William B. Shaffir

Despite various attempts to codify fieldwork practices, (Burgess, 1984a; Johnson, 1975; Schatzman & Strauss, 1973; Taylor & Bogdan, 1984), I always have been struck by the uniqueness of each of the field-research projects I have undertaken. At the same time, although each has presented its own challenges for gaining access to the setting and its participants, requiring different tactics, each also has been characterized by a common range of concerns relating to my attempts at securing entry, namely (a) despite my anxieties and fears that I will be rejected, people are more cooperative about participating in the research than I anticipate; (b) their cooperation reflects less their estimation of the scientific merits of the research than their response to my personal attributes; and (c) the research always has involved varying degrees of pretense and dissimulation. This chapter examines the problems related to entering the field in three research projects. The first project, focusing on the Chassidim (who are ultra-Orthodox Jews) was begun in 1969 in Montreal when I entered graduate school and has occupied my interest to this day. The second and third projects also are related to the sociological study of Jews and Jewish communities. During 1979–80 I conducted field research in two yeshivas in Jerusalem that were engaged in the activity of transforming secular Jewish males into observant Jews. The third study, also conducted in Israel, during 1985–86, examined the religious defection of ultra-Orthodox Jews (*haredi*) and the process by which they negotiated interaction in a culture with which they previously had minimal contact. I begin by considering how each of the research populations

Source: *Experiencing Fieldwork: An Inside View of Qualitative Research*, 1991, Sage Publications, pp. 72-81.

was located and how I involved myself with them. I next discuss my style of self-presentation in the earliest stages of the research to ease the entry process and to gain some measure of cooperation. I conclude by observing that successful entry to the research setting, and securing the requisite cooperation to proceed with the study, depend less on the execution of any scientific canons of research than upon the researcher's ability to engage in sociable behavior that respects the cultural world of his or her hosts.

Entering the Setting and Initiating Contact

I often have found the advice and suggestions for negotiating entree usually offered in texts and articles on field research to be only moderately helpful. Although certain general rules of thumb may be offered (Lofland & Lofland, 1984), the uniqueness of each setting, as well as the researcher's personal circumstances, shape the specific negotiating tactics that come to be employed.

I have come to regard the so-called getting-in phase of the research as a process that involves educating others about my research intentions. However, the first task faced by all researchers is to locate the people to be studied. This presents little problem when the research population is confined to a particular setting or situated within demarcated boundaries, as was indeed the case in my studies of the Chassidic and newly observant Jews. It took little time to find the addresses of the Chassidic institutions in Montreal; moreover, I was familiar with the Chassidic neighborhoods in the city. Locating the *chozrim betshuvah* (the newly observant Jews) was hardly a problem, as a booklet I purchased listed the names, addresses, and pedagogical approaches of all of the institutions catering to such persons in Jerusalem. By contrast, defectors from the *haredi* circles could not be identified through any institutional address and, for a time, proved most difficult to find.

In retrospect, I realize that the entry process in each of the three studies was characterized by two central features: first, that people were more receptive to participating in the research than I anticipated; and second, despite this realization I am usually very uneasy and anxious during the beginning of the research because I expect the worst from people in terms of cooperation. I have learned to cope with mild states of anxiety and uncertainty and now accept these as part of the field research adventure.

Accounts of fieldwork are highly selective in what they reveal about the researcher's emotional experiences in the field. Not unlike the practitioners of other crafts, our accounts deflect attention from, or even entirely omit, admissions we perceive as less than appropriate. My earliest encounters with the Chassidim were filled with considerable tension and nervousness. Feelings of self-doubt, apprehension, and uncertainty are what I recall most vividly about those first months in the field. I can clearly recall feeling completely overwhelmed during my initial visit with them. This was easily attributable to the wide gulf separating our respective life-styles and reflected in virtually every relevant dimension, including dress, values, and ideals. Although such feelings eventually diminished and disappeared, they directly influenced my earliest days in the field. Elsewhere I have written about my initial foray into the Chassidic community (Shaffir, 1985), and the following excerpt points to my anxieties at the very beginning:

> During my first visit ... the Hassidic area appeared deserted. The enclave was located at the end of a narrow dirt road and there were two poorly maintained structures which served both as synagogues and *batei-midrashim* (study halls) for the Satmarer and the Klausenburger. ... A handful of Satmarer children played on a nearby bridge throwing stones into a stream and a few *bakhurim* (teenage yeshiva students) were standing on the porch of the synagogue. As I came closer, the youngsters stopped playing. They noticed my skullcap, which made it obvious that I was Jewish. I had intended to enter the synagogue, but I suddenly became apprehensive and walked past without talking to anyone, all the while berating my cowardice. When I came back on the following morning, I could hear voices chanting. Walking closer to the synagogue, I saw a room filled with some forty teenage boys; they all had flowing earlocks and were dressed in long black coats, black trousers, white shirts, and black hats. ...
> It took me but a moment to recognize how uncomfortable I would feel standing among them dressed in white jeans and a multi-coloured sports jacket. And what would I do once inside? Pray with them? Perhaps. Participation in prayer, however, would require feigning familiarity with the chronology and rituals of the prayer service. I decided to begin the research on the following day.
>   On my third trip to the Hassidic colony, I took the plunge and entered the synagogue. Nothing happened. At first, no one acknowledged my presence. Finally, a few youngsters and *balebatim* (married men) nodded to me and offered me a place to sit. Then everyone stared, especially the younger children, who positioned themselves close to me and waited to see whether I donned my *tefillin* correctly and recited the appropriate prayers. I felt anxious and entirely out of place.

I am often struck by the sheer amount of time and energy that was spent meeting with Chassidim and learning to feel relaxed, though never entirely at ease, in their company. I have little doubt that my successes in meeting Chassidic Jews and becoming intimately acquainted with their world, and with the institutional organization of the hassadic community, was related directly to the frequency with which I visited with them at home and in their institutions and committed myself to their company.

In contrast to my initial forays among the Chassidim, my first contacts with newly observant Jews encouraged me and led me to believe that the study would proceed smoothly. After all, I was familiar with the students' culture and background, and could relate to their search for life's meaning and purpose. If the Chassidim did not understand about universities and graduate degrees, the *chozrim betshuvah* were familiar with sociology and academic research.

As I did not intend to pass as an interested newcomer and wished to observe the full range of student interaction, I decided to inform the head of one yeshiva about my planned research. (I had once conducted covert research among a Chassidic sect, and found the experience both confining and morally distasteful.) He listened patiently to my introduction and replied: "Make yourself at home. Come to classes. Eat here and we can even find you a place to sleep." Elated by this response, I immediately sought out the head of a different, but similar, institution, presented my credentials, and hoped for a similar greeting. His facial reactions did not exactly exude interest and hospitality, and his response confirmed this suspicion: "If you've come to do research," he said, "don't do it here. I don't want it and I don't know who needs it." Despite this response, a number of students were interested in the research and encouraged me to return. Like others, I have found that gatekeepers' approval of the research does not guarantee that cooperation will be forthcoming from others in the setting, and that subordinates in a hierarchical arrangement can disregard the wishes of their superiors and enthusiastically support and assist in the research.

People who believe they have important stories to tell are usually eager to share their experiences with willing listeners. Much like born-again religious converts, many of the newly observant were eager to take to proselytizing, and saw me as a potential recruit. Such enthusiasm was reflected in their willingness to meet with me to talk about their pasts, how divine Providence intervened in their lives, and their future aspirations. Despite the relative ease with which I met people, I generally expected to be refused when requesting to meet with someone. Yet I can only recall one individual who refused outright to be interviewed. My suspicion that I was not fully welcomed resulted from a basic misinterpretation: I mistook an indifferent reaction for a negative one. As much as I wished for people to be curious and enthusiastic about my research, the majority could not have cared less. My research did not affect them, and they had more important matters to which to attend.

Former *haredi* Jews proved to be far more elusive than I had anticipated. I quickly learned that there was no institutional framework within which to locate such persons. Thus I arranged a meeting with a journalist who recently had written a sensitive piece on the topic and who claimed that she located respondents through an ad in her newspaper inviting former *haredim* to contact her. The similar ad that I inserted yielded only one individual who claimed to know of no others like himself. Although he did not lead me to further contacts, my conversation with him sensitized me to the pain, anguish, and desperation that characterized his departure from the ultra-Orthodox world – a theme that proved central in the account of every former *haredi* I was to meet.

The snowball technique that proved so effective for meeting Chassidic and newly observant Jews was largely unhelpful in the *haredi* project. Ex-*haredim* with whom I met suspected that there were others like themselves, but they did not know where to find them. Although at first I was suspicious of this claim, I gradually appreciated the extent to which former *haredim* were cut off from their previous circle such that they knew little, if anything, about other individuals who had defected recently. The important exception was Chaim (a pseudonym), whose name I received from an ex-*haredi,* the only informant offered by the journalist. At the end of my conversation with him, I asked whether he knew of others like himself with whom I might meet. "Yes, I do," he replied, "I have names and telephone numbers. How many people do you want to meet?"

As my relationship with Chaim evolved, I thought of him as my "Doc." Much like William F. Whyte's (1943/1981) informant, who had an intimate understanding of Cornerville, so too did Chaim possess a flair for analyzing the intricate circles within *haredi* society and the problems involved in leaving it. Chaim would provide me with more than names and telephone numbers; he always included some interesting background information about the particular individual and offered how the person's circumstances either added to or reinforced dimensions of the exiting process.

Regardless of the research, the process of entering the field and becoming connected consumes enormous amounts of time and energy. Despite my success in gaining entry, the process for me is accompanied by bouts of anxiety. Until I feel that I have achieved some level of acceptance, I find myself consumed by the research, and constantly thinking about the appropriate tactics for gaining a fuller measure of rapport and acceptance. Though nerve-wracking and exhausting, the entry process is also extremely challenging and is connected intrinsically with the adoption of particular roles involving the presentation of self.

The Tactics of Self-Presentation

By its very nature, field research requires some measure of role-playing and acting. In order to be granted access to the research setting and to secure the cooperation of his or her hosts, the researcher learns to present a particular image of himself or herself. The proffered image cannot be determined in advance but instead reflects the contingencies encountered in the field. Moreover, as fieldwork accounts attest, the kinds of roles that are assumed are hardly static, but are evolving constantly. As R. Wax (1971) has observed, the researcher eventually discovers that the value of any particular role is measured best by the vantage point it gives to the observer or participant who plays it.

Because I find outright dissimulation both morally distasteful and difficult to execute, I try to be as up-front about my research interests as possible. I never pretended to be interested in becoming a Chassidic or newly observant Jew, but, instead, identified myself primarily as a sociologist who came to do research. Despite a commitment to conducting research overtly, deception is, nonetheless, inherent in participant observation. Gans (1968) draws attention to this when he writes: "Once the field worker has gained entry, people tend to forget he is there and let down their guard, but he does not; however much as he seems to participate, he is really there to observe and even to watch what happens when people let down their guard" (p. 314). I found such a measure of deceit was unavoidable, especially during the early stages of my research; it would have been both unwise as well as unmanageable to share all of the research interests, ideas, and plans with those I planned to study.

Presentation of self as well as the research are not organized in a vacuum but are shaped by the people in the setting with whom the researcher interacts. My earliest encounters with the Chassidim were with members of the Lubavitch sect, who are well-known among Jews for their proselytizing zeal. My suspicion that Lubavitchers' cooperation would be enhanced if they believed that I had a personal stake in the research was confirmed during one of my first conversations. A Lubavitcher asked me: "Exactly why are you so interested in Chassidim? Is it just for the university or are you yourself interested?" I instinctively recognized the advantage of including a personal motivation in my reply, which was not entirely untrue, and before I had a chance to formulate a reply the man explained: "You see, if it is just for school then I can answer your questions one way. But if I know that as a Jew you are also interested in this, then I will answer your questions differently."

By projecting both personal and academic interests, I was attempting to display a particular image that I suspected would be received favorably. Indeed, it was. I can think of numerous ways in which I modified my behavior in the expectation that this would enhance my acceptance among the Chassidim; for example, I wore a black felt skullcap, the kind worn by the ultra-Orthodox, I donned phylacteries when visiting the yeshiva in the mornings, and even traveled to New York to attend Lubavitch Chassidic gatherings. Although these actions admittedly included elements of dissimulation, I was, in fact, also gradually drawn to the Chassidim as a Jew. I was not simply the calculating researcher carefully planning how best to execute the research. I was that, but also more. At times my self-presentation was as much influenced by personal considerations and commitments as it was by academic ones.

A tactic that I have found especially useful is to downplay my academic status. This approach was virtually forced upon me in the Chassidic research. I discovered very early on that the vast majority to whom I introduced myself did not have the faintest notions about universities and doctorate degrees. I quickly saw the advantage in eliminating the word *sociology* from my vocabulary – it seemed to confuse more than clarify – and simply explained that I was a student at a local school and, being expected to write something, I chose to write about the Chassidim. I am convinced that this introduction hardly mattered. It made the Chassidim neither more favorably disposed to the research nor more likely to react negatively toward it. The vast majority simply could not understand why anyone wanted to write about them.

Irrespective of the researcher's declared purpose, members of a group quickly develop their own explanations for the sudden appearance of a stranger. The Lubavitcher Chassidim interpreted my presence as witness to the success of their proselytizing zeal in the larger Jewish community. The Satmarer Chassidim, one of the most extremist sects, interpreted my presence differently. During one of my first visits to their synagogue, I was asked if I had come to recite the *kaddish,* the memorial prayer for the dead. After all, what other reason could someone like myself have for reciting the afternoon prayer in their synagogue? As my first months among the Chassidim revealed, the researcher does not simply appropriate a particular status, but discovers that he or she is accorded a status by the hosts that reflects their understanding of his or her presence.

Although I introduced myself as a sociologist and researcher to all of the *chozrim betshuvah* and former *haredim,* I did so only as a matter of form. Even though I was sometimes quizzed about the purpose of the research and whether names would be mentioned in any publications, such concerns were raised by a small minority. The majority, I think, considered it odd that anyone considered their experiences worthy of investigation in the first place. My personal credentials seemed to outweigh the academic ones for purposes of securing entry and gaining cooperation (Dean, Eichhorn, & Dean, 1969; R. Wax, 1971).

I think of myself as a shy person, and I have used this quality advantageously in my field research. I have no desire to be at the center of things, always involved in conversation, and have learned to exercise patience before approaching people to chat or for an interview. At the same time I try to be friendly, polite, and engaging. I seem to have a sense of when it is appropriate to engage people in conversation, and when it is best to leave someone alone. Much like comedians who are withdrawn and reserved offstage but perform well before an audience, I am able to camouflage my anxieties and uncertainties once in the field. I try coming across during the interview as calm, relaxed, and confident. In fact, I try to ensure that the encounter takes the form of a casual conversation. Despite a calm exterior, the interview, for me, is an intense experience, one that is exhausting mentally and for which I prepare in advance. I never feel compelled to focus on the research topic immediately, and prefer, in fact, to begin with some general item, thus enabling me to assess the person's character and demeanor quickly.

Learning to conduct field research, including the informal interview, requires both skill and tact. Each researcher adopts a style with which he or she feels comfortable and that yields results. I usually pretend to know less about the topic than I actually do. Although I may phrase questions along the lines of "I don't know if this makes sense," I usually have determined from others that my line of questioning is relevant. I can usually sense when the discussion becomes too personal and threatening and can steer it in a different direction. I also have become skilled at utilizing my sense of humor to inject some levity into tense and anxious situations. It is in this respect that some measure of deception characterizes the research process.

Conclusion

Despite the tension and aggravation that I experience at the beginning of a new field research project, this period is also filled with excitement and challenge. It is a time during which new people are met, relationships are established, and hypotheses are generated, all of which require me to put my research skills to a new test. The intensity of this exercise is particularly maximized during the first weeks or months in the field as I attempt to identify the pieces of the puzzle, as it were, and imagine how they may be fitted together.

Researchers frequently pretend to participate more fully in a community's activities when in fact they are detached observers. And often they ask deceptively innocent questions to gather data that would not otherwise be readily available. Such deceptive practices, I believe, are as inherent in field research as they are in day-to-day life. More blatant and outright dissimulation is rarely necessary. Cooperation depends less on the nature of the study than on the perception informants have of the field researcher as an ordinary human being who respects them, is genuinely interested in them, is kindly disposed toward them, and is willing to conform to their code of behavior when he or she is with them. In short, the skills in using commonplace sociability (friendliness, humor, sharing) are as much a prerequisite in conducting field research as they are in managing our affairs in other settings and situations unrelated to our professional work.

Author's note: I would like to thank Jack Haas and Roy Homosty for valuable comments on an earlier draft of this chapter.

Author's Related Publications

Shaffir, W. (1974). *Life in a religious community: The Lubavitcher Chassidim in Montreal.* Toronto: Holt, Rinehart and Winston of Canada.

Shaffir. W. (1983). The recruitment of *baalei tshuvah* in a Jerusalem yeshiva. *The Jewish Journal of Sociology*, 25(1), 33-46.

Shaffir, W. (1983). Hassidic Jews and Quebec politics. *The Jewish Journal of Sociology*, 25(2), 105-118.

Shaffir, W. (1985). Some reflections on approaches to fieldwork in hassidic communities. *The Jewish Journal of Sociology*, 27(2), 115-134.

Shaffir, W. (1987). Separation from the mainstream: The hassidic community of Tash. *The Jewish Journal of Sociology*, 29(1), 19-35.

Shaffir, W., & Rockaway, R. (1987). Leaving the ultra-orthodox fold: The defection of haredi Jews. *The Jewish Journal of Sociology, 29(2)*, 97-114.

Shaffir, W. (in press). Conversion experiences: Newcomers to and defectors from orthodox Judaism *(chozrim betshuvah and chozrim beshe' aylah)*. In T. Sobel & B. Bet Hallahmi (Eds.), *Tradition, innovation, conflict: Religion in contemporary Israel.* New York: SUNY Press.

23

Lesu: Introduction & First Night Alone

Hortense Powdermaker

Introduction

Lesu is a village on the east coast of New Ireland, an island in the southwest Pacific. About two degrees from the equator and part of the Bismarck Archipelago (southeast of New Guinea), it is under an Australian mandate.[1] The island is about two hundred miles long with an average width of twenty miles; a low range of mountains, three thousand feet at the highest altitude, runs through the center. Lesu, approximately eighty miles from the northern end of the island, had a population of 232 at the time of my field work, April 1929 to February 1930.[2] The village was part of a linguistic unit of four other villages (Ambwa, Langania, Libba, and Tandis) which I visited to attend rites and secure ethnographic information. Occasionally I went to a village in an adjacent linguistic unit for a special ceremony. The people were Melanesian – tall, black, with bushy hair – members of the Oceanic Negroid race. Their homogenous society belonged to a late Stone Age culture. I was the first anthropologist to study this society, then relatively uninfluenced by modern civilization. German Catholic missionaries had been in the southern part of New Ireland, as well as in other parts of the archipelago, and had written about the religion and the *Malanggans,* ritual carvings connected with mortuary rites. But no missionary had lived in the linguistic unit where I worked. A few people in the village were technically members of a Methodist mission (Australian in origin), but appeared unaffected by its teachings in any significant way. A "mission boy" in his teens held services on Sundays, but was without influence. Writing was unknown; no one had been to school and pidgin English, spoken mainly by young men and children, was the only language other than Melanesian.

Source: *Stranger and Friend: The Way of an Anthopologist,* 1966, Secker & Warburg, pp. 49-59.

Technological influence from outside was slight and implements were primitive – stone axes, wooden digging sticks and spears, sharp sea shells for scraping taro (a tuber vegetable). Rituals were performed in traditional manner and native customs were followed. The exceptions to the latter were cannibalism and murder, both forbidden by the Australian Mandated Government. Occasionally a few men left their villages to "sign on" for three years of work on a coconut plantation on New Ireland or a nearby island, but they brought little cultural innovation back with them. At the time of my study, none of the men were away from Lesu. Government patrols made infrequent brief visits to the villages. In general, native life was traditional and had a coherence and logic of its own. I was able to participate rather fully in it.

First Night Alone

This was my first night in Lesu alone. As I sat on the veranda of my thatched-roofed, two-room house in the early evening, I felt uncertain and scared, not of anything in particular, but just of being alone in a native village. I asked myself, "What on earth am I doing here, all alone and at the edge of the world?"

I had arrived two weeks earlier, accompanied by the Australian government anthropologist and a young English anthropologist (working on another island), who had met my boat in Rabaul, the capital of the Mandated Territory of New Guinea; they had generously offered to help me get settled in Lesu. When we met, the expression on their faces was, "Oh, my God!" I was a young woman, essentially urban, and obviously knew nothing about how to live in a primitive village. Their help in setting up my housekeeping was invaluable. The introduction by the government anthropologist was good because he was known to the natives through his occasional patrols, and he was well liked. The Englishman, an expert in pidgin English, gave me daily lessons in it. Pidgin is not bad English, but is a limited combination of English and native words, with a construction of its own. In this area a few German words were also in the vocabulary. My teacher was good, and I was able to practice immediately.

Both men supervised the finishing of my house (begun before my arrival for visiting government patrols), the building of a privy, the making of a primitive shower, adding a room to the cook-house for a servant's bedroom, and all the other details of settling in. Compared to the one-room village huts whose floor was the ground, my house seemed luxurious. It was raised from the ground and had two windowless rooms with a wide veranda between them and a narrow one around the sides of the house, One room was for sleeping and the other for keeping supplies. I worked, received company, and ate on the wide section of the veranda. The thatched roof was an advantage in the tropics.

Ongus, the *luluai,* an Australian-appointed chief, was a well-built, intelligent-looking man, obviously in command as he directed the unloading of my boxes and bales and the finishing of my house. I was lucky that he was well respected by the Lesu people. I knew that in the past there had been no chiefs and that authority had rested with the important elders. The Australian Mandated Government had appointed a chief in each village, in order to have a representative with whom to deal when they made patrols.

During these first days I was busy unpacking and settling in. Almost everyone in the village was in and around the house gazing with wonder, admiration, or amusement at my folding army cot, kitchen equipment, sewing basket, a ring of safety pins which particularly fascinated two old men, an oil lamp with a gas mantle, a portable typewriter, and all the other odds and ends which I thought necessary to existence. When I unrolled a thin mattress for the army cot, the English anthropologist was scornful. I replied serenely that I belonged to the comfort school of anthropology. I could see no reason for being more uncomfortable than necessary. He seemed to believe that discomforts were essential. During this time I made no real contacts with the native peoples, although I had a feeling that they were friendly. We smiled at each other, exchanged greetings in pidgin English, and I played a little with two babies. One responded with delighted coos; the other wailed loudly.

I had two servants, selected in Rabaul by the government anthropologist to accompany me to Lesu. The man, nick-named Pau, was a short, middle-aged Papuan with an unusual characteristic of extensive baldness. He came highly recommended as a cook and his experience included cooking for the Germans before World War I, as well as recently for Australians. He was responsible for the kitchen and for the shooting of birds for dinner. Taiti, the woman, a Melanesian, about thirty-five years old, had lived and worked in Rabaul for many years. She took care of my house, did the laundry, mending, and other such chores. Their wages, fixed by the Mandated Government, were, by Western standards, ridiculously little: two dollars a month plus a blanket and rations. Taiti had appeared willing to leave her half-caste Chinese husband in Rabaul. I knew nothing about Pau's marital life, but he seemed not to have any wife at this time. Both servants were still strangers to me.

My real contacts were limited to the two anthropologists; we talked about anthropology and gossiped about anthropologists. I was still primarily in my own modern world. In a couple of weeks, when my house was finished, Ongus, the *luluai,* and my anthropologist friends knew that a feast must be held to mark the occasion. The people in each hamlet of the village contributed piles of yams, taro, and bananas which they placed on the ground in front of the house. I noted that the women and small children sat together on one side and the men on the other side. Ongus made a speech about how the house was "finished good" and then distributed the food and my contribution of Virginia Emu Twist tobacco to the men. Fortunately, an anthropologist in Sydney had told me tobacco would be my best currency, and I had purchased a hundred dollars worth of it.

A day or two later, my anthropologist friends left me to return to their own work. As I waved good-bye, I felt like Robinson Crusoe, but without a man

Friday. That evening as I ate my dinner, I felt very low. I took a quinine pill
to ward off malaria. Suddenly I saw myself at the edge of the world, and *alone.*
I was scared and close to panic. When I arrived I had thought the place was
lovely. Everything seemed in harmonious accord: the black natives, the
vividness of the sea and of the wild flowers, the brightly plumed birds, the tall
areca palm and coconut trees, the delicate bamboo, the low thatched-roofed
huts, the beauty of the nights with the moon shining on the palm trees. But
now the same scene seemed ominous. I was not scared of the people, but I
had a feeling of panic. Why was I here, I asked myself repeatedly.

There seemed to be no adequate reason: anthropology, curiosity, career –
all seemed totally unimportant. *Why* had I come? I began to think of all the
events which had preceded my arrival here. I had been envious of fellow
students in London who had done field work, who had their people, while I
had none. Towards the end of my studies, I had selected the Mafulu who
lived on top of a mountain in New Guinea to become "my" people, partly
because I liked the idea of being perched on a mountain top and partly
because an adventurous solicitor, Robert Williamson, had published in 1912 a
grammar of their language and some ethnographical data, both superficial but
of potential usefulness to a beginning field worker. Malinowski had then
arranged that the Australian National Research Council invite me to make the
study. Their grant included the payment of all expenses, plus £100 (then
the equivalent of about $500) as a personal stipend, for such items as
cigarettes, toothpaste, and so forth.

Many months of preparation followed. First, I made a long, detailed
outline – forty odd pages – of all I wanted to find out, and this was discussed
in a small graduate seminar. I went to see a doctor at the School of Tropical
Medicine (to whom Seligmann gave me an introduction) to learn a few simple
rules about how to maintain good health in the tropics; the important ones
were to see *always* that water was boiled, to sleep under a mosquito net and to
take the nightly quinine pill as a prophylactic against malaria. I shopped for
mosquito boots and other appropriate clothes. Farewell parties were given. I
had gone home the preceding summer to say "good-by" to the family. Finally
in December, 1928, I boarded a P. and O. ship.

Just before leaving I had received a cable from Radcliffe-Brown, chairman
of the Australian National Research Council, to postpone my arrival in
Sydney for a month because he would not be back from the field until then.
Having kissed everyone good-by, I felt it would be an anticlimax to wait in
London, and decided to sail as planned and stop over in Ceylon for a month.
India seemed too vast for a month's visit.

I remembered the ship's dull English passengers who took their bridge
and deck tennis with religious seriousness, while I studied the Mafulu
grammar with equal seriousness. Some evenings I danced. I was pleased to
learn that Geza Roheim, the Hungarian anthropologist and psychoanalyst,
and his wife were in first class on their way to Australia. I was in cabin class,
but saw them frequently. I enjoyed their company, but wondered that
Roheim seemed to know exactly what he would find among the Australian

aborigines. I left the ship at Colombo and was met by a Singalese prince, a former student at the London School of Economics, who drove me in great style – a string of chauffered cars – to the Y.W.C.A., the only place I could afford. It was fortunately attractive, surrounded by spacious lawns and tall trees. Ceylon was interesting, but I had a sense of marking time until I should board a ship again and be on my way to Sydney.

When I arrived there, I went immediately to the anthropology department at the university to see Radcliffe-Brown, the chairman, and pick up mail. I found a letter from the government anthropologist advising (which meant commanding) me not to go to the Mafulu, because of the difficulties of securing porters to carry boxes and other luggage to the mountain top. Later I learned that the Mandated Government also feared the isolation of the Mafulu and was anxious about its responsibility for the first woman to work alone in its Territory. The government anthropologist suggested in his letter that I go to Lesu, a village in New Ireland, and I duly accepted his suggestion.

Lesu sounded like a good place and actually, I had no alternative, since I knew I should be dependent on the Government for practical help in transportation after I reached the islands. The next boat did not leave Sydney for a month and I settled in a one-room apartment, with an efficiency kitchen which looked very American. Much of my time was spent in the university library reading everything I could find on the Bismarck Archipelago, all written in German by missionaries.

A daily tea in Radcliffe-Brown's office brought me in touch with him and the other members of his department. I had great respect and admiration for him, but could not play the worshiping role which he seemed to need. Ian Hogbin, who had returned from his first field work in the Solomons, taught me how to use a Graflex camera that the department was lending me, and helped me shop, mostly at Woolworth's, for a year's supply of gifts for the Melanesians, whose pattern of reciprocal gift-giving was well known. Camilla Wedgwood, whom I had known in London, Lloyd Warner, and a few others were in the small anthropology group at the university. Some one in Baltimore had written to distant cousins in Sydney who were most hospitable. I enjoyed the company of my new friends, but, again, I was marking time. Occasionally, I had a horrible feeling that I might go on traveling forever, arriving places, meeting pleasant people, and shopping for equipment. Field work seemed to recede further and further away. I was truly glad when the S.S. *Montoro* of the Burns Philip Line was ready to sail. It was a small cargo boat carrying supplies to the islands and copra (dried coconuts) from them, and a few passengers.

I shall never forget the day the *Montoro* sailed from Sydney. It was supposed to leave at 9:00 a.m.; three friends who had come to see me off stayed until it actually left at four in the afternoon. The waiting was exhausting; I begged my friends to leave, but they insisted on staying. Radcliffe-Brown sent roses, and a note cautioning me not to forget to type my notes in duplicate and to send the extra copies to him as often as possible, just in case anything happened to me. One of the Australian Council's field workers had died in the field and another anthropologist was then writing up his notes.

I shared an inside cabin with two women. One was Mrs. O'Hara, weighing about two hundred pounds, good-natured, not too bright, amusingly vulgar, and taking the round-trip of the islands. Mrs. Bacon, my other cabin-mate, was the young, pretty wife of a government official on her way to Rabaul to rejoin her husband. Mrs. O'Hara regaled us with funny tales of the late Mr. O'Hara and confided her hopes of finding another husband on this trip. The three of us managed to get along fairly well in our small hot cabin, as the boat sailed up the east coast of Australia and crossed the equator, stopping frequently at islands to load and unload cargo. Other passengers included a few planters, traders, missionaries, gold miners (gold had been discovered in New Guinea), and a few minor government officials. Everyone was curious about me. As I sat on the deck putting finishing touches on cotton dresses that I was expecting to wear in the field, I answered their questions facetiously and said I was a modiste, interested in studying the latest style in straw skirts. It was obvious that none of the questioners had any interest in, or curiosity about, the Melanesians. Much of the time I had to escape from the women's never-ending tales about the danger of being raped by native men.

Finally, after eight days, came Rabaul, situated in a cove and hemmed in by mountains. The heat was oppressive. When I complained, the English anthropologist, who had met my boat, said sternly that people there did not talk about the heat. He took me shopping and I bought oil lamps, gallons of kerosene, tinned butter, jars of marmalade, many other grocery staples, a dutch oven, and a few cooking utensils. Shopping was sociable, as if I had met the store keepers on a big picnic, but had not been formally introduced. Tea parties, drinks, and dinners with government officials and their wives were more formal. Everyone gave me advice, and I tried to conceal that I was falling asleep and not hearing all of it. I had started taking quinine daily and it had the usual first effect of causing sleepiness and partial deafness. The Melanesians I saw were most disappointing. The servants looked sullen and furtive. The police boys with white caps perched on top of their bushy hair seemed slightly ridiculous.

After four days of Rabaul I was glad to go back to the S.S. *Montoro,* which had finished its unloading and loading and was ready to proceed to Kavieng, the capital of New Ireland. Soon we were there and for the first time I felt that I might be approaching the end of my traveling. Xavieng was small, not hemmed in as Rabaul was, and cool breezes were blowing. We were met by the District Officer, who invited us to stay at his home for a few days while we arranged for transportation by lorry over the rough road to Lesu. I spent much time in a hot warehouse, collecting my many bales, boxes, trunks, and so forth, and added to them by doing still more shopping. The small group of Australians in Kavieng were hospitable, but I had the feeling of being inspected. The worst crime I could be accused of was snobbishness. I had to be a friendly young woman, as well as an anthropologist with a new Ph.D., and I had to listen carefully to all advice and give an impression that I could handle any practical situation that might arise with the "savages."

Finally we were off. The road followed the winding curves of the east coast, up hill and down hill. Miles without any sign of human habitation, and then suddenly we would pass through a village and I would have a glimpse of tall black men in their loin cloths at a feast, and a group of women sitting on the ground chatting and playing with their babies. They looked attractive and quite different from the Melanesians I had seen in Rabaul. Sometimes the road passed through a plantation with its orderly rows of coconut trees, owned by an Australian. Always there was the sea on one side and the bush on the other. After eighty miles, we arrived at Lesu. About four months had passed since I had left England,.

Now I was sitting on my veranda, presumably ready to begin work, yet in a panic. I asked myself again, why am I here alone? I had to admit that no one had compelled me to come, that the expedition was not only voluntary but intensely desired. There could be only one explanation: I must have been mad. I quickly decided that although I may have been mad, I did not have to remain so. I would go home on the next boat which would leave Kavieng in six weeks. This brought some relief and I felt I could stick it out for that short time. The newspapers had publicized my being the first woman to go alone into the field in this area, and I now saw future headlines, "Anthropologist Leaves Field After Six Weeks Because She Is Scared!" But even that was better than being mad.

While I was immersed in gloom, visitors arrived: Ongus, the *luluai*, who had competently directed the finishing of my home, with his wife, Pulong, and their adolescent daughter Batu. With Pulong and Batu I had only previously exchanged greetings. They presented me with a baked taro, and I asked them to sit down. Ongus and his daughter spoke pidgin English but Pulong did not. As we talked, Ongus gave me some words of the native language which I wrote down, and he told me a few stories about the former German administration (before World War I), which had been hated. He also told me a little about himself – how, when young, he had gone away to work for a few years on a plantation in New Guinea, where he had learned his pidgin English. He added that now he would never leave Lesu again. At the end of a few hours he said that he would soon call all the people together so that I could explain to them what I planned to do. He mentioned that they were very curious. At the end of the evening I felt at home not only with Ongus, but also with Pulong and Batu, who had said very little. When they were leaving Ongus said that I should "sing out" if I needed anything and he would come immediately. Their house was directly opposite mine.

I was no longer alone. I had friends. I went to bed and fell asleep almost immediately. No more thoughts of madness or leaving entered my mind. Several years later I learned that a definition of panic is a state of un-relatedness.

Notes

1. Before World War I, New Ireland was called Neu Mecklenburg and belonged to Germany. The spelling of the village name on old government maps and publications is Lossu. Lesu approximates the native pronunciation of the word more phonetically.
2. The field work was financed by the Australian National Research Council.

Section Two
Sampling in the Field

24

Sampling in Ethnographic Field Work

John J. Honigmann

Two Kinds of Sampling

An ethnographer cannot avoid selecting some people, objects, or events for study, thereby renouncing, for a time at least, the possibility of studying others. From a vast range of possibilities, he takes up work in a particular tribe, village, or town; questions certain respondents; employs a few informants; observes some artifacts, situations, or behavioral events, and makes observations at restricted times. If the word "sampling" is used so broadly, then field workers are constantly sampling the universe of people, situations, objects, and behavioral events with which they are occupied. Seldom, however, do they keep track of how they drew a sample or report its composition. Even statements as general as my pseudonymous list of principal Kaska Indian informants and subjects (Honigmann, 1949:27) and Margaret Mead's (1928:250-252) "neighbourhood maps" identifying the adolescent and preadolescent girls she observed, are rare. An anthropologist characteristically extends his remarks beyond his sample and talks about "the" Kaska Indians and Samoan girls or about child rearing, quarrels, and pottery techniques in general – as though he had studied the community, category, or topic exhaustively. The usual spoken implication is that for his problem, the sample adequately represented a larger universe of actors, topics, culture patterns, techniques, or other units under study and therefore could provide reliable information about that universe as it existed at a particular time. A statistically conscious observer might object and point out that for a sample to be considered in a strict sense representative of the universe whence it came, it must have been selected in a suitable manner. Anthropologists are likely to respond by protesting that it is

Source: *Handbook of Method in Cultural Anthopology*, 1970, Columbia University Press, pp. 266-281.

not they who decide what persons or events to use as source of data; such decisions are practically made for them when certain individuals volunteer their help, some groups extend welcome, and some techniques happen to be accessible to observation (Festinger and Katz 1953:173). That units force themselves on a researcher's attention is merely a figure of speech. It overlooks the field worker's readiness to respond positively or negatively to certain cues in the field situation and ignores his active involvement in deciding how to respond to environmental opportunities or when to surrender to unbreachable limitations.

However strongly some stimuli "compel" the ethnographer's attention, it will repay him to be aware of the character of his sample, beginning with the basic distinction between nonprobability and probability methods of drawing it. The first term refers to sampling in the general sense in which I have so far used the word. Probability sampling designates a method that specifically intends every unit in the universe under study to have the same known probability of being studied. If the universe totals 100 people, houses, hours, or garden plots, and we want to study 10, then the probability of any unit being included in the sample is 1 in 10. Actual selection of a probability sample follows definite rules, the most important one requiring the units of the sample to be drawn at random; hence the familiar name for such sampling, random sampling. The unparalleled advantages of probability sampling, which recommend it for certain kinds of social science research, will be pointed out in due course. My object in this chapter is to review both types of sampling as they have been or can be applied in ethnography. I shall develop, first, how anthropologists use and defend use of nonprobability sampling methods in studies of culture and then review random sampling. Since certain procedures connected with defining the universe to be sampled before actual sampling begins are common to both probability and non-probability sampling, they will be mentioned in both places.

Nonprobability Sampling

Selecting a Place to Work

If cultural anthropology is ultimately concerned with achieving generalizations applicable to man in general, then sampling begins when an ethnographer chooses to explore the lifeways of one social aggregate rather than another and, having made that choice, narrows down his objective to look for a locality to settle in. John Beattie (1965:3-13) chose Bunyoro on the advice of an Africanist after discovering that another anthropologist had already begun to work with the group of his first choice. Out of the many local communities constituting Bunyoro, he sought one that, as far as he could judge at the time, was "reasonably representative ... as typical as possible of rural Bunyoro." Judgment sampling of this sort, which seeks to meet specific criteria, is most likely to be successful when it is informed by expert knowledge. Beattie, being a novice, gained such knowledge from others, a relatively rich literature undoubtedly assisting him in making his choice. He also wanted a community off the main roads and away from bureaucratic centers, yet reasonably accessible. Criteria for selecting a site may follow logically from the research problem and accompanying theory. Southall and Gutkind (1956:ix-x) in their survey of Kampala sought two areas for their sample survey, one to represent the densest type of uncontrolled and primarily African urban settlement in the Kampala area and the other an intermediate situation representing a transition toward maximal density from a previously rural comunity. In 1952 I went to Pakistan to study the impact of U.S. informational films on rural audiences, the country itself having been designated for me by an agency in the State Department (Honigmann 1953:2). Available time would permit me to pay reasonably close attention to only three villages and I determined to concentrate them in West Pakistan. Here I sought to sample as much of heterogeneous territory as possible by studying one village in three of the most populous provinces out of the ten or so political units then constituting the country's west wing. This allowed me to include three major languages in my sample; for, I asked myself, if the country possessed several languages how did films containing only Urdu narration communicate their content? When it came to selecting villages, logistics and a sufficient degree of isolation from urban influence became critical guides in judging suitability. In Karachi, Lahore, Peshawar and an upcountry town, I sought to make contacts with knowledgeable people who could recommend a village that would be accessible to a mobile unit carrying projection equipment. Guarantees of welcome and a place to live also influenced my decision where to settle. Specifications for an eligible unit to study may be even more explicit, like those Whiting and his associates (1966: chap. 6) demand for a primary social unit or P.S.U. (cf. Firth 1951:49). Defined as a stable social group located within a larger social group, consisting of about thirty mutually interacting families set off from the larger society by some social factor in such a way that they conceive of themselves as a kind of social unit, a P.S.U. must provide the investigators with variables both antecedent and consequent to child rearing. It represents a culture "cut down to manageable size." Factors of temporal stability and spatial homogeneity listed in decreasing order of importance are: territorial unity; membership in a common kinship group, like a clan; membership in a common school district; common religion; membership in a common economic association; membership in the same social class; and membership in the same recreational group.

Once he settles down in a locality and begins to work, an ethnographer has no way of knowing how the behavior patterns and artifacts he observes represent the social system's larger culture, except as reading or informants extend his knowledge. Yet he may title his monograph to refer to the culture or social system as a whole, only in the prefatory pages incidentally designating the precise universe he investigated.

Selecting People to Study: Judgment and Opportunistic Sampling

Further sampling occurs when the field worker chooses steady informants, perhaps following criteria like those Tremblay (1957) specifies for key informants or else working with whoever turns up and shows a readiness and ability to provide information. Note that I am not so much drawing a distinction between the degrees of intensiveness with which an anthropologist works with people – the informants who are steadily employed and may become practically surrogates of the field worker compared to those only casually observed or engaged in conversation. I am stressing the deliberateness with which any subjects are chosen. Informants selected by virtue of their status (age, sex, occupation) or previous experience, qualities which endow them with special knowledge that the ethnographer values, are chosen by a type of nonprobability sampling best called judgment sampling. The ethnographer uses his prior knowledge of the universe to draw representatives from it who possess distinctive qualifications. He may, for example, select informants or subjects according to class strata, occupational status, sex, age, or length of residence in the community. Spindler (1955:10-11) to a large extent employed judgment sampling in obtaining sixty-eight adult Menomini males, all recorded as being at least one-half Menomini Indian. He selected subjects "to represent all degrees of observable socioeconomic status from the richest to the poorest; and all degrees of cultural participation," or acculturational status. While he would have preferred to draw his sample by some random method, he knew it to be even more important to have subjects of different economic and cultural status with whom he could establish rapport sufficient to obtain the intimate social and psychological data his research problem demanded. He later allowed his subjects a hand in choosing additional respondents:

> At each sociocultural level, a few known individuals, friendly to me, were treated with first then a minimum of three names of other persons was obtained from them and at least one of these persons was obtained as a case, using his acquaintance with the first subject as a means of introduction. These cases in turn designated other possibilities. A number of other cases were "picked up" as contacts were made in many casual conversations.

Spindler recognized the possibility of bias serious enough to affect the outcome of his research arising from the possible selection of persons corresponding to certain personality types. Unconscious selection of persons to whom he could relate, he acknowledges, would have tended to reduce the variability of personality types in his sample. However, inspection of his data gave no evidence that such selection actually operated, except for the fact that only four people he chose declined to cooperate with him. Another example of judgment sampling comes from my own experience. In Frobisher Bay, Baffin Island, I had available abundant payroll records of the town's largest employer of Eskimo labor, the government. My wife and I sampled them for only four months, July and December (1962) and March and May (1963). We sought to cover the year without over-representing the summer season when employment is very high and winter when jobs are scarce (Honigmann and Honigmarm 1965:70). Definite limits restrict the extent to which judgment sampling can be applied before the field worker knows something about the composition of the universe being investigated. The population may have to be carefully stratified to allow sufficient representation for important constituent categories, as well as explicitly defined, for example to determine who is a Menomini Indian or what summer and winter are at the latitude of Frobisher Bay. Anthony F. C. Wallace (1952:40-41) is exceptionally clear concerning the way he went about choosing a sample that represented the age and sex distribution of Tuscarora Indians, to whom he proposed to administer Rorschach tests. His census revealed a total of 353 persons sixteen years and older who were sociologically Tuscarora. (He specifies the conscious rule by which he decided who in that sense was a Tuscarora.) Then he calculated the number of records necessary to preserve in the sample the same proportions that existed in the population at large, calculating these figures on the expectation that he could deal with a total of about 100 persons (or Rorschach records). He first allowed an informant to select individuals of requisite age and sex. Later, as Wallace got to know more people, he himself suggested subjects for testing. He justifies logically his belief that these methods of selection introduced very little bias, though once his guide shocked him by commenting on twenty persons who had already been tested, saying they represented the "better element" of Tuscarora society. Apparently the assistant used the word "better" to describe people whom he personally knew and liked and therefore had chosen. This revelation distressed Wallace less than the thought that "better element" might have referred to socio-economic levels, to which he had given no consideration in preparing his sampling design.

Nonprobability judgment sampling demands a clear-cut definition of the universe about which the sample is intended to provide information. Such a decision is often difficult to make. What is the community and where are its boundaries? (See Leighton *et al.* 1963:40.) How are people in a P.S.U. connected? How shall a Tuscarora Indian be defined? What situations are likely to be most rewarding with certain kinds of information? I will have more to say about the critical judgment required in designing sampling frames in the section devoted to random sampling.

If the concept of sampling is strictly limited to some such *deliberate* selection of typical or representative units, then an anthropologist's partly self-selected informants or subjects for observation are not obtained by sampling at all. However, I have already indicated that I propose to ignore such strict usage. The term "opportunistic sampling" is available for the familiar process by which field workers find many of the people who provide them with ethnographic information. Such sampling follows no strict, logical plan (Parten 1950:242-245). The perimeters of the sampled universe are poorly drawn and the procedure itself is so situationally variable, as well as being idiosyncratically influenced by the personal qualities of the particular ethnographer, that it becomes well-nigh impossible for another person to replicate. I recall one use of opportunistic sampling during my first ethnographic trip to West Pakistan. The abundant visitors who voluntarily came to my home served as respondents for innumerable questions; I sought to plumb their motivations and other personality characteristics, and in some cases begged them to take the Rorschach test. Occasionally I solicited my guests with my interview schedule (that had been prepared for a random sample) to learn if they had attended the motion-picture showings and if so what they had seen and heard. Responses from such opportunistically selected subjects were kept separate from those of randomly selected subjects. Subsequently I compared both samples, as I will report later in this chapter. My wife and children also utilized invitations to the homes of relatively well-to-do or high-ranking families as opportunities to observe certain aspects of domestic life and to obtain other information, though success in such matters depended on the extent to which hosts were bilingual or could be conveniently interviewed through a bilingual relative. Such opportunistic sampling can also be called chunk sampling, meaning that the researcher resourcefully seizes any handy chunk of the universe that promises to reward him with relevant information: he observes whatever children or mothers are available, visits receptive households, tests willing adults, records remarks he overhears or has volunteered to him, and attends almost any public meetings, church services, and entertainments that he happens to hear about. But since this method calls for acting opportunistically in all such situations, we might as well call it opportunistic sampling.

Judgment and opportunistic, nonprobability sampling represent degrees of deliberateness exercised in choosing informants, subjects, situations, or behavioral events. One type does not exclude the other. Opportune social contacts may be exploited for the special knowledge they possess, as my wife and I did with the lawyers, farmers, teachers, Islamic scholars, women, and political leaders we met in Pakistan. The information provided by such casually selected respondents is interpreted or evaluated according to the status he or she represents and it possesses limited value until significant dimensions of the person's status have been identified. I shall have more to say about identifying opportunistically selected people or situations and about interpreting the information they provide. Such procedures, which in effect convert opportunistic into judgment samples, have been called distinctive of ethnographic field work.

Selecting Behavior and Situations to Observe

I have spoken about sampling places and people in nonprobability fashion but only incidentally have I mentioned sampling behavioral episodes themselves (which, to be sure, always include people). An ethnographer from time to time deliberately assigns himself to observe particular situations and events. Undoubtedly he initially learns much about an as yet unfamiliar culture by seizing convenient opportunities to study behavior and artifacts that catch his eye and ear. Casual observations of cattle returning to the village, men plowing, carpenters repairing a cart wheel, and mothers interacting with children eventually serve him to construct ethnographic statements about agriculture, industries, and child rearing. Informants may themselves be asked to sample by reporting cases of certain kinds of behavior they have observed, thereby extending the ethnographer's observational range. The photographs and drawings of objects in published monographs report "typical" samples chosen by nonprobability methods. "Typical" in this sense means that an object has been selected for illustration because the author judges it characteristic of the class of objects to which it belongs. In the same way, a typical wedding, game, or other behavioral event may be written up at length. (On the other hand, an episode occurring only once during the researcher's presence in the community is better reported as a single case without any assumption about its typicalness unless informants provide comparative information.)

Sampling for behavior can be quite systematically organized when the ethnographer goes into the field equipped with a carefully planned research design. Whiting and his associates (1966: chap. 5) in a field guide they prepared for studies of socialization in five cultures list a number of observations to be made of children, the object of which is to learn about prescribed situations that arise in various settings in which children spend their day and about how they respond in such situations. "Settings" means general cultural activities limited by time and place (e.g., sleeping, breakfast, playing in the schoolyard after school, etc.), and "situations" designates specific social conditions that instigate responses. Twelve situations likely to promote responses are specified, including assaults, insults, hurts, encounters with difficulties, requests for help, and reprimands. The manual contains procedural rules for identifying such situations and responses in culturally specific terms as well as instructions for classifying the data. An observer is told to construct a schedule of a child's typical day in the P.S.U. where he is working and where he is able to identify specific children. The schedule will indicate settings to be sampled for the situations they contain. He is instructed to make twelve five-minute observations on each child spaced as widely as possible over time and setting to yield a one-hour sample of each child's behavior. The field worker has a problem of distributing his time among the various settings in a way that will maximize observation in settings yielding the richest data and still cover a representative sample of the child's activities. In general, he is told to divide his time in proportion to the time children spend in each setting, to under-sample settings (like sleeping) where the twelve situations occur rarely or where response varies little, and to over-sample settings where situations occur abundantly and response varies greatly. He is also advised to photograph and even to take movies of the most frequent settings a child encounters in a community. The twelve five-minute observations are expected to indicate frequency with which the twelve prescribed situations arise and the probability with which each type occurs.

The data will later permit cross-cultural analysis of differences in the probabilities of occurrence as well as differences between subgroups and individuals belonging to the P.S.U. The fact that instructions had to be altered after the ethnographers had reached the field and begun to report on problems facing them in their various locations indicates the difficulty anthropologists face in preplanning their sampling and general research designs before learning something about the culture.

Evaluating Nonprobability Sampling in Anthropology

Nonprobability sampling in ethnography along with associated practices like reliance on nonquantitative procedures and on unimodal patterns of behavior undoubtedly constitute the most debated technique in the field worker's armamentarium. Not only do persons in adjacent disciplines voice skepticism but also, particularly when certain lands of research like national character studies are involved, anthropologists themselves (Mandelbaum 1953:182). Critics point out that judgment and opportunistic sampling allow no way of knowing precisely the degree to which a sample corresponds to the universe it represents and therefore casts doubt on the reliability, perhaps even the general validity, of the information it provides. To argue that a sample of six hundred Vassar College girls mostly of middle-class background adequately reflects the predominantly middle-class culture of the United States doesn't compensate for the lack of any empirical information about, say, lower-class girls (Codere 1955:65-67). Wallace (1952:42) sampled to ensure a representative age and sex distribution in his adult Tuscarora protocols but did he not invite serious bias to enter his sample by allowing his assistant to select 43 percent of the tested subjects? Bias so introduced may indeed be minor, but the degree to which those subjects represented the Tuscarora adult universe in other than age or sex characteristics must remain clouded by some doubt. Many anthropologists have been troubled by such criticism. Yet most of us continue to use judgment and opportunistic samples and I would not dream of suggesting we cease. We use such samples not primarily because our field problem is usually so enormous and our time so limited that we can't afford to use the several probability samples that our multi-faceted research would require in order to be clearly representative. Our adherence to traditional anthropological field-work methods of sampling rests on the assumption that the questions put in research can frequently be satisfactorily answered through samples selected by nonprobability methods.

Why should we expect that nonprobability sampling will work in the study of technology, social structure, and idea systems as anthropologists commonly pursue such topics? What logical reason do we have for believing that judgmental and more casually chosen samples will provide an ethnographer with satisfactory factual information about particular cultural systems? As a minimum definition of satisfactoriness, I would demand that the empirical propositions in an ethnography be objectively replicated in a high proportion of cases. While some notable differences of fact have indeed arisen between anthropologists who have reported on the "same" culture, when the few restudies we have are considered, the extent of agreement between professional investigators who have reported on the "same" culture (given a loose, unstandardized criteria of agreement) seem to outweigh disagreements.[1] This indicates that anthropological sampling works and is to a tolerable degree reliable, given the current standards of ethnographic reliability and my qualitative method of appraising reliability. The question I ask is: Why does it work as well as it does? A general answer holds that a common culture is reflected in practically every person, event, and artifact belonging to a common system. In a community, nearly every source of data an ethnographer consults – each informant, subject, event, and artifact – in some degree or in some way reveals consistencies with many other sources (corresponding to the same or a different type) that he consults. Accounts of child rearing by several informants partially fit together with one another and agree with observed instances of child rearing. The fit may not be as perfect as the interlocking of pieces in a jigsaw puzzle, but such an analogy is nevertheless useful. A Sindhi landlord's actions, though vastly different from his tenant farmer's, meshes with certain aspects of the latter's, and the landlord's luxurious rural dwelling is in some respects comparable to the tenant's hovel or referable to the tenant's labor, passivity, powerlessness, etc. It is with such consistencies and comparable aspects abstracted from the sample that we build up an integrated picture of a culture. No two reporters use the same facts in the same way, but some of the same facts recognizably appear in different anthropologists' treatments of the same culture or social system. Use of judgment and opportunistic samples in field work is predicated on the researcher's primary interest in the *system* of behavior rather than in the way behavioral traits or individuals with specific characteristics are distributed in a known universe whose systematic nature is either taken for granted or ignored (cf. Kroeber 1957:193). If the system is composed of subgroups, then such subgroups are sampled for whatever information they can contribute concerning the whole system.

The person who has most tried to explain how traditional anthropological sampling works is Margaret Mead.[2] Confining her discussion mainly to the selection of people by nonprobability methods, she points out the vital importance of identifying informants by salient characteristics they possess which are capable of affecting the validity of information they produce. (The same rule, as I will bring out later, applies to certain kinds of cultural products.) Hence accomplished ethnography calls for "skill of evaluating an individual informant's place in a social and cultural whole and then recognizing the formal patterns, explicit and implicit, of his culture expressed in his spontaneous verbal statements and his behavior" (Mead 1953: 646). When the sample is a human being, his identification is made in terms of more than his representative status or social characteristics.

> ... the validity of the sample depends not so much upon the number of cases as upon the proper specification of the informant, so that he or she can be

accurately-placed, in terms of a very large number of variables – age, sex, order of birth, family background, life-experience, temperamental tendencies (such as optimism, habit of exaggeration, etc.), political and religious position, exact situational relationship to the investigator, configurational relationship to every other informant, and so forth. Within this extensive degree of specification, each informant is studied as a perfect example, an organic representation of his complete cultural experience. This specification of the informant grew up historically as a way of dealing with the few survivors of broken and vanished cultures and is comparable to the elaboration with which the trained historian specifies the place of a crucial document among the few and valuable documents available for a particular period. ... (Mead 1953:645-655)

Again like a historian working with documents, an anthropologist drawing information from expressive cultural products like novels or films notes salient characteristics of their authors "so as, in the end, to be able to discount ... individual differences" (Mead 1961:19). A single life history is repre-sentative of a community's culture to the degree that the individual it portrays has been involved in experiences common to other (not necessarily all) individuals. To that degree, the subject's life history becomes a model of his culture which the anthropologist can use in building *his* model (Mead 1953:653). Even a relative stranger, like the Hudson's Bay Company manager serving an Indian community in northern Canada, or the visiting missionary, becomes representative in the sense that he is capable of providing infor-mation about the Indians' culture, but his special cultural and social position must be known and carefully considered in appraising what he says or does (Mead 1951b: 77).

Such diverse sources of data open ethnography to the charge that it relies on unstandardized modes of procedure and is haphazard or impressionistic in its approach, charges that Mead (1955) takes pains to rebut when she emphasizes that an anthropologist in his work follows rules different from those employed in other social sciences but doesn't operate totally without discipline. The ethnologist who combines information from novels, from living informants, and even utilizes his own personal experience in another culture to construct his final model of the culture or social personality may have sampled informants and behavioral settings opportunistically, but he did not do so haphazardly if he kept in mind what his sources represented. Safeguards in anthropological sampling include cross-checking information one receives from different sources, using every datum to test the soundness of the model as it is built and comparing each to data employed before, examining it for inconsistencies, contradictions, and in-congruities. "Anthropological sampling is not a poor and inadequate version of sociological or sociopsychological sampling, a version where *n* equals too few cases," Mead (1953:654) claims, "*it is simply a different kind of sampling.*"

With so much importance put on identifying salient characteristics of human samples in field work, it becomes imperative for the ethnographer to keep records of the people he studies – not merely their names but generous amounts of biographical and other data relevant for understanding information they provide. Indexing of field notes not merely by categories like those given in the *Outline of Cultural Materials* but by names is essential so that the full set of notes referring to any individual can be used to augment formal biographical data available about him and thus round out knowledge of him that will help to place any particular behavior or statement referring to him in the fullest possible, meaningful context. What X tells me on one occasion is apt to assume special significance once I know certain of his previous behavior and have retrieved it from my records. In this way, long-term research in single communities will someday benefit through comprehensive data banks established for persons and for entire families.[3] When the ideal of full, individual identification becomes unrealizable, as in studying a large community like a nation or city involving many subjects who therefore must remain for the most part anonymous, other methods can be employed to achieve a similar result. Mead (1953:652) suggests random sampling, or "positional studies in which small complex parts of the total structure are carefully localized and intensively studied," like organizations or several shops in a factory. Or else "the intensive analysis of segments of the culture which are unsystematically related to each other and overlap in a variety of ways" are consulted (in Russian national cultural studies such segments have included novels, proceedings of the Communist party congress, and controls on Soviet industry). Rhoda Metraux (1943:88) also speaks of positional sampling used to interview specific groups for information about food habits, including grocers and persons waiting in line to register for ration cards. In a heterogeneous social system, therefore, work in any sampled subgroup is done knowing, or while learning, salient characteristics of that subgroup with respect to the whole, just as in sampling persons or cultural products. Special attention might have to be given to a subgroup if its members are playing a particularly decisive political role in a nation.

Anthropological methods of sampling, Mead (1952:402-403, 1953:655) maintains, are logical as long as the fieldworker expects mainly to use his data not to answer questions like "how much" and "how often" but to solve *qualitative* problems such as discovering what occurs, the implications of what occurs, and the relationships linking occurrences. Anthropological sampling serves the ethnologist who is primarily engaged in searching for patterns that occur and recur in diverse sets of social relations, "between employer and employee, writer and reader, and so on," including between parents and children (Mead 1953:655). Such patterns can be constructed from information provided by identified living informants augmented by bits of data obtained from cultural productions, like paintings, plays, or movies. The latter data are "cross-integrated" with observed behavior and statements provided by informants (Mead 1951a: 109, 116). She illustrates from linguistics: "If one wants to know the grammatical structure of a language, it is sufficient to use very few informants about whom the necessary specified information has been collected; if one wants to know how many people use a certain locution or a particular work in preference to another, then sampling of the wider type is necessary. ..."

Mead's account of judgment sampling stops short of demonstrating how the information so obtained is utilized in ethnographies in ways that avoid undue overgeneralization. It hardly suffices to be told that "any cultural statement must be made in such a way that the addition of another class of informants previously unrepresented will not change the nature of the statement in a way which has not been allowed for in the original state-ment" (Mead 1953:648), or to be warned that the representativeness of the informants must be included in statements, as for example, " 'These statements are made about the culture prevailing in the rural south among people living in communities of less than twenty-five hundred people.'" Can all new information by hitherto unrepresented samples be anticipated? How precisely can samples be identified in ethnographic statements? I doubt if such rules can regularly be followed when large amounts of information must be reported. Such criticism, however, may be unfair, for one of the crucial problems in traditional anthropological method, and one we understand very poorly due no doubt to the extent to which a personal element is involved, is precisely the matter of what happens to data after they have been collected in the field and prior to the point where they turn up in the stylized prose of a monograph.

It is well to guard against using the term "anthropological sampling" without bearing in mind that no probability methods of sampling apply in anthropology only to the extent that ethnographers in fact pursue research interests like those stated, or interests consistent with ends such sampling can serve. I think it noteworthy that Mead does not defend nonprobability sampling by referring to the predominant homogeneity of small-scale com-munities which renders random sampling unnecessary (see, however, Mead 1932:10-12). Neither homogeneity or heterogeneity by itself constitutes a sufficient basis for choosing between probability or non-probability sampling methods. We may safely assume that in any community, regardless of whether it is large or small in scale, individuals embody or enact culture differently, and so do families. To that extent, a degree of heterogeneity is universal. A research problem that seeks to capitalize on internal ("intra-cultural") variations of behavior between a fairly large number of individuals or families in communities of any scale would undoubtedly find probability sampling advantageous.

Probability Sampling

Selecting a Sample[4]

A probability sample is called for whenever it is useful to know within precise margins of error how often units (people, artifacts, activities, attitudes, or opinions) with particular features occur in a universe of such phenomena that is too large or for some other reason difficult to investigate *in toto*. The word "features" covers any question that can be incorporated in an interview schedule and any variable to which an observer can give attention. The carefully planned process of selection used to obtain a probability sample comes close to creating a miniature, unbiased replica or cross-section of the sampled phenomena. Due to the underlying mathematical theory of probability sampling,[5] such samples can be employed with considerable, known confidence for the light they throw on the universe from which the sample was drawn. Laws of chance or probability, rather than expert knowledge or self-selection, govern the way representatives of that universe are chosen. The very role that chance plays in drawing the sample can be known. Put another way, the probability sampling tells us what percent of the time we can expect our sample to be representative of the universe from which it is drawn. Such practical and mathematical advantages are important reasons for the widespread use of sampling in science. In what follows I will be mainly concerned with random sampling, the best known method of probability sampling. In this method, each unit in the sampled universe enjoys an equal chance of being drawn.

In preparing to choose a probability sample by random selection, the first step is to construct a sampling frame. A sampling frame is the sampled universe drawn together in some convenient fashion for sampling. It often differs from the target universe, that is, from the total population which the anthropologist may be studying. In a moment I will bring up some of the problems connected with generalizing from the sampled universe to the target universe. Here it suffices to say that all the safety we enjoy in making statistical inferences from the random sample to the sampled universe disappears once we extend knowledge gained from the sample beyond the sampling frame to the target universe. The sampling frame may consist of a stack of newspapers, a herd of cows (if the object is, say, to discover milk yield), a street map of a city, or a list of people. A satisfactory census or other enumeration of people may already be available in the community or at some capital to serve as a sampling frame. If not, or if the census is suspected to be incomplete, the field worker will have to make his own enumeration. He can often save time in doing so by utilizing available knowledge, as Fortes and his coworkers (1947:177) did when the Ashanti survey began its enumeration using lists of household heads taken from the tax rolls. Often it proves too difficult or impossible to construct a sampling frame that coincides with the target universe which the ethnographer is studying. Baeck (1961:162) was interested in the consumption patterns of well-to-do Congolese in Leopoldville but restricted himself to drawing a sample of government clerks earning incomes above a certain figure who were also household heads. He used a payroll list as his frame. His sample, of course, included no other occupations that may have been represented among well-to-do Congolese. Peter Marris (1961:xii-xiv) would have preferred to sample households in Lagos, but because he found no adequate list of such units he had to settle for individuals drawn from a census. In Pakistan I wanted to know about both men's and women's presence at, and reaction to, the motion pictures shown in the three villages I had selected, but purdah did not permit me to construct sampling frames including women's names. In Frobisher Bay we wanted to know about Eskimo drinking but could best find out about Eskimo men who had received permits to deal with the Territorial liquor store. We used a 100 percent sample of such people (Honigmann and Honigmann 1965:204 ff.).

There is danger of error whenever the researcher generalizes beyond the sampling frame. To avoid or reduce such error, the ethnographer may specify the relationship between the sampling frame and the target universe, for example, the degree to which well-to-do Congolese are represented by government clerks earning above a certain figure. He may decide to restrict his conclusions to the sampled universe, at that point shedding all interest in the target universe. We did this to a large extent when under the heading of "Eskimo drinking" I confined most of our discussion to purchases made by permit holders in Frobisher Bay, merely indicating that there were some teetotalers and that a small, unknown amount of illegal home-brewing occurred. The ethnographer may also, if time permits, increase the number of sampling frames in order to cover as large a portion of the target universe as possible. In Leopoldville, for example, he might have added to the payroll list a tax list of household heads and drawn from it a random sample of householders who pay amounts above a certain figure. If one employs the sampling frame to make wider generalizations, it can be done by basing what is said on well-founded knowledge of the target universe and of the subject matter being studied. Thus because many Pashto-speaking male respondents in Pakistan failed to understand the film track's Urdu narration, it was even less likely that Pashto-speaking mature women would; their seclusion, I reason, has allowed them little opportunity to learn Urdu. Often the sampling frame represents a more or less satisfactory compromise between studying the target universe directly and utilizing available sources of information or working within time limits available to the ethnographer. Compromise cannot go to all lengths. Frames must possess some relevance to the problem being investigated if they are to be useful. For a researcher interested in the inheritors of land, a list of *all* taxpayers or households won't do; he needs a sampling frame of persons who have inherited land or a list of estates whose owners he can track down to solicit the required information (cf. Leach 1958). One is justified in wondering what Geoffrey Gorer (1955) accomplished by way of getting to know about "English character" with a sampling frame consisting of 10,524 questionnaires returned by persons who in response to an appeal published in a popular newspaper, consented to complete such an instrument.

Sampling frames are sometimes hard to construct because the universe itself (e.g., well-to-do Congolese in Leopoldville) is conceptually ambiguous. Much thought has to be given to formulating rules concerning what is to constitute the frame and why. Are men working away from the village to be included in the household? Should I include members of satellite villages in the universe to be sampled? What time limits are sufficient or required for my problem? Solutions to such questions depend on the research objectives and on knowledge of relevant factors in the community's culture and history. For example, in Frobisher Bay it was very desirable to have data on liquor purchases that went back before the date when new regulations entered into force; such data would enable me to tell what difference, if any, the regulation made. Obviously previous knowledge of an area and its history will provide valuable guidance both for constructing sampling frames and for generalizing beyond them (cf. Smith 1963). If the essence of art lies in applying skill to overcome limits imposed by one's tools, materials, and personal resources, then designing a sampling frame calls for considerable art.

The sampling frame contains all the units or observations that will be sampled; the sample contains the number of units actually studied (including those that can't be found or refuse; to collaborate). Step two in collecting a sample consists in determining how many such units are needed (assuming that circumstances do not permit a 100 percent sample) and then randomly drawing that number from the frame. Sample size depends on the amount of variability in the sample and the degree of confidence that the research wishes to establish for his results. In general, the larger the sample, the smaller the probable error and the greater the confidence attached to the results. However, beyond a certain size, gains to be expected rapidly decline, making large samples relatively inefficient to use. Listing units in the frame and assigning each a serial number or numbering houses and blocks permits convenient sampling by use of a table of random numbers (Wallis and Roberts 1956: 631 ff.), for to draw a large number of cases by lot would be a clumsy, time-consuming procedure. A list or series of items, like pages or newspapers, can be random-sampled by numbering them or numbering areas of the page and lines of type. This is an appropriate place to point out that sampling pages, newspapers, or printed lines by selecting units at regular intervals is not true random sampling because the selection of each unit fails to be independent of the others. Regular-interval sampling is random only if the arrangement of the series is free from bias, for example, if the pile of newspapers has been mixed so that choosing every seventh does not result in only Sunday papers being drawn. Similar precautions must be taken in stopping to question people or vehicles at regular intervals, when the interviewer must also be cautious that he does not depart from the sample design and unconsciously show partiality in making his selection. In sampling a list of names at regular intervals, danger lies in oversampling the initial letter and omitting the least common letters. Returning to random sampling procedures, a numbered grid placed over a large-scale map allows random selection of places to be visited for investigation. In two-stage or multi-stage sampling, once such places are randomly chosen their constituent units are again random-sampled. Peter Marris (1961:xiv) contemplated drawing a grid over a plan of Lagos and sampling the squares. However, the density of population made this unthinkable; each square would have included too many people to sample further and an adequate sampling frame would have been hard to construct.[6]

No matter how carefully drawing occurs, bias resulting in a misleading sample, one that under- or over-represents certain kinds of units, cannot be completely eliminated. Failure of people to respond or to be located, inaccessibility which deters an interviewer from going to certain places, and the readiness of some respondents to cooperate all contribute to bias. I respect the fortitude of my Pathan assistant in a large North-West Frontier village as he patiently accompanied me on long treks across hot fields in search of respondents whose wells and fields we had located through inquiring in the market place. Even then we couldn't locate an unallowably large proportion (26 percent) of the sample which had been chosen from a voter's list, the validity of which I came to doubt (Honigmann 1953:57).

Stratified Random Sampling

The simplicity characteristic of simple random sampling disappears when the basic method which I have described is applied in more complex circumstances, for example, in national samples of public opinion. It would be merely academic for me here to go into such variations of random sampling as area or cluster sampling.[7] However, I will briefly describe one well-known variation, stratified random sampling, because it is likely to be helpful in ethnographic research. This type of probability sampling occurs when the universe under study is heterogeneous; that is, the units vary in characteristics which are apt to be significant for the problem being studied. For example, a population contains persons of different ages or members of different ethnic groups. These features, the investigator suspects, might influence other features that he is studying. He takes care to draw a sample that will proportionately represent the likely significant features in the universe. He divides the sampling frame into strata or categories (cells), each homogeneous with respect to a certain characteristic. Then he draws a random sample of proportionate size from each cell. In a small Sindhi village of about five hundred persons my initial census of males eighteen years old or more revealed a population stratified in six tiers: noncultivating landlords; cultivating landholders; tenant cultivators; craftsmen and tradesmen, including domestic servants; Marwari, a Hindu enclave; and Brahui-speaking transients living on the settlement's outskirts. My sample of forty subjects represented each of these categories in proportion to its weight in the total population. Circumstances, however, made it impossible to complete interviews with each designated respondent, the suspicious Brahui putting themselves beyond reach (Honigmann 1953: 10-11). Constructing a frame for stratified random sampling obviously requires prior knowledge about the composition of the universe so that its probably significant characteristics can be defined. To a very large extent I relied on my Sindhi-speaking assistant for such knowledge.

Advantages and Disadvantages of Probability Sampling

Major justification for using probability samples in any discipline lies in the precision with which they allow inferences drawn from the sample to the sampled universe to be statistically grounded. Speaking less exactly: when sampling is used to control for bias, one is relatively safer in generalizing from the few to the many. As I pointed out, such safety vanishes upon leaving the sampled universe (or sampling frame) in order to extend results to a larger aggregate of which the frame itself is but a part, unless one knows precisely how the frame fits the target universe. Probability sampling can conveniently and confidently answer questions concerning the frequency with which features are distributed in a large population: the number of people who possess certain amenities in their homes, are gainfully employed, possess certain cognitive and emotional traits as measured by the Rorschach test, or immigrated to the community in various years. The technique need not involve people directly. It can, for example, be effectively used to discover the number of times a certain value or sentiment is expressed in newspaper editorials and reports of political speeches during an election campaign (Garrett and Honigmann 1965). Beyond such descriptive use, probability methods are even more important for the way they lend themselves to discovering predictive relationships in a given universe. Do mental health ratings vary with income or with other indicators of socioeconomic status? (Srole *et al.* 1962:32ff., 210ff.) Hypotheses following from such questions can often be confidently tested with the aid of samples drawn by some method of random selection.

Probability sampling may be to some extent inappropriate when the aim of research is to understand a social or cultural *system* to whose operation or dynamics individual actors or artifacts offer only clues. When interest then lies in discovering the logical relationship that exists between norms, statuses, organizations, or patterns of overt behavior, both deviant and non-deviant, the incidence of those phenomena is not a crucial question. Such a problem is little concerned with generalizing data from a few to the many units comprising a universe. Research problems, however, rarely correspond solely to quantitative or qualitative matters. It is rare that results obtained through one procedure can't be enlightened by results obtained in another way. Consequently, it will more often than not be advantageous to apply probability methods along with other field-work techniques. At least, one will be wise always to weigh carefully the possibilities in using or not using probability sampling and in estimating its relative advantages and disadvantages.

A latent function of probability sampling deserves attention. The careful planning it requires forces an investigator to give much thought to what he wants to learn about, and why. Therefore it is especially appropriate to problem-oriented research where it helps in defining the crucial variables which, in turn, are often few enough to allow an adequate – sampling frame to be efficiently constructed.

Turning now to disadvantages, the care and time required to construct sampling frames which in the end probably don't fully cover the target universe must certainly be taken into account (Hill 1963:8, Parten 1950: 111-112, 225-226). Perhaps it would be more efficient to sample opportunistically, carefully identifying the pertinent characteristics of the informants, particularly if precise estimates of frequency are unimportant. Furthermore, in culturally unfamiliar social systems, an adequate sampling frame can't be constructed until much preliminary study has been done. By that time the knowledge to be gained by probability sampling may be very small pickings indeed, especially if research is not problem-oriented. The relatively few variables involved in problem-oriented research constitute an advantage that allows an adequate sampling frame to be efficiently constructed. In comparison, it is very difficult if not impossible to sample by probability techniques for all the information that is pertinent when studying a total culture. In our study of town-dwelling Eskimo in Frobisher Bay we would have needed a staff of several people and much more time than we had to cover by probability sampling all the sources we actually explored; that is, to sample the local radio station's output, school-attendance records, aims and goals of the town's various organizations, activities and learning opportunities in the various shops, earnings and expenditures, amount of fresh food that full- and part-time hunters brought in, attitudes of Euro-Canadians toward Eskimo, child rearing, and so on.[8]

Although several large-scale random sample surveys have been successfully conducted under conditions of extreme suspicion and fear (cf. Southall and Gutkind 1956:235), in some parts of the world people randomly selected for interviewing would very likely so often refuse to answer questions that the proportion of uncompleted interviews would destroy the sample's representativeness. There will always be some people in a random sample who refuse to provide information for which they are solicited or who will be unavailable for interviews. They, in fact, did not have a chance equal to that of the more willing of the sample to be interviewed. Confidence in the results of a random sample is seriously impaired if the proportion of non-collaborators becomes too high, say 10 percent of the total sample or more (Cochran, Mosteller, and Tukey 1954). The implication then is that those who responded constitute a select and unrepresentative selection. In a study of sexual behavior they are, perhaps, the high performers, exhibitionists, or extroverts who distort what actually occurs in the universe (cf. Himelhoch and Fava 1955: chaps. 7-11). Resistance to being interviewed, I suspect, is likely to be frequently encountered in relatively small-scale communities. When it occurs, it springs not only from hostility or suspicion but also from inexperience with, and little taste for, the kind of introspection, reporting, and forethought that people in a different type of society so effectively manage when they are asked to respond to a host of apparently unrelated questions (Lerner 1958:147). We failed largely to overcome such unwillingness in Frobisher Bay Eskimo and as a result could barely complete even a simple household census.

Probability and Nonprobability Samples Compared

It is interesting to look at two experiments in field work which employed both probability and nonprobability samples under controlled conditions. A hypothesis I tested with data obtained in three Pakistan villages predicted that random and opportunistic samples would be significantly different in composition (Honigmann and Honigmann 1955). Results show that male subjects appearing in the combined opportunistic samples for the three villages differed in socio-economic status from those in the combined random sample. The combined random sample shows 9, 60, and 31 percent of the respondents coming from the upper, middle, and lower socioeconomic respectively. In comparison, the opportunistic samples drew 17, 46, and 37 percent of the respondents from those strata. Apparently, by querying men who came to our attention, spoke English, and proved to be willing informants we had especially shown a bias for the uppermost stratum. Why lower-status men were also over-sampled is not clear. I can only suggest that my intention to avoid unduly representing high-status people made me zealous in contacting men from the opposite end of the continuum. I also compared the Sindhi and Punjabi to see if the random and opportunistic samples would be different not only in composition but in two types of response: attendance at the film performances and number of people showing correct awareness of the government presenting the films. (For this purpose I did not use data from the North-West Frontier Province village where sampling had proven to be very difficult.) Differences at the .05 level of probability or lower occurred with respect to both types of response. This suggests, by the logic of probability sampling, that I would have been mistaken had I relied solely on the opportunistic sample to inform me about the behavior of village population from which those helpful and informative men came.

Among Cree Indians in Attawapiskat in 1955 I used Card II of the Behn Rorschach Test to discover whether information obtained from a random adult sample (N=20) in response to a controlled stimulus would differ significantly from adults opportunistically selected (N=23) (Honigmann and Carrera 1957).[9] I predicted that the samples would differ in respect to eight scored response categories (e.g., animal content, human content, total responses, incidence of color, incidence of rejection). Differences between the means of the random and opportunistic samples turned out to be statistically nonsignificant. However, a second test hints that the stimulus itself was nondiscriminatory; for when the two Cree Indian samples were compared to ninety-six undergraduate college students, no significant differences showed up between means of those two groups.

From these experiments it is possible to conclude that the more homogeneous the universe, the more likely it is that probability and non-probability samples will manifest similar characteristics and results. The reason is clear: the small variability in the universe means that all respondents are likely to respond in similar ways to the same situation.[10] The more stratified the universe, the more likely that probability and nonprobability samples drawn from the same strata will respond similarly. Again the reason is clear: the relative homogeneity within each stratum means that all respondents coming from it are likely to respond in similar ways to the same situation. Presumably anthropologists in small-scale homogeneous communities take advantage of the community's slight variability when they sample opportunistically and generalize from the sample to the population at large. When Margaret Mead, speaking of large-scale heterogeneous social systems, advises carefully identifying pertinent characteristics of opportunistically chosen informants, she is in effect saying that the anthropologist who confronts considerable variability must create and sample more categories in which variability is reduced. Sampling opportunistically from homogeneous strata reduces the possibility that different results would be obtained between probability and nonprobability samples.

Bibliography

Baeck, L., 1961. An expenditure study of the Congolese *Evolues* of Leopoldville, Belgian Congo. In Aidan Southall, ed., *Social change in modern Africa*. London, Oxford University Press.

Beattie, John, 1965. *Understanding an African kingdom: Bunyoro*. New York, Holt, Rinehart and Winston.

Cochran, William G., Frederick Mosteller, and John W. Tukey, 1954. Statistical problems of the Kinsey report. *Journal of the American Statistical Association* 48: 673-716.

Codere, Helen, 1955. A genealogical study of kinship in the United States. *Psychiatry* 18:65-79.

Deming, W. Edwards, 1960. *Sample design in business research*. New York, Wiley.

Festinger, Leon, and Daniel Katz (eds.), 1953. *Research methods in the behavioral sciences*. New York, Dryden Press.

Firth, Raymond, 1951. *Elements of social organization*. London, Watts.

Fortes, M., R. W. Steel, and P. Ady, 1947. Ashanti survey, 1945–46: an experiment in social research. *Geographical Journal* 110:149-179.

Garrett, Sue Gena, and John J. Honigmann, 1965. *Pakistani values revealed in the 1964 national election*. Manuscript.

Goldfrank, Esther S., 1948. The impact of situation and personality on four Hopi emergence myths. *Southwestern Journal of Anthropology* 4:241-262.

Gorer, Geoffrey, 1955. *Exploring English character*. London, Cresset Press.

Hansen, Morris H., William N. Hurwitz, and William C. Madow, 1953. *Sample survey methods and theory,* Vol. 1, *Methods and Applications*. New York, Wiley.

Hill, Polly, 1963. *The migrant cocoa-farmers of Southern Ghana*. Cambridge, England, University Press.

Himelhoch, Jerome and Sylvia Fleis Fava, 1955. *Sexual behavior in American society*. New York, Norton.

Honigmann, John J., 1949. *Culture and ethos of Kaska society*. Yale University Publications in Anthropology, No. 40.

–. 1953. *Information for Pakistan, report of research on intercultural communication through films.* Chapel Hill, Institute for Research in Social Science, University of North Carolina. Mimeographed.

–. 1964. Survival of a cultural focus. In Ward H. Goodenough, ed., *Explorations in cultural anthropology.* New York, McGraw-Hill.

Honigmann, John J. and Richard Carrera, 1957. Another experiment in sample reliability. *Southwestern Journal of Anthropology* 13:99-102.

Honigmann, John J. and Irma Honigmann, 1955. Sampling reliability in ethnological field work. *Southwestern Journal of Anthropology* 11:282-287.

–. 1965. *Eskimo townsmen.* Ottawa, Canadian Research Centre for Anthropology, University of Ottawa.

Kerlinger, Fred N., 1965. *Foundations of behavioral research.* New York, Holt, Rinehart and Winston.

Kish, Leslie, 1953. Selection of the sample. In Leon Festinger and Daniel Katz, eds., Research methods in the behavioral sciences. New York, Dryden Press.

Kroeber, A. L., 1957. *Ethnographic interpretations 1-6.* University of California Publications in American Archaeology and Ethnology 47, No. 2.

Leach, Edmund R., 1958. An anthropologist's reflections on a social survey. *Ceylon Journal of Historical and Social Studies* 1:9-20.

Leighton, Dorothea C, John S. Harding, David B. Macklin, Allister M. Macmillan, and Alexander H. Leighton, 1963. *The character of danger.* New York, Basic Books.

Lerner, Daniel, 1958. *The passing of traditional society.* New York, Free Press of Glencoe.

Mandelbaum, David G., 1953. On the study of national character. *American Anthropologist* 55:174-187.

Marris, Peter, 1961. *Family and social change in an African city.* London, Routledge and Kegan Paul.

McCall, D., 1961. Trade and the role of wife in a modern West African town. In Aidan Southall, ed., *Social change in modern Africa.* London, Oxford University Press.

Mead, Margaret, 1928. *Coming of age in Samoa.* New York, William Morrow.

–. 1932. *The changing culture of an Indian tribe.* Contributions to Anthropology, No. 15. New York, Columbia University Press.

–. 1951a. Research in contemporary culture. In Harold Guetzkow, ed., *Groups, leadership and men.* Pittsburgh, Carnegie Press.

–. 1951b. The study of national character. In Daniel Lerner and Harold D. Lasswell, eds., *The policy sciences.* Stanford, Stanford University Press.

–. 1952. Some relationships between social anthropology and psychiatry. In Franz Alexander and Helen Ross, eds., *Dynamic psychiatry.* Chicago, University of Chicago Press.

–. 1953. National character. In A. L. Kroeber, ed., *Anthropology today.* Chicago, Chicago University Press.

–. 1954. The swaddling hypothesis: its reception. *American Anthropologist* 56:395-409.

–. 1955. Effects of anthropological field work models on intercultural communication. *Journal of Social Issues* 11 (No. 2): 3-11.

–. 1961. National character and the science of anthropology. In Seymour M. Lipset and Leo Lowenthal, eds., *Culture and social character.* New York, Free Press of Glencoe.

–. 1964. The idea of national character. In Roger L. Shinn, ed., *The search for identity: essays on the American character.* New York, Harper.

Mead, Margaret, and Rhoda Metraux, 1953. *The study of culture at a distance.* Chicago, University of Chicago Press.

Metraux, Rhoda, 1943. Qualitative attitude analysis. In Margaret Mead, ed., *The problem of changing food habits*. National Research Council, Bulletin 108.

Parten, Mildred, 1950. *Surveys, polls, and samples*. New York, Harper and Row.

Riley, Matilda White, 1963. *Sociological research, Vol. 1, a case approach*. New York, Harcourt, Brace.

Smith, Raymond T., 1963. Review of family structure in Jamaica: the social context of reproduction, by Judith Blake. *American Anthropologist* 65:158-161.

Southall, Aidan, 1961. *Social change in modern Africa*. London, Oxford University Press.

Southall, Aidan W., and Peter C. W. Gutkind, 1956. *Townsmen in the making*. East African Studies, No. 9.

Spindler, George D., 1955. *Sociocultural and psychological processes in Menomini acculturation*. University of California Publications in Culture and Society, Vol. 5.

Srole, Leo, Thomas S. Langner, Stanley T. Michael, Marvin Opler, and Thomas A. C. Rennie, 1962. *Mental health in the metropolis*. New York, McGraw-Hill.

Tremblay, Marc-Adelakd, 1957. The key informant technique: A non-ethnographic application. *American Anthropologist* 59:688-701.

Vidich, A., and J. Bensman, 1954. The validity of field data. *Human Organization* 13 (No. l):20-27.

Wallace, Anthony F. C., 1952. *The modal personality structure of the Tuscarora Indians*. Bureau of American Ethnology, Bulletin 150.

Wallis, W. Allen, and Harry W. Roberts, 1956. *Statistics: a new approach*. New York, Free Press of Glencoe.

Whiting, John W. M., *et al.*, 1966. *Field guide for a study of socialization in five societies*. New York, Wiley.

Zelditch, Morris, Jr., 1962. Some methodological problems of field studies. *American Journal of Sociology* 67:566-576.

Notes

1. 1 believe Kroeber originally made this point.
2. Her views mainly appear in Mead 1951b, 1953, 1954, 1955, 1961; and Mead and Metraux 1953:1-53. See also Zelditch 1962.
3. For an example see the use Goldfrank (1948) makes of such information in analyzing versions of myths.
4. In describing how probability samples are selected I follow mainly Parten 1950:116-122 and Riley 1963: 284-287.
5. For the theory of sampling see any of the following: Deming 1960; Hansen, Hurwitz, and Madow 1953; Kerlinger 1965: chap. 4; Kish 1953; Wallis and Roberts 1956: chaps. 4, 10, and 15; also Naroll's chapter on statistical inference in this volume.
6. For more on the mechanics of drawing samples see Parten 1950:265-272, 277-280.
7. For information on these and other methods see Hansen, Hurwitz, and Madow 1953 or Parten 1950.
8. I forbear going into arguments concerning the validity of responses obtained by use of questionnaires. For discussions of this question see Vidich and Bensman 1954 and Zelditch 1962.

9. The Wenner-Gren Foundation for Anthropological Research supported the field work in Attawapiskat.
10. I am indebted to Donald R. Ploch for the following conclusions and for a very critical and helpful reading of the section dealing with probability sampling.

25

Decision Taking in the Fieldwork Process: Theoretical Sampling and Collaborative Working

Janet Finch and Jennifer Mason

O ne of the key ways in which qualitative or fieldwork methods differ from social surveys is in the sampling or selection of the people and situations that are studied. In surveys, such decisions are made once-and-for-all at the beginning of a project, and follow formalized statistical procedures for sampling. In fieldwork, such decisions are taken at various stages during the course of the project on the basis of contextual information. To outsiders who are not privy to the changing contextual basis of this project, research decisions can look rather ad hoc.

In this chapter we are going to discuss the questions of whether and how decisions about fieldwork sampling can be taken in a systematic way. We will use our experiences of working together on the research study of Family Obligations to provide the contextual information necessary for a discussion of systematic decision taking.[1] At the time of writing we are at the mid-point of this study with most of the data collected but much of the formal analysis still to be done, so we cannot relate to our sampling strategies to our final analysis. However, what we have tried to do is to reflect the blend of practical and intellectual considerations that form the basis of decision taking in the fieldwork process, at a stage when these are fresh in our minds.

We begin by briefly describing the Family Obligations project before outlining the principle of theoretical sampling, which represents a possible model of systematic selection in qualitative research. In the main part of this paper we discuss how we attempted to develop and apply this principle in our own research and we use our experience to suggest more generally the problems and possibilities of this approach. A further important theme in our

---

Source: *Studies in Qualitative Methodology*, 1990, vol. 2, pp. 25-50.

discussion is the extent to which working collaboratively facilitates systematic qualitative research.

The Family Obligations Project

Our project involves investigating patterns of support, aid and assistance, of both practical and material kinds, between adult kin in a survey population based in the Greater Manchester area. As well as being interested in patterns of support, we are exploring concepts of obligation and responsibility to assist one's relatives, the circumstances in which these come into play, and the processes through which these are related to actions. We have used a conceptual framework for studying family obligations based on a contrast between two different ways of conceptualizing obligations: as moral norms and as negotiated commitments (Finch, 1987). On the one hand, family obligations might be seen as part of a structure of normative rules that operate within a particular society, and which simply get applied in appropriate situations. On the other hand, they might be seen as agreements that operate between specific individuals and are arrived at through a process of negotiation. This negotiation may be explicit, or more likely may be covert. We would argue that a full understanding of what family obligations mean and how they operate almost certainly contains elements of both of these.

Our perspective suggests that these norms are not really like rigid and precise rules that must be followed, or that are imposed on passive individuals. Rather they are general guidelines for "proper" or "correct" behavior toward one's relatives, which "everyone is aware of," but that need to be interpreted or tailored in specific situations. It is at this level of interpretation that the notion of negotiated commitments comes to the fore: if it is the case that norms are not sufficiently detailed or universally applicable to be used straightforwardly in concrete situations among relatives, then in what ways are actual commitments and responsibilities negotiated? This part of our perspective casts "negotiation" in broad terms, allowing not only for "round the table" explicit negotiations, but also for other processes by which particular patterns of obligation become "obvious" to members of kin groups.

We are not going to discuss the substantive issues in the project here, but it is necessary to give some detail so that we can explain the nature of the decisions that we had to take about selection and sampling. The perspectives upon the study of family obligations that we have outlined here guided the overall planning of the project, and led to a research design that included both a large-scale quantitative survey and also a second stage of qualitative fieldwork, mainly based on in-depth interviews. In the survey we were concentrating solely upon data about normative beliefs, and at the second stage we wanted to use qualitative techniques to understand more about the complexity of beliefs, as well as the relationship between beliefs and actions, and how people actually negotiate commitments with their own relatives.

It is this second stage that we discuss in this chapter, as this was where we were trying to put theoretical sampling into practice. We planned to use the survey population as a sampling frame from which to select individuals for more detailed study. We had a total survey population of 978 randomly selected individuals over the age of eighteen, of whom 85% had agreed at the time of the survey that they would be willing to be reinterviewed.[2]

We, therefore, had the possibility either of choosing another randomly selected group for more detailed study or of targeting particular subgroups. A further consideration was that we hoped to be able, in some cases, not only to reinterview a survey respondent, but also to interview members of his or her kin group, thus building up a more complete picture of negotiations within families. In a sense, therefore, we were operating two levels of selection: interviewees from the survey population, then the kin groups of some of those interviewees. There was a limitation of numbers in that we had budgeted for 120 interviews at this second stage, but other than that we were free to be guided by theoretical considerations, and by our preliminary analysis of the survey data, in deciding whom to interview. However, we needed a strategy that was very flexible so that we could: (1) change direction as we went along if necessary, (2) leave open the possibility of doing more than one interview with some respondents, and (3) maintain the possibility of interviewing other members of the kin group.

We had, therefore, in effect set ourselves the task of being both flexible and systematic in our selection of interviewees for the qualitative stage. In practice this seems commonly to be the aim of much fieldwork based research, and certainly sits comfortably with a strategy of theoretical sampling.

A Guiding Principle: Theoretical Sampling

What are the main themes in the existing literature on fieldwork that can help to guide our thinking on this process? In addition to the emphasis upon selection as an on-going process, the two important themes seem to be first the interplay of theory and data, and second that the analysis of data is a process that continues throughout the project rather than occurring as a discrete phase after the data collection is complete. Theory should guide data collection and the on-going analysis of data should feed back into theory, which in turn guides the next phase of data collection. Most fieldwork researchers would acknowledge that this is the model to which they aspire, but as other commentators have noted this process is often not put into practice very effectively, leaving (and there are often) quite serious gaps between theory and data (Hammersley and Atkinson 1983, p. 174).

The concept of theoretical sampling is probably the most common way of translating this model of the research process into guidelines about selection of research situations or informants. Certainly this is the concept that guided our own thinking and it forms a central focus of this chapter. We offer an account of our own experience of trying to put into practice the notion of theoretical sampling, and use this to draw out some general principles about how qualitative research can be done in a systematic way.

The term "theoretical sampling" is generally associated with Glaser and Strauss's treatise on the discovery of grounded theory (1967), but its logic and practice has become part of a tradition of qualitative research (Bertaux 1981; Schwarz and Jacobs 1979; Baldamus 1972; Hammersley and Atkinson 1983). Essentially, theoretical sampling means selecting a study population on theoretical rather than, say, statistical grounds. The underlying logic is one of analytical rather than enumerative induction which were distinguished many years ago by Znaniecki in the following way:

> Enumerative induction abstracts by generalisation, whereas analytic induction generalises by abstracting. The former looks in many cases for characters that are similar and abstracts them conceptually because of their generality, presuming that they must be essential to each particular case; the latter abstracts from the given concrete case characteristics that are essential to it and generalises them, presuming that insofar as they are essential, they must be similar in many cases (Znaniecki 1934, pp. 250-251).

This means that theoretical sampling involves a search for validity of findings, rather than representativeness of study population. However, for some degree of generalization to be made about the consequent research findings, it is vital that the processes of theoretical sampling (as well as data presentation) be *systematically* carried through and documented.

Yet when viewed apart from its context, certain aspects of theoretical sampling can appear ad hoc and unsystematic. In particular, from a positivist standpoint, where research decisions are made in advance of operationalization and tested through hypotheses on a randomly sampled population, the continual making of decisions throughout the course of the research can itself appear very unsystematic. Of course this is partly because the two endeavors are not entirely comparable: qualitative researchers following theoretical sampling are generally looking to build theory from data rather than to test hypotheses on representative populations. At the same time, however, we are not suggesting that qualitative researchers have license to be unsystematic in their decision making simply because it cannot be done in "one go." Rather, we would emphasize that the validity of the qualitative researcher's interpretations depends in part upon the quality and relevance of their in-process decisions.

But what does this actually mean in practice? How is theoretical sampling *done?* Given that such importance is placed upon in-progress decision making in particular research settings, then it is inappropriate to set down in advance a series of general rules about how to make informed and systematic decisions. Instead we describe below what we did, and on what basis we made our decisions. As well as giving a more situated feel for theoretical sampling, this will in a sense provide the data from which to extrapolate some more general observations at the end.

A Guiding Practice: Collaborative Working

A vital part of the way in which we have put theoretical sampling into practice in the Family Obligations project has been through collaborative working. Neither of us had worked in a close collaboration of this kind before, and, therefore, part of our task was to develop ways of working together effectively. Janet Finch had set up the project and organized the survey fieldwork[3] and Jennifer Mason joined her at the stage when that was completed. It had been agreed that we each would take an equal share in planning and conducting the qualitative fieldwork, but we wanted to ensure that our contributions were fully integrated with each others' and that the fieldwork would be a genuine collaboration. We tried to achieve this in a number of ways.

Joint Discussions and Planning

From the beginning we held regular joint discussions about our plans, strategies and practice. Our early discussions centered on ways of working together, how often we should meet and so on. We decided at that time always to take decisions together about overall strategy and practice. This may seem a rather obvious point to make about collaboration, but we know from our own contacts with other researchers, as well as from a few published accounts, that decisions are not always taken openly and explicitly in research teams, leaving the opportunity for misunderstandings and disagreements to arise about what strategy is actually being followed (Platt 1976; Bell 1977; Porter 1984).

Division of Labor

One aspect of our practice that we have always discussed, rather than assumed, is our division of labor. Jennifer Mason was employed for three years full-time on the Family Obligations project, and Janet Finch, who holds a full-time university teaching post, had arranged to have one year seconded to the research project. This meant that our first year of working together could involve collaboration on a full-time basis for both of us. One of the reasons Janet Finch had set up the project timing and staffing in this way was so that she could maintain a full involvement in the fieldwork stage, and the research process that we discuss in this chapter all took place during that time.

Therefore, when discussing our fieldwork division of labor we could take an equal share of the tasks. As a result, we were able to organize ourselves to conduct half of the interviews each, as well as to structure in time to keep up to date with what the other was doing. Some of the procedures we used to maintain an ongoing preliminary analysis of the fieldwork are described later.

Collective Research Diary

One of the mechanisms that we used to achieve this was a collective research diary. We agreed at an early stage that we would record all substantial discussions that we had about the research, and would always give each other a copy of any notes that were made individually. In each of our joint meetings, we would agree that one of us would take notes and produce a record of the meeting, so that our collective research diary is made up of contributions from both of us.

It is this collective research diary that forms the basis of our discussion here. We have decided to include extracts from this diary and we have kept these in their raw state with no editing, so that readers can see the actual process of decision taking at work. When these notes were written, we had no idea that we might publish them in this way, and they were written solely for our own use although we did anticipate reflecting on them and using them in our analysis. We have little idea whether our procedures match other people's since personal research diaries of this kind are seldom made publicly available. Equally, we know little about the actual day-to-day procedures that people use to work collaboratively, and how far ours are distinctive. We have decided to include our raw notes as extracts because of the lack of discussion in the literature about these issues, although the importance of making public the research process in this way has been noted by others (Stenhouse 1980; Burgess 1984).

Initial Selection of Interviewees

We shall deal with issues of selection as they occurred chronologically telling our story in the order in which things actually happened, but also drawing out theoretical points as we go along. Figure 1 provides a "map" of the sequencing of events in the story.

The first set of decisions that we had to make concerned which people in the survey population would be chosen for more detailed study. We also had to decide how many to select. There were a number of interwoven considerations here concerning: principles of selection; the possibility of having subgroups and how many of these we would realistically include; strategies for selection to retain maximum flexibility especially to accommodate successful attempts to move outward to some interviewees' kin. Extract A is taken from the record of the planning meeting in which we talked through all these issues.

Extract A: Notes from the Record of Planning Meeting 5/8/86
(recorded by Janet Finch)

Our final decision was as follows:
  We will begin selecting interviewees from two sub groups: people who have

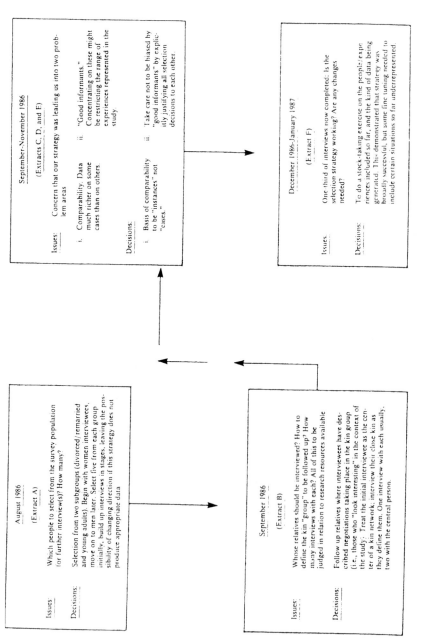

August 1986

(Extract A)

Issues: Which people to select from the survey population for further interview(s)? How many?

Decisions: Selection from two subgroups (divorced/remarried and young adults). Begin with women interviewers, move on to men later. Select five from each group initially, build up interviews in stages, leaving the possibility of changing direction if this strategy does not produce appropriate data

September 1986

(Extract B)

Issues: Whose relatives should be interviewed? How to define the kin "group" to be followed up? How many interviews with each? All of this to be judged in relation to research resources available

Decisions: Follow up relatives where interviewees have described negotiations taking place in the kin group (i.e., those who "look interesting" in the context of the study). Treat the initial interviewee as the center of a kin network; interview their close kin as they define them. One interview with each usually, two with the central person.

September-November 1986

(Extracts C, D, and E)

Issues: Concern that our strategy was leading us into two problem areas

i. Comparability. Data much richer on some cases than on others.

ii. "Good informants." Concentrating on these might be restricting the range of experiences represented in the study.

Decisions:

i. Basis of comparability to be "instances" not "cases."

ii. Take care not to be biased by "good informants" by explicitly justifying all selection decisions to each other.

December 1986-January 1987

(Extract F)

Issues: One third of interviews now completed. Is the selection strategy working? Are any changes needed?

Decisions: To do a stock-taking exercise on the people/experiences included so far, and the kind of data being generated. This demonstrated that strategy was broadly successful, but some fine tuning needed to include certain situations so far underrepresented.

Decision-Taking Sequence

been divorced and/or remarried; young adults (under 25 at the time of the survey).

We will begin with women, until we have our selection procedures running smoothly and have decided on the merits of employing a male interviewer.

We will begin with five from each group, randomly selected from our list of people who meet these criteria. If we have a refusal, we will replace it with another name, selected randomly.

We will build up from there, seeing how far we can get with the kin groups of each, and adding more names from our sample. Our final aim will be to have qualitative data not only from people whose current, recent life experience has involved a renegotiation of family relationships (the basis of the above categories) but also people whose experience is close to the stereotypic norm of family life. If we do not pick up such people via kin groups, we may select from a different sub group of our sample, such as people with large kin networks who were once married or "women in the middle" (of a younger and older generation). We also want our final selection to have a reasonably good social class spread, and therefore we may select interviewees at a later stage which enable us to do that. Social Class I may be a case in point.

This strategy also opens the possibility of finding some other sub group, or individuals with particular characteristics who emerge as important during the course of earlier interviews.

The reasoning which lies behind this strategy included the following considerations:

1. A target sample of sixty individuals at the second stage means that four sub groups (i.e., fifteen in each) looks like the absolute maximum. But if we are successful in interviewing kin, then the number selected from the sample will be smaller than sixty. Our strategy of two main sub groups therefore seems realistic.

2. Our two sub groups are selected on the basis of life experience, and we have focused on people where their family relationships are likely to have undergone some renegotiation, which makes issues of obligation more explicit. They are also sub groups which seem to be significant in terms of social change, in that the rules of family obligations are currently probably being written/rewritten – because of divorce/remarriage becoming an increasingly common experience and because of pressures which seem to be creating longer periods of non-independence for young people.

3. We considered principles of selection based upon views expressed in the interview, especially people who gave "standard" answers and people who were in "deviant" minorities. We rejected this because: it seemed less important than the other principles of selection and we didn't want to multiply sub groups; we can probably get a lot out of the interviews themselves in relation to these issues; the second stage interviews are to concentrate upon experience rather than beliefs.

4. We considered adding a third group which would effectively be a control group, composed of people whose experience seems near to the stereotype norm. Although we agreed that it is important to build in the principle of comparison between typical and atypical experience, we decided not to select these initially as a former control group, because: we want to maintain maximum flexibility; to add a third group would mean that we reduce the numbers in the other two at an earlier stage; we may well pick up people

whose experience is close to the norm *via* the interviewees initially selected on the other criteria. So we decided instead to treat this as a gap filling exercise at a later stage.

5. Part of the reason for rejecting a formal control group was that this concept derives from an underlying logic which doesn't really fit this stage of the project. We aren't aiming at generalisation based on represenativeness, etc. Instead, we think that our agreed strategy is actually quite faithful to the principles of inductive logic. Indeed, we have left our options open to select cases which emerge as key in the course of our interviews.

It can be seen from this extract that we decided to sample initially from two subgroups: people who had been divorced and/or remarried, and the youngest age group in our population, namely people aged eighteen to twenty-four at the time of the survey. The reasons for this are centrally concerned with theoretical sampling. We quickly rejected the idea of a randomly selected subgroup on the grounds that we were not trying to use our qualitative data to make generalizations based on representativeness (although the survey data of course could be used in that way). Since fieldwork was principally to be concerned with understanding the process of negotiation between relatives, we decided that it would be much more useful to focus upon individuals who might currently or recently have been involved in processes of negotiation and renegotiation of family relationships. We hoped that talking to these individuals would give us access to family situations in which those processes would be most visible. The two groups that we chose seemed to fulfill these criteria.

It is important to underline (as we have found that people sometimes misunderstand what we are saying about our selection strategy) that we did not select these two as comparison groups in the orthodox sense. We were not seeking straightforwardly to compare the experience of young adults and divorced people, but were using both groups as a "way in" to the kind of family situations that we did want to study. We were, for example, very interested in the care of elderly people and how responsibilities for that develop over time within families, but we did not select an elderly subgroup because we hoped that our selection strategy would lead us to such situations in the kin group of the young people and the divorced people whom we had selected. In this sense, we were selecting kin groups (or at least situations in kin groups) as the focus of our study, rather than individual. We recognized, of course, that this strategy might not work, and it can be seen from Extract A that we built in the possibility of reviewing and revising our strategy during the course of the fieldwork.

The major principle that we used to guide our selection, therefore, was theoretical significance: we chose to focus on those groups that would enable us best to evaluate and develop the theoretical ideas and concepts with which we began the project. However, it can be seen from Extract A that we were also juggling with a number of other considerations that helped to shape our overall strategy. We will comment briefly on these.

1. Although we were not aiming at statistical representativeness in this fieldwork study, we did want to ensure that we included a range of experiences of family life. We wanted to include some situations (like divorce) which would be a minority experience and others that were more routine and typical. Further, we could see from our survey data that some subgroups in the population had answered our questionnaire in a distinctive way, and we wanted to ensure that their personal experiences were reflected in our qualitative study. People in Social Class I were one example mentioned in the Extract. There were other groups – for example, people who have experienced unemployment – whose experience we also wanted to include because of its public importance in contemporary Britain. At this initial stage we decided to wait and see if our selection strategy based on two subgroups would lead us to a good range of situations which included all of these. If not, we left open the possibility of rethinking our strategy at a later stage.

2. The inclusion of the experience of non-white people presented us with particular problems since the survey population had only a small number of respondents from ethnic minorities (the refusal rate having apparently been high among these groups). We were also aware that we might want to change slightly the format of our interview to make it appropriate to distinctive cultural experiences, and that we might wish to seek advice on this. At the initial selection stage, while we were strongly committed to not producing an ethnocentric piece of research, we decided that we would come back to the issue of specifically selecting some non-white interviewees at a later stage in the fieldwork, after we had gotten our procedures operating smoothly.

3. We took a similar decision in respect of interviewing men, although for completely different reasons. We wanted to include both women and men in our study, both in our initial selection of interviewees and as relatives of those selected. However, since we would be conducting interviews in people's own homes, and because we were two female researchers, we were conscious of issues about personal safety and felt that it would be unwise for either of us to go alone into the homes of unknown men (McKee 1983). We considered various possible strategies, including employing a male interviewer, but at this stage in the project we felt dissatisfied with all of the possible solutions. We decided, therefore, that the first group of interviewees selected would be all women, thus buying ourselves time to get our interview procedures running smoothly before we tried to solve the problem of men.

The skeptical reader might accuse us of having put off a great many decisions and conclude that we were unclear about what we wanted to do and unwilling to make firm choices. However, the whole point about trying to achieve an interplay between theory and data, and the logic of analytic induction that underlies fieldwork procedures, is that decisions cannot be taken in a final and irrevocable form before any data are collected. This is because we cannot know in advance of studying some actual cases what are (to put it in Znaniecki's terms) the essentials that we would want to abstract in order to compare them with other cases and to test and refine our generalizations. What we were trying to do at the initial stage of selection was to decide *where to look* for the processes of negotiating obligations in families, rather than to prejudge *what* we would find. In these decisions about where to look we were trying to be guided in a systematic way by theory, while maintaining the flexibility to look elsewhere at a later stage if we had gotten it wrong, and to be able to build in, at a later stage, the comparisons that would emerge as most significant on the basis of our initial cases.

These principles of selection had to then be translated into practical strategy, and we decided that we would proceed by selecting small numbers of people from each subgroup. We actually selected five at a time from each subgroup, giving ourselves the opportunity to assess how many actual interviews we were achieving, and how many relatives we were following up, before going on to select some more initial contacts. We had a total list of 117 young adults who were willing to be interviewed again and 112 people who had been divorced and/or remarried. Each time we selected from these lists we did so using a table of random numbers, since we did not want to develop more detailed criteria about whom to follow up. This, of course, still left open the possibility that at a later stage we could "search" for people who had a particular combination of characteristics that we might wish to include. For example, we could look for people who were unemployed as well as in the young adult group if this experience was not being included in the cases we had initially selected.

At this initial stage we think that our procedures do demonstrate a fairly successful attempt to be both systematic and flexible. We recognize that the actual detail of what we did could not be straightforwardly translated into a different project. We had, for example, a great deal of prior information about potential interviewees based on the survey questionnaires, probably far more than is usually available at the beginning of a piece of fieldwork. But we think that the underlying logical procedures that we were using can certainly be translated to other contexts.

Selecting Kin Groups

Our procedure for sampling individuals from the survey population proceeded as described. After the first five sampled from each group, we continued sampling in small bunches, substituting refusals by another random selection from the same subgroup. Having set the wheels in motion in this way we had to decide whose relatives we would like to include in our study. Developing criteria for identifying kin to be followed up proved to be the selection task that we found most difficult and we will discuss it in detail in this section. Extract B shows how our initial thinking on this issue developed.

Extract B: Notes from Record of Planning Meeting 23/9/86
(recorded by Jennifer Mason)
Interviews with Members of the Kin Group-Discussion of Rationale and Strategy
Whose Kin Group Do We Want to Study?

We discussed the pros and cons of either using our respondent as the central person and examining their kin group, or of using them as a way into a variety of kin groups. We decided on the former strategy because:

we will then have survey data on all the people whose kin groups we are examining, because they will all have been survey respondents.

there is a logic of selection whereas if we were to get deflected into other kin groups it would all become very haphazard.

interviews with relatives will thus be used to elucidate our survey respondents kin group and the negotiations within it.

Which Relatives to Select
After a fairly detailed discussion we decided to use the following selection principles:

we will try to interview relatives with whom negotiations have taken place (i.e., where our survey respondents has told us about these).

we will exclude those in "crisis situations" on ethical grounds.

people with whom there has been close contact at some time in the past, i.e., where there has been some kind of negotiation, but where there is now little or no contact.

This is a way of selecting people with whom we might expect our survey respondent to be negotiating, but where negotiation appears to be absent, *without* necessarily limiting ourselves to primary kin.

By following these selection principles we will be being more precise about who we follow up than if we simply interviewed all "significant others" (i.e., significant from our survey respondent's point of view).

How Many Interviews With Each?
As with all the issues we discussed today, we had implicit assumptions and rationales about how many interviews we would want with different types of respondent, and once we had made them explicit we came up with the following:

With our survey respondent we want to know about her/his relationships in all directions, because it is her/his kin group we are studying. With other relatives, although we will have to understand something about their relationships in all directions in order to understand their relationship with our survey respondent and his/her kin, we are interested chiefly in their relationship with her/him. Therefore, *generally we will want:*

one interview only with relatives of our survey respondent, *except:*

where relatives are clearly "significant others" as far as she/he is concerned, in which case they are likely to have more to say about relationships with her/him. In these cases we will want two interviews.

where relatives fall into either our divorced/remarried or young adult categories, in which case we will want two interviews to further our understanding of issues relevant to these categories.

As far as interviews with spouses are concerned, we will only want one because we are less interested in the conjugal tie than in other aspects of kinship. Furthermore, it is neat and tidy to finish the third interview with our survey respondent at the same time as finishing the one with the spouse (i.e., where these interviews are conducted simultaneously). Also, the inter-personal point about feeling awkward because we (including Social and Community Planning Research), will have made three visits to the household by this time.

At this stage we had no idea how successful we would be at gaining access to relatives: we thought it quite possible that our interviewees would decline to pass us on, and even if they agreed, that relatives might refuse to be interviewed. Beyond that unknown element, our major concern at this stage was to decide upon the appropriate balance between getting very detailed information from a very small number of kin groups, and including a range of different experiences in our study. Given the practical limitation of having budgeted over 120 interviews, we could not do both.

Looking back on our research diary from that period, we seem to have resolved that issue (although this is not spelled out in the notes) by going back to look at the purpose of studying kin groups, that is, by working through from the logic of our theoretical ideas and the research issues upon which we were focusing. Certainly our notes do record that we clarified that our purpose in studying kin groups was to understand the process involved in negotiations between kin over financial and material support. We, therefore, felt that we needed to include a range of experiences to help us to generalize about these processes. On the other hand, the whole purpose of studying kin groups rather than individuals was to get accounts of the same issues from different parties involved, and we needed to try to interview enough people from each kin group studied to give us a rounded picture.

We decided to try to follow up the kin group of those people where the initial interview had revealed examples of negotiations between relatives over issues concerning financial or material support. In that sense we were selecting for more intensive study the kin groups of people who "looked interesting" in relation to the issues that we wanted to study. While in the end we stuck to that strategy, it was this particular issue that subsequently gave us cause for concern as we shall explain shortly.

The more practical issues to be resolved at this stage concerned how to define a kin group and how many interviews to have with each person. Our reasoning on both these issues can be seen in Extract B. We decided that in each case we would treat the person who had been in the survey population as the center of a personal kin network, and would focus on that person's significant or close kin as she or he defined them, rather than trying to be passed ever outward along chains of kin. Having taken that decision to focus on clearly defined kin "groups" centered on an individual who had been in the survey, the question about how many interviews to conduct followed fairly straightforwardly: we would do two more with the key person and one each with his or her relatives since our aim was to generate a detailed set of data on the group which centered on our key person. We anticipated that we might sometimes want two interviews with certain relatives for special reasons, but in the event we did not do this.

The disadvantage of this strategy is that it closed off the possibility of following through other relationships that looked relevant to our concerns if they did not involve the key person in the kin group. This did indeed occur. There were several instances where we interviewed a sister or a cousin of our key person who would themselves have made excellent subjects for detailed study. Extract E (see below) shows that we did go on noticing these examples and paused to consider whether our strategy should be changed. However, we continued to reason that we were prepared to sacrifice those possibilities in order to create a systematic selection strategy that would enable us to study a range of different situations. Other researchers might have taken a different decision but we felt any other approach would have led us into a series of ad hoc decisions which, in the end, would be difficult to justify.

Problem 1: Comparability

Equipped with a reasonably coherent selection strategy, we, therefore, began identifying interviewees whose relatives we would like to follow up. However, we felt a continuing concern to formalize and crystalize our thinking on these issues. The first issue that concerned us was comparability. In each case we were making decisions for good reasons, and following the principles that we had articulated, but we were concerned that these might result in a set of interviews that could be difficult to handle as comparable cases. We would have two interviews with some people, and one with others; with some people we would be following through their relatives and with others we would not. We resolved this by deciding to turn an apparent weakness to good effect. Extract C shows how we reasoned this through.

Extract C: Janet Finch's Research Notes for 27/10/86
The principle of *instances rather than cases* as the basis of comparability seems to be particularly suited to this project, since we are searching for a range of experiences and social phenomena, and we don't know in advance of the first interview which are present for a given interviewee. We concentrate on those which we do find, but that means that the idea of comparability between cases does not fit this study in any event. Because people have different experiences,

we have data on different topics from each person. The principle of taking "instances" as the basis of comparability in a way just goes one step beyond saying that we will have to count up how many interviewees have had a given experience, and that this will be less than the total number in the study. To put together instances of an event from each "side" of it, plus accounts given by third parties gives a more rounded picture. We will need to be able to justify third party examples in terms of taking these accounts *as seriously as* accounts of personal experience, but of course *not the same as* them. Third party accounts are important to us precisely because people are distanced somewhat from the circumstances and therefore they reflect a more "public" view of the situations, reflecting something of how the public morality of obligations gets applied in particular instances, I suspect.

   This approach is of course *not the only way* in which we should use examples from our data. I would anticipate that we will want to present it in different forms, and that another obvious one is extended discussion of individual cases (which might be individual people, or kin groups). Obviously the people on whom we have got the most data are likely to be the most suitable candidates for this, although that might not always be the case. My idea about comparability of instances is not to close off other methods of analysis, but simply to see a way through the problems created by the need to present some of the data in aggregated form (i.e., not *just* as a series of individual cases) and the particular issues of comparability that we seem to be building in.

Our idea was that much of our analysis should proceed, not on the basis of comparing each individual person or "case" with another but on the basis of comparing "instances" or examples in our data of particular circumstances in which we are interested. To take one example: people who have temporarily moved back into a parent's home after divorce. Instead of simply counting the number of people interviewed who themselves have moved back and comparing their experiences, we could search in our data for all examples of this happening: people who themselves had done it, people who had been the "receiving" parent, examples given of third parties doing it. Of course, for some of the instances we would have much more detailed data than for others, and for some we would have accounted from more than one party to the arrangement. Some would be personal accounts and some would be second hand accounts. That variability obviously would have to be acknowledged in the way we used the data, but in principle we could draw together a range of instances in this way from wherever they occurred in our data.

   The principle of instances rather than cases as the basis of comparability seemed to be particularly suited to our project, since we were searching for a range of experiences and social phenomena, and we did not know in advance of the first interview which would be present for a given interviewee. Again, this comes back to analytic rather than enumerative induction, because it is based on the validity of instances or processes, rather than the representativeness of the sample, as a means of generalizing and of making sociological statements. Furthermore, it illustrates ways in which we were linking our strategies at this stage to ideas about how we would use and write up the data in our formal analysis.

Problem 2: Good Informants

We resolved the question of comparability to our own satisfaction but fairly soon after this we began to be concerned about another issue connected with selection criteria for following up kin. The core of the problem here was that we were worried that we were being seduced into following up the kin groups of people whom we found interesting to interview and who made it easy for us to spot situations apparently concerning negotiations in their kin group. Some of our respondents made very "good informants" in the sense that they talked about their families using concepts that were quite close to our own, whereas others presented material in a more bland way that did not highlight issues like reciprocity, conflict, compromise, working things through, talking things out, and so on. However, this latter group might well be involved in negotiations – in the broad sense – about kin support. Were we in danger of missing the full range of experiences open to us by tending to follow up the people who were – on our distinctive definitions – most articulate and interesting?

Although the detail will vary in different projects, this must be an issue commonly faced by field researchers who want both to use "good informants" and also to produce a rounded picture of the situations they are studying that does not systematically exclude certain kinds of informants or experience. Extracts D and E show our attempts to resolve this issue. We discussed it on several occasions without getting very far before we decided that Jennifer Mason (who had originally spotted the significance of this issue) should spell out the nature of the problem on paper (Extract D). Janet Finch then responded (Extract E). As a procedure we found this a helpful way of moving beyond our verbal discussions where, on this issue in particular, we had been tending to go round in circles. In these notes, we had reached the stage where we were able to discuss concrete examples of interviews that had been completed. In the extracts these are referred to by their interview numbers.

Extract D: Jennifer Mason's Research Notes 3/11/86
Further Thoughts on Following Up Kin Groups
I have been concerned lately about the implicit criteria I am using during and after interviews to make decisions about whether people's kin groups are worth following up. After talking with Janet we agreed that I should try to make my worries explicit by writing them down.

My main worry has been that there is a danger of only following up the kin groups of articulate respondents – "good informants" – for example 01 or 110. I think my problem is that respondents like this approach some of the issues we are interested in in an analytical way – they are able to reflect and philosophise about their kin relationships – which means that they draw out interesting situations, relationships, etc. to tell us about. In fact, in both of these cases, there are situations which we could presumably identify as interesting even if they were not articulated to us in this way: e.g., sharing accommodation. But I suppose I am concerned that conceptual issues might sway us into following up a kin group – e.g., things like reciprocity, independence and dependence, conflict and tension, giving and lending - and that not all of our initial contact respondents will articulate these. However, their behaviour and kin relationships may still be bounded by/governed by these sorts of issues. So, for example, 101 did not make sharing accommodation sound half as interesting as 110, or 106.

These worries were thrown into relief a bit for me in considering 108 because I had just about made the decision during the interview (exactly as I had made the converse decision with 110), that her kin group would not be worth following up. Yet "objectively" there seemed to be some interesting features: e.g., her relationship with her mother, the effective dissolution of the family home when our respondent bought a house with her boyfriend and her mother moved into warden assisted housing at the age of sixty, examples of cohabitation vs. marriage, her mother's role in caring for her parents before their death a couple of years ago, her mother's widowhood at the age of forty and her consequent retraining and employment as a book keeper, our respondent's consequent close relationship with her grandparents, her determination to marry on the same day as her grandparents, using her grandmother's wedding ring, etc! But all of these things were not articulated in a way which made them sound inherently fascinating. Would 01 have made them sound interesting for us?

I think my nagging doubt is that if we are not careful we will systematically exclude certain types of kin groups, or at least the kin groups of certain types of initial contact respondent, i.e., those who do not reflect or are not fascinated by the intricacies and ambiguities, etc. of family relationships and/or those who are unable or unwilling to articulate these.

Extract E: Janet Finch's Research Notes 5/11/86
Following Up Kin Groups: My Response to Jennifer's "Further Thoughts"
We are trying to use 108 as the focus for deciding more clearly our principles for who not to follow up. But when I listened to this tape, I found it rather interesting, and can identify a number of issues which might well make it worth following through her kin group. (Issues listed in detail at this point.)

So for me, 108 doesn't perhaps present quite the perfect example of the dilemma which Jennifer wrote about, because I think 1 find it intrinsically more interesting. It may be that there is a general lesson to be learned here: she did the interview, but I have only listened to the tape. It may well be that it is easier to listen for and find interesting issues to pursue when you can listen to the tape without having been influenced by the nature of the interaction. If the interview interaction was difficult, or even just not specially exciting, it may well be more difficult to get enthused about it afterwards than it is for someone who comes to it fresh. So that probably means that we should certainly involve each other actively in any decision *not* to follow up a kin group – whichever of us has not done the interview may be able to spot more interesting possibilities.

My conclusion therefore is that we should probably follow up the kin of 108 working on the criteria which we have already established. But Jennifer's note about the danger of not following up less articulate respondents does convince me that there is a potential problem which I had perhaps been a bit slow to recognise.

What worries me now is: if we recognise that some people's kin groups may be more interesting (to us) than they seem at first sight, are we *ever* going to have a reason for not following up (other than the separate sets of reasons to do with not probing around in crisis situations, etc.)?, i.e., does this effectively amount to a decision to follow up everyone whom we reasonably can? In some ways that would be the easiest strategy to operate and to justify, but I don't feel wholly comfortable about it. I think I am worrying mainly about the best use of our limited resources, in that the more kin we follow up, the fewer kin groups overall we can study. Since material from kin groups (where we do succeed in getting it) is essentially bound to be used as case study material, because we are not attempting to select groups in a way which would make them comparable with each other, then I suppose I have a niggling feeling that I want to get the *best cases* which we can, and which will enable us to understand social interaction and social process but which of course will not in any sense be representative. I don't feel inclined to shift from the strategy of treating our initial contact as the "centre" of a kin group and not to keep snowballing on infinitely with her relatives, and then theirs. To have a cut off of that kind is bound to produce some examples of individuals whom we would have been very happy to see as the contact person themselves (a recent example for me would be 08, who is the cousin of 01, who has a very interesting situation in her own right) but I think I accept that as a consequence of our strategy.

The main way in which we worked through to a solution of the problem of good informants was to capitalize upon having two researchers working coilaboratively. Since only one of us was normally present at an interview (and if we were both present, only one of us took an active role and the other was purely an observer) we found that the person who had not conducted the interview was often able to see more clearly the merits of following up a particular case. That person was less likely than the person who had done the interview to be over enthused by a particularly good interviewee, or to dismiss the situation of a more difficult interviewee as being not worth following through. In other words, the other's judgment was unlikely to be clouded by issues connected with having had the responsibility for maintaining the interview as a successful *social* interaction. In this way we were able to take decisions on a case by case basis and to continue to select certain kin groups for detailed study, but not others. It can be seen from Extract E that at this point there was some danger that we should slide back into following through all possible cases, on the grounds that it was just too difficult to distinguish between one and another. But the process of working through the issue with each other and on paper enabled us to confirm that our selection strategy remained appropriate.

From this point onward we adopted a procedure where we always documented the pros and cons of following up the relatives of each interviewee individually. After each interview, but prior to transcription, the person who had conducted it listened to the tape, and produced a family tree,

summaries of information given about relatives, and a life story chart. This
material, together with the tape, was then passed to the other and formed the
basis of a joint discussion about following up kin. This means that in each case
both of us listened to the interview tape, and took the next decision
collaboratively on the basis of a preliminary analysis. In this way, we felt that
we could ensure that we were being as systematic as possible in our choices.

Stock Taking Exercise

Alongside this developed a more cumulative strategy of discussing each case
not just on its own merits, but as part of a growing data set. In this way we
tried to keep an eye on the range of experiences that we were studying, and to
identify obvious gaps. We formalized this, about halfway through the
interview stage, in a stock taking exercise. Again, this was premised upon
analytic induction, the logic now being that we should both plug the gaps and
begin to seek for "negative instances." As Hughes has pointed out, analytic
induction involves:

> A strategy which calls for the investigator to search deliberately for instances
> that negate his (sic) hypothesis and, using these, to refine the hypothesis
> further. ... In practice, the process of analytic induction proceeds by
> formulating a rather vague generalisation and then revising it in the light
> of contrary evidence, so that there is a continual process of redefinition,
> hypothesis testing, and a search for negative cases until a point is reached
> where a universal relationship can with some confidence be established
> (Hughes 1976, p. 128).

Our stock taking involved a preliminary but systematic categorization
both of characteristics of people and kin groups in the study, and instances of
kin support and negotiation in the interviews done so far (41 completed
and 17 firmly arranged, out of a target number of 120). On the basis of
this, we were able to assess and modify our strategy for the second half
of the qualitative stage. Janet Finch did the detailed work of itemizing and
categorizing the range of situations already present in our data, and Extract F
comes from the record of the meeting where we discussed this stock taking
document and used it as the basis for the last major stage in refining our
selection strategy.

Extract F: Notes From The Record Of Planning Meeting 14 and 15 January 1987
(recorded by Jennifer Mason)
We used Janet's "taking stock exercise" as a discussion document for
our meeting, taking each point in turn. The following are the major points
arising:

1. Categories to Include
    We decided that, overall, our present strategy for sampling is working fairly

well, but that we need to refine it a bit to ensure that certain categories of people are included:

a. Men. We agreed, perhaps a bit reluctantly(!) that we cannot simply continue to rely on being passed on to men via the kin groups of our "key" women. We need to select some men who have also been survey respondents, not least so that we can then gain access to their kin groups, hence not filtering out this possibility at the start by only selecting women. We acknowledged that this would raise again the unresolved problems of personal safety we discussed a few months ago. We decided that the best strategy would be to go together to interview men and, where that was not possible, to approach a male colleague with experience of field research with a view to his being a "minder." We talked about the possibility of employing a man to do the interviews with men, but agreed that this would be an inadequate substitute for us, given our familiarity with the objectives, perspectives, data already collected on the project.

b. We agreed that unemployment was an important enough contemporary issue, with implications for our work, for us to include some unemployed people in our sample. Although we cannot tell who is currently un-employed from the questionnaires, which are now a year old, we agreed that we could select people who were unemployed at the time of the survey, and had been for some time, e.g., over a year. If it transpired that they were no longer unemployed such people would nevertheless have experience of a fairly lengthy, and recent, period of unemployment. We agreed to confine this to the under forties or fifties, to prevent the conceptual difficulties with unemployment in later life.

c. Ethnic Minorities. We agonised over this, feeling that in some ways it would be racist to exclude them, but also to include them on different terms. We agreed that if we were to include people from ethnic minorities they should certainly be people who fitted into our two main sampling categories: young adults and divorced/remarried. Finally we decided that we would get a list of the people involved, and literally take out the questionnaires and examine them to see just exactly what we have got, and what the nature of the situation is. We also agreed that Janet would approach a personal contact with a view to our interviewing him and his wife as a sort of pilot interview. This would enable us to see if our questions made sense, and to discuss with them what sorts of modifications would be appropriate for the different ethnic minorities.

d. Social Class I, IV and V. We reaffirmed that we want to get a range of experience in our study, whilst also not making any claims as to the representativeness of our qualitative study group for the general population. Thus, we agreed there was a need for us to gain more people from classes IV and V, to offset the clustering we have at the moment in the middle (II and III). Weight is added to this when we looked at the housing tenure distribution, and our overwhelming bias towards owner occupation. We felt that a conscious attempt to gain people from classes IV and V would help offset this. We also agreed that our survey data made Social Class I (men especially) look interesting enough to warrant a conscious selection strategy here too. Weight was added to this by Janet's "hypothesis" that the continuance of "friendly and civilised" contact following divorce might be a middle class phenomenon (nicknamed the Posy Simmonds phenomenon).

e. Divorce and Widowhood. Janet's suggestion that widowhood might help to throw some light on our understanding of divorce seemed compelling, and we agreed that we should try to include some widows - especially those under fifty years old where this is less common and in a sense more comparable with divorce (does not conflate issues of ageing and widowhood, etc.). We agreed that divorce continued to be a worthy focus and sampling strategy for us, not least because our divorced survey respondents have led us into kin groups displayed a good spread of other "situations" we are interested in. If Janet's "Posy Simmonds" hunch about middle class divorce is right, then our SCI respondents might prove interesting here too. We talked about the possibility of refining our strategy of centering on our "key" respondent as far as divorce was concerned, so that for example if we were to discover a divorced person in their kin group we could possibly follow them up in their own right, that is by treating them as another key person with a kin group. We decided that this would be perfectly valid, and indeed that we could "look out" for some of our other categories and situations in this way too. Now that we are almost halfway through the qualitative bit, and are in a position to reflect on where we are going in the light of where we have been, we felt that there was less danger of losing our focus than there might have been last year in a strategy which allows us to follow up someone who is not necessarily a key figure in our initial contact's kin group, but who is, for example, divorced and of interest in their own right.

f. Elderly. We agreed that we wanted to keep on the look out for elderly, and particularly fit elderly, people in the kin groups, but not to modify our selection strategy in this respect. One of the problems with doing the latter is the danger of our crashing in on a crisis situation which would, in any event, lessen our potential for following up kin given our strategy of non intervention in crises.

g. Step Children and Step Grand Parenting. We agreed that given our interest in divorce and remarriage, this was actually a fairly central issue and we should give it a higher priority. We discussed ways of identifying step parents from the survey questionnaires – i.e., by choosing people who are (divorced or) remarried and who have children listed under "spouse kin." We agreed that we should look out for step parenting situations in the kin groups, but also at the selection stage in the questionnaires.

2. How Many to Sample For Each Category

We agreed, given the fairly heavy commitment of our resources involved, that it would be acceptable to treat men as a "minority group" in our sampling strategy. Partly, we felt this justifiable because our female respondents *are* yielding men in their kin groups. We agreed that we should continue sampling until we have achieved ten men - five divorced/ remarried, and five young adults. These ten men can include people in Social Class IV and V, and unemployed (which in fact they do), and we agreed that we should monitor refusals very carefully during this phase, so that where men in these categories refuse we can replace them with other men in these categories.

That would leave us with the following to achieve: ethnic minorities, Social

Class I, adult stepchildren/parents, young widowed. We agreed that we would be best to leave until later the sampling decision about young widowed and step children, when we will be in a position to see what we have achieved in these respects from the kin groups. We decided we should target about three or four SCIs, probably men but they could be women (Janet has one potential in her five male divorced/remarried survey candidates). We agreed that we would be lucky to get three ethnic minority initial contacts, at most.

Most of these precise decisions about sampling numbers cannot be made very effectively at this stage, and we agreed that a good strategy would be to allow ourselves a further "taking stock" exercise when we can assess how well "represented" our categories are, and whether there is a case for including other groups/categories/situations. When we are at a stage where we are beginning to feel confident of ideas/theories being generated, we could therefore adjust the sampling a bit in line with the logic of analytic induction.

At this point we were able to be much more focused about selection issues than was possible at an earlier stage. While we were pleased to be able to confirm that the strategy we had been pursuing was generating the kind of data we had hoped for, we were able to engage in some fine tuning. For example, we came back to the categories of respondents whose experiences we wanted to include, but where we had decided at an earlier stage to delay a decision. Thus, we decided actively to seek out examples of people who had been unemployed since we were not picking up examples of these in our existing strategy; but by contrast we concluded that we did not specifically need to seek out elderly interviewees, since we were successfully including their experiences through following them up as relatives within our existing subgroups. We also finally took a decision about men, confirming that we needed to include some as the focal person of a kin group (not just as relatives of women) and resolved the practical problems of security by opting for the labor intensive strategy of accompanying each other to initial interviews with men about whom we had no information beyond the survey interview. We also agreed upon a strategy for selecting people from ethnic minority groups, leaving open the possibility that we might go beyond our two major subgroupings in the case only, to make sure that some non-white experiences were included in our study. This arose solely from the fact that we had a very small number of survey respondents from whom to make a selection; but in principle we were able to confirm that our basic strategy of selecting from the two subgroups of young adults and divorced/remarried was leading us to examples of negotiations within families, and all other selections were made from *within* those two subgroups.

Another slightly different issue that emerged from our stock-taking exercise was that we had so far been interviewing people from a rather narrow social class range, namely, from the middle of the range as defined in orthodox terms. From the point of view of reflecting a range of social experiences in our data, it seemed important to broaden that and we agreed that we should seek out respondents within our main subgroups who fell into classes I, IV, and V. The value of having undertaken a systematic stock-taking exercise at the midway point in the fieldwork is very clear in this instance, since neither of us had realized that our interviewees were bunched in this way. If we had relied upon our informal and intuitive knowledge built up in the course of interviews, we would not have identified this problem until it was too late to do anything about it.

The principle of analytic induction is very explicitly followed in another set of decisions that we took at this time concerning our interest in families that had been reconstituted through divorce and marriage. In the interviews that we had already completed we had plenty of examples of renegotiation of relationships with the person's own relatives, but very few of continuing relationships with relatives of the former spouse. The common pattern seemed to be to cut off contact completely. The "rather vague generalization" with which we began (to put in in Hughes' terms) was that there would be circumstances under which relationships with former in-laws would continue in a renegotiated form. The data that we had collected in the first half of our fieldwork suggested that we should modify our hypothesis to: active relationships with in-laws continue in a renegotiated form after divorce only in unusual circumstances, if at all.

Thus, our data were helping us to modify our theory and that in turn enabled us to test our revised theory further. We decided to do this in two ways. First, we would search for negative instances, which in the context of our modified hypothesis meant that we would seek out those situations where we were *most* likely to find continuing relationships after divorce. In discussing where to look for these we brought to bear our wider knowledge of social theory and of other studies and decided that the desire to continue "friendly and civilized" relationships after divorce is probably a phenomenon associated with the intellectual middle classes. We christened it the "Posy Simmonds" phenomena in our notes: *Guardian* readers will be familiar with this kind of "civility" in the cartoons of Posy Simmonds. This confirmed that we should specifically select some interviewees from Social Class I.

Second, we decided to try to refine our theory further by testing out whether the process of cutting off from in-laws is a consequence of divorce specifically or whether it is a result of the tie that previously bound the people together having been removed. If it were the latter, people who had been widowed would undergo a similar process to the divorced; if the former, the pattern of relationships with in-laws after divorce or widowhood would be very different. This reasoning led us to a decision to select some "young widows" (of either sex) for interview, to test out this distinction by comparing widows and divorcees whose family circumstances were otherwise quite similar.

Extract F shows that we translated these modifications into a selection strategy for the second part of the fieldwork in which we were able to be quite precise about the numbers we were seeking in each category. In terms of the balance between being systematic and being flexible it is clear that we were able to be systematic in a much more overt sense at this stage than we had been at the beginning of the process. But we were still able to retain a degree of flexibility as our notes indicate, we built in the possibility of further stock taking at a later stage. We did in fact repeat the exercise when we were about three quarters of the way through our interviews – this time Jennifer Mason doing the itemizing and categorizing but we made no significant changes at that point.

Conclusion

In telling the story of our own project we have made a number of points about how the principles involved in theoretical sampling can be applied and we will not repeat them here. We make no special claims to methodological virtue but we think that it is quite possible to produce a selection strategy in field research that is systematic rather than ad hoc, while maintaining a level of flexibility that is essential within this research paradigm. We have shown how we selected cases to study for their theoretical significance, worked through problems associated with comparability, applied the principle of analytic induction, and made systematic appraisals of the data that we were generating as we went along – all of these within the normal practical constraints of money, time, and, in our case, a concern about the personal safety of the researchers.

We shall conclude by highlighting some of the more general principles that can be drawn from this description of our research process.

1. It is clear that analysis of some kind is constantly taking place, and forms the basis for decisions about strategies, within the overall parameters set at the beginning through a particular theoretical perspective. Different levels of analysis can be relevant here, for example, listening to interview tapes, making a preliminary assessment of each case, itemizing and categorizing characteristics and situations. Preliminary forms of analyses such as these are the raw materials from which informed decisions are made. Theoretical sampling, therefore, encompasses a good deal more than processes generally considered to constitute sampling.

2. Leading on from the first point, this means that decisions made on this basis are not ad hoc. Rather they are both situated and informed. Some decisions simply cannot be made at the very beginning of the research enterprise without loss of theoretical and data sensitivity, yet each time a decision is made it is important to be clear about the principles underlying it, the reasons for it, possible alternatives and so on. On the one hand, informed decisions are part of a process of sharpening or modifying – underlying principles leading to theory that is grounded in data. On the other hand, this is only possible because to recognize that informed decisions have to be made continually is to acknowledge that the research process takes the researcher through changing contexts. These result from the data being generated, and from continuing exposure to other researcher's theories and findings in relation to her or his own.

3. The implication of this is that delaying some decisions until a later stage of the research process, rather than taking them all at the beginning, is a positive rather than a negative feature. However, this is not a license for the researcher to be ad hoc, and to make decisions simply off the top of her or his head. In essence, what must be gained from any situated description of informed decisions is a lesson in how to be systematic. This is rather more of a challenge than to be systematic in a positivistic sense, because informed decisions made in-progress can easily appear ad hoc and inconsistent if the researcher cannot be entirely clear about the changing contexts of those decisions, their purposes and consequences, and the principles underlying them. In the absence of this vital contextual information, it is dangerously easy for researchers to telescope decisions made into a positivistic model, by suggesting that they had sorted out most of the issues at the very start.

4. Being systematic in preliminary analyses of one's data in this way represents the beginning of a cumulative development of principles of analysis. Therefore, as well as it being important to record both decisions and contexts for an expose of the practicalities of theoretical sampling, these very records form excellent documents for use in the early stages of the formal analysis of data.

5. Collaborative working methods are, we have found, a positive bonus in all of this. We have been able at each stage to have real discussions about decisions and issues as they occur, and kept records of these discussions as well as our individual endeavors. However, if some of the processes involved in being systematic seem more obvious in a collaborative working context, they do not have to be exclusive to it.

Acknowledgments

We would like to thank Bob Burgess, Caroline Dryden, John Hockey, and Sue Scott for reading and commenting on an earlier version of this chapter. Also thanks to colleagues present at the meeting of the qualitative methods study group in the Department of Social Administration at the University of Lancaster, where we discussed an early version of this paper: Nick Derricourt, Joy Foster, Anne Williams.

Notes

1. This study is supported by a grant from the Economic and Social Research Council, 1985-89. The total grant was £121,000 of which about £50,000 represented the cost of the fieldwork and data processing for the large-scale survey which formed part of the study.

2. The survey was conducted in the Greater Manchester area and was based on the electoral register in forty cluster sampled wards. A response rate of 72% was achieved, making a total of 978 completed interviews. At the end of the

questionnaire respondents were asked, "It is possible that a researcher on this project might want to come back in some months' time. Would you be willing to give another interview?" Eighty-five percent said they would be willing.

3. The survey fieldwork was organized and conducted through Social and Community Planning Research, and we would like to gratefully acknowledge Gill Courtenay's contribution and support in this stage of the project.

References

Baldmus, G., 1972. "The Role of Discoveries in Social Science." In T. Shanin (ed.), *The Rules of The Game*. London: Tavistock.

Bell, C., 1977. "Reflections on the Banbury Re-study." In C. Bell and H. Newby (eds.), *Doing Sociological Research*. London: Allen and Unwin.

Bertaux, D., 1981. *Bibliography and Society*. Beverly Hills, CA: Sage.

Burgess, R.G., 1984. "Autobiographical Accounts and Research Experience." In R.G. Burgess (ed.), *The Research Process in Educational Settings: Ten Case Studies*. Lewes: Falmer Press.

Finch, J., 1987. "Family Obligations and the Life Course." In A. Bryman, B. Bytheway, P. Allatt, and T. Keil (eds.), *Perspectives on the Life Cycle*. London: Macmillan.

Glaser, B. and Strauss, A., 1967. *The Discovery of Grounded Theory*. Chicago: Aldine.

Hammersley, M. and Atkinson, P., 1983. *Ethnography: Principles and Practice*. London: Tavistock.

Hughes, 1976. *Sociological Analysis: Methods of Discovery*. London: Nelson.

McKee, L. and O'Brian, M., 1983. "Interviewing Men: 'Taking Gender Seriously.' " In E. Gamarnikow et al. (eds.), *The Public and The Private*. London: Heineman.

Platt, J., 1976. *The Realities of Social Research*. Brighton: Chatto and Windus/Sussex University Press.

Porter, M., 1984. "The Modification of Method in Researching Postgraduate Education." In R.G. Burgess (ed.), *The Research Process in Educational Settings: Ten Case Studies*. Lewes: Falmer Press.

Schwarz, H. and Jacobs, J., 1979. *Qualitative Sociology: A Method to the Madness*. New York: Free Press.

Stenhouse, L., 1980. "The Study of Samples and the Study of Cases." *British Educational Research Journal* 1-6.

Znaniecki, F., 1934. *The Method of Sociology*. New York: Farrar and Reinhart.

Section Three
Observing in the Field

26

Roles in Sociological Field Observations*

Raymond L. Gold

B uford Junker has suggested four theoretically possible roles for sociologists conducting field work.[1] These range from the complete participant at one extreme to the complete observer at the other. Between these, but nearer the former, is the participant-as-observer; nearer the latter is the observer-as-participant. As a member of Junker's research team, I shared in the thinking which led to conceptualization of these research roles. After the work of the team was completed, I continued the search for insight regarding processes of interaction learning in field observation in a special study of my own.[2] A considerable portion of this study was devoted to exploration of the dimensions of Junker's role-conceptions and their controlling effects on the product of field study.

My aim in this paper is to present extensions of Junker's thinking growing out of systematic interviews with field workers whose experience had been cast in one or more of these patterns of researcher-subject relationship. All of these field workers had gathered data in natural or nonexperimental settings. I would like in this paper to analyze generic characteristics of Junker's four field observer roles and to call attention to the demands each one places on an observer, as a person and as a sociologist plying his trade.

Every field work role is at once a social interaction device for securing information for scientific purposes and a set of behaviors in which an observer's self is involved.[3] While playing a field work role and attempting to take the role of an informant, the field observer often attempts to master hitherto strange or only generally understood universes of discourse relating to many attitudes and behaviors. He continually introspects, raising endless questions about the informant and the developing field relationship, with a view to playing the field work role as successfully as possible. A sociological

Source: *Social Forces*, 1958, pp. 217-223.
*Read before the nineteenth annual meeting of the Southern Sociological Society, Atlanta, Georgia, April 13, 1956.

assumption here is that the more successful the field worker is in playing his role, the more successful he must be in taking the informant's role. Success in both role-taking and role-playing requires success in blending the demands of self-expression and self-integrity with the demands of the role.

It is axiomatic that a person who finds a role natural and congenial, and who acts convincingly in it, has in fact found how to balance role-demands with those of self. If need be he can subordinate self-demands in the interest of the role and role-demands in the interest of self whenever he perceives that either self or role is in any way threatened. If, while playing the role, someone with whom he is interacting attacks anything in which he has self-involvement, he can point out to himself that the best way to protect self at the moment is to subordinate (or defer) self-expression to allow successful performance in the role. In other words, he uses role to protect self. Also, when he perceives that he is performing inadequately in the role he can indicate to himself that he can do better by changing tactics. Here he uses self as a source of new behaviors to protect role. The case of using role to protect self from perceived threat is one of acute self-consciousness, a matter of diminishing over-sensitivity to self-demands by introspectively noting corresponding demands of role. The case of using self to protect role from perceived threat is one of acute role-consciousness, a matter of diminishing over-sensitivity to role-demands by introspectively indicating that they are disproportionately larger than those of self. Both cases represent situations in which role-demands and self-demands are out of balance with each other as a result of perceived threat, and are then restored to balance by appropriate introspection.

Yet, no matter how congenial the two sets of demands seem to be, a person who plays a role in greatly varied situations (and this is especially true of a sociologist field observer) sometimes experiences threats which markedly impair his effectiveness as an interactor in the situation. When attempting to assess informational products of field work, it is instructive to examine the field worker's role-taking and role-playing in situations of perceived, but unresolved, threat. Because he defines success in the role partly in terms of doing everything he can to remain in even threatening situations to secure desired information, he may find that persevering is sometimes more heroic than fruitful.

The situation may be one in which he finds the informant an almost intolerable bigot. The field worker decides to stick it out by attempting to subordinate self-demands to those of role. He succeeds to the extent of refraining from "telling off" the informant, but fails in that he is too self-conscious to play his role effectively. He may think of countless things he would like to say and do to the informant, all of which are dysfunctional to role-demands, since his role requires taking the role of the other as an informant, not as a bigot. At the extreme of nearly overwhelming self-consciousness, the field worker may still protect his role by getting out of the situation while the getting is good. Once out and in the company of understanding colleagues, he will finally be able to achieve self-expression (i.e., finally air his views of the informant) without damaging the field role.[4]

Should the situation be such that the field worker finds the informant practically inscrutable (i.e., a "bad" informant), he may decide to persevere despite inability to meet role-taking and role-playing demands. In this situation he becomes acutely role-conscious, since he is hypersensitive to role-demands, hyposensitive to self. This partial breakdown of his self-process thwarts his drawing on past experiences and current observations to raise meaningful questions and perceive meaningful answers. At the extreme, a role-conscious field worker may play his role so mechanically and unconvincingly that the informant, too, develops role-and-self problems.

The following discussion utilizes these conceptions of role and self to aid in analyzing field work roles as "master roles" for developing lesser role-relationships with informants.[5] While a field worker cannot be all things to all men, he routinely tries to fit himself into as many roles as he can, so long as playing them helps him to develop relationships with informants in his master role (i.e., participant-as-observer, etc.).

Complete Participant

The true identity and purpose of the complete participant in field research are not known to those whom he observes. He interacts with them as naturally as possible in whatever areas of their living interest him and are accessible to him as situations in which he can play, or learn to play, requisite day-to-day roles successfully. He may, for example, work in a factory to learn about inner-workings of informal groups. After gaining acceptance at least as a novice, he may be permitted to share not only in work activities and attitudes but also in the intimate life of the workers outside the factory.

Role-pretense is a basic theme in these activities. It matters little whether the complete participant in a factory situation has an upper-lower class background and perhaps some factory experience, or whether he has an upper-middle class background quite divorced from factory work and the norms of such workers. What really matters is that he knows that he is pretending to be a colleague. I mean to suggest by this that the crucial value as far as research yield is concerned lies more in the self-orientation of the complete participant than in his surface role-behaviors as he initiates his study. The complete participant realizes that he, and he alone, knows that he is in reality other than the person he pretends to be. He must pretend that his real self is represented by the role, or roles, he plays in and out of the factory situation in relationships with people who, to him, are but informants, and this implies an interactive construction that has deep ramifications. He must bind the mask of pretense to himself or stand the risk of exposure and research failure.

In effect, the complete participant operates continually under an additional set of situational demands. Situational role-and-self demands ordinarily tend to correspond closely. For this reason, even when a person is in the act of learning to play a role, he is likely to believe that pretending to have achieved this correspondence (i.e., fourflushing) will be unnecessary when he can actually "be himself" in the role. But the complete observer simply cannot "be himself"; to do so would almost invariably preclude successful pretense. At the very least, attempting to "be himself" – that is, to achieve self-realization in pretended roles – would arouse suspicion of the kind that would lead others to remain aloof in interacting with him. He must be sensitive to demands of self, of the observer role, and of the momentarily pretended role. Being sensitive to the set of demands accompanying role-pretense is a matter of being sensitive to a large variety of overt and covert mannerisms and other social cues representing the observer's pretended self. Instead of being himself in the pretended role, all he can be is a "not self," in the sense of perceiving that his actions are meaningful in a contrived role.

The following illustration of the pretense of a complete participant comes from an interview with a field worker who drove a cab for many months to study big-city cab drivers. Here a field worker reveals how a pretended role fosters a heightened sense of self-awareness, an introspective attitude, because of the sheer necessity of indicating continually to himself that certain experiences are merely part of playing a pretended role. These indications serve as self-assurance that customers are not really treating *him* as they seem to do, since he is actually someone else, namely, a field worker.

> Well, I've noticed that the cab driver who *is* a cab driver acts differently than the part-time cab drivers, who don't think of themselves as real cab drivers. When somebody throws a slam at men who drive only part of the year, such as, "Well, you're just a goddamn cab driver!," they do one of two things. They may make it known to the guy that they are not a cab driver; they are something else. But as a rule, that doesn't work out, because the customer comes back with, "Well, if you're not a cab driver what the hell are you driving this cab for?" So, as a rule, they mostly just rationalize it to themselves by thinking, "Well, this is not my role or the real me. He just doesn't understand. Just consider the source and drop it." But a cab driver who *is* a cab driver, if you make a crack at him, such as, "You're just a goddamn cab driver!" he's going to take you out of the back seat and whip you.

Other complete participant roles may pose more or less of a challenge to the field worker than those mentioned above. Playing the role of potential convert to study a religious sect almost inevitably leads the field worker to feel not only that he has "taken" the people who belong to the sect, but that he has done it in ways which are difficult to justify. In short, he may suffer severe qualms about his mandate to get information in a role where he pretends to be a colleague in moral, as well as in other social, respects.

All complete participant roles have in common two potential problems; continuation in a pretended role ultimately leads the observer to reckon with one or the other. One, he may become so self-conscious about revealing his true self that he is handicapped when attempting to perform convincingly in the pretended role. Or two, he may "go native," incorporate the role into his self-conceptions and achieve self-expression inthe role, but find he has so violated his observer role that it is almost impossible to report his findings. Consequently, the field worker needs cooling-off periods during and after complete participation, at which times he can "be himself" and look back on his field behavior dispassionately and sociologically.

While the complete participant role offers possibilities of learning about aspects of behavior that might otherwise escape a field observer, it places him in pretended roles which call for delicate balances between demands of role and self. A complete participant must continually remind himself that, above all, he is there as an observer: this is his primary role. If he succumbs to demands of the pretended role (or roles), or to demands of self-expression and self-integrity, he can no longer function as an observer. When he can defer self-expression no longer, he steps out of the pretended role to find opportunities for congenial interaction with those who are, in fact, colleagues.

Participant-as-Observer

Although basically similar to the complete observer role, the participant-as-observer role differs significantly in that both field worker and informant are aware that theirs is a field relationship. This mutual awareness tends to minimize problems of role-pretending; yet, the role carries with it numerous opportunities for compartmentalizing mistakes and dilemmas which typically bedevil the complete participant.

Probably the most frequent use of this role is in community studies, where an observer develops relationships with informants through time, and where he is apt to spend more time and energy participating than observing. At times he observes formally, as in scheduled interview situations; and at other times he observes informally – when attending parties, for example. During early stages of his stay in the community, informants may be somewhat uneasy about him in both formal and informal situations, but their uneasiness is likely to disappear when they learn to trust him and he them.

But just when the research atmosphere seems ripe for gathering information, problems of role and self are apt to arise. Should field worker and informant begin to interact in much the same way as ordinary friends, they tend to jeopardize their field roles in at least two important ways. First, the informant may become too identified with the field worker to continue functioning as merely an informant. In this event the informant becomes too much of an observer. Second, the field worker may over-identify with the informant and start to lose his research perspective by "going native." Should this occur the field worker may still continue going through the motions of observing, but he is only pretending.

Although the field worker in the participant-as-observer role strives to bring his relationship with the informant to the point of friendship, to the point of intimate form, it behooves him to retain sufficient elements of "the stranger" to avoid actually reaching intimate form. Simmel's distinction between intimate content and intimate form contains an implicit warning that the latter is inimical to field observation.[6] When content of interaction is intimate, secrets may be shared without either of the interactors feeling compelled to maintain the relationship for more than a short time. This is the interaction of sociological strangers. On the other hand, when form of interaction is intimate, continuation of the relationship (which is no longer merely a field relationship) may become more important to one or both of the interactors than continuation of the roles through which they initiated the relationship.

In general, the demands of pretense in this role, as in that of the complete participant, are continuing and great; for here the field worker is often defined by informants as more of a colleague than he feels capable of being. He tries to pretend that he is as much of a colleague as they seem to think he is, while searching to discover how to make the pretense appear natural and convincing. Whenever pretense becomes too challenging, the participant-as-observer leaves the field to re-clarify his self-conceptions and his role-relationships.

Observer-as-Participant

The observer-as-participant role is used in studies involving one-visit inter-views. It calls for relatively more formal observation than either informal observation or participation of any kind. It also entails less risk of "going native" than either the complete participant role or the participant-as-observer role. However, because the observer-as-participant's contact with an informant is so brief, and perhaps superficial, he is more likely than the other two to misunderstand the informant, and to be misunderstood by him.

These misunderstandings contribute to a problem of self-expression that is almost unique to this role. To a field worker (as to other human beings), self-expression becomes a problem at any time he perceives he is threatened. Since he meets more varieties of people for shorter periods of time than either the complete participant or the participant-as-observer, the observer-as-participant inclines more to feel threatened. Brief relationships with numerous informants expose an observer-as-participant to many inadequately under-stood universes of discourse that he cannot take time to master. These frustratingly brief encounters with informants also contribute to mistaken perceptions which set up communication barriers the field worker may not even be aware of until too late. Continuing relationships with apparently threatening informants offer an opportunity to redefine them as more congenial partners in interaction, but such is not the fortune of a field worker in this role. Consequently, using his prerogative to break off relationships with threatening informants, an observer-as-participant, more easily than the other two, can leave the field almost at will to regain the kind of role-and-self balance that he, being who he is, must regain.

Complete Observer

The complete observer role entirely removes a field worker from social interaction with informants. Here a field worker attempts to observe people in ways which make it unnecessary for them to take him into account, for they do not know he is observing them or that, in some sense, they are serving as his informants. Of the four field work roles, this alone is almost never the dominant one. It is sometimes used as one of the subordinate roles employed to implement the dominant ones.

It is generally true that with increasingly more observation than participation, the chances of "going native" become smaller, although the possibility of ethnocentrism becomes greater. With respect to achieving rapport in a field relationship, ethnocentrism may be considered a logical opposite of "going native." Ethnocentrism occurs whenever a field worker cannot or will not interact meaningfully with an informant. He then seemingly or actually rejects the informant's views without ever getting to the point of understanding them. At the other extreme, a field worker who "goes native" passes the point of field rapport by literally accepting his informant's views as his own. Both are cases of pretending to be an observer, but for obviously opposite reasons. Because a complete observer remains entirely outside the observed interaction, he faces the greatest danger of misunderstanding the observed. For the same reason, his role carries the least chance of "going native."

The complete observer role is illustrated by systematic eavesdropping, or by reconnaissance of any kind of social setting as preparation for more intensive study in another field role. While watching the rest of the world roll by, a complete observer may feel comfortably detached, for he takes no self-risks, participates not one whit. Yet, there are many times when he wishes he could ask representatives of the observed world to qualify what they have said, or to answer other questions his observations of them have brought to mind. For some purposes, however, these very questions are important starting points for subsequent observations and interactions in appropriate roles. It is not surprising that reconnaissance is almost always a prelude to using the participant-as-observer role in community study. The field worker, feeling comfortably detached, can first "case" the town before committing himself to casing *by* the town.

Conclusions

Those of us who teach field work courses or supervise graduate students and others doing field observations have long been concerned with the kinds of interactional problems and processes discussed above. We find such common "mistakes" as that of the beginner who over-identifies with an informant simply because the person treats him compassionately after others have refused to grant him an interview. This limited, although very real, case of "going native" becomes much more understandable to the beginner when we have analyzed it for him sociologically. When he can begin utilizing theory of role and self to reflect on his own assets and shortcomings in the field, he will be well on the way to dealing meaningfuly with problems of controlling *his* interactions with informants.

Beyond this level of control, sophistication in field observation requires manipulating informants to help them play their role effectively. Once field worker learns that a field relationship in process of being structured creates role-and-self problems for informants that are remarkably similar to those he has experienced, he is in a position to offer informants whatever kinds of "reassurances" they need to fit into their role. Certainly a field worker has mastered his role only to the extent that he can help informants to master theirs. Learning this fact (and doing something about it!) will eliminate nearly all excuses about "bad" or "inept" informants, since, willy-nilly, an informant is likely to play his role only as fruitfully or as fruitlessly as a field worker plays his.[7]

Experienced field workers recognize limitations in their ability to develop relationships in various roles and situations. They have also discovered that they can maximize their take of information by selecting a field role which permits them to adjust their own role-repertoires to research objectives. Objectively, a selected role is simply an expedient device for securing a given level of information. For instance, a complete participant obviously develops relationships and frames of reference which yield a somewhat different perspective of the subject matter than that which any of the other field work roles would yield. These subjective and objective factors come together in the fact that degree of success in securing the level of information which a field role makes available to a field worker is largely a matter of his skill in playing and taking roles.

Each of the four field work roles has been shown to offer advantages and disadvantages with respect to both demands of role and self and level of information. No attempt has been made in this report to show how a sociological conception of field work roles can do more than provide lines of thought and action for dealing with problems and processes of field interaction. Obviously, however, a theory of role and self growing out of study of field interaction is in no sense limited to that area of human activity. Learning to take and play roles, although dramatized in the field, is essentially the same kind of social learning people engage in throughout life.

In any case, the foregoing discussion has suggested that a field worker selects and plays a role so that he, being who he is, can best study those aspects of society in which he is interested.

Notes

1. Buford Junker, "Some Suggestions for the Design of Field Work Learning Experiences," in Everett C. Hughes, et al, *Cases on Field Work* (hectographed by the University of Chicago, 1952), Part III-A.

2. Raymond L. Gold, Toward a Social Interaction Methodology for Sociological Field Observation, unpublished Ph. D. dissertation, University of Chicago, 1954.

3. To simplify this presentation, I am assuming that the field worker is an experienced observer who has incorporated the role into his self-conceptions. Through this incorporation, he is self-involved in the role and feels that self is at stake in it. However, being experienced in the role, he can balance role-demands and self-demands in virtually all field situations, that is, all except those to be discussed shortly.

4. An inexperienced field worker might "explode" on the spot, feeling that role and self are not congenial in this *or any other* situation. But an experienced field worker would leave such a situation as gracefully as possible to protect the role, feeling that role and self are not congenial in *this* situation only.

5. Lesser role-relationships include all achieved and ascribed roles which the field worker plays in the act of developing a field relationship with an informant. For example, he may become the "nice man that old ladies can't resist" as part of his over-all role-reportoire in a community study. Whether he deliberately sets out to achieve such relationships with old ladies or discovers that old ladies ascribe him "irresistible" characteristics, he is still a participant-as-observer who interacts with local old ladies as a "nice man." Were he not there to study the community, he might choose *not* to engage in this role-relationship, especially if being irresistible to old ladies is not helpful in whatever master role(s) brought him to town. (Cf. any experienced community researcher.)

6. "In other words, intimacy is not based on the *content* of the relationship ... Inversely, certain external situations or moods may move us to make very personal statements and confessions, usually reserved for our closest friends only, to relatively strange people. But in such cases we nevertheless feel that this 'intimate' *content* does not yet make the relation an intimate one. For in its basic significance, the whole relation to these people is based only on its general, un-individual ingredients. That 'intimate' content, although we have perhaps never revealed it before and thus limit it entirely to this particular relationship, does nevertheless not become the basis of its form, and thus leaves it outside the sphere of intimacy." K. H. Wolff (ed.), *The Sociology of Georg Simmel* (Glencoe, Illinois:, The Free Press, 1950), p. 127.

7. In a recent article on interviewing, Theodore Caplow also recognizes the key role played by the field worker in structuring the field relationship. He concludes, "The quality and quantity of the information secured probably depend far more upon the competence of the interviewer than upon the respondent." "The Dynamics of Information Interviewing," *American Journal of Sociology*, LXII (September 1956), 169. Cf. also the studies by Junker and Gold, *op. cit.*

27

Fieldwork: The Basic Arts

Harry F. Wolcott

There may be kinds of information that are in fact vital to the task of anthropological analysis but that are fairly consistently excluded from our field notes – in other words that we have conventional criteria for identifying observations as data that are inappropriate for the kinds of hypotheses and theories we wish to develop in our analysis. The frequent assertion that anthropology is an art as well as a science might depend precisely on the unsystematic or unreflecting way in which we accumulate part of our basic data.

– Fredrik Barth Preface to *The Social Organization of the Marri Baluch,* x

This chapter is as close as I come to presenting a fieldwork manual. It brings me perilously close to dwelling on the techniques and strategies of fieldwork as craft, although I will focus on the less systematic aspects related to the experience rather than on data gathering per se. At the same time, behind every strategy or technique employed in fieldwork there needs to be sound human judgment – an artistic decision guided in large measure by what passes as ordinary courtesy and common sense. I have made "Courtesy and Common Sense" my first subheading, to precipitate out some pervasive elements in fieldwork before dealing with topics more customarily addressed in such discussions. Under the un-conventional subtitles "Being There," "Getting Nosy," and "Looking Over Others' Shoulders," I then review fieldwork's major dimensions: participant observation, interviewing, and archival research.

Courtesy and Common Sense

On first thought, participant observation would seem to be the obvious choice as a starting place for discussing the basic arts involved in fieldwork.

Source: *The Art of Fieldwork,* 1995, pp. 86-121.

On second thought, centering on participant observation hopelessly confuses whatever is unique to fieldwork with the display of everyday courtesy and common sense.

A fieldworker can easily offend through inappropriate behavior, comment, or question. But fieldworkers are not clairvoyant; they, too, are subject to making social errors. If it takes thoughtful explaining to get out of a tight or embarrassing predicament that one shouldn't have gotten into in the first place, that is certainly not an art limited to those who do field research. Nor are those who do fieldwork necessarily gifted in the handling of human relations. I have heard colleagues reportedly successful at fieldwork ask rhetorically, "Can you imagine *me* doing participant observation?" and a voice inside me whispers, "Well, frankly, now that you mention it. ..."

Presumably the human relations aspect of fieldwork is enhanced for those to whom such qualities as empathy, sympathy, or at least everyday courtesy and patience, come naturally. I see no evidence that such qualities can be taught, or that they show themselves to be particularly abundant among the practitioners of certain disciplines to the exclusion of others. The consequence of anthropology's supposed humanizing message seems not, in my experience, to be any more or less evident in the everyday behavior of anthropologists than of ordinary folk. If it were, then to be a member of an anthropology department would be the envy of members of every other department on the campus.

The idea of "participant observation," which James Clifford characterizes as a predicament transformed into a method (1988:93), can raise a straightforward question: How does one go about being artful when assuming so obvious a role? I recall a colleague in the 1960s who flat-out rejected any proposal he was asked to review that explained, or attempted to explain away, the question of method with the simplistic response "participant observation." Michael Moerman, writing in the postmodern heyday, has observed that participant observation, "once anthropology's secret shame," had subsequently become "the fashionable focus of its self-absorption" (1988:68). Nevertheless, participant observation will surely continue to occupy the preeminent role Russ Bernard ascribes to it as the "foundation of anthropological research" (1988:148). It is all encompassing, yet, Bernard continues, it is "not really a method at all." Rather, it is "a *strategy* that facilitates data collection in the field – all kinds of data, both qualitative and quantitative" (p. 150). Employing it as a strategy requires common sense. Viewed as a strategy, participant observation needs to be examined in terms of what it is that brings fieldworkers into a setting in the first place and whether they are well situated to learn whatever is to be learned. This is where many qualitative researchers get off on the wrong foot, somehow confusing the fact of their physical presence with the hope that simply by "being there" they will be able to observe or experience what they are interested in observing and experiencing. Two questions to ask in that regard are, "Can whatever I want to study be 'seen' by a participant observer at all?" and, if so, "Am I well positioned to observe those phenomena?" These questions need to be followed by a third one: "What are my own capabilities for participating and observing in this situation?" Many descriptive studies intended to be pursued through participant observation have elected a time-consuming approach with only an outside chance that the researcher proposing them will ever have the opportunity to "see" whatever purportedly is to be observed.

To illustrate: Years ago I remember talking with a student who had heard of an Alaskan village where television was about to be introduced. Intrigued with the possibilities of ethnographic inquiry and the tradition of village studies, the student asked whether I thought ethnography would "work" as the appropriate research strategy for a study of the impact of television on village life and, if so, how I would approach it.

My personal reaction was, "Why bother?" The broad sweep of a community study did not seem warranted with such a narrowly focused and poorly posed question. I replied that on a well-funded project one might assign an ethnographer to *every* family, or, lacking such generous funding, one might assign a lone researcher to any household willing to have a longtime observer. In either case, the purest observer would not want to influence the results and therefore would be hesitant to describe the study as one on TV's impact, yet a live-in observer in a village household might prove far more entertaining than TV fare, the researcher's presence creating the very kind of distraction that dedicated participant observers try desperately to avoid. It looked to me like a low-yield investment of researcher time to catch a few possible comments and to record some TV watching. Even then, at the end of the year how would anyone actually assess "impact"? The proposed project seemed to illustrate what Fredrik Barth has described as a tendency to confound *process* and *change* (Barth 1994a:76).

Granted that the village had been without TV before, was the occasion for introducing it all that interesting? It was not the inefficiency of the research strategy that bothered me so much as the mismatch between the magnitude of the problem and the magnitude of the investment in time and resources to study it. A year devoted to a study of village life in modern Alaska ought to be a provocative experience and rich source of data. A commitment of that sort seemed to warrant a more imaginative scope of work than tracking TV viewing and attempting to assess – or guess – its impact. I gently asked whether the student could think of any other ways to get relevant information if the social impact of TV was his burning issue?

Another example illustrates the complex cross-over (or heavy residue) from tightly designed quantitative studies to the creative use of qualitative ones. This time *sampling* was the bugaboo. A student in a seminar I was presenting overseas was interested in studying what she called "discovery learning." In my suggestion that participants engage in some modest field research during the course of the seminar, she saw an opportunity to try her skills at classroom observation. But she had become distraught over a major obstacle she foresaw and made a special appointment to discuss it with me. "I have always understood that any school or classroom in which I do observations must be selected by random sample," she explained. "What if the school and teacher I happen to draw isn't using discovery learning?" Her faith in sampling procedures for subject selection was as profound as her misunderstanding of when to apply them. Common sense should have guided her to a setting where she was likely to find the phenomenon of interest; questions of frequency and distribution were beyond the scope of her proposed inquiry.

I was intrigued that this student felt bound so rigidly to sampling procedures in spite of the fact that hers was to be an exploratory case study. It signaled that my explanations about qualitative research were not powerful enough to dispel her previously held beliefs about how "research" is supposed to be conducted. There was room for some teaching here, but there was also a challenge for me to try to learn what I could about the beliefs associated with "research" from my workshop participant. Might that be where the real art is in all inquiry: recognizing what might be learned as situations present themselves? If so, then, as anthropologist Mariam Slater once caricatured it (1976:130), whether or not you eat soup with a chicken head floating in it is rather incidental to the business at hand. What counts in fieldwork is *what is going on in your mind.*

Even to describe participant observation as a "strategy" may be going too far, except to prompt researchers to seek an opportune vantage point for seeing what they want to observe. The element of strategy turns on two complementary questions to be reviewed over and over:

- Am I making good use of the opportunity before me to learn what I set out to learn?
- Does what I have set out to learn, or to learn about, make good use of the opportunity presenting itself?

What is going on in the researcher's mind is critical to all this. If nothing is going on, not much is likely to come out of the experience except experience itself, with a possible residue of "empathy, a rapport high, and headnotes," in Roger Sanjek's terms (1990:238). This is not unlike actors whom we criticize for simply "mouthing words" rather than getting into their role. (I address this issue more fully in Part Three, "Fieldwork as Mindwork.") It may seem strange thus to separate mind from body, but the distinction helps to underscore the difference between what others observe us doing as we go about fieldwork – how we get around and conduct ourselves – from what is going on in our minds as we go about it.

How researchers move their bodies around is not what makes art out of fieldwork. Nevertheless, one can offer suggestions as to how to move about with sufficient grace as to be perceived graciously by those with whom we hope to interact. I have identified four areas of social behavior that seem especially important for the successful and satisfactory conduct of field-work – its *performance* aspects, if you will. None is unique to fieldwork. I regard them collectively as no more than the demonstration of everyday courtesy and common sense.

1. *Gaining entrée and maintaining rapport.* These two terms, joined so often as to have become a single and sometimes trite phrase in fieldworker accounts, mask a great deal of the angst associated with fieldwork, especially among those who have never done it and who worry that they may not be successful in achieving its personal dimensions. I remember a young graduate student in anthropology who returned from a difficult (not impossible, just difficult) year of fieldwork in the Canadian Far North anxious to communicate to his fellow students not only how terribly important this aspect of fieldwork was but also that these were critical aspects for the *duration* of fieldwork, not just a pair of tasks to be attended to first thing on arrival.

Maintaining rapport presents a continuing challenge through the very presence of an intrusive and inquiring observer forever wanting to know more and to understand better. The long-term nature of fieldwork, and the likelihood of both physical and emotional/intellectual isolation, exacerbate interpersonal tensions: Fieldwork can be its own worst enemy. I know because I've been there. No one was stealing my mail during the year of my induction into fieldwork as village teacher on a Canadian Indian reserve. There simply were times when there was no mail for anyone to bring, or only unimportant mail when important mail hadn't been sent. A couple of families *were* regularly relieving the school of a few gallons of fuel oil; I needed to maintain perspective more than I needed to maintain rapport, for I had not been sent to the village as an agent of the government with a primary responsibility for safeguarding that fuel supply.

2. *Reciprocity.* There is an art to gift giving. There is something of an art to gift receiving. These arts are by no means unique to the conduct of fieldwork, but fieldwork entails a subtle kind of exchange, one that often involves gifting across cultural boundaries where exchange rates may be ambiguous or one wonders what to offer in exchange for intangibles such as hospitality or a personal life history. Whether, and how much, to pay key informants, for example, always presents a problem. Grant-rich investigators are concerned that they may offer too much, while resource-poor graduate students are concerned that any payment at all is a further drain on already overtaxed resources. Employing local field assistants, or choosing a dwelling to rent or a family with whom to reside, invariably puts researchers at risk of siding with factions or otherwise being accused of being partial, parsimonious, or extravagant – and perhaps all of these at once.

Conventional wisdom cautions fieldworkers to remain as neutral as possible, especially when new to a site, but that option is not always open in the field. Conversely, one must learn how to manage being "put upon" by those who recognize the inherent fieldworker vulnerability to requests, when success depends on being able to make requests of others. If as fieldworker I am unsure what I may need from you by way of help or information at some future time, I have to be cautious in turning down requests you make of me at present. At the same time, I dare not fully reveal how vulnerable I feel, lest you impose unduly. Such decisions are not made easily. Along with extending the depth of one's understanding, long-term commitment extends both the depth and the duration of one's vulnerability.

One-shot interviewers or pollsters have it easy. At most, they may be hit up for a cigarette or a ride to town. They don't stay around long enough for requests to start escalating, as they inevitably do over time. Questions such as whether to pay a standard rate for interviewee time ought already to have been worked out as a matter of project policy. On the other hand, a request for food, money, medical assistance, or a job can put a resident fieldworker in an awkward bind, damned if you do, damned if you don't. In the abstract, a firm policy seems advisable ("Sorry, I just don't loan money – to anyone."), but in the world of diplomacy, everything remains negotiable, and fieldwork requires the art of diplomacy. One seeks knowledge in the professional role of researcher but prays for wisdom in the personal roles that make it possible.

3. *A tolerance for ambiguity.* Another admonition that becomes trite in the saying but essential in the doing is the need to remain as adaptable as one is humanly capable of being, to exhibit a "tolerance for ambiguity." In terms of priorities, perhaps this point deserves mention first, yet one can hardly claim that all fieldworkers exhibit this quality or that only fieldworkers need it.

There is no way anyone can train or prepare another for all the vagaries of fieldwork any more than one can train or prepare another for the vagaries of life. Of course, there is no way one can pass on to another the quality of tolerance, either: Merely saying it does not make it so. But there have been times in my own fieldwork (and life) that with nothing more than the cliché to sustain me, I have managed to eke out just a bit more patience than I thought I could muster. Someday the admonition to develop a "tolerance for ambiguity" may be helpful in your own work (and life). Simply suppressing a too-hasty comment or reaction is a good step in this direction.

Fieldworkers would hardly go wrong to take "tolerance for ambiguity" as their *professional* mantra if it is not by nature a personal one. I have seen it treated exactly that way in a summer workshop designed to help prepare teachers for assignments in the Alaskan bush. I was unable to think of any other phrase that might someday have proven more helpful. The workshop instructor used the expression so often that participants groaned every time he repeated it, and they presented him with a special T-shirt designed with that slogan on it. By the following winter, I assume that his message took on more significance as daylight hours and patience shortened and the realities of bush living began to take their toll.

I have heard the phrase "life shock" in reference to a related problem. Those of us who make our entry into the real world via protected mainstream lives and respectable academic routes. – the usual pool from which field-workers are recruited – are not necessarily well versed in the harsher realities associated with life itself. During those years we spent in the library *studying* about life, everybody else was knocking about in it. We may never have witnessed anyone dying, the sort of thing genteel folk do in hospitals, out of sight. We were even less likely to have witnessed a birth, especially in my day. The ragged and deformed may also have remained out of sight. All those statistics we read – poverty, illness, accidents, violence, abuse – may suddenly materialize for a fieldworker whose most traumatic experience to date had been a ticket for speeding.

The ambiguity comes in the meaning of human life, which proves not to be endowed with such universal reverence as we ourselves have been schooled to believe. "How many children do you have?" you inquire of your Ndebele informant in southern Africa. "Six, maybe five," he responds, leaving you to wonder if he really does not know how many children he has. But that is exactly why he has answered with such calculated ambiguity. When he last saw his children, there were six. In the interim, something may have happened to one of them, even if they all were OK this morning. And anyway, one does not want to provoke fate by taking anything for granted.

Not even natural disasters – fires, floods, earthquakes – shake us from our Western belief, or faith, that essentially we humans remain in control. We have the proof. Even our language comforts us: fireproof, earthquake proof. Foolproof! Fieldwork can sorely test the belief that we exert such control. A tolerance for ambiguity is an essential element in the art of participant observation.

4. *Personal determination coupled with faith in oneself.* Self-doubt must be held in check so that you can go about your business of conducting research, even when you may not always be sure what that entails. In part this means being able to maintain balance in the face of what anthropologists have termed "culture shock." Michael Agar describes it this way:

> The shock comes from the sudden immersion in the lifeways of a group different from yourself. Suddenly you do not know the rules anymore. You do not know how to interpret the stream of motions and noises that surround you. You have no idea what is expected of you. Many of the assumptions that form the bedrock of your existence are mercilessly ripped out from under you. (Agar 1980:50)

And that's only half of it; whatever shocks you probably was not what you originally set out to understand. The complexity of your task grows before your eyes, with more and more you want to understand as you realize you understand less and less. At such times you cannot help wondering if any fieldworker before you has confronted anything quite like this!

Rest easy – no one about to undertake fieldwork can ever answer exactly what will be encountered or exactly what is to result from a descriptive inquiry. If they could, there would be no point in doing the research this way, for our studies are constructed in the doing. Even hard-nosed experimentalists recognize, as Ludwik Fleck observed 60 years ago, that if a research experiment were well defined, it should be altogether unnecessary to perform it (Fleck 1979[1935]:86). The more that is known about a topic, the less likely a qualitative broadside of the kind that results from fieldwork may be best suited to explore it further. There is a becoming level of uncertainty in this work, but you must be prepared for the unsettling experience of constantly having to set and reset your course.

Should you feel so baffled by what confronts you that the only recourse you see is to record "everything," you will realize that certain "everythings" take precedence over others. What do you see and hear that strikes you as most important? How might you direct the attention of a newcomer to this setting? How can you best distill its essence for a reader who will only be able to "see" through your eyes or "hear" through your ears? Description is the starting point, Square One. You need never be at a loss as long as you remember you can always go back to description when you feel stuck.

Being There

Used in its broadest sense, participant observation is so all-encompassing that it can refer to virtually everything qualitative researchers do in pursuing descriptive/naturalistic inquiry, cultural anthropologists do in pursuing ethnography, sociologists do in pursuing a field study, and so forth.

Here I take participant observation in a somewhat narrower sense that makes it the complement to interviewing rather than inclusive of it, although that still leaves it to cover any field activity not specifically related to some form of interviewing. Its essence is captured, although oversimplified, in the phrase "being there." In a chapter with that title, Clifford Geertz offers a lighthearted image of the "proper" role of the fieldworker:

> What a proper ethnographer ought properly to be doing is going out to places, coming back with information about how people live there, and making that information available to the professional community in a practical form ... (Geertz 1988:1)

Somewhere between "going out to places" and "coming back with information ... ," every fieldworker has to achieve some workable balance between participating and observing. There is always a question of whether those two processes constitute discrete functions or are hopelessly intertwined in the very act of anyone being anywhere, but it is comforting to have our own special label for what we do to reassure ourselves that *our* being there is different from anyone else's. That self-conscious role is what we examine when discussing participant observation – how we can realize the potential not simply of "being there" but of being so agonizingly self-conscious about it.

How to participate effectively, how to observe effectively (especially that), how to keep the one from interfering with the other, and how to get others to act "naturally" while we try to appear nonchalant about our own presence – those are the confusions and challenges of the *participant* dimensions of the participant observer role. They, in turn, are confounded by the perennial problems of the process of observation. Those include what to look at, what to look for, and the never-ending tension between taking a closer look at *something* vs. taking a broader look at *everything*.

Many sources are devoted to the topic of field observations and participant observation (two recent additions are Adler and Adler 1994, and Jorgensen 1989). I, too, have joined in efforts to demystify that which cannot necessarily be explained, in a recently revised paper, "Confessions of a Trained' Observer" (HFW 1994a[1981]). My purpose in that writing was to help neophyte fieldworkers recognize what the problems are, rather than to offer simple solutions for resolving them. Each of us addresses the problems in specific ways in specific cases; there are more-or-less appropriate adaptations, not definitive answers. But no old-timer is going to forsake an opportunity to offer a bit of advice. My suggestions here underscore the dilemmas and inventory the options that confront the participant observer.

Doing Better Participant Observation;
Using Participant Observation Better

- You may tell others you are "just observing" and may satisfy their curiosity, but do not believe for a minute that there is any such thing as "just observing." A lens can have a focus and a periphery, but it must be pointed somewhere, it cannot "see" everywhere at once; in Kenneth Burke's aphorism, "A way of seeing is a way of not seeing" (1935:70). Our marvelous human eye has its scotoma, its blind spot; the analogy to fieldwork has been duly noted (for example, by Crapanzano 1980:ix).

  When you are not sure what you *should be* attending to, turn attention back on yourself to see what is it you *are* attending to, and try to discern how and why your attention has been drawn as it has. What are you observing and noting; of that, what are you putting in your notes, at what level of detail; and at what level are you tracking your personal reactions to what you are experiencing? Kleinman and Copp (1993) suggest that note taking is not complete until you go back over your notes to make "notes-on-notes." The point is to ensure that you are coupling your analysis to your observations (rather than putting that task off until later), and to help you remain attentive to your own processes as a human observer. Don't worry about all that you are *not* getting; focus on what you *are* getting: Observe yourself observing.

- Review constantly what you are looking *for* and whether or not you are seeing it or are likely to see it. You may need to refocus your attention to what is actually going on and discard some overconceptualized ideas you brought into the field (such as "watching" decision-making or "observing" discrimination). Begin by looking for recurring patterns or underlying themes in behavior or action. That should include patterns of things *not* happening as well as things that are happening. The latter kind of observations are most likely to be made comparatively, for example, "Back home this would be a major source of stress, but here no one seems to concern themselves." You will probably catch yourself becoming prematurely evaluative, particularly when righteous indignation tells you what people *should* be doing but are not. In case you don't recognize it, that's culture at work. Yours, not theirs! Tracking your own "shoulds" and "oughts" may provide valuable insight into your own processes as an observer.

Another kind of comparative question that can help focus your observations is to reflect on what a fieldworker of another persuasion within your discipline, or schooled in a different discipline entirely, might find of interest in a setting. Take the economist's concern for the allocation of scarce resources, for example. Questions addressing the distribution of resources can prompt fresh insight for a fieldworker who may not have thought about what is in short supply in a seemingly affluent community (for instance, time) or what seems to be in abundance (perhaps time, once more) in one stretched for resources.

In the course of opportunities for fieldwork, watch also for recurring themes in your own evolving career that lend focus and continuity to it. A common thread running through my own work is a focus on cultural acquisition. In any setting where I am an observer, I find myself asking, What do people (individually, collectively) have to know to do in order to do what they are doing here? And how do they seem to be transmitting or acquiring that information, especially in the absence of didactic instruction?

· I doubt that any observer can sustain attention for any great length of time. Be prepared to discover that observation itself is a mysterious process. At the least, it is something we do "off and on," and mostly off; we cannot meaningfully sustain passive attention. We compensate for that by "averaging out" our observations, reporting at a seemingly constant level of detail that implies we are keener at this than we are. A realistic approach for the fieldworker is to recognize and capitalize on the fact that our observations – or, more accurately, our ability to concentrate on them – are something comparable to a pulse: short bursts of attention followed by inattentive rests.

Capitalize on the bursts. Be especially observant about capturing little vignettes or short (but complete) conversational exchanges in careful detail. You could never capture all the conversation you hear about you, and you neither want nor need to. But what conversation you do record needs to be recorded in sufficient detail that you can report it verbatim. Beginners often gloss their observational efforts in a way that leaves them with no *reportable* data. Every statement they record is paraphrased *in their own words,* rather than in segments of conversation as actually spoken. A guideline I suggest is: What you do record, record in sufficient detail that, should the need arise, you would be able to report it directly from your notes. I am not suggesting that you actually report that way – fieldnotes don't usually make for great reading – but I urge you to record pertinent information at that level of detail. Otherwise, why bother?

- Try to assess what you are doing (that is, your participation), what you are observing, and what you are recording, in terms of the kind of information you will *need to report* rather than the kind of information you feel you *ought to gather*. (More on this idea of remaining goal-oriented is coming in Chapter 9.) If you think you might need certain information, by all means record it, but keep asking yourself whether or how you intend to use it.
- Reflect on your note taking and subsequent writing-up practices as a critical part of your fieldwork "work." There is a balance to be struck with writing up fieldnotes. For some, note taking is one (and perhaps the only) activity in which they feel they are really "doing" research. They may be tempted to overwrite because of the satisfaction note making brings. I worry about them less than I worry about those who resent the time that must be devoted to writing and who procrastinate and thus make the task increasingly formidable. If you are one of the latter, I suggest you try to discover how short you can make entries that nonetheless satisfy you for their adequacy, and then find a way to make that level of note making part of your daily routine (e.g., finishing up yesterday's notes while having your second cup of morning coffee). However you approach it, you must make note making sufficiently "doable" that you always do it, rather than put it off. It may prove to be a chore, but it need not become a dreaded one if you follow the simple rule of keeping your entries up to date. There isn't much sense to go out and get more if you haven't digested what you took in last time. (For more on fieldnotes, see Sanjek 1990; for more on writing them, see Emerson, Fretz, and Shaw 1995.)

Most of what you observe will remain in a form that Simon Ottenberg calls "headnotes" (1990:144-146), but some of it must make it into written jottings, whether simple or elaborate, that will eventually prove invaluable. Your elaborated note making also provides a critical bridge between what you are experiencing and how you are translating that experience into a form in which you can communicate it to others. Make a practice of including in your notes not only standard entries about day, date, and time, accompanied by a simple coding system for keeping track of entries, but also reflections on and about yourself – your mood, personal reactions, even random thoughts – that may later help you recapture detail not committed to paper but not "lost," either. Note taking is not the only kind of writing for you to consider at this stage. There is something temporary about any kind of notes that effectively says the "real" writing will come later. What is to prevent you from doing some of that "real" writing as fieldwork proceeds? Instead of putting everything in an abbreviated note form, take time frequently to draft expanded pieces written in rich detail in such a way that they might later be incorporated into your final account. Disabuse yourself of any idea that as long as you are doing fieldwork, note taking is the only kind of writing you should do.

The key to participant observation as a fieldwork strategy is to take seriously the challenge it poses to participate more, and to play the role of the aloof observer less. Do not think of yourself as someone who needs to wear a white lab coat and carry a clipboard to learn about how humans go about their everyday lives. If you find you are comfortable only by remaining distant and aloof, why do you insist on describing yourself as a participant observer? Perhaps a more formal approach will get you what you want to know, far more efficiently. Fieldwork entails more than data gathering. If you just want "data," turn your emphasis to activities that get you data. Semistructured interviewing might be a good compromise. If that doesn't do it, turn to more structured forms of interviewing (to be discussed next) that lead to questionnaires and surveys. Consider also the possibility that you may not have a natural affinity for fieldwork, especially if you begin to feel that it is getting in your way rather than helping you *make* your way.

At the time this manuscript was undergoing its major revisions (academic year 1994-95), I had the good fortune to be corresponding with Peter Demerath who, with his wife Ellen, was conducting fieldwork in Papua New Guinea. The Demeraths were more dramatically situated than any other beginning fieldworkers I knew at the time, and I was anxious to solicit their thoughts on the essence of fieldwork while they were deeply immersed in it. Peter's response gives a sense of the fieldworker's participation as performance, making oneself "believable."

> When I think of the "art" in fieldwork, and ways in which the artist rather than the scientist is called for, I think primarily of how much of what we are trying to do here is to present, or compose, both personas and projects that are appealing and attractive (or at least comprehensible) enough, so that people will talk with us and ultimately participate in our research. In this sense, perhaps much of the art of fieldwork lies in effective public relations.
>
> We find that we do many things – housework, pumping water, chewing betelnut, playing soccer and volleyball, chatting, greeting, poling a canoe, eating sea turtle stew after having just seen the animal slowly and painfully butchered – with an eye on how these things are perceived by the people here. We hope they will regard us and our actions as attractive (or non-threatening) to the extent that they will regard us as fellow human beings. It seems to us that the anthropologist must constantly attend to the "composition" of this public persona, and perhaps this is one of the areas where the art of fieldwork is visible. (Peter Demerath, personal communication, February 1995)

The Demeraths did not go halfway around the world to chat, play volleyball, or pump water, and ordinarily they would have had no opportunity at all to pole canoes or eat sea turtle stew. They were doing whatever intuition and common sense guided them to do as "fellow human beings," participating in the activities of others in the hope that those others would participate in their research. Their strategy addresses the concerns reviewed at the beginning of the chapter: gaining entree and maintaining rapport, reciprocity, a tolerance for ambiguity, and personal determination coupled with faith in themselves. There are no guarantees. But any experienced fieldworker will recognize that this is what genuine *participant* observation entails.

Getting Nosy

A ready topic for debate among experienced fieldworkers is whether interviewing or participant observation is the key dimension in the work; which is "more important"; and which logically should precede the other when initiating a new inquiry. Again, the best answer seems to be "It depends." Interviewing, the other major fieldwork activity to be discussed, includes a broad spectrum of activities, but it is easier to define. Participant observation remains as the residual fieldwork category that includes anything that is not some kind of interviewing.

I distinguish between the two in recognition of the profound difference in what fieldworkers do when engaging in participant observation – used here in the sense of experiencing – and interviewing. It is the difference between passively accepting what comes along, information that is virtually handed to us, and aggressively seeking information by "getting nosy."

In the simple act of *asking,* the fieldworker makes a 180-degree shift from observer to interlocutor, intruding into the scene by imposing onto the agenda what he or she wants to know. That does not make questioning a sinister business, but there is a quantum difference between taking whatever happens to come along and taking charge of the agenda. The difference might be likened to the contrast between being served an institutional or hosted meal and ordering from the a la carte menu of a restaurant. In the first case, one takes what is offered; in the second, one makes personal preferences known.

There are artful ways to conduct interviews, artful ways to ask questions, artful ways to make informants more comfortable when using a tape recorder, artful ways to check the accuracy of informant responses. Decisions about how much to record from informal conversations, how much to transcribe from formally recorded ones, or how long to conduct interviews in the course of an inquiry, all require judgment calls. One needs to develop a "sixth sense" about which data may ultimately prove most useful, toward the objective of accumulating less data rather than more. I will highlight a few points deserving of special mention, but I offer no magic formula for turning a poor interviewer into a better one. We all can improve our interview style by attending as carefully to our own words recorded in transcribed interviews as we attend to the words of our interviewee.

Longtime fieldwork allows a researcher to develop a keen sense of what, when, and under what circumstances it is appropriate to ask something, and when it is better to remain quiet. That requires distinguishing between what you would like to know and how to go about making that interest known. Sometimes that means holding questions for later; sometimes it means holding them forever; as often, it means recognizing the moment to raise a question because circumstances open a window of opportunity on a normally taboo or sensitive issue.

I recognize a cultural norm that guides my own behavior in this regard, one that makes *all* fieldwork a dilemma for me and rears itself on every occasion when I want to interrupt with a question, even in ordinary conversation: Do not intrude. In *Halfway Home,* novelist Paul Monette describes the reluctance to intrude as "the first WASP commandment." This is why the most thorough and inquisitive of researchers might be aghast at the suggestion that they ought to seek the same level of intimate information about their own colleagues or students at home that they feel professionally obliged to achieve in the field. Anthropologist Fred Gearing reveals the uneasiness he felt from the first moments of his introduction to fieldwork:

> During the next several days 1 sought out certain Indians, and we talked. Our conversations were typically low-keyed, filled with long silences. I never quite felt that I was intruding, but was never fully confident that I was not. (Gearing 1970:9)

Asking does more than merely intrude, however – at least when it goes beyond exchanging pleasantries of the day. And even exchanging pleasantries can lead to unexpected awkwardness, as when a friendly Thai asks, "Where are you going?" in the custom of a people for whom this, rather than our innocuous "How are you?" is the proper greeting in passing. Our questions as fieldworkers become increasingly intrusive as we seek to understand what is going on. Too easily we may put informants on the defensive by insisting or implying that they should be able to explain not only *what* is going on but *why*. In framing our questions we also tip our hands in ways that subtly influence the future course of our work. While we almost routinely insist that we are interested in "everything" about the lives of our informants, our questions belie that claim by revealing that some "everythings" are of more consequence than others.

Years ago, writing what turned out to be a spectacular chapter on interviewing in general but was intended only as a methodological preface to their pioneer study of male sexual behavior, Alfred Kinsey and his colleagues pointed out that although their questions were on sensitive topics, the very act of questioning can make *any* topic sensitive. (Kinsey, Pomeroy, and Martin 1948:Chapter *2)*. Through interviewing, we risk turning any topic about which we express interest into a sensitive one, inadvertently alerting informants to issues of our special concern. At the same time, local issues of purely academic concern to us may be fraught with political or economic overtones for respondents. We cannot naively assume, for example, that informants are delighted to be asked about the value of their personal possessions, the size of their livestock herds, or the amount they pay in taxes (Christensen 1993).

Let me offer an illustration of the difficulties in obtaining sensitive information. I was invited to comment on a redrafted proposal for researching

condom use in AIDS prevention among minority populations. Indicative of
the influence qualitative approaches now exert – even among agencies that
insist on final reports with totally quantifiable results – researchers in the
process of applying for a grant had been directed to augment their essentially
quantitative approach by including semistructured interviewing among their
data gathering strategies. I noted that the way the interview schedule had
been designed required the researchers to introduce the topic of condoms
early in the interviews. Thus interviewers were likely to lead respondents to
answer along socially acceptable lines that did not necessarily square with
actual behavior.

The underlying question is one of the most difficult in nondirective
interview strategies: how to find out what you want to know without framing
questions in a way that you, rather than your informants, introduce and
pursue topics? How can the context remain theirs, rather than your own? In
this case, with one-time interviews, some possibilities presented themselves.
Interviewers might ask respondents to name (free list) all the "safe sex"
practices they could think of, returning to those of special interest to the
project only later in the interview, and perhaps prompting with other
practices not mentioned. Or they might provide a comprehensive list of their
own, "burying" items of concern to the researchers, as, for example, a list that
included but did not specifically highlight condom use. In addition, specific
questions on that topic could be introduced near the end of each interview, so
that interviewers (and coders) would be able to track when, where, and how
in the course of an interview the topic was formally introduced.

It has taken years for me to become so bold that I risk the disapproval
of dental hygienists by looking them directly in the eye and stating flatly
that I do not now and never intend to floss! Why would a minority
respondent, answering intimate personal questions about sexual practices,
want to disappoint a researcher by claiming to be socially irresponsible about
the risk of transmitting a disease as devastating as AIDS? Further, if you tell
interviewers what you think they want to hear, maybe they will go away
sooner. Interviewing is not all that difficult, but interviewing in which people
tell you how they really think about things you are interested in learning, or
how they think about the things that are important to them, is a delicate art.
My working resolution to the dilemma of assessing what informants say is to
recognize that they are always telling me *something*. My task is to figure out
what that *something* might be.

What interviewing can do, of course, is introduce efficiency into fieldwork. That "efficiency" can reach a point in which fieldwork itself – the
participating kind that is the focus of this discussion – may be eliminated
altogether. If the questions to be asked can be tightened up enough, perhaps
the principal investigator need not enter the field at all. Research assistants,
even contract pollsters, can get the needed information.

One cannot do participant observation without "being there," although, as
pointed out in the previous chapter, fieldwork consists of more than "just"
being in the field. On the other hand, one can conduct fieldwork through

extensive interviews that do not assume or require residency on the part of the fieldworker, if sufficient time is allowed for research in depth, as with the collection of life history data. I think most qualitative researchers consider participant observation and interviewing to be complementary, but that does not require drawing on them equally or necessarily even drawing on both of them at all in every study. Fieldworkers invest more heavily in whichever of the two better accommodates their research style and their research question.

Some fieldworkers do little or no *formal* interviewing, maintaining instead a casual, conversational approach in the manner of Gearing's "low-keyed conversations." Mike Agar takes a strong position that underscores his ethnographic concern with meanings: "Ethnographic question-asking is a special blend of art and science. ... Ethnography without questions would be impossible" (1980:45). If his statement is too strong to apply to all fieldwork, we must at least recognize that fieldworkers who ask no questions are sorely tempted to become their own informants.

I take interviewing to include any situation in which a fieldworker is in a position to, and does, attempt to obtain information on a specific topic through even so casual a comment or inducement as, "What you were telling me the other day was really interesting. ..." or "I didn't have a chance to ask you about this before, but can you tell me a bit more about. ..." To categorize the major types of "asking" in which fieldworkers engage, I offer the following list. Descriptive titles make the categories seem obvious, yet each is worthy of the scholarly attention it has received in the extensive literature devoted specifically to aspects of interviewing:

- Casual or conversational interviewing
- Life history/life cycle interviewing
- Semistructured (i.e., open-ended) interviewing
- Structured interviewing, including formal eliciting techniques
  - Survey
  - Household census, ethnogenealogy
  - Questionnaire (written or oral)
- Projective techniques
- Standardized tests and other measurement techniques

The list could easily be expanded or collapsed, depending on one's purposes. My bias toward ethnographic research shows through with the inclusion of two categories. One is the category for household census and ethnogenealogy, once a mainstay in initiating community studies and still a good starting place when conducting them. Another is the category for projective techniques. That category accommodates the once-fashionable fieldwork practice of collecting Rorschach or Thematic Apperception Test protocols (see, for example, Henry and Spiro 1953), as well as more recent interests in projective interviewing such as the Spindlers' Instrumental Activities Inventory (1965) or Robert Textor's work in Ethnographic Futures research. There has been a longtime practice of asking informants straightforward but nonetheless projectively aimed questions about the foreseeable future: "Ten years from now, what do you think things will be like?"

Work in educational research leads me to include as a separate category the kind of tests associated with schooling, and thus my inclusion of the category "Standardized tests and other measurement techniques." For the fieldworker, however, such measurement techniques should be regarded as *a special type of interview*. What makes standardized tests different from other forms of interviewing is that the interviewee supplies an answer already known to the person administering the test. As a general rule, fieldworkers ask questions to find out what informants know and know about, not to "test" their knowledge. The questions we ask, the manner in which we ask them, and what we do with the information given are intended to signal our interest in and regard for what people know. In spite of experiencing too many years under the tyranny of testing in their own lives, practitioners of the *art* of fieldwork never, *never* "put down" those among whom they study. Fieldworkers as attuned to the art of teaching as to the art of fieldwork are able to follow that practice in their classrooms as well. It is critical to keep in mind that testing is a very special kind of interviewing, designed for assessment in terms of normative standards. Although fieldwork cannot help but have evaluative overtones, formal testing arises out of a quite different tradition, and one hopes that fieldworkers make nontraditional use of whatever test data they collect.

One way we show appreciation for what informants tell us is the serious respect accorded to the information they provide. I felt I had conveyed that idea to two African field assistants assigned to help me conduct a questionnaire survey in my study of the beer gardens of Bulawayo (HFW 1974). As soon as we started interviewing, however, I heard each of them roaring with laughter at responses to the questions they posed, in marked contrast to the studied reactions they had displayed during an earlier practice session. Out in the real world – we were conducting our interviews in urban, municipally operated beer gardens – their better judgment took over. It was risky to ask anything of total strangers, they explained, and if you wanted to keep respondents talking, you had better make sure they understood how appreciative you were of their responses. They weren't laughing *at* their respondents, they wanted me to understand, they were laughing *with* them. And how were *my* somber interviews going, they inquired tactfully?

The convenience of gathering any type of systematic interview data is always undertaken at the risk of losing rapport, although we can never anticipate exactly what anyone's reaction will be. For every individual too busy to talk, someone else may be reluctant to bring the interview to a close. For someone annoyed with questions too personal, another may insist on volunteering far more, and far more personal, information than that requested. Adherents of particular approaches have their stories to offer as testimonial. Chances are that approaches and questions that make the researcher uncomfortable will have a similar effect on respondents.

I know that fieldworkers have sometimes gone out of their way not to appear too inquisitive, too "pushy," too calculating in their approach, too like teachers giving examinations, journalists tracking down a story, or government agents ready to impose more taxes or exert more control. Most people are uncomfortable with the notion of a "file" being kept on them, a universal and growing discomfort as we realize how commonplace this has become in an age of information processing. The experienced longtime fieldworker is not likely to make his or her first appearance at the door with a questionnaire to be answered. The researcher who does show up at the door with a questionnaire is not likely to stick around to learn any more than what is asked on the questionnaire form.

Do I seem to be advocating a fieldwork approach, particularly in regard to interviewing, in which "slow is beautiful" and therefore "fast is bad"? Frankly, when thinking about what fieldwork can and cannot accomplish, that *is* my position. Issues surrounding the topic of interviewing help me to clarify it. There are things one can learn quickly by asking direct questions revealing of what one wants to know. There are things one can ask directly without much assurance about the answer. There are things about which we do not ask, guided by our own standards, or about which interviewees do not offer answers, guided by theirs. And there are underlying questions, often the kind of question that undergirds social research, that can neither be asked nor answered directly (for example, "Please tell me your world view," or "Why do we have schools at all?" or "When everyone seems so dissatisfied, why do you continue with your form of government?").

In a hurry-up world, with technologies that devour information byte by byte, there is constant pressure to get the facts and get on with it. Fieldworkers are in an excellent position not only to get facts but to be able to put facts in context. But fieldwork is a grossly inefficient way simply to gather factual data. When time is of the essence – as it is so often perceived to be – then fieldwork as represented here is out of the question, even when field-based research for collecting necessary data is essential. It is only the integrity of the label *fieldwork* that I seek to protect, however. There is no mandate that says if you can't devote at least a year, you shouldn't bother to go into the field at all. I agree with Russ Bernard, who *insists* on participant observation in the conduct of all scientific research about cultural groups and who argues more generally that "it is possible to do useful participant observation in just a few days" (1994b:140).

Contemporary fieldworkers have responded to the need for speed by incorporating survey-type techniques into their standard repertory, although there is nothing new about having to compress a heavy dose of fieldwork into a short period of time. As with any human activity, there are times when everything seems to be happening at once, or a brief foray is all that time or resources allow. Robert Redfield was so pleased with a 3-day field survey he conducted in 1941 with his then student and field assistant Sol Tax that he coined the term Rapid Guided Survey. However, the document that resulted from the work retained "Report of a 3-Day Survey" in its title, and the researchers had a clear idea of the information they sought, for their fieldwork was then in its seventh year (see Rubinstein 1991:297, 304). At that, they attributed their success at least in part to sheer luck.

Rapid Appraisal or Rapid Rural Appraisal became more commonplace in development projects in the Third World during the 1970s and 1980s when Appropriate Technology was the buzzword; Rapid Rural Appraisal itself has been recognized as a form of appropriate technology. Today there are numerous variations on "R.R.A." in both name and application, including Rapid Anthropological Assessment, Rapid Ethnographic Assessment, and Ethnographic Reconnaissance. Practicing anthropologists have their own handbook, *Soundings* (van Willigen and Finan 1991; see also Beebe 1995), that outlines and illustrates a number of "rapid and reliable" research methods. These procedures can retain something of a fieldwork flavor through what is described – or rationalized – as an iterative and exploratory team approach. In this approach, the research begins with (but moves rapidly beyond) preliminary observations and semistructured interviews with key informants. These preliminary data are used to guide the construction of appropriate survey or questionnaire instruments, the entire process to be completed in a limited time.

To an old-time and old-fashioned ethnographer like me, terms like *ethnography* or *fieldwork* join uneasily with a qualifier like *rapid*. Then again, I've never been in a hurry to do things. My motto, to "Do less, more thoroughly," may be nothing more than rationalization for my preferred and accustomed pace. Perhaps I envision a fieldwork entirely of my own making, having mistakenly accepted pronouncements about its duration (such as "one year at the least, and preferably two") as minimum standards when today's fieldworkers regard them as impractical and unnecessary. Russ Bernard now proclaims *three months* as the minimum time "to achieve reasonable intellec-tualized competence in another culture and be accepted as a participant observer" (Bernard 1994b:151). I heartily agree that *any* amount of time a researcher in our "rushy culture" (Dianne Ferguson's phrase) can devote to participant observation should prove useful for gaining a sense of context. But I am concerned whenever participant observation is simultaneously portrayed and faulted as a quickie exercise. Similar efforts have been directed at determining how *few* informants one really needs in gathering technically reliable information about a cultural domain (e.g., Bernard 1994b:Chapter 8; Romney, Weller, and Batchelder 1986). It is hardly surprising that these researchers are strong advocates for the efficiency of formal procedures and structured interview schedules. I hope Bernard has not inadvertently fore-shortened the acceptable period for fieldwork for those who will carefully misread his statement to reassure themselves that the three months he says is adequate to *establish* oneself in the field is all the time one needs to devote to a study.

Although I am not an advocate for finding faster ways to do fieldwork, neither am I committed to making fieldwork more time-consuming simply for its own sake. Time in the field is no guarantee of the quality of the ensuing reports. Nor need efforts to speed things up and find ways to get better data in less time be seen as detracting from efforts to make interviewing a better art as well. With that in mind, I offer some suggestions about interviewing, accompanied by a reminder that this topic has been well served in the vast "methods" literature, including early statements still brimming with cautions and insights (e.g., Paul 1953) and more recent how-to-do-it monographs (e.g., Seidman 1991; Spradley 1979). My comments relate especially to semi-structured interviewing of the sort that virtually all field researchers employ, whether constructing a rapid survey or embarking on a long-term inquiry into world view.

Doing Better Interviewing; Using Interviews Better

- *Recognize listening as an active and creative role.* I once heard the late educational historian Lawrence Cremin eulogized for his capacity as a "creative listener," a phrase that lingered in my mind as both an unusual compliment and a wonderful insight into the art of interviewing. Creative listener. Certainly that includes being an attentive listener. But it seems to imply more, a listener able to play an interactive role, thereby making a more effective speaker out of the person talking. An interview ought to be a satisfactory experience for listener and speaker alike.

  I regard myself as a listener, but that is not the same as being a creative listener. I confess that I frequently tire of listening, although surely Cremin must have experienced some of those same feelings, especially after assuming the role of college president. There are a few individuals for whom I seem to play the role of creative listener, and there are a few individuals who play that role for me; on either end of such conversations, I find the interaction not only satisfying but intensely stimulating. To consciously strive to become a creative listener seems a wonderful talent for any fieldworker to develop, especially anyone who depends on semistructured interviewing as a major field technique.

- *Talk less, listen more.* If the idea of creative listening seems too elusive, try simply talking less and listening more during any interview. As an easy first step, practice waiting one thousandth of a second longer before intruding on a momentary pause to introduce a comment or new question. Inter-viewers are reminded to distinguish between a "pregnant" silence and a dead one. A lengthened pause on the researcher's part may be enough to prompt the interviewee to pick-up the conversation again. Our own conversational patterns display a certain inertia: A conversation in motion tends to remain in motion. Silence poses a threat. We can become our own worst enemies during the interview process by rushing to fill in the pauses. If the researcher does not immediately plug the gap, the interviewee is likely to do it instead, without even realizing why.

- *Make questions short and to the point.* If necessary to repeat, do exactly that. Do not expand or elaborate, for in doing so you are likely either to start an answer or to change the question. This is usually done inadvertently, in the spirit of helping both the respondent and the dialogue. If you study interview protocols – and I particularly urge you to study your own – you are likely to discover that one simple question usually becomes two or three competing and increasingly complex ones through the course of the solicitous prompting that follows.

- *Plan interviews around a few big issues.* Successful interviewers return again and again to develop dimensions of an issue, rather than detailing myriad little questions to ask. For initial interviewing, anthropologist James Spradley recommended what he termed Grand Tour questions (Spradley 1979) of the sort, "So, tell me something about yourself or "How did you happen to get here?" The interviewer might then have several major topics in mind to which attention can be turned repeatedly in minor variation. For example, family and kin might be the central topic in the interviewer's mind, to be translated into more detailed questions about each family member, sometimes with a simple prompt such as, "Can you tell me anything more about that?"

- *As soon as possible after an interview, write it up.* Transcribe the interview, if it was taped, or index its contents (topics discussed and their location on the tape) if you do not intend to make full typescripts from each interview. If it was not taped, all the more reason for fleshing out your brief notes while your informant's words remain fresh in your mind. Then "study" the transcript, or listen to the tape, both to see how you are doing as an interviewer and to immerse yourself in what you are learning from and about your informant. If time allows (as it should), do not proceed with the next interview until the previous one has been processed. Always be thinking about how you intend to use the information, both for the immediate purpose of guiding future interviews, and for your eventual incorporation of the material into your final account.

- *Anticipate and discuss,* the level of formality you plan for the interview. If you intend semistructured interviews to be more formal than earlier dialogues – to be more than casual conversations that happen to be recorded – explain any shifting ground rules so your informant understands what may otherwise appear as a personality change that has suddenly come over you. Formal taped sessions can provide opportunity for a different kind of exchange, one in which the person being interviewed is clearly "in the know," and the researcher is the person who wants to find out. Michael Agar calls this the "one down" position, with the fieldworker assuming a subordinate role as learner rather than the one-up role assumed by the scientifically oriented hypotheses tester (Agar 1980:69).

Recognize nonetheless that the person with the tape recorder ought to remain in charge of the setting. You may need to think through whether you can live with that. Perhaps you will have to give way to egalitarian urges to make the exchange more evenly reciprocal. Be advised that when you listen to the tape you may discover that *you* were the one being interviewed.

I have always felt that a formal interview is and ought to be a special, asymmetrical form of conversation, one party seeking information, the other providing it. Work toward achieving that format if it suits your style and purposes. Explain that in your formal interviews you want your interviewee's words and explanations recorded, even if your informant wants it understood that some comments may be declared "off the record." Offer to turn off the tape recorder any time your interviewee prefers to speak off the record, desires a break, or wishes to discuss the interview process with you. You might also suggest that if your questions prompt similar questions your informant might like to ask of you, they can be noted for discussion later.

Conversational approaches in tape-recorded interviewing are less efficient, and may not be necessary if your informant understands how you distinguish between ordinary conversation and a formal interview in which you will take special care to record the interviewee's exact words. You may have to overcome an urge to be more casual, but both you and your informant probably need to remember that your association, while friendly, is essentially professional. Someday you will go away, and you intend to take the interview with you.

Make informants aware of the importance of their interviews to your work by your actions as well as your expressions of appreciation. Better to err on the side of being too formal than to create the impression of being too casual. Try to use a tape recorder, if possible. Augment that with brief notes, if possible. Conduct the interview in private, if possible. Formalize the occasion with a formally arranged appointment that you yourself (rather than an assistant or secretary) have arranged, if possible, perhaps even suggesting in advance the major topics you would like to discuss. And leave the tape recorder running after the formal interview ends, if possible, in the likelihood that although the interview is finished, your informant may not be.

If such formality seems the very antithesis of the kind of interpersonal exchange you want to foster, then follow your intuition to find a style more suitable. There is no rule against being more interactive, no rule insisting that somewhere in your report you must include the words of your informants. Perhaps the idea of "capturing" someone else's words precisely is precisely the kind of fieldworker you did not want to become. As integral as formal interviewing is to fieldwork in general, you must always consider the possibility that it is not for you.

- If you are not under the gun to work through your interview data as rapidly as possible, see how long you can hold off before you develop a questionnaire or a tightly structured interview schedule. The question of when and how interview schedules are developed reveals a major difference between fieldworkers and survey researchers. The survey researcher typically enters the field with a prepared schedule. Fieldworkers are more likely to administer such an instrument near the conclusion of the field research, when they know the questions that have yet to be asked and have a clearer idea of how best to ask them. The exception might be a household census or similar inventory through which the researcher also introduces the research project, gathers relevant basic demographic data, and looks for knowledgeable informants willing to be interviewed in depth. Even under those circumstances, try to keep the interview open. Ask as few specific questions as necessary, and include an open-ended question or two to invite respondents to say what is on their mind or to help provide context for the research topic.

A maxim directed at quantitative researchers (although too seldom heeded) holds in our work as well: Behind every question asked, there ought to be a hypothesis. We don't have to be that sticky about formalizing hypotheses, but data should never be gathered simply for the sake of gathering them or because it is so easy to add another question or two. If it doesn't really matter whether respondents own their own home, graduated from high school, or have ever been arrested, don't ask. If it does matter, give ample opportunity for them to explain, and include their explanations in the information you record. That's the difference between hit-and-run surveys and the fieldworker who intends to stick around to try to figure out how things fit together.

• Invite informants to help you become a better researcher. Agar's notion of the interviewer in the one-down position can be extended to the research process itself. Keep in mind that your interviewees have "views" about your interview techniques as well as about the scope of your questions. Don't fish for compliments, but a direct question such as "Do you have any suggestions about these interviews?" may prove immediately helpful as well as lend insight into how the interviewee is feeling as a participant in the research process. A further question can get directly at content: "Are there topics we might explore that I haven't asked about?" Should you get no response at first, you nonetheless are emphasizing the extent of your interest and effort at thoroughness and your respect for the intelligence of your informant; suggestions may follow later.

• Search for patterns in responses, not only for what is there but for cutoff points in discussion, or topics consistently skirted or avoided – on your part as well as on the part of your informants. Don't forget to go back through *all* your interviews if you work with an informant over a period of time. I have often discovered that informants gave important information, and important clues to what they felt was important, in early interviews. Everything was new, coming at me so fast that I failed to pick up on much of the information and clues the first time around.

In studying interview protocols, I find it useful to distinguish between what informants are telling me and what else, if anything, they may be *trying* to tell me. In one sense, everything an informant tells you can be taken as a fact – a linguistic fact, if no other kind. But informants make choices, sometimes leading us, sometimes leading us astray. Occasionally I find myself anticipating what they will say next, as a way to assess whether my informant and I are on the same wavelength. I believe it important to be able to quote back to informants, in their exact words, topics mentioned or alluded to in earlier conversations. There may also be times, however, when an ambiguous reference to an earlier topic is a more appropriate way to reintroduce it. That approach keeps you from leading the discussion or from phrasing questions in such a way that the only response needed is a yes or no.

- Finally, do not become so committed to the qualitative dimensions of responses that you fail to count and measure those aspects that warrant being counted and measured. Keep your research purposes clearly in mind in deciding what and how much to analyze. Carefully recorded language, for example, lends itself to rigorous analysis, but the rigor can set up an illusive smoke screen of carefully conducted but totally inappropriate analyses, lending an aura of science but indicative of a poor artistic choice. Behind every decision intended to advance science lies an opportunity for exercising sound human judgment.

Looking Over Others' Shoulders

Data gathering is not limited to information that fieldworkers gather through participant observation and interviewing while actively on site. There are additional, often critical, sources of information, especially but not limited to personal documents and other written records. This third category, archival research, concludes this review of the basic arts in the fieldwork part of fieldwork.

I used to think there was a degree of art involved in searching out information in a library; today I am willing to concede that task to science. I watch in dismay as students run enormous computer searches on unfamiliar topics, perhaps hoping that if they can press the right combination of keys at their terminal, information will spew forth like coins from a slot machine. Given the exponential increase in recorded information, we can be thankful that the technologies that helped create problems are also available to help resolve them.

There is still some art required in using archives, however. The most obvious art clearly parallels the problem one faces in the field: How wide a swath to cut, how deep to burrow; in short, "What counts"? "No depth of commitment and sense of responsibility will ever be enough to permit any individual to do what is there to be done," Margaret Mead cautioned fieldworkers a quarter of a century ago (1970:258), and today it is quite thinkable that a fieldworker determined to get a thorough grounding in library research might, in Mead's words, be so "attracted by the in-exhaustibility of the task" (p. 258) as to never leave the library at all. As with everything else about fieldwork, one needs to recognize how to focus and when to stop.

Libraries and the proliferation of information are everybody's problem, but those attracted to fieldwork probably are not going to get stuck in the library. We still hear arguments about whether we should go into the field well informed or should consult what others have said only after forming our own impressions. I believe the better argument can be made for being well informed, as long as being informed is accompanied with the same healthy skepticism befitting all scholarly research. That is the first of the three suggestions discussed below for making the most artful use of secondary sources.

Making the Best Use of the Work of Others

- *Be as skeptical of anything you read as you are of anything you are told.* A lesson we learn too well as schoolchildren must be cast aside in scholarly pursuit, that printed texts are sacred texts. Most certainly, what earlier fieldworkers have reported may no longer be true, even if it was accurate at one time. Skepticism is absolutely essential to all aspects of fieldwork, including any use made of printed sources.

  A skeptical stance does not give license to demean all prior efforts, however; academics sometimes get carried away in their truth-seeking zeal. It is tempting, for younger scholars especially, to find fault with earlier reports and "bring down the elders." I think it far more constructive, and more consistent with a spirit of inquiry, to take the position that earlier researchers did not quite get it right, just as future researchers will probably show that we did not quite get it right, either. If it is any comfort, know that fieldwork's "greats" continue to take their licking, as in this passage from Clifford Geertz, "Firth, not Malinowski, is probably our best Malinowskian. Fortes so far eclipses Radcliffe-Brown as to make us wonder how he could have taken him for his master. Kroeber did what Boas but promised" (1988:20).

  A healthy skepticism must always be maintained, even when everything seems to be checking out perfectly, past with present, established landmark studies with your own embryonic inquiries. While Ron Rohner and I were doing our fieldwork on the Northwest Coast, Ron discovered an excellent informant in Bill Scow and was sometimes surprised at how consistently Bill's accounts validated the early work of Franz Boas. But one of Ron's questions stumped Bill one day, and he explained, "I can't answer that one, Ron. I'll have to look it up." Only then did Ron realize that the old informant and the young anthropologist were using the same references; an earlier descriptive ethnography had now become a prescriptive one!

- *Look far afield for all you might include as "the work of others."* Sometimes anthropologists join the "stack rats" to do their work entirely through library scholarship, but fieldworkers are more likely to be sensitive to any suggestion that they never, or hardly ever, go to the library. Whether they spend much time in the library or not, most fieldworkers make use of a vast array of materials in addition to the customary library resources. (See Hill's useful guide for conducting original archival research "with quality and dispatch," 1993.)

Personal documents are especially high on the list of non-library sources: correspondence, diaries, travelers' journals, any sort of written account that might never find its way into a formal collection but can be invaluable to understanding everyday life or special events. Government records, newspaper accounts, surveyor reports – there is no end to the possible resources to be considered. Similarly, fieldworkers examine, and frequently collect, artifacts of all sorts, things in addition to words.

Fieldworkers need to think creatively about available sources of information that are not ordinarily regarded as data, to avoid falling victim to habits that find us invariably gathering the same limited information in the same limited ways. In my study of a school principal, for example, I was interested in getting some sense of how the principal's professional relationships with other teachers and administrators overlapped with his personal relationships among family and friends (HFW 1973). An opportunity to get some "hard data" on the topic occurred when his oldest daughter announced her forthcoming wedding. I asked the principal if he would be willing to review the wedding list and say something about everyone invited, paying particular attention to invitations extended by the parents of the bride rather than to the young couple's own social network. I might have obtained similar information by going over the list of people to whom the principal and his wife regularly sent Christmas cards. Personal documents such as these are not likely to end up at the Smithsonian, yet they are a ready source of data about social networks. Wouldn't a list of the telephone numbers frequently dialed, or a directory of e-mail correspondents for anyone who keeps such a record, provide similar insight into professional and/or personal networks?

- *Think about new ways to use data easily at hand.* The previous point emphasized looking at sources of data easily overlooked, so that we do not take too constricted a view of what constitutes data. The complement to that is to be equally creative about using readily available data in unusual ways.

It may, for example, be easier to document, and even to discern, patterns or trends by looking at the frequency or space devoted to certain kinds of events in the local newspaper over a period of years than by having to rely solely on the impressions of older informants. Margaret Mead was able to give a historical perspective to her interest in child training by comparing the range and detail of topics discussed in government manuals throughout a period of several decades. The changing tables of contents in introductory texts in fields like anthropology or sociology provide an excellent basis for watching the evolution of those disciplines. Old catalogues or photographs offer evidence of changing fashions in clothing, hair style, and the like. That such sources of data exist is hardly a revelation, but it doesn't hurt to remind fieldworkers to remind themselves that participant observation and interviewing are not the only ways to get information. Such extraneous sources also invite researchers to compare what they are being told with sources less susceptible to being re-interpreted with a knowing backward look.

This chapter has reviewed some basic arts in fieldwork, as perceived by a fieldworker committed to a personal investment of sufficient duration that data gathering is subordinated to insight born of, or informed by, direct experience. Potential problems were recast as challenges to be recognized and reckoned with. I turn next to examining some related problems from what might be called the dark side of fieldwork. Given the focus of the book, I refer to them as the Darker Arts.

References

Adler, Patricia A., and Peter Adler, 1994. Observational Techniques. In *Handbook of Qualitative Research*. Norman K. Denzin and Yvonna S. Lincoln, eds. Pp. 377-392. Thousand Oaks, CA: Sage.

Agar, Michael H., 1980. *The Professional Stranger: An Informal Introduction to Ethnography*. New York: Academic Press.

Barth, Frederick, 1966. Preface. In *The Social Organisation of the Marri Baluch*. Compiled and analyzed from the notes of Robert N. Pehrson by Frederick Barth. New York: Wenner-Gren Foundation.

Barth, Frederik, 1994a. A Personal View of Present Tasks and Priorities in Cultural Anthropology. In *Assessing Cultural Anthropology*. Robert Borofsky, ed. Pp. 349-361. New York: McGraw-Hill.

Beebe, James, 1995. *Basic Concepts and Techniques of Rapid Appraisal*. Human Organization 54(1):42-51.

Bernard, H. Russell, 1988. *Research Methods in Cultural Anthropology*. Newbury Park, CA: Sage.

–. 1994b *Research Methods in Anthropology: Qualitative and Quantitative Approaches*. 2nd ed. Thousand Oaks, CA: Sage.

Burke, Kenneth, 1935. *Permanence and Change*. New York: New Republic.

Christensen, Garry, 1993. Sensitive Information: Collecting Data on Livestock and Informal Credit. In *Fieldwork in Developing Countries*. Stephen Devereux and John Hoddinott, eds. Pp. 124–137. Boulder, CO: Lynne Rienner Publishers.

Clifford, James, 1988. *The Predicament of Culture*. Cambridge, MA: Harvard University Press.

Crapanzano, Vincent, 1980. *Tuhami: Portrait of a Moroccan*. Chicago: University of Chicago Press.

Emerson, Robert M., Rachel I. Fretz, and Linda L. Shaw, 1995. *Writing Ethnographic Fieldnotes*. Chicago: University of Chicago Press.

Fleck, Ludwik, 1979. *Genesis and Development of a Scientific Fact*. Chicago: University of Chicago Press. [Translated from the text originally published in German in 1935.]

Gearing, Frederick O., 1970. *The Face of the Fox*. Chicago: Aldine.

Geertz, Clifford, 1988. *Works and Lives*. Stanford, CA: Stanford University Press.

Henry, Jules, and Melford E. Spiro, 1953. Psychological Techniques: Projective

Techniques in Field Work. In *Anthropology Today*. Alfred L. Kroeber, ed. Pp. 417–429. Chicago: University of Chicago Press.

Hill, Michael R., 1993. *Archival Strategies and Techniques*. Newbury Park, CA: Sage.

Kinsey, Alfred C, Wardell B. Pomeroy, and Clyde E. Martin, 1948. *Sexual Behavior in the Human Male*. Philadelphia: W. B. Saunders Company.

Kleinman, Sherryl, and Martha A. Copp, 1993. *Emotions and Fieldwork*. Newbury Park, CA: Sage.

Mead, Margaret, 1970. The Art and Technology of Fieldwork. In *Handbook of Method in Cultural Anthropology*. Raoul Naroll and Ronald Cohen, eds. Pp. 246-265. Garden City, NY: Natural History Press.

Moerman, Michael, 1988. *Talking Culture: Ethnography and Conversation Analysis*. Philadelphia: University of Pennsylvania Press.

Ottenberg, Simon, 1990. Thirty Years of Fieldnotes: Changing Relationships to the Text. In *Fieldnotes: The Makings of Anthropology*. Roger Sanjek, ed. Pp. 139-160. Ithaca, NY: Cornell University Press.

Paul, Benjamin D., 1953. Interview Techniques and Field Relationships. In *Anthropology Today*. A. L. Kroeber, ed. Pp. 430-451. Chicago: University of Chicago Press.

Romney, A. K., Susan Weller, and W. H. Batchelder, 1986. Culture as Consensus: A Theory of Culture and Informant Accuracy. *American Anthropologist* 88:313-338.

Rubinstein, Robert A., ed., 1991. *Fieldwork: The Correspondence of Robert Redfield and Sol Tax*. Boulder, CO: Westview Press.

Sanjek, Roger, 1990. On Ethnographic Validity. In *Fieldnotes*. Roger Sanjek, ed. Pp. 385-418. Ithaca, NY: Cornell University Press.

Sanjek, Roger, ed., 1990. *Fieldnotes: The Makings of Anthropology*. Ithaca, NY: Cornell University Press.

Seidman, I. E., 1991. *Interviewing as Qualitative Research: A Guide for Researchers in the Social Sciences*. New York: Teachers College Press.

Slater, Mariam, 1976. *African Odyssey: An Anthropological Adventure*. Garden City, NY: Anchor Press/Doubleday.

Spindler, George, and Louise Spindler, 1965. The Instrumental Activities Inventory: A Technique for the Study of the Psychology of Acculturation. *Southwestern Journal of Anthropology* 21(l):1-23.

Spradley, James P., 1979. *The Ethnographic Interview*. New York: Holt, Rinehart and Winston.

van Willigen, John, and Timothy L. Finan, 1991. Soundings: Rapid and Reliable Research Methods for Practicing Anthropologists. NAPA Bulletin #10. Washington, DC: American Anthropological Association.

Wolcott, Harry F., 1973. *The Man in the Principal's Office: An Ethnography*. New York: Holt, Rinehart and Winston.

–. 1974. *The African Beer Gardens of Bulawayo: Integrated Drinking in a Segregated Society*. New Brunswick, NJ: Rutgers Center of Alcohol Studies. Monograph 10.

–. 1981a. Confessions of a "Trained" Observer. In *The Study of Schooling: Field Based Methodologies in Educational Research and Evaluation*. *Thomas* S. Popkewitz and B. Robert Tabachnick,

–. 1994a. Confessions of a "Trained" Observer. In *Transforming Qualitative Data: Description, Analysis, and Interpretation*. Pp. 149.–172. Thousand Oaks, CA: Sage.

28

Cracking Diamonds: Observer Role in Little League Baseball Settings and the Acquisition of Social Competence

Gary Alan Fine

I t is an axiom of sociological methodology that the form of data collection one employs will affect the data that one is able to collect. Research is thus dependent upon the constraints imposed by one's methodological choices. This is well attested to in general discussions of methodologies, but less notice has been given to this point when examining strategic approaches within a methodology. In the case of participant observation, which pre-supposes that the observer will interact intensely with those being studied, this argument is worth making explicitly. The role one chooses to adopt in dealing with research subjects will influence the speed and adequacy with which the researcher is able to "learn the ropes" in the situation under observation, and this will influence the type of information which will be collected. Further, the explanation of that role to the group being examined will provide assistance and constraints in learning the mechanisms by which the group operates. Participant observation assumes that the researcher can, with time, learn the ropes of the group under examination and, as a result, can become part of the group's interaction system. Thus, it seems of particular importance to examine the interrelationship among the observer's role (as seen by members), the explanation of that role, and the behavior of members as a result of that explanation and their observation of the observer. This will allow us to understand how the observer becomes adjusted to the chosen field setting.

Although sociologists are generally knowledgeable of the national culture in which their research is embedded, this does not imply that they examine

Source: *Fieldwork Experience: Qualitative Approaches to Social Research,* 1980, St. Martin's Press, pp. 117-132.

their own subgroups; in fact, this reflexive orientation toward one's membership groups has not often been attempted. The sociologist's modus operandi is to choose a relatively underexplored group of theoretical or descriptive interest and detail its social processes, traditions, and behavior patterns. Thus, the sociologist assumes an outsider's position in regard to the group, and learning appropriate modes of behavior typically is problematic.

Research with children's groups, the focus of this selection, poses interesting issues in this regard. Central is the biological fact that all adults have once been children. Children's cultures do vary across time, through space, and through environmental and demographic differences; still, children's cultures tend to be rather conservative, and their content changes slowly (Newell, 1963; Opie and Opie, 1959). Thus, one might suppose that adults could recall the dimensions of children's culture and would readily feel comfortable dealing with children on the children's own terms. However, by the end of adolescence, adults have become blissfully unaware of what passes in the more secret realms of preadolescent society. What was once central has been discarded as childish and not of practical utility for accomplishing "adult" tasks.

That childlore has been forgotten poses no difficulty for the average adult, except perhaps in disciplining offspring, and adult ignorance may actually provide children with needed room to grow. However, for the participant observer this lack of knowledge poses a frustrating barrier to research rapport and understanding. Because adults believe that they are familiar with children's behavior and talk, despite all they have forgotten, this difficulty may surprise the neophyte participant observer, who expects immediate understanding and acceptance and finds instead a feeling of awkwardness in the early stages of research.

The process by which the researcher acquires competence in dealing with children is tied to the role adopted. As noted above, this assertion is applicable to all participant observation environments, although we shall focus only on the relationship between role and social competence in regard to children's societies, and shall use this example to an understanding of how the researcher comes to learn the ropes in a semifamiliar situation.

This study is based on three summers of intensive data collection in five Little League baseball "major leagues" in Massachusetts, Rhode Island, and Minnesota.[1] The primary methodological technique employed was participant observation; the author (and, in one league, a research assistant) interacted with the players and coaches over the course of the Little League season (see Fine and Glassner, 1979 for further details). Two teams in each of these leagues were observed in detail. During practices and games, the participant observer stayed with the team in the dugout or on the field and attempted to maintain as much contact as possible with the players in nongame situations. While the original intent was to examine the processes and content of interaction in the Little League setting, the research focus was expanded to include an examination of how children act when adult supervisors are not present. Particularly in the final year of research, efforts were made to learn about that side of children's life hidden from adults. This emphasis produced special obstacles for the participant observer which would not have been present if only "public behavior" were to be examined.

The five communities which were examined represent distinct social environments: (1) Beanville,[2] an upper-middle-class professional suburb of Boston, Massachusetts, (2) Hopewell, an exurban township outside of the Providence, Rhode Island, metropolitan area – consisting of small towns, oceanfront resorts, farms, and a campus of the state university, (3) Bolton Park, an upper-middle-class professional suburb of St. Paul, Minnesota, similar to Beanville except for geographical location, (4) Sanford Heights, a middle-to lower-middle-class suburb of Minneapolis, consisting primarily of developers' tract homes, and (5) Maple Bluff, an upper-middle-class neighborhood within the city limits of St. Paul, examined by Harold Pontiff. These five communities are not intended to represent a random sample of locations in which preadolescents live and congregate; however, they do cover a substantial range of environments, and they guard against making generalizations on the basis of a single idiosyncratic community.

Culture and Roles

Adult researchers can choose from a number of roles when conducting observation among children. Roles for research of this type include supervisor, leader, observer, and friend (Fine and Glassner, 1979). The role that the adult researcher adopts will have implications for gaining acceptance and for discovering the rules of appropriate behavior in children's groups.

Supervisor

The supervisor is a researcher who has direct authority over the child and yet lacks any direct, positive contact. Such figures include authoritarian teachers, camp supervisors, and religious instructors. Generally, this role provides access to a relatively restricted range of preadolescent behavior. The preadolescent attempts to follow the dictates of the authority when under observation; thus, there may be a marked difference in behavior between situations in which the supervisor is present and those in which the supervisor is absent. The children are thus managing the impressions the adult gains of them, with the intent of avoiding negative sanctions. The behavior that is being observed may be natural, but it will not constitute the range of behaviors that preadolescents engage in. Within the context of this research role, it is unlikely that the barriers between adults and children can be eliminated. Adults will find it impossible to feel comfortable in collecting private information from children, although they may feel secure in the position of authority this role implies.

Leader

The leader can be differentiated from the supervisor by the presence of positive contact, although legitimate authority remains. Were the social researcher to become a Little League coach, the role that would be adopted would necessarily be that of the leader. Many professionals who regularly deal with children adopt this role – teachers, camp counselors, or coaches. A wider range of behaviors is legitimate here, and even if preadolescents overstep the line, some tolerance will be shown by the adult; however, the normative frame of reference will be that of the adult. Preadolescents may even feel constrained to act "properly" in order not to embarrass their adult leader. Preadolescents' affection for and affiliation with their adult leader may prevent their revealing their private behavior – which may be contrary to their desired presentation of self (Goffman, 1959). Their respect may, in effect, serve as a research barrier for the adult who wishes to acquire social competence. While the adult leader will have free access to a wide range of children's activities, the line between adult behavior and children's behavior remains strong, and the adult must behave in accord with adult prescriptions rather than those of children.

Observer

The observer role is the inverse of the leader role. The observer is an adult without formal authority and affective relationships. While preadolescents do not consciously behave in a particular fashion to obtain approval, neither do they admit the observer into their confidential circle. This is unlike the situation of the leader, in which preadolescents conspire to protect the adult role. Preadolescents have no motivation to allow the observer to learn of the social contingencies by which their group operates. By preadolescence, children are well socialized in the nuances of impression management and realize that some of the activities in which they regularly engage are frowned upon by adults. Thus, preadolescent groups will sometimes post a lookout for adults and will quickly change the subject when an adult is present. The pure observer has little more right to witness preadolescent behavior than any member of the general public, although this may vary according to the way in which the observer presents the research role. Further, because of the lack of positive affect and intense relationships, questioning about private and sensitive topics becomes problematic. The observer may witness behavior, but its meanings and motivations may not be self-evident and may remain hidden or be explicated only through the observer's knowledge as a former preadolescent and a current member of adult society. Thus, the observer, through a combination of choice and role, remains an outsider, destined not to acquire the competence to behave as a preadolescent.

Friend

The fourth major type of participant observation role, and the one emphasized in this research, is to become a friend to one's subjects and interact with them on as intimate a level as possible. One can never fully achieve the position of a peer, because of demographically based social requirements. There is value in being able to differentiate oneself from one's subjects – a feature which allows for a wider range of behaviors by the researcher than might be legitimate otherwise, such as asking "ignorant" questions. However, the adult who is able to transcend or bracket most of the status-based role requirements of adulthood may acquire greater social competence, leading to access to the recesses of children's culture. The friend role is conducive to the development of trust, although this trust must be cultivated by the researcher. Preadolescents may be willing to suspend their usual manner of dealing with adults, but this extraordinary relationship will take a substantial period of time to develop. Often special note is taken of the relationship – to signify its differences from other adult-child relationships. This was impressed upon me at one point in my research experience when one preadolescent labeled me an "honorary kid," to signal to a friend of his, with whom I did not have a relationship, that it was appropriate to talk freely in my presence. While that felicitous phrasing occured only once, many similar messages were conveyed by my preadolescent friends to their friends that I was an acceptable participant in their sexual and aggressive discussions. The key to this role is its explicit expression of positive affect combined with a relative lack of authority and a lack of sanctioning of preadolescent behavior. In turn, adopting the friend role suggests that the participant observer has the desire to acquire preadolescent social competency. The observer's acceptance will depend partly on the extent to which his or her behavior is congruent (though not identical) with that of preadolescents. Thus, there is a need for the adult to learn the ropes early in the research process – a process in which one's newly acquired preadolescent friends will provide sympathetic support.

Development of the Friend Role

In any research endeavor, one must obtain access to the scene one wishes to examine. In gaining permission, it becomes necessary to present a rationale of why one wishes to be present. This is not only a feature of participant observation but applies to any long-term relationship. One needs some justification or "cover" to explain one's actions. In nonresearch situations, one may be able to cite the sponsorship of an acquaintance or the existence of some biographical interest that would immediately legitimate one's presence – an explanation that makes sense in terms of the structure of the setting. These natural explanations are routinized and conventionalized and are not problematic; further, in natural interaction the explanation that the participant gives will be the one that he or she explicitly accepts – the real reason for the person's presence. From this, two issues emerge that relate to the acceptance and acceptability of any explanation of presence: (1) its acceptance by the others in the situation and (2) its acceptance by the participant. In participant observation these two features may become problematic, and in settings where one deals with several distinct groups of participants, each with its own criteria for acceptance and its own level of understanding, this issue becomes especially difficult – as the researcher may be forced to take sides in an explanation of presence.

One of three basic approaches is typical in explaining the participant observer's presence (we are assuming, for simplicity's sake, that the subjects may be taken as a single group). First, the participant observer may provide the research subjects with a rather complete and detailed explanation of the purposes and hypotheses of the research; this we shall term "explicit cover." Second, the researcher may explain that research is being conducted, but be vague or not completely candid about its goals; this we shall term "shallow cover." Finally, the researcher may deliberately hide the researcher role from the subjects – a situation we shall term, with apologies to our intelligence apparatus, "deep cover." The explicitness of explanation may relate to any of the research roles described above. Since our Little League research involved the use of the friend role, it is this that we will deal with in the subsequent discussion.

Explicit Cover

While this approach may seem at first to be the most ethically responsible, it creates methodological problems. The observer presents the research role as objectively as possible, but this may not provide an adequate explanation for the research subjects, who lack experience with sociological investigations. There is danger in telling subjects too much about one's research goals, and this danger consists of more than the expectancy effect by which knowledgeable subjects attempt to confirm or deny the researcher's hypotheses through their timely actions. The explanation given may, if sufficiently explicit, prove limiting to the subjects, who may feel compelled to reveal only that behavior under study and may exclude the researcher from areas outside of this range of interest. Further, by presenting the research endeavor as more formal than it is (considering the flexible nature of grounded research), the effect may be to make intimate friendships less likely. The relationships which do develop under such a circumstance are likely to be utilitarian ones, based on the formal research bargain. Because of this, the researcher may find it difficult to become comfortable investigating topics outside of the stated research bargain.

Shallow Cover

The approach adopted for my Little League research was shallow cover and involved the "sin" of omission. While it was explicitly mentioned and reaffirmed that the author was a social psychologist interested in observing the behavior of preadolescents, this was not expanded upon in detail. The researcher claimed that he wished to discover what children said and did, and that he would spend as much time with them as possible. This vague bargain permitted informal bargains to be struck with many individuals – explanations which at times differed substantially from each other. This allowed some players to treat the researcher as an intimate, sharing their dirty stories and vile exploits with him; allowed other boys to use the researcher as a protector against the bullying of their peers; provided isolates with someone to talk to about their baseball concerns; and gave parents and coaches an opportunity to describe their frustrations in raising children.

Shallow cover makes explicit one's structural role, and as such, the researcher's credibility as a role inhabitant cannot be undermined. However, since the research interests are not specified, individuals may feel deceived when they learn that the researcher's presumed interests at the beginning of the research were not the "real" topics. No matter how vague the researcher attempts to be, subjects develop ideas about what is being tested – ideas that can be cruelly or benignly disconfirmed and that will affect the researcher's access to the subjects. Shallow cover is perhaps the most frequent approach and may account for the fact that occasionally after a research account is published (Gallagher, 1964; Vidich and Bensman, 1964), subjects will feel betrayed by the researcher when the ambiguous cover is made explicit. The sociologist is still seen as a researcher, and in that the subjects were not defrauded, but the topics of study were not what subjects defined them to be. In such a situation, some subjects may feel deceived, while others may not – either because their expectations were not similar or because the explanations given to them differed materially.

In shallow cover, one has sufficient flexibility to create a research bargain that will allow a wide range of situations and behaviors to be examined. Since the researcher may initially be interested in a wide range of topics or unsure of a precise set of interests, the research problem can be narrowed or changed while still maintaining the research bargain. Because of the nature of the research explanation, expanding my focus from what occurs in Little League fields and dugouts to what preadolescents do in their leisure time was not problematic because of the initial explanation. Once the final report of my research findings is made available to the subjects, we will have the opportunity to determine how well they believe the research bargain has been upheld.

Deep Cover

In research studies in which subjects are not aware that they are under investigation, the position of the researcher is structurally equivalent to that of the undercover intelligence agent, although presumably there is a different set of motives. In that situation the researcher may witness a wide variety of behaviors, but simultaneously may find it difficult to inquire about any of these behaviors without the cover being suspect. A cover that is blown in such a situation – when subjects discover that their new member is actually a professional observer – may have profound implications. This uncovering discredits not only the research (as is true when one's shallow cover is blown) but the researcher as well, and perhaps the entire scientific enterprise.

In the case of research with preadolescents, deep cover is impossible to maintain since adults cannot "pass" as prepubescent (although this has been attempted with adolescents (Tornabene, 1967). However, one can live a false existence if one pretends to portray a role other than a researcher while surreptitiously taking notes about preadolescents (e.g., Sherif's position as a camp custodian in his summer camp studies: Sherif and Sherif, 1953; Sherif et al. 1961). This deception, while generally innocuous, can be sustained only for a short period of time for two reasons: (1) the frustrations that affect the role performer and (2) the limitations that are built into the role in terms of lack of access to the meanings that events have for the participants. The researcher learns about the operation of the group through a process of induction, generalizing from behavior to what these behaviors must mean for the group. Thus, while legitimate group members may believe that the researcher knows as much about the rules of the game as they do, actually the researcher knows less and finds no easy way of discovery.

The research announcement that the participant observer chooses to make affects the observer's ability to feel comfortable within the field setting. In this regard, deep cover is the most problematic, since the research is in danger of being unmasked at any point. In addition to learning the exigencies of proper social interaction, the researcher must be careful that discrediting information is hidden. This uncovering can occur with dramatic and potentially devastating suddenness, and in at least some accounts the problematic feature of deep cover has led the researcher to terminate participation in difficult situations (Wallis, 1977). While explicit cover promotes personal comfort in the field – since there is little discrepancy between public and private roles and questioning can be done openly – if the researcher decides to change the focus of the investigation, a feeling of anxiety may develop as the research bargain is altered and the observer must acquire new social competencies (such as the ability to talk about preadolescent sexual behavior as well as baseball). It is the third approach which seems most conducive to acquiring situational competencies. Shallow cover avoids possible discrediting, and because of the open focus on the researcher's role, it allows for questioning of the norms and appropriate behaviors of the group, both in public and in private. Generally, the more congruent the observer's desired social role is with the role as seen by informants, the more rapidly will the observer feel comfortable in the chosen setting; this consideration is important in choosing a research bargain.

Developing Trust

Despite the explanations that are given as justification for the observer's presence (we shall focus on shallow cover), individual participants may attempt to use the researcher for their own purposes (Johnson, 1975). This manipulation will influence the research arrangements and may facilitate or hinder the collection of data. Thus, while the adult with children will *always* be treated as some kind of adult by children (and the concept of *"honorary kid"* implicitly acknowledges this), there are services which the researcher-friend can provide in exchange for information. The observer may provide rewards for the preadolescents; may be used to satisfy some psychological needs (such as being able to tell their story); or may be dealt with as a friend – and in this case, the rewards are supplied by the mere presence of the researcher. In turn, the researcher looks for interactional rewards: status and information, fulfill-ment of the researcher's psychological needs, and enjoyable and emotionally satisfying friendships with the subjects. The development of social exchange patterns between researcher and subject allows for successful participant observation.

The behavioral content of preadolescent society varies in the extent to which it may normatively be revealed in the presence of adults. Some behaviors, such as playing baseball, are performed unhesitatingly in the presence of adults. This public behavior is easily observed and readily explicable with the aid of informants. The fact that preadolescents have little trouble spending time with adults indicates that there is a wide range of public behavior options available, and some parents believe that their offspring have no clandestine behavior.

The traditional adult concept of preadolescent socialization suggests that preadolescents strive to master the adult culture and that deviations imply the incompleteness of this learning. However, as Speier (1973) has pointed out, children can be profitably described as maintaining a culture of their own, separate and distinct from that of adults. He extends the argument to suggest that adult-child contact can be seen as an example of culture contact. On the basis of my research, I agree with Speier that this separate culture is a sizeable part of children's interaction, although preadolescents are competent to deal with adults using the adult-sanctioned culture. This concept of dual cultures is not unique to children but applies also to adults who are members of one or several subcultures. The culture of childhood may be seen as one of the numerous subcultures in contemporary heterogeneous society.

The research question involves *obtaining access* to this secretive culture – a process which is time-consuming and demands the development of trust. Preadolescent culture is akin to a deviant subculture in that its participants strive to keep the content hidden from their adult guardians. They do this for two pragmatic reasons. First, there is a desire to maintain a morally proper "face" in front of adults – that is, to manage the impressions their parents have of them. Second, the rough edges of children's culture must be hidden if the child is to avoid punishment. For example, one boy in Sanford Heights was grounded for a week when his mother heard from his sitter that he told a peer (in a phrase that psychoanalysts would find delightfully symptomatic) that "my cock has teeth." It is pragmatically necessary that adults be kept ill informed about the sexual and aggressive content of this culture.

The observer of children, like the researcher who studies deviant groups, finds that trust is essential. Polsky (1967) argues that the researcher who seeks acceptance by a criminal group must: (1) become willing to break some laws (if only as an accessory to crimes and not reporting information to the authorities), (2) make his or her contacts believe these intentions, and (3) prove that these acts are consistent with relevant beliefs. In the case of preadolescents, the issues are structurally similar. The participant observer may be, as I was, tested. This testing appears to be a precondition for acceptance in the private settings of the group. One key area in which this testing by preadolescents occurred was in determining my reaction to rowdiness (see also Glassner, 1976). This constellation of behaviors included shouting, shoving, fighting, insulting, and arguing. Repressing my adult desires to intervene at the slightest provocation led to my being allowed to observe other occasions, as an adult who knew how to behave around children.

On one occasion, I was in a Sanford Heights park with a group of preadolescent boys who, over a period of about five weeks, had begun to trust me. Suddenly, these boys spotted a group of girls they did not know, seated around a park bench near a thermos of water. One of my companions felt that it would be great sport to bother them (and simultaneously pay attention to them). He and his friends plotted to rush them, steal their thermos, and pour out the contents, disrupting their gathering. After a short period of insults between boys and girls (mostly about their physical attractiveness), the plan was put into effect – with the expected screaming and squealing on the part of the girls. At one point, several of the girls turned to me (busily taking notes and appearing, I assume, furtively guilty) and asked me, as the adult presumably in charge, why I didn't stop them. This reasonable question placed me in a difficult situation as a participant observer. Since no serious harm seemed to be occurring, and since I felt from various cues (such as the boys not looking at me) and prior actions that the behavior was natural and not being done for my benefit, I decided not to intervene, and said only that I was not in charge and had no control over their behavior. The boys were gleeful at hearing this, and shortly, with their mission completed (and the beginning of cross-sex contact begun), left the scene of battle. In retrospect, that occasion seems a significant step in my acceptance as an honorary preadolescent and indicated to the boys that I would not restrain them excessively – that I knew "my place" in the group. After that time I began to hear more detailed accounts of "making out"; one boy even used my recorder to tape a mutual masturbation session, and then returned the tape to me without commenting on what was taped.

Total acceptance is impossible, and I was fortunate to have been accepted by a handful of boys in the leagues who felt they could trust me (which never really occurred in Bolton Park or Maple Bluff). After I had won the trust of several boys in Beanville, they would tell me how they had just mooned[3] at passing traffic on a nearby street. The first time this occurred, I felt exhilarated for having been trusted sufficiently to be told about this example of preadolescent deviance, and yet somewhat frustrated for not having seen it in its natural context. When a similar revelation occurred several times without warning, I came to realize that this was an important part of the relationship; it was necessary that I not witness the actual mooning in order to protect both parties from embarrassment. Similar events happened in the other locations. In Hopewell, I heard about egging houses (throwing eggs at homes), but never witnessed it. In Sanford Heights many pranks and sexual acitivites were discussed in my presence, but despite attempts to go with the boys when they played pranks or to attend boy-girl parties, this never seemed possible. The barriers between adult and child are too powerful to be totally erased, although I was privy to a lot of dirty talk and verbal reconstructions of sexual and aggressive events. Adults can never really be treated as children, despite the behavioral competencies which they feel they might have re-acquired. Indeed, the adult will not feel comfortable behaving as a child, despite the possible benefits such a total role enactment would bring. Although sociologists can learn what constitutes proper behavior of the subjects, a very different set of behaviors may be expected of researchers.

The Key Informant

Crucial to learning the ropes and acceptance by a preadolescent group is the sponsorship of a "key informant." This individual is frequently cited in the sociological literature as the "hero" of the research – the person without whom the research could never have been conducted, or at least, not in its present form. In the course of this research, I gained the assistance of several boys who can properly be termed key informants. In Beanville, for example, without the assistance and sponsorship of a twelve-year-old named Rich Janelli, who suggested techniques of gaining rapport with his friends, I might have given up in frustration early in the research. These key informants expended their time, energy, and prestige to help me – although they gained prestige among their peers for having access to the observer. Within any population there may be several potential key informants. One criterion for this position is that the individual has a central position in the social structure of the group, which implies access to persons and knowledge. One can distinguish between two components of the key informant role: that of *sponsor* and *source*. Needless to say, these two components need not be embodied in the same individual. In the course of this research, many adult coaches and parents acted as sponsors, allowing me to gain access to their charges, but were unable, despite their best intentions, to provide much information about the nature of children's culture. Some low-status preadolescents provided a wealth of information, but little aid in gaining entry to the group of which they are nominally a part. It is the convergence of ability and willingness to supply the researcher with information and entry that is the mark of the key informant. In reviewing my research, it is difficult to determine why those individuals who became important to the research behaved as they did. One element which seems to characterize these boys is a sense of security in their social positions. Like Doc in Whyte's (1955) research, Rich, Justin, Whitney, Tom, and Frank in my own research were leaders in their groups, and they recognized this. They were socially self-confident, and this self-confidence allowed them to bridge the gap between adult and child and caused them to feel secure in their social authority and competence over a friendly, yet ignorant, adult. They were preadolescent teachers, willing to suggest ways I should act or react (i.e., don't be shocked; don't be too pushy; don't ignore the middle-status group members). This point is important in research with children, in that it represents something of an inversion of the normal relation between adult and child. It also represents placing trust in an adult, when normally, because of the topics being considered, that trust would be misplaced.

Thus, this research is in the debt of Rich Janelli from Beanville, who invited me to one of his private parties as "one of the boys," and to Tom Jordan, who was willing to assure his Sanford Heights peers that they could talk about girls in my presence, and in fact, on one of these occasions explained to his peers the proper techniques of "frenching." These individuals also gained from our relationship. Justin, Whitney, and two of their friends were taken from Hopewell to see a Boston Red Sox game; Frank and Tom were taken to see *Star Wars* in Sanford Heights; and neither group was rebuked for most of their antics in the process. Over the course of the research I came to be very good friends with these boys. We developed relationships of exchange which were balanced, even though different commodities were involved (including their desire to be immortalized through my writings and my desire to relearn how to be a preadolescent).

The role that I adopted with these boys was complex. Friend is certainly a part, as is big brother, student, journalist, and protector. However, with each boy my role had to be somewhat different. This factor is at the core of participant observation research. The basic interactionist perspective is not that of a single, simple, immutable role but a continual shaping to fit an ongoing relationship. This affected the way in which my knowledge of preadolescent culture was acquired.

Summary

There is a relationship between the role that researchers choose to employ and their ability to gain acceptance and rapport in the group. In every research setting this relationship will take a somewhat different form, owing to the nature of the research roles that can be adopted and the modes of behavior that group acceptance requires.

The position that researchers must adopt in regard to preadolescent subjects can be seen in this light. Because of physical appearance, social knowledge, and status, researchers are forced to operate within the role boundaries which constrict adults. Although the researchers may know how preadolescents do behave, other standards are applicable to their own behavior. While these behavior constraints are not grossly restricting, the range of permissable behaviors is narrowed by the researcher's self-image, the subjects' image of the researcher, and the normative expectations of other adult onlookers. Similar constraints on participant observers operate in all cases in which the researcher's own membership group is not being examined.

These research roles are not reified constellations of behavior. Rather, they are guides which channel action. As researchers learn the expectations of the group under study, behavioral options undergo continuous change as rapport is gained, relationships are negotiated, and new situations are encountered. The behavioral options available to researchers who study children are altered during the research, although this change does not necessarily imply an increase or decrease in the absolute number of options. At the outset, before researchers have acquired a behavioral competence in dealing with the group, a wide range of researcher roles are available. Researchers choose among these possibilities, thus affecting the manner in which the group will be known and how the group will react. For example, once positive relationships have developed, a researcher cannot easily retreat to the role of uninvolved observer. However, as research roles are developed, these roles allow for considerable flexibility and a feeling of comfort in the research setting.

The basic argument is that behavioral interaction acquired through participant observation is learned in ways similar to those of natural interaction. These social understandings are transmitted as a function of the social relationships which have developed between participant observer and subject – and these relationships, in turn, depend on the researcher's understanding of situational proprieties.

Obviously we are not dealing with a simple cause-and-effect relationship; the observer's social competence in the group affects the treatment by the group, and this treatment, in turn, expands and refines the observer's social competence. Learning the ropes in a group different from one's own is a continuous process, affected by the situated motives of both researcher and subject. However, by carefully considering the choice of role announcement, the researcher's acquisition of social competence can be supported by subjects' perceptions of the research goals.

Notes

1. Since a large majority of our preadolescent subjects were male (approximately 98 percent), we shall use masculine terminology exclusively. Differences between boys and girls were not examined in this research.
2. All names of persons and places are pseudonyms.
3. In this prank, preadolescents quickly pull down their trousers and briefs while facing away from oncoming traffic. See Licht (1974) for a psychiatric analysis.

References

Fine, G.A., and B. Glassner. "Participant Observation With Children: Promise and Problems." *Urban Life,* (1979), 153-174.

Gallagher, A., Jr. "Plainville: The Twice-Studied Town." In A.J. Vidich, J. Bensman, and M.R. Stein, eds., *Reflections on Community Studies.* New York: Harper & Row, 1964, pp. 285-303.

Glassner, B. "Kid Society." *Urban Education,* 11 (1976), 5-22.

Goffman, E. *The Presentation of Self in Everyday Life.* New York: Doubleday, 1959.

Johnson, J.M., *Doing Field Research.* New York: Free Press, 1975.

Licht, M. "Some Automotive Play Activities of Suburban Teenagers." *New York Folklore Quarterly,* 30 (1974), 44-65.

Newell, W.W. *Games and Songs of American Children.* New York: Dover, 1963. (Orig. 1883.)

Opie, I. and P. Opie. *Lore and Language of School Children.* London: Oxford University Press, 1959.

Polsky, N. *Hustlers, Beats, and Others.* Garden City, N.Y.: Doubleday, 1969.

Rynkiewich, M.A., and J.F. Spradley. "The Nacerima: A Neglected Culture." In J.F. Spradley and M.A. Rynkiewich, eds. *The Nacirema.* Boston: Little, Brown, 1975, pp. 1-5.

Sherif, M., and C.W. Sherif. *Groups in Harmony and Tension.* New York: Harper & Row, 1953.

Sherif, M., O.J. Harvey, B.J. White, W.R. Hood, and C.W. Sherif. *Inter group Conflict and Cooperation: The Robbers Cave Experiment.* Norman, Okla.: University of Oklahoma Book Exchange, 1961.

Speier, M. *How to Observe Face-to-Face Communication.* Pacific Palisades, Calif.: Goodyear, 1973.

Tornabene, L. *I Passed as a Teenager.* New York: Simon & Schuster, 1967.

Vidich, A., and J. Bensman. "The Springdale Case: Academic Bureaucrats and Sensitive Townspeople." In A.J. Vidich, J. Bensman, and M.R. Stein, eds., *Reflections on Community Studies.* New York: Harper & Row, 1964, 313-349.

Wallis, R. *The Road to Total Freedom: A Sociological Analysis of Scientology.* New York: Columbia University Press, 1977.

Whyte, W.F. *Street Corner Society.* Chicago: University of Chicago Press, 1955. (Orig. 1943.)

29

Getting On the Door and Staying There: A Covert Participant Observational Study of Bouncers

David Calvey

Introduction

This chapter discusses a covert participant observational study of door supervisors, or bouncers as they are more traditionally called, in the leisure and entertainment sector of Manchester, England. The fieldwork was conducted between January and June 1996. Similar to Westmarland's experience of police work (Chapter 2), the research involved substantial physical threat to the researcher. However, unlike Westmarland's experience, mine was a covert study, carried out without the knowledge of bouncers, club and pub owners and customers. This chapter discusses my experience of physical threat and highlights the ways in which bouncer/researcher relationships were enhanced by shared experience. However, at the same time there were important ethical issues involved in the research. The implications of the covert nature of the research are still ongoing and I have deliberately allowed some years to pass between the completion of the fieldwork and publication, as I feared recrimination by the door community if my research role was discovered. The experience of threat continuing after the fieldwork is completed and when one may be working in totally unrelated research areas is not uncommon or indeed new. Wallis's (1976, 1977) experience of studying Scientology followed him for years after the work was completed. This chapter contributes a recognition of the need to be aware of the longer-term consequences of research upon researchers themselves in terms of physical risk and threat.

The research discussed in this chapter was a sociological ethnography of

Source: *Danger in the Field: Risk and Ethics in Social Research*, 2000, Routledge, pp. 43-60.

door work that explored cultural practice, work culture and social organisation. My interest in studying this area grew out of being employed as a working bouncer for a local 'door' agency in pubs and clubs throughout the Manchester region. I had trained in martial arts for several years prior to undertaking the research and so was physically equipped to study this field. Due to recently completing a local authority DoorSafe (door staff training) course I had made a number of useful initial contacts and had negotiated access to a local door agency. Throughout the study other contacts were made which allowed greater access to this occupational setting. The chapter is organised into five broad sections. The first section is concerned with outlining the backdrop to the study by examining the professionalisation and occupational imagery of bouncers and bouncing and the regulation of door work. The second section discusses the intellectual orientation of the approach adopted in the study and the third section describes two key ethnographic episodes from the fieldwork. The penultimate section reviews the dual concepts of nomadic ethnography and the covert research role as strategies that articulate the management of research danger. The final section offers some reflections on ethical dangers and proposes a reflexive position for ethnographic research. In this way the chapter raises issues which are relevant beyond the study of door work to all research involving fieldwork in physically threatening contexts with potentially physically dangerous groups.

The Professionalisation and Regulation of Door Work: from folklore and mythology to big business

Bouncers are often typified as aggressive and unintelligent heavies and this image can be seen as part of their mythologisation as icons of masculinity. The categorisation and typification of bouncers in this way conventionally frames their perception and interpretation by others. Classically, they are the 'men of honour' when on your side and the 'heavies' when not on your side. Doors can be both opened and slammed shut. Put simply, bouncers can make or break your night out, with the club or pub effectively becoming their monopoly. However, in the United Kingdom, an occupational transformation is currently occurring: job title, job description and occupational image have shifted from that of bouncer to door supervisor, door steward and door security operative. As an occupational group the people who do this work are beginning to present themselves as undertaking a trained and professional form of labour, one which shuns the previously mythologised notion of 'bouncer'.

Bouncers have both traditional and contemporary associations with criminality in the shape of organised criminal gang activities and, particularly in the contemporary context, the sale of popular 'dance drugs' throughout the entertainment and leisure industries. At the same time, the 'night-time economy' and 'cultural industries' (Lovatt and O'Conner 1995) of many cities have experienced a boom, evidenced in the number of new pubs and clubs opening. Dance culture is now an integral part of the cultural industries and the lifestyle of a significant section of some communities. As a result, large numbers of door staff are in demand, dramatically increasing the number of private security agencies providing this service. The 'bouncing classes' currently represent by far the biggest private security operation in the UK. In 1996 an estimated 2,000 security companies were recorded with 50,000 door personnel. These figures are an estimate by the GMB union, quoted in the *Guardian,* April and May 1996.

The bouncing classes are composed primarily of males, although the proportion of female bouncers is increasing. If these men were the 'lads' of the counter school culture (Willis 1977), now that they are grown up they are doing door work. Most commonly, door work forms part of the informal economy, although professionalisation of the industry aims to reduce that. The drive for professionalisation, however, has evolved simultaneously with the rise of gangsterism and the widespread sale of 'dance drugs'. Bouncing has become an important source of employment and 'doing the doors' is now big business.

In an attempt to regulate door work, local authority door supervisor registration schemes are organised collaboratively by city councils to enable door staff to work in premises licensed for public entertainment throughout the United Kingdom. There are also attempts by unions to unionise the group and provide in-service training. Part of the rationale behind regulation is to make the work less dangerous and more open to scrutiny. However, the professionalisation of door work has gone hand-in-hand with its criminalisation. So widespread are the connections between club culture, drugs and door work that the Home Office conducted policy research into the area by the Police Research Group (Morris 1998). This research highlighted the way that door supervision was subverted by organised criminal factions involved in drug dealing in the dance culture, summed up in the commonly-used phrase 'control the doors, control the floors'.

The regulation of door work was started in the early 1990s. The implementation of Manchester DoorSafe happened in 1994. Many of the bouncers I had contact with during the study viewed the scheme ritualistically as a bureaucratic requirement to get 'badged up'. Employment was restricted by the City Council if you failed to display a DoorSafe badge when doing the doors. Such a process is part of the wider surveillance of both door work and the use of city spaces. However, there are still concerns over the trustworthiness of door staff among several club and pub owners in Manchester, who want police to act as door staff, as they do in parts of the United States, to deter drug dealers and violent thugs. Currently, police chiefs in Britain are opposed to the idea, but the debate continues.

The European-style reshaping of the leisure and entertainment sectors of Manchester has, ironically, brought with it gangsterism. The extension of licensing laws and the development of a cafe society provides opportunities for door agencies to monopolise doors and develop drug within venues. It has long been the case that bouncers, affiliated to organised criminal fraternities, have colluded with drug dealers, but this has become more acute due to the recent growth of the dance drug scene, which in turn is linked to the internationalisation of club culture. There has been much local, and indeed national, press interest in bouncers and bouncing in Manchester. Various popular dance clubs have closed in Manchester city centre due, in part, to drug and gang problems. Others have opened up with new, supposedly strict, door systems. This environment of cultural, social and occupational change makes the study of bouncing an interesting, rich and emergent area. The bouncer is at the centre of these changes, managing the door, managing their own role and monitoring their own occupational transformation. To study this area is to step into a dangerous world where attempts at regulation have not been as successful as was hoped.

Methodological Concerns and Bouncing: ethnomethodologically-inspired ethnography and covert participant observation

The objective of this section is to ground the version of participant observation that I practised in the study, within my intellectual orientation. Participant observation can usefully be seen as a tool embedded within an ethnomethodologically-inspired ethnography (Calvey 1993). Such an approach uses ethnography, and in this case a covert style, as a basic methodological strategy while departing from traditional styles. My ethnography, in terms of logic and reasoning, is inspired by an ethno-methodological program (Garfinkel 1996) on which there is a dedicated literature.[1] Briefly, this approach involves taking the issue of description seriously. It starts and stays with the research participant's perspective and is grounded in the 'lived experiences' of the participants. Thus the central objectives of this ethnography are to describe as faithfully as possible the natural setting of door work in a manner which does not trivialise, diminish or caricature the observed phenomena. This ethnographic mode is one of a wide range of styles.[2] This means of studying the social world utilises participant observation as its main methodological tool.[3] The important point here is less about method than about methodology. Namely, the researcher is embedded within the setting and the socially interactive nature of his/her role is explicitly accepted. It is the very character of this method that produces the duality of the research role and the dilemma of being simultaneously an insider and an outsider.

In terms of taking a covert role, some argue that such a stance is ethically indefensible. However, given my concern with authenticity and the lived experience of this dangerous work, it would have been nearly impossible to gain access any other way. My defence of the methodology adopted in the study revolves around certain premises being taken seriously. First, my central concern is with attempting adequately to describe, understand and explicate participants' accounts of their world in a spontaneous and emergent manner. Second, this examination is done whilst abstaining from, bracketing or being indifferent to, all corrective moral judgments of the adequacy, value or success in the way participants perform their work. What needs to be kept in mind is the difference between academic and street ethics and the corrective tendencies of the former on the latter. Third, immersion is a condition in this type of embedded role and, last, ethnography is a temporal, contingent and practical matter. An overt role would have been inappropriate for this topic as the participants are reluctant to give any information about their work activities to external agencies. Even if they did it would be highly selective and artificial. Covert participant observation was the richest way to engage with the participants in any meaningful sense. To get closer to and understand the experience of being a bouncer, one needed to do minimum damage to the natural settings of bouncing. The practical concerns, and the aim to understand the setting without disturbing it, problematised the issue of informed consent. From start to finish I was placed in an ethical dilemma and also in personal jeopardy, as a direct result of my use of covert methods. A key priority was to carry out the research with minimum damage to myself.

Ethnographic Episodes

The objective of this section is to outline two key ethnographic episodes that display and articulate the ethnographic condition and my experiences of physical risk during this study. The dominant source of data for the research was covertly tape-recorded conversations (a tape recorder was concealed in my jacket) and field notes of incidents which occurred as I worked alongside the bouncers. The two ethnographic episodes, one at a gay pub and the other a dance club, are drawn from a diverse range of door modes or contexts that I worked on during the six-month fieldwork period. The episodes are taken from the early and latter periods of the fieldwork respectively. It must be stressed at the outset that, although such ethnographic episodes form a rich picture of the fieldwork settings, they are limited in that they serve merely as snapshots or vignettes of that world. The episodes represent critical incidents on the door from which to analyse the concept of danger in the field and they can be understood as a routine part of door work. So while these particular events provide more insight than others they also capture the dangerous character of this fieldwork in general and its consequences.

Ethnographic episode 1. Site X: a case of assaults, take-overs and swimming lessons

This research site was a recently-opened gay pub in the heart of the area of Manchester city centre known as 'the gay village'. It had six door staff and extended hours at the weekend until 2am. It has since become a popular venue in this fashionable area of the city. The area as a whole has experienced a boom of pubs, clubs and restaurants and has become economically strong as a business district. It has a 'gay friendly' door policy and selection process that has to be sensitively managed by door staff.

Here I recount my first night on this door which was carried out early on in my fieldwork. The experience of the night was an ethical baptism of fire in which I witnessed two assaults. The first involved a fellow bouncer punching a customer in the face after he refused entry to him. I was standing on the door alongside the action. The second assault followed on from the former. The customer who had been assaulted had a relationship with a gay bouncer who worked on the door of another club in the village. This bouncer was a senior member of a Manchester gang running the doors in the area. He took revenge on our member of staff, assisted by a team of eight other bouncers, by breaking his nose and throwing him in the canal. This assault was not resisted by our door team. Such a response was interpreted as a public demonstration of weakness resulting in a 'take-over bid' for our door. We had been seen to 'lose our bottle' in the face of conflict and hence our appropriateness for doing that door was questioned. The rival bouncers had clearly won the show of strength and put in an immediate offer to our management to run the door.

The fear for my team was of the door being perceived as an 'easy door' where other bouncers, gangs and aspiring local 'hard men' would impose pressure via a range of humiliation and intimidation tactics. Door respect was at stake. The police arrived, alerted by customers concerned by the enforced swimming lesson, but they gained no information or statements from the bouncers. Everyone, including me, had seen and heard nothing. Traditionally, information has never been given by bouncers to the police. One bouncer described one of the cardinal rules as, 'if the police are there nobody has seen fuck all'. It turned out that the dispute between the bouncers was deep rooted and linked to the assaulted bouncer attempting to gain membership in the dominant gang that controlled and monopolised the city-centre doors. The assaulted bouncer was removed from his post and the door agency found him work on another door away from the city centre. The management stated that he was temporarily suspended but he never returned. It was clear they were put under gang pressure to do this.

Such insider information would have been difficult for me to obtain by other methods, in particular overt ones. It was important that I was seen and treated as a working door person so I could understand the way the work was carried out and the constraints of the job. The feeling of physical danger was acute in terms of what I had witnessed and, marginally, been involved in. However, I resisted making a classic category mistake of conflating contexts and imposing corrective meanings. The work involved threat, violence and intimidation and the choices the bouncers made involved street values and ethics. This was people doing door work not in academia.

Ethnographic episode 2. Site Y: a case of visits and vests

Working at Club Y was a high-status job because this was a dance-oriented club. Greater credibility and a door track record were required to gain employment here. The job gave me continued access to bouncing employment and was hence an important factor in securing continued access to the field. In essence, this door would open other doors. It took me a lot of canvassing of the door agency to get this one. The weekend I worked at the club was the occasion of its reopening after two weeks of intensive security precautions. The close-down had been due to successive take-over bids, violent incidents and intimidation tactics by various Manchester gangs, all interested as it was a new dance club in the city.

As a result the door staff had effectively lost control of the door. The club became a melting pot of gang interest and activity. The owners, a large multinational brewery chain, closed the club for two weeks to formulate a new security strategy. As part of these efforts £25,000 was spent on new measures including closed-circuit television. These measures were also intended to regain customer confidence after the close-down.

The owners of Club Y wanted a 'clean' door and were willing to recruit a new door team and enlist the full support of the police to stop the intimidation and halt gang infiltration on the doors. It was clear by the set-up of the door team that trouble was expected. All of the ten door staff, including myself, were fitted with bullet-proof vests. On fitting me with a vest the CID (Criminal Investigation Department) officer noted that it would stop bullets from most types of guns. One doorman later quipped that if guns were pulled 'he ain't gonna be around anyway'. This comment filled me with a certain amount of fear about my first night in the club but this gave way to my quest for richer data. However, there was an atmosphere of tension and apprehension all through the opening weekend. It became a question of when, rather than if, there was going to be gang interest and trouble over the re-opening.

Because my working knowledge of the gang structure, and particularly of the leaders or 'heads', was limited, I stressed to the head door person that I needed to be clearly told who had any form of privileged entry. I did not want to make mistakes on any door, but least of all on this door, on this night. At the same time I did not want the head door person to know too much about my concerns, so I had to be subtle in seeking advice. It is vital for door people to 'know the score' in terms of who controls the door so they can manage entry accordingly; the irony then being that to keep out gang members you need to employ gang members. Thus, being and staying on the door at such clubs requires a current working knowledge of gang organisation, including who are the leaders, and the ongoing gang ranking. This knowledge is part of the interactional management of respect enacted on the door between the door staff and the customers. Mismanagement could have severe repercussions for that individual and possibly for the whole door team.

The first night was generally regarded as uneventful. This was commonly perceived by the door team as the 'quiet before the storm'. The second night the club had a visit from a very senior Salford gang leader who monopolised doors throughout the Manchester area. All the door team, except me, recognised him. Their reactions told the story. When he arrived, one of the senior doormen hid behind the main door whilst nervously spying through the peek hole and firmly pronouncing that he was not going outside. The visit was a business one, made just before the club was due to open for the night. The gang leader arrived with his driver and parked outside the club. His driver then told the head door person to get into the car so the gang leader could talk with him. The other bouncers waited for the news inside the club and held an emergency meeting about the situation. Meanwhile customers had begun queuing outside. At this stage the safety of the door team was prioritised over that of the customers.

There was fear and apprehension building throughout the discussions held by the door team. The door buzzer started ringing more frequently as the customer queue grew. The team eventually agreed to open the doors of the club. It was a waiting game and the night suddenly started to turn into a very long one for everyone. The night continued without event until during the latter part of the night two young black men arrived at the front door. It was felt, after assessment of closed-circuit television, that they had guns in their possession. There was considerable panic and confusion amongst staff as to who they were and whether or not they actually had guns. There were certain significant assumptions made about the race of these men by the bouncers regarding their connection to dominant gangs in the city centre. These assumptions were illustrative of the racist nature of some of the door practices as young black men, mainly of Afro-Caribbean origin, were often discriminated against as a potential threat to the door team (Mungham 1976). Door teams are ethnically constructed according to which gang or coalition have an active interest in them. According to most of the door team the bravado with which the young men approached and demanded entry suggested that they were 'carrying'. Moreover, in terms of physical confrontation there were only two of them facing a full door team of ten. This convinced the door team of their intent. The front door was closed and temporarily locked with nobody, including customers, being allowed out. Indeed, one female customer, who needed to leave immediately, was flatly denied and allowed to vomit in the corner of the club. At this stage, most of the door team were huddled in the middle pay booth section trying to view the closed-circuit television monitor to see if they recognised the men. Indeed, for fear of possible shooting, nobody stood near the middle of the door but to either side. The head doorman was asked to go outside and investigate. He summed up the collective anxiety of the team by saying, 'I don't want to get no bullet over no bullshit.' The two men then left in a car. At no point were the police called. There is a traditional cynicism towards them amongst bouncers, and on this occasion there was a hesitancy to call the police as the club had just re-opened.

Despite the apparent dissipation of danger after the two men had left, the situation developed further when they returned to the club shortly after it had shut, demanding entry and attempting to force the front door open. At this point the club manager called a state of emergency, put the entire door team, remaining bar staff and DJs in a locked cellar and called the police for assistance on his mobile phone. Such was the level of intimidation that the club was abandoned in favour of personal safety. The intruders succeeded in damaging the front door but had left before the police arrived. The main question raised for the bouncers by this incident was whether these men were connected to the earlier visit of the Salford gang leader or were part of a rival gang displaying their interest.

The police stayed on site until everyone was off the premises. They suggested to the bouncers that we had better keep our vests on until we got home. Some of the door team were visibly shaken by the chain of events. Whilst the dangerous events were in progress I prioritised my own survival over sociology, but the tape was kept running throughout. Walking home with my vest on filled me with extreme anxiety about my personal safety and turned the brief journey home into a paranoid nightmare. Managing threats was a routine part of the job of being a bouncer but at this point I felt very vulnerable. Events had clearly illustrated that my role as a bouncer could result in serious injury and it took some time for my adrenalin and stress levels to subside when I returned home. Taking a side was one thing, the threat of being removed from one was another.

On reflection, to gain access to such observations it was vital that I had credibility as a working door person and had a door history. The concept of collective trust is integral to doing door work, encapsulated in the doorman's slogan 'watch my back'. More specifically, this trust is a fragile one involving high levels of suspicion and cynicism. This type of trust and risk management was not questioned or challenged by door staff, it was simply a condition of the work.

Danger and All That: a case of the nomadic ethnographer

The nomadic role that I adopted arose from my need, driven in part by personal safety concerns, to move constantly around door settings. The rationale behind the nomadic role was two-fold. First, I wanted to draw on a wide range of settings for the research in order to do comparative analysis. Second, it diminished my chances of being discovered, as personal bonds were not given time to form, nor intimate biographical questions asked by door staff or regular customers. It was a paradox getting close to participants without allowing them to get too close to you. In short, the dangerous nature of this research necessitated that I adopt a nomadic ethnographic role. Thus I constantly engineered appropriate exits as I moved around various work sites. These self-created exits were usually based on issues of pay, personality conflicts with management and inappropriate hours. In the event that my cover was blown and my denial that I was anything other than an ordinary bouncer was rejected, I had rehearsed a cover story stating that I was linked to covert police surveillance. Merely stating that I was an academic would offer no or very little protection. When asked where I lived I had standard responses such as 'local', 'not that far away' or as a last resort 'the city centre'. I never provided a precise location. If I gave a phone number it was a mobile rather than home one.

This vagueness was rarely questioned. Strangely, this dangerous work was undertaken without knowing the surnames or addresses of your colleagues. But this did not matter and was taken as normal. As long as your colleagues were there to 'watch your back' when it mattered the rest was academic. That is not to say that friendships did not develop or that they were irrelevant. Indeed, door work features a lot of bonding and comradeship and due to the nature of the work close friendships develop, but it can also be a temporary line of work, in which one forms passing attachments to colleagues. In these circumstances I had to keep control of the information that my colleagues received about me. This meant limiting the opportunities for them to have access to personal information. For example, my partner kept a safe distance from the doors I worked. Such a distancing strategy was more problematic in the post-field experience but one which had to be sensibly maintained. After all, to the men on the doors, I had merely finished doing door work with them. Consequently, I was regularly asked when I was coming back or which door I was working.

Communication was kept on a first name basis only. Pay was in cash in an envelope with your first name on the front and no formal documentation. This suited me well because the less they knew about my biography the better for my personal safety. The flow of information from friends and students I knew also had to be controlled. Angst about my research role was compounded when I received some press coverage in the official newspaper of the University of Manchester Student Union. The article was titled "Work Experience' and made reference to the first of the ethnographic episodes mentioned above. It read:

> Conscientious as ever, members of staff at the Sociology Department have been doing undercover research into the life of those much-maligned guardians of the door, Bouncers. At least, Biteback presumes that's why some tutors have been working on the door at Pub X in town. They wouldn't be moonlighting, would they?
>
> (*Mancunion* Issue no. 13, 29/1/96)

As this newspaper had a large local student circulation and the piece was published in the early part of my fieldwork, I was concerned about my cover being blown by students. Fortunately this did not happen, although I was sensitised to the possibilities of such an occurrence.

During the fieldwork I maintained key contacts although I was involved in various shifting and temporary friendships with door staff. These relationships had to involve careful boundary maintenance. On the one hand it was necessary to display a bouncer's interaction rituals (Goffman 1967) including dress code, non-verbal codes and war stories in the appropriate argot – this is what I refer to as the 'bouncer self'. The constitution of a bouncer's subjectivity, self-image and identity is tied up in complex ways with these social practices that are expected and taken for granted in door work. The 'bouncer self' is embedded in masculinity and is accurately displayed in and through the interactional management of respect on the doors. On the other hand the duality of the research role is paramount. The difference between self and other must remain and not become blurred during the research process. By this nomadic fieldwork method I built an adequate picture of the field, wherein observations were drawn from various sites. A single ethnographic immersion at one door would have involved thick description but would have lacked analytic breadth. At the same time the nomadic approach also protected my personal safety and protected the boundaries between my bouncer and non-bouncer roles.

Post-mortems, Hangovers and Reflections on Ethical Dangers

The research dangers I experienced were physical, emotional and ethical. The experience of physical danger and the routine management of conflict, both real and supposed, came with the research territory. It was more than simply a feature of the research setting. Importantly, it was integral to understanding the context of violence in which the participants lived and worked and which became normalised. A 'hardness passport' (James 1973) was required for entry into the bouncing game and once achieved was never questioned. In addition to the physical danger that I encountered, emotional risk was also an aspect of the research. These emotional dangers centered on the threat to my sense of self in the research process and the ongoing management of personal relationships, loyalties, obligations and confidences that developed. This became stressful the longer the fieldwork continued because I began to know more about the settings. Moreover, as time went on, the more participants assumed that I knew about the bouncing world. This is not sociological romanticism running riot, discovery would have meant 'door justice' in the shape of a 'good kicking'. Fortunately, this did not happen.

In terms of ethical dilemmas, I witnessed various criminal events such as assault, drug taking, theft of entrance money and the withholding of information from the police. It is difficult to plan for such events in the sense of taking legal advice and guidance beforehand but I became increasingly aware of the sensitive situations I was becoming embroiled in during the research. I was also offered, and refused, various drugs by doormen and frequently had to physically restrain customers. Such incidents were 'all in a night's work'. There was no time to stop and think about how to respond to them, except retrospectively. It is important to locate these ethical dangers as in the normal run of the job and my concern was in trying to understand the routine orientation of the participants to such events. As the ethnographic episodes display, the expectations of the role and my personal ethics could clash. This had to be negotiated in an occasioned and emergent manner by distancing myself as much as practically possible from such events whilst still performing the dual fieldwork role.

The Post-fieldwork Experience and Self-management

I would like to stress here that these multiple aspects of danger were experienced throughout the research, including during the post-fieldwork stage. Importantly, this shifts the picture of fieldwork away from a simplified chronology, often presented in traditional methodological literature, to a more complex and dynamic account. For me the research not only involved getting on and staying on the door but, once the study ended, staying out. After the fieldwork was completed, I was still treated as a bouncer by my erstwhile colleagues and was asked to work on doors, was queried as to where I was working and asked about old door relationships. The research role might have ended for the researcher but not for the researched. My story of who I was had to be sustained both throughout the study and after it. It was as if the study had no closing date.

Doing the door is a way of life and a lifestyle. By doing the job I had become part of the bouncers' community and in the post-fieldwork period many privileges were extended to me, including free entry into local clubs and pubs. These practices are seen by the door staff as legitimate social and economic fringe benefits (Mars 1994) of the job. You know you are distinguished from the crowd and observed as such. You are not just another punter but a punter who is also an ex- or current bouncer. Managing the post-fieldwork experience was not only a case of wearing two hats but also being competent at the impression management that goes with it. Moreover, because it was in a violent context the research involved more foresight, planning and skilful manoeuvre (Sluka 1995) than other contexts might have done. It could not be treated, and I certainly did not treat it, lightly. I partly enjoyed the seductive 'buzz' from working on doors from 'the inside' but I was simultaneously relieved eventually to melt back into the anonymous crowd. When one senior doorman of Manchester's largest night club, which was run by a dominant gang and has since closed down, stated I was now 'in the firm', as I picked up my wages, I definitely decided it was time to close the study. The double-edged character of my research, in simultaneously using and exposing the self, was a high-risk methodology. I refer to it as 'sub-aqua ethnography' – dangerous due to the constant fear of discovery. The field experience of getting on, staying on and leaving the door has been a powerful one.

In such a covert role there is also the issue of my over-identification, emotional attachment and collusion with the subject. However, this is only a serious problem if one holds on to a traditional concept of the objectivity of the fieldworker. For me, the issue is one of entitlement, in the sense of being able to talk adequately about bouncing and bouncers whilst, in my case, being a temporary and particular version of one. It is not to say that ethics can be relativised away or that professional codes of conduct need not apply. The question is in viewing ethics more broadly as situational and case contingent. A re-orientation is required that places ethics as part of the ethnographic condition. That is, ethics as part of the ethnographic setting rather than extracted from it and given honorific status.

This research account is a contribution to the developing literature on the dangers of research. It supports the attempts to de-marginalise danger and bring it from the periphery to the centre. It is my contention that research danger can be usefully conceptualised as a positively disruptive influence on traditional and conventional methodological accounts. It moves debates from simplified ideas of taking a side (Becker 1998) to issues of mixed loyalties and shifting identities in fieldwork. Ethical frameworks need to be understood as a dynamic and empirically-informed and continuous process. Codes of ethical practice are idealisations. In terms of my research I ran the risk of academic alienation because of the methodology which I employed, in spite of the pioneering nature of the investigation. Covert research always requires clear justification and explication as a research tool, but is nonetheless still criticised.

Ultimately, the topic dictated that the research be conducted covertly as the level of access, and hence analytic richness, which I gained would have been seriously diminished otherwise. Many sociologists would whole-heartedly reject all covert research on ethical grounds as violating the principles of informed consent, privacy and trust. Indeed, it is professionally frowned upon. However, it is one that I would vigorously defend on the grounds of both methodological necessity and appropriateness. Moreover, as with Fielding's (1981) contentious study of the National Front, topics need to be investigated analytically despite personal preferences and political tastes. In fact, more investigative social research should be done on controversial areas, although not blindly.

Reflexive Ethnography

My aim in this chapter is not to offer formulaic and prescriptive advice for the ethnographic research process but rather to reflect on some particular problems I encountered. My approach is neither to unify nor to integrate the varieties of sociological reflexivity (Slack 1993) into schematic meta-theories that gloss over serious differences. Rather it has been to frame and distinguish some of the features of a reflexive research position. My reflexive ethnography involves types of phenomenological and ethnomethodological engagement, immersion and participation. Reflections about the self and others in the study which I include here are deeply autobiographical. Such an approach serves to make the researcher less omniscient and more ordinary.

Hence, part of the reflexive position is the application of scepticism through-out the process of inquiry.

Lovatt and Purkis (1996) stress that the duality of the research role produces a web of connections, tactics and identities, including auto-biographical motives, which must be part of the foreground rather than relegated to the background. They add that the conventional sociological text is approaching its sell-by date and other creative modes of representation should be explored. I fully support such a diagnosis. In my work I have aimed to avoid the position of the privileged ethnographer. What is crucial is an understanding of the privileging game (Stanley and Wise 1993) and the resistance to it in social research.

This call for a reflexive position is about achieving a sensible and reasoned balance between 'desk work' and fieldwork, with the former emerging from the latter. What ethnographers practice and what they preach can vary significantly; there is plenty of mediodological gesturing around. The reflexive nature of social research is a condition of the discipline and should not be used as a justification for academic introspection. My conception of reflexive research involves a certain type of democratisation. The spirit of experimentation can become self-regarding, pompous indulgence in which more is learned about the fieldworker than the field. In my opinion this tendency should be rigorously resisted throughout the fieldwork process. Instead we need to conceptualise and characterise the reflexive nature of the fieldwork process beyond the crude duality of taking sides.

A Final Note

In terms of fieldwork strategies, a number of lessons can be learned from this case study about the safeguards needed when planning 'dangerous' research (for example the use of practical equipment like mobile phones, the careful choice of setting, letting someone know your whereabouts). Moreover, one has to become artful and skilled in impression management in the field (for example creating cover stories and exits when necessary, and coping with interaction rituals). Similarly, the ethical landscape needs to be contemplated before entry, although not in an obsessive way that would limit entry to the research setting. I have argued in this chapter that diverse and threatening topics and groups should not be ruled out because of ethical dilemmas. Such groups need to be understood as part of social life just as much as 'safer' groups and contexts. This chapter raises general issues which should be of use to researchers within general social research, popular cultural studies and criminology who are interested in observing other potentially dangerous groups or activities, such as football violence or gang culture. Similar personal safety concerns would be of importance in the planning process and in carrying out fieldwork.

The chapter may also be of more general use to social researchers or students thinking of undertaking ethnography in any field. In sum, my call here is for more types of reflexive ethnography, which involve a form of passionate sociology as an imaginative pursuit (Game and Metcalfe 1996; Morgan 1998). I hope to have presented door work not as exotica or subjugation but both as a type of work and an important part of popular culture. Although I was a professional stranger (Agar 1980), I have attempted to offer a brief glimpse of the reality which engages bouncers and to do so on their own terms. This has been done with a view to the research constituting a beginning and not an end in itself (James 1973). Ultimately, even if you have no intention of staying, you should at least be prepared to make the journey (Hobbs 1995). My journey was a rich one in many senses. The bouncer identity is constituted by and tied up with ideas about violence and masculinity that require exploration in future studies of the area. My study has attempted to both demystify and de-romanticise the status and process of doing ethnography as well as to celebrate creative social research. The motivation was not to produce corrective analysis but to produce a faithful account of the rich social world of bouncers and bouncing.

As I was conducting the fieldwork my partner remarked: 'When you put that jacket on, your bouncer head comes on.' I reflected on this as an appropriate subtext for a description of my dualistic ethnographic journey. In saying this I am not being so naive as to claim that my temporary stay in their world entitles me to make uncontested claims on bouncers' behalf or, patronisingly, that I had become one of them. After all, bouncing was, and remains, a way of life and not just a sociological category. However, I have gained an empathy for and engaged with bouncers and bouncing. My approach is one sociological path amongst many. I hope that this study encourages others to take more risks and to be creative on their journeys.

Notes

1. There is a wide literature on ethnomethodology including: Sharrock 1989; Garfinkel 1967, 1996.
2. There is a wide literature on ethnography that discusses its diversity and problematic issues: Van Maanen 1988; Atkinson 1990; Stanley 1990.
3. There is an extensive prescriptive literature on participant observation: Whyte 1952, 1984. There is also a more limited literature that specifically discusses the problems of covert participant observation: Blumer 1986; Adler and Adler 1987; Lee 1995.
4. There is an interesting literature on violence mainly drawn from criminology, social psychology and gender studies: Short and Wolfgang 1972; McVicar 1974; Hobbs 1988, 1995. There is a growing literature on masculinity mainly drawn from various fields that can be related to this topic: Collinson 1996; Denby and Baker 1998.

Bibliography

Adler, P. and Adler, P. (1987) 'The Past and Future of Ethnography', *Journal of Contemporary Ethnography* 16, 1: 17–86.

Agar, M. (1980) *The Professional Stranger,* London: Academic Press.

Atkinson, R (1990) *The Ethnographic Imagination: textual constructions of reality,* London: Routledge.

Becker, H. S. (1998) *Tricks of the Trade: how to think about your research while you're doing it,* Chicago: Chicago University Press.

Bittner, E. (1973) 'Objectivity and realism in sociology' in G. Psathas (ed.) *Phenomenological Sociology,* New York: Wiley.

Blumer, H. (1986) *Symbolic Interactionism: perspective and method,* London: University of California Press.

Calvey, D. (1993) 'The Organisation of Work Culture: The case of a high-tech salesforce', unpublished PhD thesis, Department of Sociology, University of Manchester.

Collinson, D. (1996) *Men as Managers, Managers as Men: critical perspectives on men and masculinity,* London: Sage.

Denby, S. and Baker, C. (1998) 'How to be Masculine in the Block Area', *Childhood* 5, 2: 151-75.

Fielding, N. (1981) *The National Front,* London: Routledge & Kegan Paul.

Game, A. and Metcalfe, A. (1996) *Passionate Sociology,* London: Sage.

Garfinkel, H. (1967) *Studies in Ethnomethodology,* Englewood Cliffs: Prentice Hall.

–. (1996) 'An Overview of Ethnomethodology's Program', *Social Psychology Quarterly* 59:5-21.

Goffman, E. (1967) *Interaction Rituals,* Chicago: Aldine.

Hertz, R. (1997) *Reflexivity and Voice,* London: Sage.

Hobbs, D. (1988) *Doing the Business,* Oxford: Clarendon Press.

–. (1995) *Bad Business,* Oxford: Oxford University Press.

James, P. (1973) *A Glasgow Gang Observed,* London: Eyre Methuen.

Lee, R. M. (1995) *Dangerous Fieldwork,* London: Sage.

Lovatt, A. and O'Conner, J. (1995) 'The City and the Night-time Economy', *Planning Practice and Research,* July.

Lovatt, A. and Purkis, J. (1996) 'Shouting in the street: popular culture, values and ethnography' in J. O'Conner and D. Wynne (eds) *From the Margins to the Centre,* Aldershot: Arena.

McVicar, J. (1974) *McVicar by Himself,* London: Arrow.

Mars, G. (1994) *Cheats at Work: an anthropology of workplace crime,* Aldershot: Dartmouth.

Morgan, D. (1998) 'Sociological Imaginings and Imagining Society', *Sociology* 32: 647–63.

Morris, S. (1998) *Clubs, Drugs and Doormen,* Paper 86, Crime, Detection and Prevention Series, London: Home Office.

Mungham, G. (1976) 'Youth in pursuit of itself in G. Mungham and G. Pearson *Working Class Youth Culture,* London: Routledge & Kegan Paul.

Redhead, S., Wynne, D. and O'Conner, J. (1998) *Club Cultures Reader,* Oxford: Blackwell.

Reed-Danahay, D. E. (1997) *Auto/Ethnography: rewriting the self and the soul,* London: Berg.

Sharrock, W. (1989) 'Ethnomethodology', *British Journal of Sociology* 40: 657-77.

Short, J. F. and Wolfgang, M. E. (1972) *Collective Violence,* Chicago: Aldine.

Slack, R. (1993) "Varieties of Sociological Reflexivity', unpublished PhD thesis, University of Manchester.

Sluka, J. A. (1995) 'Reflections on managing danger in fieldwork: dangerous anthropology in Belfast' in C. Nordstrom and A. Robben (eds) *Fieldwork Under Fire,* London: University of California Press.

Stanley, L. (1990) 'Doing ethnography, writing ethnography', *British Journal of Sociology* 24:617-27.

Stanley, L. and Wise, S. (1993) *Breaking Out Again: feminist ontology and epistemology,* 2nd edition, London: Routledge.

Thompson, H. (1967) *Hell's Angels,* New York: Random House.

Twemlow, C. (1980) *The Tuxedo Warrior,* Chichester: Summersdale.

Van Maanen, J. (1988) *Tales of the Field: on writing ethnography,* London: University of Chicago Press.

Wallis, R. (1976) *The Road to Total Freedom: a sociological analysis of Scientology,* London: Heinemann Educational.

–. (1977) 'The moral career of a research project' in C. Bell and H. Roberts (eds) *Social Researching: Politics, Problems, Practice,* London: Routledge & Kegan Paul.

Whyte, W. F. (19S2) *Street Corner Society,* Chicago: University of Chicago Press.

–. (1984) *Learning from the Field,* London: Sage.

Willis, P. (1977) *Learning to Labour: how working class kids get working class jobs,* Farnborough: Saxon House.

30

Uncovering the Ethnographer

Odette Parry

There can be few more literal claims to 'doing fieldwork' than that posed by a participant observation study inside a naturist club. Some colleagues and friends alike delighted in the double entendre to which this research seemed particularly prone. For example, they seldom wasted an opportunity to ask about the 'state of the raw data', the 'extent of the progressive focusing' and the processes 'of fleshing out the bare bones of the initial findings.'

On account of its novelty and subject matter I suspect that the study drew a lot more attention than that usually experienced by postgraduate students embarking on their MSc theses. If, however the responses of my peer group and some staff members at the university to the project was mild bemusement, this was outshadowed by the reactions of naturists themselves upon our first meetings at the club. Whilst the former group approached me with respectful curiosity, to many of the latter group I assumed the characteristics of a freak. Academics who had previously passed me unnoticed in the corridor would stop and say 'you're the postgrad doing work on nudists', and club members would approach me at the club and say 'you must be the sociology student who's come to spy on us.' Whilst this is a feature common to many studies in the early stages of fieldwork, the nature of the setting itself appeared to continually exaggerate routine problems associated with carrying out a research project.

Whilst outlining the problems encountered during the fieldwork in my research diary, I came to re-evaluate the nature of the research bargain. It seems that this bargain is too often presented as unequal in terms of reciprocation. It is often assumed that once access has been granted the researcher has, at least potentially, access to the necessary data which when collected and processed will provide him or her with the goods. These goods usually take the form of a postgraduate title (MSc or PhD), a number of

Source: *Enter the Sociologist,*1987, Avebury, pp. 82-96.

academic publications or a satisfied employer and future research contracts. From this point of view the respondents are the providers and the researchers are the receivers; not unlike the parasite and his/her host.

The other side of this coin is often neglected. The researcher, for example, is seldom seen in the role of giver. In the literature our attention is usually drawn to the input of the researcher in terms of his/her ability to secure the needs of the project and overcome its attendant problems. For example, when discussing access, Lofland (1971) advises that gatekeepers are only interested in what will help or harm them. Seldom has such concern been shown for the researcher; that is, what will harm him or her.

This account sets out to go some way towards redressing the balance. It does this by taking issue with a number of problems routinely encountered by researchers and illustrates their resolution through the example of my own experience of doing ethnography in the naturist club.

The Setting

All researchers experience problems which are particular to the group of people they are studying. These problems arise out of the unique characteristics of the research setting. Naturists are a particularly difficult group to work with because whilst they see their activities as natural, normal and healthy, they simultaneously recognise that social nudity is generally taboo in our society and is therefore unacceptable to many non-naturist groups. This makes them wary of outsiders or intruders, who do not share their perspective on naturist activities or entertain notions of decent exposure.

Naturists reject the 'conventional wisdom' that social nudity is associated with sexuality and argue instead that naturism is 'the practice of naked but non-sexual activity'. In order to maintain a respectable perspective on nudity, naturists erect strong physical and social barriers around their activities and within clubs construct what Weinberg (1970) has described as a 'situated morality'. This situated or constructed morality denies legitimacy to alternative definitions which present naturism as unrespectable behaviour.

Naturist clubs are located away from areas of dense population and are enclosed by tall boundary fences, walls and/or trees and shrubbery. They are open only to members (and their guests), with clubs exercising strict membership requirements, which favour families at the expense of single applicants. They are particularly wary of admitting single men to clubs because this, they argue, would upset the sexual balance of membership and may therefore be threatening to female members and their husbands. Married applicants will only be considered eligible for membership if their spouses are prepared to join also and accompany them to the club regularly.

Members themselves also erect strong social barriers around the club. They address each other by first name only and seldom either meet each other ouside of the club or divulge any information about their non-club lives. Similarly club members rarely tell non-naturists about their club membership or naturist activities: many do not tell their parents and, in some cases, older members do not tell their grown up children. If they do tell others about their activities, they are forbidden to disclose the location of their club.

Inside the club strict regulations apply to the practice of acceptable nudism: 'Outside, on appropriate premises, in daylight hours in amenable weather conditions'. Some clubs have rules which forbid any clothing to be worn (with the exception of menstruating women who must wear bikini bottoms) even temporarily if the temperature drops. In those clubs which do allow clothing to be worn during cooler spells male members tend to put on track suit tops or tee shirts and women, track suit tops or blouses, leaving the lower part of the body unclothed. These patterns of partial dress serve to differentiate naturist activities from those of non-naturist groups.

Inside clubs, there are also informal norms which relate to interaction and which serve to maintain a minimal level of eye contact between participants. These restrict the development of familiarity between strangers, particularly when this applies to single male applicants. Through such practices, members construct a club morality which sets their activities apart from the activities of outside groups and allows them to maintain a definition of naturism as a respectable pursuit.

Getting In

The naturist club was not initially the intended focus of the research project. Similar to the experiences of other postgraduates, the substantive topic was derived from a series of exploratory ventures (some necessary, but many red herrings), the majority of which were eventually discarded.

The original intention was to examine attitudes toward the human body and take issue particularly with the conventional wisdom which suggests that much naked behaviour is sexually motivated. This prompted me to find some settings in which naked individuals did not construe their behaviour as sexually motivated. The question arose 'where, how and for whom does decent exposure take place?'

The first problem was finding an appropriate group of people to study and during this process several alternative situations where nudity is generally regarded as acceptable were considered, tentatively explored and then rejected. These included the changing rooms in sports centres and communal fitting rooms in boutiques and department stores. There were two main problems with these choices. On the first account I came to see myself, and even more regretfully, on occasions I suspect I was seen by others, in the odious role of voyeur. On the second account I was limited to a research population of women. I therefore sought a group of individuals who not only maintained naked but non-sexual activities for protracted periods but who were also amenable to the possibilities of observation; by a participant or an insider as opposed to a peeping Tom. Fortunately naturists are a good example of such a group.

If the first problem had been identifying a suitable group, the second was actually locating them. The easiest route to naturism in this country is through recommendation from an existing club member: without this, sheer determination and limitless spare time are necessary.

The first breakthrough came with the discovery that the traditional nudist organisation in Britain (The Central Council for British Naturism or the CCBN) calls its members 'naturists' and their choice of activities 'naturism'. If naturists prefer naturism to nudism because of the latters' association with rude, crude and lewd (New Society, 1976), they are equally confusing in their choice of naturism which more often than not calls, to the uninformed mind, notions of butterfly collecting and whole food regimes. Naturist clubs rarely advertise for members and when they do it has never, in my experience, been in health food shops or wild life journals. Fortunately at the time of my enquiry the CCBN had tenuous links with *Health and Efficiency* and this journal directed my attention to the central organisation of naturism in Britain.

The next problem was time: it took a long time to join. The CCBN take their holidays in winter and so it was two months before I received any reply to my initial enquiries. Although when it arrived the reply provided useful background information on the organisation and its membership, it was a further two months before my application to join the club could be made.

It was during these latter two months, and by complete accident, that I discovered that a lecturer in the same university faculty as myself was a club member. He was actually discovered by my supervisor who was at the time standing in a lift holding a copy of *The Nude Beach* (Douglas, 1977). Had she not so thoughtfully been returning my inter-library loan copy it is doubtful whether this contact would have been established.

However, even with a club member as a contact it seemed unlikely that my application for club membership would be accepted. There were two reasons for this, first I was single and clubs favoured married applicants and families, second, I had an ulterior motive for joining. Initially I toyed with the idea of attempting covert research by concealing the research interest. Whilst generally not condoning or supporting covert or secret research I justified my intent on the grounds that it was extremely unlikely that a club would accept me whether or not they knew about my MSc. I therefore considered that continuing covertly with my application was ethical in so far as I saw myself participating in a process that was almost certainly going to be unsuccessful. This intention was discarded when I received the application form from Elm club which required that 'I have no other reason for joining a club other than the practice of naturism'.

At this stage I wrote a letter to the secretary of Elm, explaining the reasons why I wished to join. I acknowledged that the research project might prejudice any application for membership, in which case I requested any alternative help or advice he might be able to offer. Contrary to my expectations the secretary replied:

I read your letter with interest and came to three conclusions:

1. That the basis of your thesis did not prejudice your application to join the club.

2. That there are no restrictions so far as discussing aspects and ideas of naturism with groups of individuals or individuals concerned.

3. That any material gained in such discussions should be published in the third person unless individual's permission is obtained for the use of first names only and addresses and site locations of clubs must never be revealed.

This letter was received with ambivalence. Whilst it was obviously good news for the MSc that Elm were prepared to consider the application, it had the unexpected effect of producing a situation more similar to that of a moral crisis than a successful access negotiation. Up to that point I had been convinced that the application would be unacceptable and was therefore psychologically prepared for rejection. Already I had developed alternative avenues of research by involving myself with the 'Free the Beach Campaign' which was set up and run by the CCBN to secure legal nudist bathing in Britain.

Membership of the club depended upon the applicant meeting fairly strict criteria as well as being very determined. My motivation for going native derived from the research objective and not (as in the case of other applicants) from the desire to practice social nudism. Whilst I had visited a nude beach in Greece the previous summer (who hasn't?), the prospect of actually joining a club was terrifying. Fortunately the processes of application were lengthy and as the secretary of Elm pointed out:

Should you wish to pursue your application for membership would you please complete the attached form. An interview will be arranged with my wife and I and arrangements will be made for you to visit the club. If after your visit(s) you wish to take up the option of membership your application will be assessed on you as a person and not on the subject of your thesis.

This gave me some time in which to readjust to the new developments, and the opportunity to seek advice and reassurance from the naturist contact at work.

Before the interview arrangements were settled I was advised to provide myself with transport, as, although the site location was still unknown, the club secretary warned that it was outside the route of public transport. I was then advised by telephone that the interview would take place on a main road about fifteen miles from the city, five hundred yards from a major exit, in a layby opposite a telephone kiosk. I was instructed to arrive at this venue at one thirty in the afternoon, and wait for Harry (the club secretary) who would be driving a red car. I was instructed to never divulge the address of the club or reveal the identity of Harry, his wife or any other members who I met, to any outsiders. I would argue that seldom have ethnographers entered the field with more misgivings.

I later learnt that this was an interview procedure favoured by many clubs because should a club secretary dislike the look of a prospective member, then by simply driving past, he or she is able to reject applicants without ever meeting them or revealing their identity.

The red car arrived at one thirty-five and drew up opposite. Harry got out and crossed the road. We shook hands and I was invited to join him and his wife in their car where the interview took place. I was questioned for about ten minutes to establish that I was who I said I was, what the research involved and my willingness to participate in naturist activities. Harry then accompanied me back across the road, returned to his own car and I followed them for about two miles down twisting country lanes until we reached the club.

In the Field

Before going on to describe some of the fieldwork experiences it is important to note that several unique problems are attached to the role of the participant observer in the naturist club. In an environment where participants are wary and suspicious of outsiders, new members remain under close scrutiny from established members even after their membership has been approved by the club committee. This was more apparent in my case because I was seen as a particularly unusual member. On the first account I was young, single and female. Whilst most clubs do have an allocation for single men, their motivations for joining are questioned more than those of families or childless couples. This is because clubs receive a disproportionate number of applications from single men and yet they make up only a very small percentage of total membership. On the other hand, single women rarely apply to clubs and I only met two during the course of a season's fieldwork. On the second account, no secret was made of the research and hence I was regularly approached by strangers asking 'are you the one who's looking at us?'

In a situation where, initially at least, I was regarded by most members as a freak and was therefore under close observation, and also in a setting where the level of eye contact is reduced, it was impossible to reciprocate observation. For example during my first few visits to the club I tended to sit with Harry, his wife and a small group of their friends. It was a bit of a joke that I had been adopted or, as I felt, was under Harry's supervision. Despite this I felt that whilst not unfriendly, Harry's friends were wary of my presence in the group. They never initiated conversations with me and whenever I looked up and caught them looking at me they looked away. Harry solved this problem for me by forcing his friends to acknowledge my contribution to the group. For the first two visits, whenever a group member made tea I was presented with a cup though I was never allowed to fill the kettle or wash the cups. This made me feel like a guest rather than a participant. On my third visit Harry announced, 'Odette is going to make the tea it's about time she took her turn.' Once accepted into the tea making rota my status as beginner or guest diminished and it was no longer necessary for members to keep such a watchful eye over my activities.

On an even more practical level it was difficult to make fieldnotes. A note pad and biro are particularly conspicuous items when you have nowhere to hide them. It would have been impossible to slope off to the toilet block with a pen and paper every time an event or conversation demanded recording. After three visits to the club, and very few fieldnotes to show for them, I decided to construct a questionaire in order to interview as many members as possible. Once accepted by the committee, the questionaire fulfilled three functions. Firstly, it provided me with an accepted cover; that is it established my identity as a researcher. Secondly, it enabled me to move more freely around the club than other members, simply because it gave me a legitimate reason for doing so. Lastly the back covers of the questionaires were used for recording fieldnotes.

Coming to Terms with Naturism

The second major problem encountered during the course of the research stemmed from my initial ambivalence regarding the respectability of naturism. I believe I experienced this more acutely as a female member than I would have done had I been male.

It has already been noted that more single men than women apply to join naturist clubs. It can also be argued that there are basically three categories of membership: those who want to join; those who are persuaded to join, and those who have no choice. Generally those who want to join are men, those who are persuaded are wives, and those who have no choice are children. The majority of women who were interviewed at clubs said that their husbands had persuaded them to join. For example, Gladys at Elm explained:

I didn't want to join, not for years, but he talked me into it in the end.

That women are generally less enthusiastic than men about becoming naturists suggests that they may have more difficulty in coming to terms with club activities. In other words they may take longer than men to accept the definition of naturism as 'decent, normal and moral.' Whilst children have been presented as the members with the least choice, they are provided with a protective capsule, by their parents and other members presenting the naturist way of life as normal and healthy. Generally nudism does not become problematic for children at the club until this protective shell is shattered by the opposing definitions of naturism offered by their peers and other outside reference groups. When this happens the majority of young members leave the club to seek social activities elsewhere.

The fieldnotes and interview scripts suggested that female members, on average, took one season to adjust to and accept the club perspective. It had, for example, taken Peter at Beech three years to persuade his wife to join. She described her initial reaction to club activities as:

> Really shocking, I thought they were really shocking. I was totally embarrassed, I hated every second of it.

Similarly Yvonne described how, in the beginning of her first naturist season, pilots from a local gliding club would fly over Elm. When they realised it was a naturist club the pilots would fly as close as possible to members.

> At first I thought it was horrid. Some of the members would cheer and jump up and down whilst I just wanted the ground to swallow me up.

However, as she recalled, later in that same season:

> I joined in with the others ... After all I've got nothing to be ashamed about.

The CCBN recognise that the first experiences of members can be traumatic and hence liken them to jumping into a swimming pool:

> Shocking for the first thirty seconds and then soothing from then on (CCBN: 1978).

During my first visit to Elm I determined not to prolong the agony, so I took off my clothes as quickly as possible, sat down on the lawn and proceeded to concentrate all my attention on one blade of grass. Harry and Gill respected my unspoken desire to be left alone, and so I sat for what seemed to be hours before plucking up the courage to look up and see what everyone else was doing.

My discomfort, as a new member, was certainly not unique. An American sociology student describes her first nudist experiences:

> So I closed my eyes and slowly took off my clothes. I suppose this was somehow symbolic closing my eyes that is. I felt if I couldn't see then no-one could see me (Georges, 1980).

However, unlike other female club members my situation was different. Whereas they were able to slowly adjust over the course of their first season, I was expected not only to fit in, but also to carry out the research project. What was in their case a period of transition, was in my case a season's fieldwork. On a number of occasions this caused problems which related to my personal perspective on naturism. The best example of this is illustrated by the following incident which occurred about half way through the season.

It was a cool August afternoon in mid week. Both of these factors accounted for a poor turn out at the club. Apart from myself there were two married couples, with two young children and a baby between them, and Guy, a single male member. He sat apart from the two women who were watching their husbands playing badminton. I was lying down between the two women. (It was very quiet at the club and I had almost dozed off to sleep). Suddenly I was aware that the mood had changed from lethargy to activity. Sylvia was busily rounding up the children and ushering them into the pavilion. Guy, who was now wearing trousers, was running towards the west boundary. Tom and Greg were, I realised later, hurriedly dressing in the pavilion before following after Guy. When Sylvia returned, I asked her what was happening and she told me: 'there's a man over there in the bushes watching us.' Rose joined us at this point and added: 'He must be really sick, I mean perverted.' Sylvia agreed, 'Fancy coming all the way out here to stand in the bushes and watch us.'

Rose and Sylvia defined their own behaviour as correct and proper whilst the peeping Tom was defined as sick and abnormal. Both the women had been members of the club for several seasons and had exchanged the non-naturist perspective for the one which presented their activities as decent and respectable. On the other hand, I was only half way through my first naturist season and found the incident threatening. It seemed that there were several competing perspectives to be considered. The first, that of the clothed man standing in the bushes spying on a group of naked adults and children sitting in a field on a cool August afternoon; the second, that of a group of naked adults sitting in a field on a cool August afternoon whilst being spied upon by a clothed man hiding in the bushes; and finally that of a naked sociologist sitting in a field on a cool August afternoon observing a group of naked adults and children whilst being observed herself by a clothed man hidden in the bushes.

The naturists were adamant that their perspective was correct: they described another incident where a flasher had streaked across the bottom of the sun lawn one afternoon at the club. Apparently the young man had stripped off his clothes in the bushes which surround the club and then, holding them under one arm, had dashed across to the opposite boundary. He then proceeded to make his get-away running (whilst attempting to dress at the same time) across the neighbouring fields. Rose said that the majority of members at the club that afternoon had found the incident highly entertaining.

Actually doing naturism was a problem for me both inside and outside of the club. For example, I would go to great lengths to conceal the object of my research from anyone other than sociologists. For a long time my parents were under the misapprehension that I was looking at council housing policy in Cardiff. When the title and subject of the research were eventually revealed to my mother, she smiled and said thoughtfully:

Very nice dear, I do think people should be doing more work with animals.

A situation which caused me the most discomfort during the course of the research occurred when my two lives (inside and outside the club) coincided. This happened one afternoon when I visited Elm and discovered that my university contact was on the sun lawn with his children. It is one thing to discuss social nudity academically in the privacy of one's office or in the lift, but quite another to come face to face with that person in a naturist club and then face them the following week at work.

Whilst my situation in the club was unusual, like other members I gradually came to accept a naturist perspective on nudity inside the club. Although I had determined to remain sensitive to any changes in my own outlook which evolved out of the research role, this, as the following incident illustrates, was not always the case.

During the last week of the season I spent a few days at Beech club, and during this time became friendly with a number of members. On the third day I was approached by my friends who told me about a new family at the club. This family, who were by all accounts Dutch, had arrived early that morning. My friends suggested that I interview the family to give a 'continental flavour' to the research. I was happy to do so and returned to the car for more questionaires. The Dutch couple agreed to be interviewed so I sat down and got on with the business. During the interview I learnt that Europeans on holiday in Britain may visit any British naturist club without actually being a club member. This is because the CCBN is a member of the International Naturist Federation and any IFN member is automatically an affiliated member of the British organisation. Whilst the CCBN membership does not entitle an individual to visit clubs in Britain, because of a reciprocal arrangement it does allow him/her to visit INF affiliated clubs abroad. At this point it struck me that the family who I was interviewing did not necessarily have to be naturists and then, to my embarrassment, I realised that both the couple and their children were clothed. On the other hand I was wearing my standard interviewing uniform – skin. I immediately terminated the interview and hurriedly left. Meanwhile my friends had found the incident extremely amusing; when one had controlled her laughter enough to make herself understood she said:

> Well now at least you know you're really a naturist. You don't even notice if people have their clothes on or not.

The Research Bargain

It was upon my last visit to Beech club when the exact terms of the research bargain became explicit. By this time I felt quite at ease in the naturist club. To date, very few demands had been made upon my behaviour outside of the club, the only notable exception being that it was not acceptable as a naturist to swim and sunbathe on a straight (non-nudist) beach. I discovered this after attending a postgraduate summer school, which was held in Portsmouth. The weather was beautiful and one afternoon a group of us went swimming. During my next club visit I was told off by members because I no longer had an all over suntan, or rather the all over tan was punctuated by lighter stripes indicating that a bikini had been worn.

During the last fieldwork visit to Beech, and towards the end of an afternoon's interviewing, I was approached by a member of the club's committee, who was also the president of the CCBN. This individual, who because of his official status and sympathy with the research objectives was a key informant, had been instrumental in securing access to a range of different sources, including organisational, archival records. In other words I was indebted to him for his co-operation probably more than any other individual naturist. I had just completed the last interview of the season when he appeared and said:

> Odette, this is your last visit isn't it? You must have all the information that you need. Would you agree with me now that there is nothing wrong with the human body?

After agreeing with him he continued by outlining the number of ways in which the organisation, clubs and members had co-operated in the research problem. It was further pointed out that had this co-operation not been forthcoming it was unlikely that the research could have been carried out. In order partially to repay this favour it was suggested that I should write an article, 'Naturists I have met' to be published in the house journal *British Naturism*.

Having willingly agreed to write the article and reinforced previous expressions of gratitude, I was asked again whether I totally accepted the naturist perspective of 'decent exposure'. When in answer to this I pointed out that my acceptance of naturism should be obvious through my participation in naturist activities, it was put to me:

> Well in that case you shouldn't have any objection to your picture appearing with the article.

At this point a photographer stepped out from behind a bush and took a picture of me with no clothes on. Not surprisingly, my feeble protestations about being unphotogenic and camera shy fell on unsympathetic ears. I had just admitted that there was nothing wrong, naughty, or immoral about naturism. I had also acknowledged a debt of gratitude to the respondent group: here was a perfect chance to go some way towards redressing the balance.

Guarantees of anonymity were, of course, requested and given. However, whilst the number plate of a car which was behind me was obliterated, the description which accompanied the photograph read to the effect of ... This is Odette West who is studying sociology at Cardiff University ...

That the distribution of *British Naturism* is not restricted to club members, was, for some weeks after publication of the article and picture, a source of concern for me. This stemmed, at that time, not from any personal rejection of the notion of decent exposure, but far more from the fear of discovery and hence exposure to the alternative wider perspective on social nudism.

References

Central Council for British Naturism, (1978), *Dare to go Bare,* Orpington.
Douglas, J. et al. (1966), *Purity and Danger,* Routledge and Kegan Paul, London.
Lofland, J.(1971), *Analysing Social Settings,* Wadsworth, Belmont, Ca.
New Society, (1976), 'Herbivore: Marginal Note', Sept 16.
Weinburg, S.G. (1970), 'The Nudist Management of Respectability', in Douglas, J., (ed.), *Deviance and Respectability,* Basic Books, New York, pp. 375-404.

Section Four
Field Talk: Interviews and Conversations

31

The Spoken Word

Beatrice and Sydney Webb

For much of his information about the social institution he is studying the investigator must rely on the oral testimony of those who know the facts. Sometimes this is available in a printed form, for instance in the voluminous questions and answers that make up nearly all the "evidence" taken by royal commissions and parliamentary committees, and published in the blue-books. Unfortunately the enormous accumulation thus enshrined – which has necessarily to be consulted – is of very varying evidential value, a shortcoming discussed in a subsequent chapter. For the greater part of his information the investigator must find his own witnesses, induce them to talk, and embody the gist of this oral testimony on his sheets of notes. This is the Method of the Interview, or "conversation with a purpose", a unique instrument of the social investigator.[1]

First, let us point out, for the benefit of students who dislike personal contacts, or who feel themselves unsuited for the difficult art of interviewing presently to be described, that this method of investigation is not required, and may, indeed, be impracticable, for historical research. It is, moreover, not absolutely essential even in the investigation of certain contemporary social institutions. Thus, English local government, from the seventeenth to the nineteenth century, was the pastime as well as the public work of potential "writing men"; of accomplished country gentlemen and ecclesiastics; of city merchants and provincial manufacturers; whilst many solicitors and barristers, and in later years medical practitioners, engineers, architects and surveyors, accountants and auditors have found in the complicated network of courts and councils a considerable part of their livelihood. Hence, as we have already shown, not only are the documents of local authorities bewildering in their number and variety, but there are also, for each generation during the past two centuries, rich deposits of fact in con-temporaneous literature, in law books and treatises, in parliamentary reports

Source: *Methods of Social Study*, 1932, Longmans, pp. 130-141.

and controversial pamphlets, in letters and articles in local newspapers, not to mention biographies, plays, novels, poems, and even sermons. Even the working-class co-operative movement has, for nearly a century, had its technical periodicals, its conference and congress reports and papers, its audited accounts of trading and manufacturing enterprises, together with an incessant stream of pamphlet literature, frequently written by able intellectuals bent on informing the members and on making known to the public the achievements of the movement. On the other hand, any adequate investigation into the policy of the trade union movement during the nineteenth century, or even of the movement of to-day, would be impossible without considerable personal intercourse with the leading personalities, and even with the members of the rank and file. For the trade unions, partly because of their exclusively working-class membership, and partly because they were regarded by the law and by public opinion, even down to the last quarter of the nineteenth century, as unlawful if not actually criminal combinations, had, at the time of our investigation, neither the opportunity nor the desire to put themselves on record in contemporaneous literature, or even in office documents, more than was absolutely necessary for their immediate purposes. Moreover, the average manual worker has no love for archives. What is of "no more use" is only waste paper cumbering the narrow room. How exasperating it was to the investigator, on entering the office of a powerful modern union; or the parlour of the secretary of an ancient craft organisation, to be casually informed that "only a few months ago", on removal to new premises, or on the occasion of some scare about the illegality of a particular act or decision, all the past manuscript minutes had been destroyed, whilst the various editions of the rule-books that had become obsolete had been burnt. We were sometimes able to find nothing beyond copies of the membership card and the current rules, with possibly a few statistics of membership for particular years. This was not always the case. We spent many months in minutely going through the well-kept records of (to name only some examples) the ironfounders, the boilermakers, the stonemasons, and the London and provincial compositors. We found much of historical value in the scantier documents of ancient trade clubs. But though we hunted up every bit of literature or document in local libraries, trade union offices, and members' homes – and the smallest scraps were sometimes of fundamental importance by way of verification – we had, for much of the past record of the majority of the smaller unions, as well as for their current activities, to fall back on the spoken word. Especially for the working constitution and day-by-day activities of the trade union movement, had we to rely, in the main, on our innumerable interviews with trade union officials and members, with friendly employers and their foremen, and with the agents of employers' associations – all this being valuably supplemented by what we picked up by attendance at branch or delegate meetings, open or private, or overheard in informal intercourse in hotel smoking-rooms, the bars of public-houses frequented by the workmen, and the homes of brain workers and manual workers in every trade, from one end of the United Kingdom to the other. The special obstacle to be overcome in this use of the interview was, in the case of the trade union movement, the presence, in all the witnesses, of unconscious bias in an aggravated form. For the ground we were exploring was, in fact, a permanent battlefield, upon which there was being waged, day in and day out, the endless secular conflict between the capitalist profit-makers and the manual working wage-earners, whilst within the ranks of each of the opposing forces there went on a continuous petty skirmishing between rival profit-makers for markets and men, and between rival unions for work and members. For this reason the process of "overhearing" the actual transactions on each side was more valuable than any direct hearing of testimony. What we picked up in this way could be elucidated by specific enquiries, and checked for bias by investigation in other quarters, whilst we often found it possible to obtain verification of what we had learnt from scraps of documents and incidental references in contemporaneous literature that would otherwise have been without significance for us.[2]

There are many uses of the interview. It may be a necessary passport to the inspection of documents or to an opportunity of watching, from the inside, the constitution and activities of some piece of social organisation. For this purpose the requisites are a good "introduction", brevity of statement, a modest and agreeable manner, and a ready acquiescence in any arrangement made, however inadequate or inconvenient. Above all, the student must have a clear conception of exactly which documents and what opportunities he is seeking. Do not ask for too much at the first start off; you can always ask for more; and an inch given is better than an ell refused!

But by the method of the interview is meant something more than a social gateway. The "conversation with a purpose" may be, so the American social workers say, "fact-finding", or "informing", or "motivating", according as it is designed to obtain information, to instruct or to influence the will. We use the term here solely to label a particular instrument of sociological investigation, the eliciting of facts from a competent informant by skilled interrogation. As a device for scientific investigation it is peculiar to the sociologist. It is his compensation for inability to use the astronomer's telescope or the bacteriologist's microscope.

The first condition of tlie successful use of the interview as an instrument of research is preparedness of the mind of the operator. The interviewer should be himself acquainted not, of course, with all the known facts – that would be to set too high a standard – but with all the data that can be obtained from the ordinary text-books and blue-books relating to the subject. For instance, to cross-examine a factory inspector without understanding the distinction between a factory and a workshop, or the meaning of the "particulars clause"; or a town clerk, without knowing the difference between getting a provisional order, promoting a local Act, or working under a general Act, is an impertinence. Especially important is a familiarity with technical terms and a correct use of them. To start interviewing any specialist without this equipment will not only be waste of time, but may lead to a more or less courteous dismissal, after a few general remarks and some trite opinions; at best, the conversation will be turned away from the subject into the trivialities of social intercourse. For technical terms and technical details, relating to past as well as to present occurrences and controversies, are so many levers to lift into consciousness and expression the more abstruse and out-of-the-way facts or series of facts; and it is exactly these more hidden events that are needed to complete descriptive analysis and to verify hypotheses. And note in passing that not to have read and mastered what your client has himself published on the question is not easily forgiven!

The second condition is, of course, that the person interviewed should be in possession of experience or knowledge unknown to you. This is not to say that persons without acknowledged reputations for specialised knowledge must always be ignored; and that there should be no speculative investment in queer or humble folk. It is, for example, almost axiomatic with the experienced investigator that the mind of the subordinate in any organisation will yield richer veins of fact than the mind of the principal. This is not merely because the subordinate is usually less on his guard, and less severely conventional in his outlook. The essential superiority lies in the circumstance that the working foreman, managing clerk, or minor official is himself in continuous and intimate contact with the day-by-day activities of the organisation; he is more aware than his employer is of the heterogeneity and changing character of the facts; and he is less likely to serve up dead generalisation, in which all the living detail becomes a blurred mass, or is stereotyped into rigidly confined and perhaps obsolete categories.[3]

More difficult to convey to the student is the right manner of behaviour in interviewing.

Regarded as a method of investigation, the process of interviewing is a particular form of psychoanalysis. From within the consciousness or sub-consciousness of another mind, the practitioner has to ferret out memories of past experience – "orders of thought" corresponding with "orders of things". You may easily inhibit free communication, or prevent the rise to conscious-ness of significant facts, by arousing suspicion. For instance, whilst a careful plan of examination should be prepared, no paper of questions should be apparent; and during the interview no attempt should be made to take notes. Except in cases in which your client is not merely according an interview but is consciously co-operating in your investigation, it is a mistake to bring with you a secretary or other colleague; caution is increased when a man perceives that his words are being "witnessed".

It is disastrous to "show off", or to argue; the client must be permitted to pour out his fictitious tales, to develop the most preposterous theories, or to use the silliest arguments, without demur or expression of dissent or ridicule. The competent social investigator will not look bored or indifferent when irrelevant information or trivial details are offered to him, any more than a competent medical practitioner will appear wearied by his patient's catalogue of imaginary symptoms. Accept whatever is offered: a personally conducted visit to this or that works or institution may be a dismal prospect; it may even seem waste effort to inspect machinery or plant which cannot be understood, or which has been seen *ad nauseam* before, or which is wholly irrelevant to the subject-matter of the enquiry. But it is a mistake to decline. In the course of these tiring walks and weary waitings, experiences may be recalled or elicited which would not have cropped up in the formal interview in the office. Indeed, the less formal the conditions of the interview the better. The atmosphere of the dinner-table or the smoking-room is a better "conductor" than that of the office during business hours. The best of these occasions is when you can casually start several experts arguing among themselves: in this way you will pick up more information in one hour than you will acquire during a whole day in a series of interviews.

When you have got upon confidential terms, your new friend may cite private statistics or mention unpublished documents; this should be met by an off-hand plea for permission to see them. If a direct offer be made to produce and explain documents, the interviewer has scored a notable success, and should follow it up on the spot. "I am dreadfully careless and inaccurate at figures: I wonder whether I and my secretary might come here to-morrow to look through these reports again?" will often find good-natured acquiescence.

Bear in mind that it is desirable to make the interview pleasing to the persons interviewed. It should seem to him or her an agreeable form of social intercourse. One of the authors remembers, in an early adventure in "wholesale interviewing" with a group of representative men, even telling fortunes from their hands, with all sorts of interesting results! Without such an atmosphere of relaxation, of amused interest on both sides, it will often be impracticable to get at those intimate details of daily experience which are the most valuable data of the sociologist. Hence a spirit of adventure, a delight in watching human beings as human beings quite apart, from what you can get out of their minds, an enjoyment of the play of your own personality with that of another, are gifts of rare value in the art of interviewing; and gifts which are, perhaps, more frequently characteristic of the woman than of the man.

It need hardly be added that once the interview is over, the first opportunity should be taken to write out fully every separate fact or hypothesis elicited. Never trust your memory a moment longer than is necessary is an all-important maxim. Practice will make it easy to reproduce on paper, that very evening, or on the following morning before starting out for the day's work, every phrase or suggestion that needs to be recorded, even of several successive interviews.

The investigator using the method of the interview must, we need hardly say, remember his responsibilities. In any publication he must scrupulously respect the confidence accorded to him. He must invariably suppress the name of the person who has given the information. But he must do more than this. He must exercise the utmost care to prevent his identification by those familiar with him, his circumstances, his town, or his trade. Thus, it is dangerous to mention the town in which, he lives; or to use such superlatives as "the oldest establishment", or "the largest factory"; or to describe any marked peculiarity of its location or layout. And there is one supreme rule which must always be observed. You must be careful never to use or publish anything to the disadvantage of your informant that he may have rashly or unsuspectingly let out in his conversation. Only by the strictest observance of these rules of discretion is the investigator's inquisition justified.

Notes

1. The greater part of this chapter will be found, in substance, as an Appendix to *My Apprenticeship,* by Beatrice Webb, 1926, pp. 340-355. In a recently published American work, entitled *How to Interview,* by W. V. Bingham and B. V. Moore, 1931, over 300 pages are devoted to an elaborate description of the "personal interview" as a means of "fact-finding, informing, and motivating", largely for the instruction of Charity Organisation and other social workers, but also of teachers, salesmen or canvassers for orders, policemen, journalists, doctors, and lawyers. The book contains an extensive annotated bibliography.
2. This paucity of documents and contemporaneous literature as sources of information for the investigator is no longer characteristic of the British trade union movement. The documents at nearly all trade union offices are nowadays voluminous and well preserved, and some of the larger unions have even regular Statistical and Research Departments. Though there is still no trade union journal analogous to *The Co-operative News,* there has been, during the past quarter of a century or so, a steadily increasing stream of monthly and quarterly periodicals published by the different unions in which the current statistics and some of the details of their work are recorded, whilst books and pamphlets on trade unionism abound. The statistical and other information compiled and published by the Government, which was, half a century ago, of the scantiest, has, since the formation of the Labour Department at the Board of Trade (now absorbed in the Ministry of Labour) been of the highest quality.
3. It is interesting to see a similar comment made about the German capitalist employer. "Hardly ever", says Professor Schumpeter, "can a business man analyse his business processes. He acts on his experience, on his feelings, and rightly so. If then we ask him about his business affairs, we get in reply any casual thought which happens to be in his mind, and to which he momentarily attaches importance." (*Wit studirt man Sozialwissenschaft,* by Josef Schumpeter, Munich, 1915, p. 427.)

32

Conversations With a Purpose: The Ethnographic Interview in Educational Research

Robert G. Burgess

Introduction

Talk forms a key element in social and educational research where investigators collect, analyse and report the conversations they have conducted (cf. Adelman 1981). Certainly, this was regarded as a key element of social investigation in some of the early 'methods' textbooks that were produced in Britain and the United States in the 1920s and 1930s. For example, an American field manual produced by Vivien Palmer highlighted the importance of conversation in social research (1928, pp. 168-9):

> The ability of the objects of social research to converse with each other and with the scientific investigator is so vital a characteristic of the subject matter of the social sciences that it cannot be disregarded in any well rounded study.

For Palmer argued that conversation not only generated important data but was also an important research technique. A similar view was advanced in Britain by Sidney and Beatrice Webb in their classic 'methods' text *Methods of Social Study* (1932, p. 130):

> For the greater part of his information the investigator must find his own witnesses, induce them to talk and embody the gist of this oral testimony in his sheets of notes. This is the method of the interview or 'conversation with a purpose', a unique instrument of the social investigator.

Source: *Studies in Qualitative Methodology Volume 1*, 1988: *Conducting Qualitative Research*, JAI Press, pp. 137-155.

Despite this propitious start in methodology texts, the notion of conversation as a research technique has for some years been replaced by the interview as an abstract category that textbook writers have argued has a standard format regardless of the research and the research context (cf. Moser and Kalton 1971; Goode and Hatt 1952; Cohen and Manion 1985). Such an approach presents social research in terms of a static model where interviewing is a scientific technique that is detached from the substantive and theoretical concerns of the investigator (cf. Wakeford 1981).

The consequence of this stance being taken towards interviewing results in:

> a variety of assumptions about the relationships between interviewer and respondent [being made]. It assumes that they are for practical purposes anonymous to each other and that they do not belong to the same groups and will not meet again, so that the relationship has no past and no future, and the research roles are (or should be) segregated from all other roles. (Platt 1981, p. 75)

On this basis, it is argued that the researcher has no social responsibility for the research, may manipulate the situation and the informant, and maintains a social distance from the project.

However, it is important not to provide a stereotype of the research interview as Converse and Schuman (1974) and Kahn and Cannell (1957) provide a portrait of the survey interview that is far from the static model. Indeed, writers such as Gorden (1980) point to a range of interviewing styles including a dichotomy between standardized and non-standardized interviewing. While the standardized interview is designed to collect similar kinds of information from all those interviewed, the non-standardized interview does not include identical questions for all those interviewed with the result that information cannot be summarized in a statistical form. The non-standardized interview does not follow a set pattern or routine and as a consequence Gorden suggests this is why we know little about the strategies, tactics or techniques of this kind of interview.

Yet it is this model that has relevance for researchers who engage in ethnographic research where often the researcher has direct responsibility for the project, is involved in an intense and non-hierarchical set of relationships with his or her informants and has no intention of deliberately manipulating them or maintaining a social distance from them. Indeed, studies beyond education by Oakley (1981) and by Finch (1984) indicate that researchers form intense relationships with their informants, engage in conversation with them and answer, as well as ask, questions. Similarly, in educational studies, accounts by a variety of researchers (Burgess 1984, 1986; Porter 1984; Stenhouse 1984; Measor 1985; Scott 1985) indicate that they consider it important to develop a conversational style with their informants based on the relationships with pupils, students and teachers. For example, Measor indicates that her research with teachers involved building relationships in order to get access to their lives and to their views of the world.

Similarly, in my own work I have attempted to establish relationships with teachers by developing the art of conversation. This approach follows closely the style adopted by writers such as Studs Terkel (1968) and Tom Cottle (1977), both of whom have argued against the use of the standardized interview. In his work in Chicago, Terkel found that interviews, conventionally conducted:

> were meaningless. Conditioned clichés were certain to come. The question-and-answer technique may be of value in determining favoured detergents, toothpaste and deodorants, but not in the discovery of men and women. It was simply a case of making conversation. And listening. (Terkel 1968, p. 20)

Yet such an approach raises several questions concerning what constitutes a conversation in a research project and how data are acquired. These questions need to be addressed in any consideration of the ways in which the art of conversation can be used for research purposes. Such issues arise out of a consideration of my research experience in the course of restudying an urban co-educational comprehensive school that I called Bishop McGregor School.

The Project

Initially I conducted an ethnographic study of Bishop McGregor School in 1973-4 where the focus was upon teachers and pupils and where data were obtained through observation and unstructured interviews based on conversations (see Burgess 1983, 1984). Since 1983 I have been involved in a restudy of McGregor School (Burgess 1986, 1987). The restudy has focused upon teachers and, in particular, has been concerned with the current problems that confront teachers with falling roles and redeployment; with fewer job and career opportunities; and, in the case of McGregor School, with the ways in which teachers have come to terms with working in a newly designated community college. Much of this work has been done using ethnographic methods: by participating in a variety of social situations – public meetings, working parties, committees of teachers and of governors and individual meetings organized by the head and other teachers. I have also observed meetings of school governors including those of the governors' appointments sub-committee and sat in on staff appointments. This research has also been based on numerous conversations. Some have been requested by me, while others have been instigated by teachers. Some have been pre-set while others have been spontaneous. Yet, in all cases, the conversations that are recorded either on tape or in my fieldnotes relate to principles of selection concerning people, events and themes of study (Glaser and Strauss 1967; Burgess 1982, 1984).

In some cases I have systematically tape-recorded conversations with whole departments; especially those involved in redeployment. I have interviewed all teachers in the senior management team and I have also held tape-recorded discussions with all teachers holding particular posts, such as the Heads of Year or those engaged in particular teaching, such as adult education classes (see Burgess 1985; Burgess 1988), and the Department of Education and Science Special Project Classes. Yet these encounters only account for a small portion of the talk on my project.

A chance encounter with a teacher on the corridor in the administrative block; a brief word with a new member of staff on the stairs to the common room; a short conversation with a teacher in the school grounds during a 'free' lesson; a long discussion with a deputy head in the school car park after a difficult meeting; a tip from a staff friend quietly passed to me at coffee time that I may follow up; a brief discussion with the head in a corner of the staff common room about a meeting he had been unable to attend; a conversation in a local club or pub at the end of an evening meeting. These are a few of the many conversations that constitute the data in my study. There are discussions with teachers newly appointed, 'old hands' whom I have known for ten years, members of senior management, teachers who have been promoted and those who have been nominated for redeployment. In short, the conversations that constitute the data of this project come from teachers in a range of situations: the young and old, men and women, those of low and those of high status, those who work part-time and those who work full-time. Accordingly, it is impossible to talk in an abstract way of *the* conversation in my research, as the conversations in my project include the pre-set one-hour tape-recorded discussion as well as a series of brief exchanges that are recorded in my note book. It is, therefore, the purpose of this paper to draw on some of these conversations that have occurred in my research with a view to understanding the processes and problems involved in conducting conversations in an ethnographic study.

A Context for a Conversation

For some years sociologists have pointed to the importance of physical contexts and spatial relations for social interaction among groups of participants; a situation that has been well researched in education by Stebbins (1976). Yet despite all this work having been completed, methodology texts appear to make little reference to the importance of physical context and spatial relations in conversations. Indeed, many writers convey the impression that discussions are context-free.

In educational studies Marten Shipman (1981) has drawn attention to the importance of physical context in conversations that researchers conducted with teenage boys. Shipman compares the discussions held at a similar time by Willis (1977) and by Scharff (1976) who examine the transition from school to work. In the former study most conversations with the researcher were punctuated by four-letter words while in the latter study no such language was used; a situation that Shipman partly attributes to the fact that Scharff conducted all his interviews with pupils in the Deputy Headteacher's office, while Willis worked in a variety of locales that were not linked with staff. But we might ask: does the physical context influence conversations with teachers?

Often in studies of schools, researchers have to find make-shift accommodation in stock cupboards and physics workrooms where interviews may be conducted (see Simons 1981). Indeed, in my study I have conducted tape-recorded interviews in teachers' classrooms, in department workrooms, in offices that have been on loan from a head of department and in offices that have 'belonged' to the participants. Such locations influence the degree of privacy that can be assumed. For example, dinner ladies and other teachers cannot just wander into the office of a deputy head or the head in order to hang up their coats, but this often occurs in departmental workrooms. Conducting a tape-recorded conversation in the former locations results in interruptions that are always cued by a knock on the door or by the ring of a telephone which allows my partner in the discussion to decide when to break a sentence, when to pause and when to answer the enquiry. In contrast, an interview in a departmental workroom may be out of the earshot of pupils but not always of staff who may wander in unannounced. In these situations sentences are abruptly stopped as I reach for the pause button on the recorder. We sit silent for a few moments while the teacher apologises for the intrusion, collects some books and leaves. Yet the ebb and flow of the conversation has been momentarily broken and some minutes have to be spent establishing the point we had reached prior to the intrusion. Certainly, the presence of a tape-recorder influences the beginning and end of pre-set conversations when buttons are pressed that signal the beginnings and ends of conversations. At these times individuals appear most aware of the machine, however small it may be.

Physical context also influences seating arrangements. In the office of a head or a deputy head there are comfortable chairs as well as a desk and chair. Choosing to sit around a coffee table helps to break down the fact that the tape-recorded conversation did not occur spontaneously but was pre-set. In contrast, talking to a deputy head across a desk with a tape-recorder placed beside us may give the individual I am talking to some confidence, as he or she is surrounded by props: a filing cabinet that may be consulted, a file that can be opened. Yet it also adds to the formality and communicates something about the status of individuals and the way in which they perceive themselves.

Teachers have often held detailed, intense conversations with me as we sat side by side in the staff common room. Often such informal conversations include an individual's public perception of events that are frequently within earshot of others. Here, they are contributing to a conversation where it will not be problematic if someone eavesdrops. But when I ask to meet for a tape-recorded conversation, people invariably wish to move out of the common room, where, as one teacher put it, 'I can talk in an unprofessional way', by which she meant name colleagues and provide perceptions of situations which she would wish to remain confidential until I apply pseudonyms to the transcript in order to make anonymous the material prior to publication.

As well as taking place in a physical context, conversations are also located in a social context. Some conversations arise out of ongoing situations. They spontaneously arise out of situations in which the researcher participates. For example, at a party in the staff common room at the end of term, teachers often draw me to one side in order to review the events of the past term. In the common room at morning break, I am updated on the latest events in a long-running staff saga. But not all conversations are spontaneous. For example, when the head wished 'to put the record straight' on a staff interview I had observed during the previous week I was asked, 'Do you have a minute?' After which I was invited into his office for a three- or four-minute reflection on his actions. Similarly, when conducting interviews on re-deployment in one department, I was told by a deputy head that I was running the risk of bias as I had not been to interview him. As I indicated at the time, he had not been interviewed, not because I did not wish to talk to him, but because every time I attempted to fix a mutually convenient time he claimed he was too busy to spend an hour with me. There followed a brief discussion of his perceptions of redeployment in the department concerned and an agreement that he would attempt to make himself available for a brief discussion in a lunch-hour, as he indicated, 'I would like you to see it from our [senior management's] point of view'. The lunch-hour discussion took one hour and ended with an agreement to meet again for another short tape-recorded discussion. However, I found that this conversation began at eleven-thirty in the morning and finished at two-thirty in the afternoon.

In this situation the deputy head provided a management point of view but also produced evidence which shed new light on the public account of a redeployment situation. The public account that was in circulation among staff indicated that this deputy had been personally responsible for a teacher being nominated for redeployment, yet he could give another account which was fully supported by documentary evidence that indicated others were implicated. His accusation of bias in my own work was, it appeared, a trigger to provide sufficient space for him to tell his story.

Some tape-recorded conversations are not requested by me. For example, when a member of staff did not get appointed to a post for which he had been the 'hot favourite', he was known by staff to be very angry and I was told by several people that he wanted to talk to me. I had been present at the interviews and wondered if the teacher concerned would wish to ask me questions about his interview – a situation that I hoped would not arise as I have an agreement with the governors and the head that I will not divulge information about the content of interviews to individuals. However, on meeting this teacher I found that it was not information that he wanted from me but merely the opportunity to put on to tape his feelings about the way he thought he had been handled at the interview. In his view, if too great a time period elapsed before he came to talk to me, his feelings would be modified, smoothed, and lost from sight. In turn, he also wished to talk to me about ways in which he might discover what had 'gone wrong' at his interview. The conversation that transpired drew on the fact that I had been present at the interview in question. Accordingly, assumptions were made by the teacher that indicated I knew about the interview and about who had said what. Here, the content was not repeated but used as a basis on which to advance his views. The discussion was, therefore, based on my participation in the school and a shared knowledge of the situation, both of which held implications for the data obtained (see Platt 1981).

Conversation Based on Participation

In her discussion of interviews with peers, Jennifer Platt (1981) indicates that shared membership of a social group has an influence upon the way in which relationships are established between the interviewer and those who are interviewed. In a similar way, in ethnographic research the individual's participation in the social group that is being studied may assist in establishing relationships. In McGregor School my presence is well established, but invariably not all staff have the opportunity to hear directly from me about my research. Nevertheless, individuals are quick to relay information that conveys, in some respects, details (however incomplete) about my research and about tape-recording. At a staff disco, jokes are made in the DJs commentary which include 'Bob Burgess is here tonight without his tape-recorder'. I have also figured in joking terms in the headteacher's end-of-term speech to the staff. When he was recounting the events of the year, I and my tape-recorder figured in the action, including the comment, 'Bob Burgess ends up talking to himself'. The knowledge which individuals have about me, about the role of tape-recording and the tape-recorder, eases my passage in the research.

For some individuals, tape-recorded conversations provide what they describe as 'therapy'; that is, an opportunity to talk about themselves and the situation they are in. A new member of staff, whom I interviewed after six weeks in the school, signalled that an hour's conversation with me provided an opportunity to reflect on all the problems involved in settling into a new job. It also strengthened that person's views on how to come to terms with a new job, a new situation and a new school. As a consequence, my interview technique was referred to as 'therapy' by this new staff member.

The equation of our conversations with therapy has often been noted by the head who has remarked that 'talking to you is cheaper than having your own shrink'. Furthermore, this analogy has also passed into the public domain, as demonstrated one morning when I was waiting to see the head. A head of department emerged from the head's office and remarked: 'He's all ready for you now. He's just got to pull out the couch and lie down and then you can begin'. Similarly, other teachers have commented on the style that I use in establishing conversations that allow them space to talk. Here, comparisons have been made between my research interviews that are rooted in a conversational style, and job interviews in McGregor School and elsewhere that they have found hostile, aggressive and restricting, with little opportunity for reflection and self-expression.

The conversations that I establish are therefore designed to provide an opportunity for teachers to talk about their work in their own words, using their own concepts rather than in an abstract way or in response to a set of staccato questions. Sometimes I am approached by individuals who indicate that they would like to come to talk to me about their work and their school experiences. These conversations often trade on common understandings and background knowledge which teachers assume I have acquired through my participation and observation in the school.

Conversation and Observation

In the course of conversations with teachers I frequently draw on my observation of situations so as to check out the teachers' motivations in a particular situation; or to ascertain the meanings that they attribute to social situations.

When I started my restudy in Bishop McGregor School I first joined a community development group that consisted of a number of teachers who were making plans for the first adult education classes that would be held in the school since it was designated a community college. Planning was slow as individuals gradually moved towards evenings on which adult classes would operate. However, without warning, one teacher, Liz Owen, suddenly appeared at a meeting and gave out literature that she had designed for classes that she was to teach. The advertizing material contained details of the dates on which these classes were to operate; a situation that pre-empted a collective decision by members of the group. I was puzzled as to why she had taken this course of action and therefore followed it up in a subsequent tape-recorded conversation in the following way:

> RB: My memory of the way these classes began, particularly your course on the gospels, is that we were having the community development group meetings in the first term and you were a participant in these meetings, and the thing that struck me, as someone sat around the table, was that you were very enthusiastic about getting going and getting started, so much so that you went off getting literature together and came along one week and said 'well I started putting these around' and it meant that you'd actually chosen dates and you had then said 'Right, that's when we've got to go because these dates are now made public'. Why did you work in that way? I was interested in that. But perhaps you didn't see it that way.
>
> LO: But I can remember we were asked to get started as far as I recall, and I took people at their word ...
>
> RB: Oh yes you did. I mean ...
>
> LO: I was aware that in a way I had a slightly easier task than some other

people in that I felt I could use different people. I had the Chaplain behind me. The priests who were willing to publicize things in their parishes and so on, and I decided I had my own channels of communication and could use them. I don't remember you know, that I was trying to pre-empt anything.

RB: Oh, no, no, no.

LO: ... or control the situation, at all, I just remember, just thinking that I was doing what I'd been asked to do.

RB: Oh yes, I'm not saying ... what I'm saying is that it seemed to me, as I sat round the table, that there was a lot of talk about should we do this, or should we do that or might we do this, or might we do that ...

LO: Yes ...

RB: and you were always very much coming in and saying 'well I want to put on this course and I'm going to put it on' and then one week ...

LO: Yes, I did deal with ...

RB: you turned up with the stuff. Sorry ...

LO: I did feel that, you know, that was what we were supposed to be doing, taking our own initiatives and I felt there were initiatives I could take, and that they would work, and I wanted to see if they would work, I very much wanted to prove I suppose a point.

RB: Yes.

LO: Because already there was talk about this job in the community and I think I wanted to get on and prove that there was something to be done. Perhaps 'prove' is the wrong word. I wanted to see whether there really was a market and I wanted to get on and do it.

RB: Yes, yes.

LO: That's really why I started.

RB: Yes, yes.

In this part of the conversation I started by describing a situation with a view to it being checked out and either confirmed or modified by the teacher concerned. Furthermore, I then moved on to try and get an account of the teacher's motivations for her actions. While, in public, it appeared that she had pre-empted a decision, this was not, according to her, her motive for working in this way. Instead she saw it as using her initiative and 'proving' that there was a market for courses in Adult Religious Education – a factor that was important to her in establishing evidence in support of the school having a post in Adult Religious Education for which she later applied. As such, this observation of an action in a meeting was important to follow up as it provided a lead into an analysis of events before and after the appointment of another person to the post concerned. The conversation, therefore, helped me to construct part of the story line of a series of events in my study.

Another way in which conversations can be linked to observations is when the researcher wishes to check on a sequence of events. For example, it was usual for the woman deputy head, Gillian Davies, to chair meetings of the pastoral team in the head's absence. However, on one occasion when one of the male deputies was present he appeared to oust her from this position; a situation that I checked up on in the following way when interviewing Geoff Goddard, the headmaster:

After a brief telephone interruption

RB: We were talking about ...

GG: The meeting that I arrived at half way through ...

RB: You ...

GG: I actually had an appointment in the office there, it wasn't fixed. But I had arranged with Gill that that item [on the job designation of new Heads of Year] would be held back till I arrived.

RB: Oh no, that was made clear – I was sort of leading you in by saying well you came half way through – yes, Phil had in fact chaired the meeting up until that point ...

GG: That's right ... with Gill thinking she was going to chair it.

RB: ... and together they described that all the items were to be taken then you would arrive or they would wait if they had covered the items before you arrived. How would you see that? – what do you think you were doing there that day? What was your position?

This conversation, therefore, provided a means of engaging in the process of triangulation, as it helped me to check up on several issues. First, whether, as was publicly stated, the head had deliberately been absent from the meeting. Second, how he had established the procedure that was adopted. Finally, how he perceived the situation. In addition, I also approached talking about this meeting in this way as I had anticipated that it would be difficult to get the head to talk directly about his position, given the problems associated with the meeting concerned.

A further strategy that I used to check on my observations and to get teachers to discuss their role in a sequence of events was to get them to confirm or to reject my understanding. For example, in a situation where events leading up to the possible redeployment of a teacher were under discussion, I got one head of department to talk about the numerous activities in which he had been involved in a two-day period. He described for me the activities in which he had participated and placed them in a sequence in the following terms:

JS: That was Wednesday. Because as you know what we haven't mentioned, the one thing we did positively was put the governors meeting off 24 hours, you know. So I mean, this was very important because this was the one ...

RB: The governors never met until the Thursday.

JS: Yes, but they had got the meeting down for the Wednesday.

RB: Yes, but they never actually met ...

JS: I see, they never met that Wednesday.

RB: Well if they did ...

JS: No, look, you don't get me. They were down to meet on a Wednesday. The one thing I did get which was very important, we were looking for breathing space ...

RB: Oh, you had the meeting postponed?

JS: Yes, postponed for a day. That was very important.

RB: Yes, then they met on Thursday.

JS: And the Boss accepted this.

In this extract from a conversation with Jack Spiller, a head of department, I got an account of the sequence of events and his involvement in the crucial rescheduling of a meeting that I had not previously understood, given the limitations on my participation. Accordingly, this conversation helped me to understand how the crucial rescheduling was pulled off and in turn how a teacher who was to be redeployed was saved from having to be nominated by the school governors.

Such understandings often have to be worked at within a conversation; especially when the researcher has participated in a number of social situations in the school. Often the researcher's participation results in teachers assuming a considerable background knowledge that will allow crucial gaps in our knowledge to be filled. For example, when talking to the head about redeployment I make assumptions about his ability to recognize and 'fill in' the details of a situation and he makes similar assumptions when talking to me:

> GG: Yes, yes, it got beyond the brink. I got myself four feet out beyond the end of the rope, and then that piece of the bridge which had been built, which had been carefully constructed, was pulled back and I hit the deck. Now, I am scrambling over metaphors. We moved, very slowly and steadily, towards the point where three people were being nominated for re-deployment. One person has not been nominated for redeployment that was in the position that she might have been. I don't know the full ins and outs but the union were involved. The union looked at the rule book, and despite the fact that I was Union Secretary, went to the Authority, and said 'he missed the date by three days, therefore no fight, no contest', and the Authority looked at it and decided 'right, no redeployment'. And then told me. I ended up with a considerable amount of egg on my face. I ended up very bruised inside. I ended up not liking the proceedings very much, and the reason that we had been three days late was that I wasn't prepared to do a particular thing until I had talked to a particular person. So, by acting with a degree of courtesy, I thought, I trapped myself and the Authority simply said 'you can't do it'. There was a certain amount of sympathy in the office, for the position. The result was we were over-staffed in September. As a result last year's over-staffing and this year's over-staffing have led us to face a need for redeploying twelve.

In order to understand the implications of what is being discussed in this sequence it is necessary to be familiar with the regulations and procedures relating to redeployment that the head had been involved in establishing (as union secretary) with the local education authority.

A further example concerns in-school situations; especially relationships and disputes between teachers where it is important to have an understanding if names and situations are to be applied to supposedly hypothetical situations. In a situation where two teachers had been locked into a dispute for several months one of them talked to me about it but in abstract terms as shown in the following remarks:

Teacher: Because at the end of the day, I mean if you look at principles at the end of the day, you have ... even if there were no problems whatsoever standing in your way... if party 'A' says we must have this and party 'B' says we mustn't have this, that's got to be resolved and there's no compromise in a sense, it either goes ahead or it doesn't go ahead so there's that constant negotiation until a decision is reached.

RB: But your example then, of party 'A' and party 'B'. Is it that what this really comes down to is the negotiation that takes place between you and Phil, or is it not?

Teacher: I think ... yes I think that's fairly obvious, yes.

RB: Or is it not just you and Phil?

Teacher: No, I think it is, yes it is.

Here, it was essential to have an understanding of the dispute that had taken place in order to shift the teacher from an abstract discussion. Accordingly, I inserted the other teacher's name so as to bring an abstract discussion closer to reality and in turn so that I could proceed to obtain some account of the kinds of principles that were involved in the dispute.

So far I have focused on some of the ways in which conversations are linked to observational work for the purposes of data collection. However, conversation may also be linked to observation for the purposes of data analysis, or at least to stimulate further data analysis. In my initial study of Bishop McGregor School I had been interested in the structure of groups in the staff common room (Burgess 1983, pp. 72-6), a theme that I have also followed up in the restudy.

In the first study I had focused on the dominant characteristic of particular groups in the common room, including a male sports group. On returning to McGregor it appeared to me that this group had expanded and become more prominent, principally because a full-size pool table has been located in the centre of the common room. It is the pool table that is the focus of much attention in the common room as conversations now occur not only between those who play pool but between individuals who play pool and other teachers who are sitting around in the common room.

As a result of a conversation with a woman teacher about the position of women in the school, I was helped to understand the way in which gender could be used as a principle around which to examine both the content of conversation and the structure of activities in the common room. We were talking about how men joke with women in the common room and how jokes are made by men about sexism which lead on to talking about *how* women are portrayed in staff room discussions.

Woman teacher: Oh I think that [sexism] typifies the general approach. I do think the men on this staff resent successful women or seem intimidated by them or even threatened by them.

RB: Which of these?

Woman teacher: Well I think you can feel all of them, if you are a man. I wouldn't know but I have some examples of it. I have seen examples thrown at people. Not perhaps in an obvious way, you know, face to face, but when someone has walked up to the staff room. It's taken years for them [the men] to come to terms with the fact that women are good at their job, in giving discipline.

In addition, this teacher was also aware that the male staff often made comments about women teachers, as she remarked that this is 'the general thing, or you will get laughed at, or made fun of in such a way that it won't just be a joke and dropped, it will constantly come back at you'. In response to this remark I said that I had particularly noticed this phenomenon in large staff meetings, but the teacher added other examples and in particular mentioned an end-of-term social where she felt comments were made directly against women. She remarked:

Well right at the end of term they often have a social. I must admit I avoided the last one, I just couldn't tolerate it. I had such a bad day here, and I thought I can't swallow that as well. I just couldn't be bothered to go. Because it just typifies to me all that's wrong in some ways. The way some women are treated.

In turn, this teacher also drew my attention to the sports competitions among male staff and with male staff in other schools which, she argued, was a way in which the common room association was 'upholding the masculine ideal and all the rest of it and all that is masculine'. However, she also believed that this was part of the 'normal' way of life among teachers in the school. As she remarked, 'I can't explain it. It is just something. I suppose you learn to live with it, you have to really'. For example, for this teacher the pool table was part of these phenomena; as she said:

Woman teacher: For instance, the pool table in the staff room. Now I am not against pool, but the fact that if a woman is playing, she is quickly hurried along or shoved off.
RB: Oh, really?
Woman teacher: Or comments are made to the effect that you are made to feel, you know, this is the man – this is belonging to the *men*.

For this woman teacher considered that those who played pool showed they were 'one of the lads', but she warned:

Yet if a woman tries to, not that I would like to, but if a woman did try and get in on that type of environment, she would be branded, not only by her own peer group of women in the staffroom but also by men.

It was on the basis of this conversation that I began to explore the staffroom and conversations in the staffroom in terms of the notion of a 'male domain' and male space. For example, I was already a regular attender at the end-of-term socials to which this teacher had referred, but I now began to re-examine my data concerning such occasions. On the basis of this conversation with a woman teacher I was directed towards questioning part of the routine of the staffroom in order to build up an account of gender relations in the common room (cf. Delamont 1981). Conversations that are conducted in ethnographic studies can, therefore, contribute directly to the conduct of fieldwork using observation and participant observation. But as with many strategies of qualitative research, the conduct of conversations and the data that they generate raises ethical problems for the researcher to which we briefly turn.

Some Ethical Issues

In the course of this chapter I have made reference to using conversations to get teachers to talk in a personal way so that I can record their experiences, their views and their recollections. But we might ask: to what extent does this constitute an invasion of privacy? To what extent does this involve asking people to expose private aspects of their lives? In part, researchers attempt to come to terms with this dilemma through assurances of confidentiality, anonymity and the use of pseudonyms. Yet as some classic studies (Vidich and Bensman 1968) have shown, the participants in studies can often recognize themselves. Indeed, it could be argued that if the hallmarks of ethnography include the possibility of 'telling it as it is' and providing accounts that 'ring true', then the participants should be able to recognize the real situations and events which lie beneath the changes that are made and the pseudonyms that are used.

But this poses a dilemma for the researcher, especially in some situations. For example, in the previous section of this chapter a teacher has made criticisms of male staff and the way in which male humour is used against women teachers. As a consequence I decided to use the term 'woman teacher' rather than using a pseudonym which might be linked back to a particular teacher, as I would not want her to be the subject of ridicule on the basis of the remarks that she made to me. Yet as Janet Finch (1984) has demonstrated, this strategy may offer some protection to an individual woman but it does not protect women as a group. Indeed, the kind of analysis to which I have drawn attention might worsen the situation not only for women in Bishop McGregor School but in a variety of school staffrooms. Yet to do nothing for fear of the possible harm that might result is not a 'solution' – that way the researcher is not adding to our knowledge about sexism in the staffroom. However, in this context, it is also important to consider strategies to raise awareness among women teachers and counter strategies that might be used to overcome staffroom sexism.

In other examples in this chapter I have used the word 'teacher' rather than a pseudonym to further disguise situations such as the dispute between two teachers, as I would not want any comments by me, or extracts quoted from interviews, to be used to fuel further disputes. As such, the selection of some quotations has been made so as to illustrate methodological issues but also to maintain confidentiality. However, there are some quotations that have been used that are attributed to particular teachers, such as Liz Owen. In her discussion she highlights how she was taking particular actions with the long-term objective of applying for a particular post in the school. While I have changed the name of the teacher, I have not changed the name of the post as only one such position exists in the school so it is difficult to change. In addition, if the name of another subject was substituted for the real subject it would still be identifiable to other staff at McGregor. A further factor that has also influenced my decision not to change the details of the post is the fact that it was always known publicly among the staff at McGregor that this teacher intended to apply for this job when it was advertized. In this sense, I do not feel that I have betrayed a confidence.

However, we might ask: what counts as 'confidential'? At times, in the course of conversations, teachers will say, 'and this is confidential'. But we might ask: what is actually held by the informant to be confidential – everything that is said, the name involved, or the occurrence of a particular episode? Further questions can also be raised: to whom is information confidential? To me and to the secretary who transcribes the tape? Or does it mean that sufficient confidentiality has been observed if pseudonyms are used? In some cases, individuals go further. For example, in one of the tape-recorded conversations that I had with the headteacher, we were in the middle of talking about a situation where he had already made several acute comments but without naming any names. He then paused and said: 'God help me if you quote me, I'll be up the spout'. Now such a remark puts a very clear restriction on the researcher. However, reading the transcript of the interview in which this comment appears, some fifteen months after the conversation took place, appears to put it in a different context. The situation that is being discussed is no longer 'hot news' in the school. Indeed, the issues are no longer contentious as they were when the original discussion took place. On this basis, I think extracts such as these might be reviewed periodically with a view to going back to the individual concerned to seek permission to allow the public release of a statement that has the potential to develop and deepen our understanding of the relationship between a head-teacher and a staff at a time when schools are experiencing cuts in public expenditure.

There are, nevertheless, some materials that are always confidential to the researcher and permanently lost from view. For example, in the middle of a taped conversation with a teacher I was requested to 'shut that bloody machine off'. At this point the individual told me about something that he had not done. The teacher indicated that the information should never be used and, having said that, indicated I could switch the tape recorder on again so that he could pick up the conversation at the point where he had broken off the account. Such situations pose a major dilemma for me. If the informant did not intend the information to influence my interpretation, why did he tell me at all? In some respects this appears to be an invitation to incorporate this material in some way, but if it is done without giving data and sources, the assertions may look ungrounded. This kind of situation also presents many other problems. First, the researcher colludes with the other person involved in the conversation if no material is used. Second, in this instance the data that are being withheld would dramatically change a public account of a situation, so in this sense the researcher is involved in some deception. Third, the data that are withheld would, if released, change the public view of the teacher concerned. However, as some commentators (Barnes 1983; Burgess 1985) have indicated, the 'whole truth' is unattainable in social research where a compromise becomes part of the reality of social situations in which researchers are involved.

Conclusion

The conversation allied to participant observation in ethnographic work is a way in which researchers can begin to examine how people perceive themselves and how they operate in social situations. Yet so often methodologists would have us believe that conversations cannot be used in the research process. Instead, preference is given to the standardized interview which, as many researchers have shown, does not engage with the texture of people's lives (see Terkel 1968; Cottle 1977; Oakley 1981; Wakeford 1981; Burgess 1982, 1984; Finch 1984; Graham 1984). If we are to comprehend the lives of those people who are studied in educational ethnography, it is essential that we consider how to conduct conversations with a purpose. The result will mean that rather than having the sanitized interview of the textbook writer, we shall have a series of conversations that will act as the essential catalyst to further our understanding of teachers' lives.

Acknowledgments

The research that is reported in this paper was supported by grants from the University of Warwick Research and Innovations Fund and the Nuffield Foundation to whom I am most grateful. An earlier version of this paper was presented at the annual conference of the British Educational Research Association held at the University of Sheffield in August 1985. I am indebted to conference participants and to Stephen Ball, Martin Bulmer, Hilary Burgess, Janet Finch, Martin Lawn and Jennifer Platt for their perceptive comments that have been used in revising this material for publication.

References

Adelman, C. (ed.), 1981, *Uttering, Muttering: Collecting, Using and Reporting Talk for Social and Educational Research,* London: Grant McIntyre.

Barnes, J. A., 1983. 'Lying: a sociological view', *Australian Journal of Forensic Sciences,* vol. 15, no. 4, pp. 152-8.

Burgess, H. and Burgess, R. G., 1985. 'Collaborative research and the curriculum', paper prepared for the Sociology and the Teacher Conference, St. Hilda's College, Oxford, 9-11 September.

Burgess, R. G. (ed.), 1982. *Field Research: A Sourcebook and Field Manual,* London: Allen & Unwin.

Burgess, R. G., 1983. *Experiencing Comprehensive Education: A Study of Bishop McGregor School,* London: Methuen.

–. 1984. *In the Field: An Introduction to Field Research,* London: Allen & Unwin.

–. 1985. 'The whole truth? Some ethical problems of research in a comprehensive school' in R. G. Burgess (ed.) *Field Methods in the Study of Education,* Lewes: Falmer Press.

–. 1986. 'School and community: it's so close together you can't see the join', *Journal of Community Education,* vol. 5, no. 2, pp. 5-9.

–. 1987. 'Studying and restudying Bishop McGregor School' in G. Walford (ed.) *Doing Sociology of Education,* Lewes: Falmer Press.

–. 1988. 'Examining classroom practice using diaries and diary interviews' in A. Pollard and P. Woods (eds.) *Sociology and the Teacher,* London: Croom Helm.

Cohen, L. and Manion, L., 1985. *Research Methods in Education* (2nd edn) London: Croom Helm.

Converse, J. and Schuman, H., 1974. *Conversations at Random: Survey Research as Interviewers See It,* New York: Wiley.

Cottle, T., 1977. *Private Lives and Public Accounts,* New York: New Viewpoints.

Delamont, S., 1981. 'All too familiar? A decade of classroom research', *Educational Analysis,* vol. 3, no. 1, pp. 69-83.

Finch, J., 1984. ' "It's great to have someone to talk to": the ethics and politics of interviewing women' in C. Bell and H. Roberts (eds.) *Social Researching: Politics, Problems, Practice,* London: Routledge & Regan Paul, pp. 70-87.

Glaser, B. and Strauss, A. L., 1967. *The Discovery of Grounded Theory,* Chicago: Aldine.

Goode, W. J. and Hatt, P. K., 1952. *Methods in Social Research,* New York: McGraw Hill.

Gorden, R. L., 1980. *Interviewing: Strategy, Techniques and Tactics* (3rd edn) Homewood, Illinois: Dorsey Press.

Graham, H., 1984. 'Surveying through stories' in C. Bell and H. Roberts (eds.) *Social Researching: Politics, Problems, Practice,* London: Routledge & Kegan Paul, pp. 104-24.

Kahn, R. L. and Cannell, C. F., 1957. *The Dynamics of Interviewing,* New York: Wiley.

Measor, L., 1985. 'Interviewing: a strategy in qualitative research' in R. G. Burgess (ed.) *Strategies of Educational Research: Qualitative Methods,* Lewes: Falmer Press, pp. 55-77.

Moser, C. and Kalton, G., 1971. *Survey Methods in Social Investigation* (2nd edn) London: Heinemann.

Oakley, A., 1981. 'Interviewing women: a contradiction in terms' in H. Roberts (ed.) *Doing Feminist Research,* London: Routledge and Kegan Paul, pp. 30-61.

Palmer, V. M., 1928. *Field Studies in Sociology: A Students' Manual,* Chicago: University of Chicago Press.

Platt, J., 1981. 'On interviewing one's peers', *British Journal of Sociology,* vol. 32, no. 1, pp. 75-91.

Porter, M., 1984. 'The modification of method in researching postgraduate education' in R. G. Burgess (ed.) *The Research Process in Educational Settings: Ten Case Studies,* Lewes: Falmer Press, pp. 139-161.

Scharff, D. E., 1976. 'Aspects of the transition from school to work' in J. M. M. Hill and D. E. Scharff, *Between Two Worlds: Aspects of the Transition from School to Work,* Richmond: Careers Consultants, pp. 66-332.

Scott, S., 1985. 'Working through the contradictions in researching postgraduate education' in R. G. Burgess (ed.) *Field Methods in the Study of Education,* Lewes: Falmer Press, pp. 115-30.

Shipman, M., 1981. *The Limitations of Social Research* (2nd edn) London: Longman.

Simons, H., 1981. 'Conversation piece: the practice of interviewing in case study research' in C. Adelman (ed.) *Uttering, Muttering: Collecting, Using and Reporting Talk for Social and Educational Research,* London: Grant McIntyre, pp. 27-50.

Stebbins, R. A., 1976. 'Physical context influences on behaviour: the case of classroom disorderliness' in M. Hammersley and P. Woods (eds.) *The Process of Schooling,* London: Routledge and Kegan Paul, pp. 208-16.

Stenhouse, L., 1984. 'Library access, library use and user education in academic sixth forms: an autobiographical account' in R. G. Burgess (ed.) *The Research Process in Educational Settings: Ten Case Studies,* Lewes: Falmer Press.

Terkel, S., 1968. *Division Street USA,* London: Allen Lane.

Vidich, A. J. and Bensman, J., 1968. *Small Town in Mass Society* (2nd edn), Princeton, New Jersey: Princeton University Press.

Wakeford, J., 1981. 'From methods to practice; a critical note on the teaching of research practice to undergraduates', *Sociology,* vol. 15, no. 4, pp. 505-12.

Webb, S. and Webb, B., 1932. *Methods of Social Study,* London: Longman Green.

Willis, P., 1977. *Learning to Labour,* Farnborough, England: Saxon House.

33

Is Oral History Auto/Biography?

Joanna Bornat

Introduction

I have to confess to a whole range of complex feelings when I consider the issue of the relationship between oral history and auto/biography. As an oral historian reading the newly emerging auto/biography literature, I hear problems being outlined, dilemmas presented and see constructs developed which I recognise. I feel myself reacting defensively, but at the same time am curious to find out how this literature relates to what I think I know and practice. In part I am responding in the traditional role of the academic, staking out territory, declaring possession and owning thoughts. But I am also responding as a potential subject, rebelling against the possibility that my work and my activities might become part of someone else's thinking and be resumed to me as only part of a larger scheme or, worse still, analysed and explained in a language beyond my recognition. I may be guilty of inventing a distinction which only exists in my mind but, in following the development of what seems to be a new area of interest for sociologists, I am conscious that what is being discussed sounds familiar to me. What follows is an exploration of what I, as an oral historian, sense as differences and similarities between what I think I know about and what I now see being discussed as auto/biography.

Defining Terms

I begin with definitions. Seeking a form of words which is inclusive of what seems to the most reflective thinking, I have chosen a quotation from a recent article by Liz Stanley, written for an audience of oral historians:

Source: *Auto/Biography*, 1994, vol. 3, pp. 17-30.

"Unlike oral history, auto/biography has no common method, nor a preferred form of data, nor is it programmatically based in a methodological sense, and nor does it 'belong' to one 'discipline.' Its common focus lies in the notion of auto/biography as an epistemologically-oriented concern with the political ramifications of the shifting boundaries between self and other, past and present, writing and reading, fact and fiction, and with an analytic attention to these within the oral, visual and written texts that are 'biographies' and 'autobiographies' in the widest sense of these terms. The writer or author and the researcher are certainly not treated as transparent or 'dead', but very much as agents actively at work in textual political production". (Stanley 1994, p, 89)

This definition is explicitly engaged with the issues I want to confront in this paper. It sets out the key areas of engagement and disengagement between these two discipline areas. Looking for a useful definition of oral history I have been struck by the fact that oral historians seem to be more interested in stating what oral history can do, rather than what it is (Thompson 1988, Grele 1985; Frisch 1990). In the end I have chosen a definition offered by Michael Frisch who argues that oral history is:

"a powerful tool for discovering, exploring and evaluating the nature of the process of historical memory – how people make sense of their past, how they connect individual experience and its social context, how the past becomes part of the present, and how people use it to interpret their lives and the world around them". (Frisch 1990, p. 188)

These definitions of auto/biography and oral history are at once the same and different. There is a shared interest in knowledge and how it is constructed, with references to 'epistemologically-oriented' and words like 'the nature of the process of historical memory'. They allow for the manufacture of reality, by problematising the nature of arrived at accounts, with reference to 'how people make sense of the past' and 'political production'. Each defines itself in terms of both method *and* content. They connect with notions of reflexivity, referencing the inter-relationship of 'self and other' and the role the past plays in personal explorations of life experience: each suggesting a central role for the individual in the process of understanding accounts. Finally, they both acknowledge the possibilities of a merging of categories: the individual and the social, the past and the present, fact and fiction, writing and reading.

Though there are similarities there are also differences. It is the focus on the 'doing', on its use as a 'tool' that I think provides a distinction between the tasks of oral history and auto/biography. There is scope here for openness in the process. It is perhaps a question of where theorising is placed, whether, as in auto/biography it is a goal, or whether, as in oral history it is a means. Moving on to a second difference, there is the actual method. Though each describes a process of interactions between self and society, self and described selves, I want to suggest that the interactions of oral history are by nature interrogative. Whereas the interactions of auto/biography are imposed on the texts, be they oral, visual or written, or contained within them, oral history is a process of social interaction and interrogation. A third distinction which I draw is in terms of aims. Whereas auto/biography's aim, though political in terms of its openness to debate and its interest in challenging orthodoxies, remains contained within an academic discourse, the aim of oral history is broader being unashamedly political in its instrumentality and with concern for outcomes. I will argue each of these differences in more detail, but first I want to explain where I think oral history is at present and where it has come from. I need to do this in order to make it clear that I come from an area of work that, like auto/biography, is developing and has its own history.

The Past and Present of Oral History

Elsewhere (Bornat 1993a) I have outlined some of the changes which oral history has gone through. From positivist beginnings it has reached out to more reflective and interpretative ways of working. Looking back through early issues of *Oral History* it is clear that the drive was towards collection and itemisation, what Michael Frisch describes as "more history": "a source of new information about otherwise inaccessible experience" (Frisch 1988 pp. 186-7). Innovators in England in the late 1960's were academic historians, archivists, librarians, folklorists, museum workers and broadcasters amongst others whose "primary concern (was) with research in social and political history making use of sound recordings" (*Oral History*, 1972 Vol 1, no 1, p. 5). Collectors at that time were actively interviewing for information about rural crafts, details of local history, traditional lore and belief, family life and work experience, Christian socialism, dialect speech, Oxford college servants, labour history, Welsh International Brigadiers. This was an eclectic set of interests but with a shared perspective, the collection of memories of the past through interviews.

In the United States, the goal was similar. Alan Nevins, who is credited as the founder of oral history in that country, began a series of interviews in 1948 with the aim of obtaining "from the lips and papers of living Americans who have led significant lives, a fuller record of their participation in the political, economic and cultural life of the last sixty years" (Baum 1972, p. 17). From quite an early point, however, British oral history demonstrated evidence that it aimed to fulfill another function. Michael Frisch again supplies the descriptor: this is the "anti-history" approach which assumes that "conventional historical frameworks are not only inadequate, but more fundamentally obstructive of deeper understanding. In this sense, oral history is offered as a way to bypass such obstacles, a short cut to a more direct, emotionally informed sense of 'the way it was' " (Frisch 1988, p. 186-7). George Ewart Evans, whose oral history work in East Anglia inspired the first generation of oral historians in Britain talked about his realisation of this direct and humanistic link to the past in relation to his neighbours, a retired shepherd and his wife

> "I found that they were books that walked and the whole village was living history. But I realised that although the old survivors were walking books, I could not just leaf them over. They were persons and I had to be very very careful". (Evans 1972, p. 57)

George Ewart Evans' early awareness of his informants as older people was later advanced with some oral historians' exploration of the relationship between remembering and those existential issues raised by the experience of ageing. It is perhaps a distinctive feature of oral history in Britain that what is known as 'reminiscence work' has kept in close association with oral history with each informing the other (Bornat 1993b), reinforcing awareness of the contribution which even the most frail older person makes to our under-standing of the past while underscoring the fact that most oral history practice is a dialogue about ageing.

Understanding aspects of ageing is acknowledged to be of importance to the competent and empathetic oral historian, so is an understanding that what may be given as an account is no more objectively 'true' than a written document. Oral history has moved from an obsessive concern with validity towards a more relaxed attitude which allows for interpretation and an awareness of presentation skills on both sides of the microphone. In this it has been influenced from two directions. European oral historians, in particular the Italian school, have long had an interest in the cultural and symbolic content of oral evidence. The work of Sandro Portelli and Luisa Passerini has been key in this. Sandro Portelli has developed ways of acknowledging the contribution of mythical accounts both to an understanding of the internal worlds of some informants and to explaining the history of left politics and action (Portelli 1988; 1991). Luisa Passerini writes about:

> "the impossibility of making direct use of oral memories as immediately revealing facts and events. Rather, they reveal a tension between forms of behaviour and mental representations expressed through particular narrative guises". (Passerini 1989, p. 194)

'Narrative guises' and strategies crop up in unexpected circumstances. A nurse writing about his work with older women on a continuing care ward gives an example of an account being given in the form of a traditional story. An older woman near death from heart disease talked to him about her early childhood experiences of family abuse and neglect and introduced fairy tale elements with the story of a passing 'gentleman' who asked to adopt her. Looking back on this interview John Adams suggests that this may have been a way for her to generalise painful experiences and present these in an acceptable form to her hearer (Adams 1993, p. 86-9).

The other influence has been feminist oral history. Where Michael Frisch points to oral history's two poles of 'more history' and 'anti history', feminist historians have identified the 'how' in history. It has been feminist oral historians who have shown most interest in how we work, what assumptions and motives we bring to the process and how the process is changed by and changes us. In part this influence has emerged as women oral historians have reflected on shared experience across and between generations, it is partly through a need, an urgency to tell and reveal hidden accounts, to right wrongs and to stake claims for justice. But it is also a result of having to come to terms with the limits of sharing while we reflect on the divisions of class, race, age, culture and impairment which continue to distinguish groups of women from each other, It is this tension between sharing and dividing which has led to the identification of issues relating to how we work as oral historians.

Two papers in a recent issue of *Oral History* contribute to these developing debates. Mary Stuart has been interviewing women with learning difficulties who have lived in a convent for most of their lives. Her interviews made her remember herself as a four year old, left at a convent by her mother and only returning home for holidays. She began to realise that the experience of taking part was affecting her, the interviewer. This became clear when, on asking one woman about how she felt about being interviewed, she was surprised to hear the same question being put back to her, "And how was it for you Mary?". Her conclusion is

"As participants in the creation of an oral history the process itself will change 'us' and this must not be hidden from scrutiny but must be part of that process. Our roles and our meanings and identities, as oral historians, must be investigated". (Stuart 1993, p. 82)

The other paper is by Miriam Zukas and raises the issue of interviews as friendship. She writes as a psychologist who has come upon oral history. In the process of interviewing twenty nine women about friendships she notes that she changed her usual terminology of interviewee as 'subject' to using the term "respondent". She considers the interviews as friendships but in the end she sees them as "quasi-friendships". Women confided in her easily, she felt, but she acknowledges that there was no reciprocity in what was essentially a research relationship

"I asked many more direct questions, directed the conversation much more, was more controlled about my interventions and said much less than I would have done if I had been talking to a friend" (Zukas 1993, p. 78)

Her reflection on their experience of each other's company, over questions and cups of tea, evokes the detailed analysis of interview practice by US feminist oral historians who have recently written about their recognition of differences and the limits to ideals of empowerment and partnership, in the oral history interview. Where objectives and backgrounds differ then the experience of being interviewed and of relating life history cannot be controlled or predetermined either in essentialist or democratic terms (Gluck & Patai 1991).

I have introduced some developments in what I recognise as oral history in order to illustrate ways in which it is approaching some of the issues which auto/biography commonly deals with, issues of identity, fabulation, revealing and accounting for self in the research process. Now I want to retrace my steps and gather up the three points of difference between auto/biography and oral history which I identified earlier. These are: openness, interrogation, and instrumentality. I look at each in turn.

Openness

Oral history seeks to explore and explain in a way which involves an active seeking out of lives. It therefore goes beyond the inhibitions and the social and political restraints which still determine who will participate in writing and reflecting on the self. This means that there is potentially a greater inclusivity, a greater openness: hidden histories come to light.

Over a decade ago this process began with the new histories of women in the family and community, (Chamberlain 1975; McCrindle & Rowbotham 1977, Liddington and Norris 1978; Wilson 1978, Thompson 1981; Roberts 1984, Davidoff & Westover 1986 are just a few examples). Recently we have seen histories of other previously 'invisible' groups begin to emerge. People with learning disabilities who have spent lifetimes in institutions, (Potts & Fido 1991; Atkinson 1993) or whose experiences as children and young people with physical disabilities have remained hidden because they lived apart within their community (Humphries & Gordon 1992). Oral historians can take the initiative, persuade and cajole, demonstrate with examples, encourage participation and create new biographers or autobiographers. The traditions of community publishing have done much to promote the idea of writing about oneself and a self defined community. Groups of people for whom the idea that their lives could have any wider worth and value beyond their immediate family or community found new ways to record their histories and recognition both as historians and as creative writers (Centerprise 1977; Bornat 1992; Woodin 1992).

Working with older women living in hospital recently we came up against the familiar refrain, "you wouldn't be interested in my life, I've done nothing". Part of openness lies in freeing up old skills or finding new ones. Making life story books with these women has highlighted ways in which past experience needs to be recreated and remembered if present conditions and circumstances are to be understood and needs met. Once begun, the process overwhelmed the self-doubts and inhibitions which these older women had accumulated within an institutional regime. What emerged was a compromise between privately owned knowledge and public life. The women we talked to clearly made selections, determined their own stories and created accounts which both accommodated with and challenged the presentation of themselves as hospital patients (Adams, Bornat & Prickett 1993).

Oral history opened up possibilities for self expression amongst this marginalised group of older women who thereby joined the community of historians: a truly open process.

Interrogative

Auto/biography is concerned with interrogation of the text. But oral history is wholly interrogation, a practice and method shaped by the rules, conventions and opportunities of question and answer. This means that what is produced is the result not simply of conversational exchange, but may also have a wider purpose, for both parties. The effect of interrogation may mean that what is an often told story comes out quite differently. There are as yet few examples of the difference which questioning makes to the same account. Paul Thompson includes an example from a comparison of memoirs written by Swedish working men and interviews with these same men (Thompson 1988, p. 244-5). My experience of comparing a tape, its transcription, and a written account of the same events, shows similar differences. Where the oral account is lively and responsive to the questioner the written account is pallid, literary conventions having ironed out the dialect and somehow rendered the whole piece less personal and unique (Bornat 1993a). Sandro Portelli observes:

> "The oral discourse 'runs through our fingers', so to speak, and must be 'solidified', 'frozen' if we are to hold it, however precariously. Writing, on the other hand, literally fills our hands with solid, already-frozen words. Nothing is lost, but nothing seems to be moving either". (Portelli 1991, p. 279)

The words 'interrogation' and 'questioning' have oppressive associations. Listening to tapes, the qualities of orality may help to temper such assumptions. Trevor Lummis criticises autobiography for its tendency to assume an audience (Lummis 1987, p. 83). I prefer to turn this argument on its head and to value aspects of performance within oral history. Narrators play out what are dramatic roles; they " 'take the floor' " and act as if the audience, the tape recorder is not there while they tell their stories, develop narratives or simply answer questions (Minister 1991, p. 28-9). As well as developing a presentation of self there are the qualities of voice, accent, emotion and emphasis which shade and colour the narratives. Though people may at first be embarrassed at hearing their voice on tape, they also see the print of a voice as a natural partner to the print of a face. Sandro Portelli takes this further, arguing that the taped voice has the power to become a gift to the future

> "The recorded voice ... becomes an ambiguous gateway between life and death. While an image – a dead relative's photograph ... evokes that person's

memory, the recorded voice evokes the presence ... The speaking person is both there and not there, both living and vanished". (Portelli 1993, p. 221)

In terms of the experience of being questioned it is clear that many interviewees find the process of voicing their thoughts in response to questions an enjoyable experience. Oral historians develop ways to build relationships which may be of short duration. They may want to talk about quite intimate aspects of people's lives, or they may find themselves talking to people who have not recently experienced anyone else taking an interest in their lives. This means cultivating a supportive manner without guaranteeing a lasting and deep relationship. More than likely the person being interviewed finds positive enjoyment in the experience and is able to take it for what it is. They may relish the opportunity to put themselves on the map of achievements, local or national. They may find that in talking to someone else they are able to connect their life into a meaningful whole for the first time. They may welcome the chance to express quite deep emotions with someone who has no personal expectations. While oral historians are ever mindful of the ethics of the life history interview, there are many examples from the oral history literature of the interviewee's positive involvement in the process of question-ing, and of deliberate management of an interview on the part of the interviewee (Bornat 1993a; 1993b).

A Political Instrumentality

The origins of oral history in Britain lie in that period of the late 1960s with those who, in the main, identified themselves with social and political change. It traces its roots back to areas of research and teaching which challenged the established order of things. This was the search for alternative explanations to the 'official' view of the past, the 'people's history' of GDH Cole, Raymond Postgate, the Webbs and others. It sees itself as connected to that part of sociology which immersed itself in the life of communities, and elicited accounts directly through testimony, witness and the detailed observation of everyday life. Challenges to authority in education came with student action, 'sit ins', 'free universities', moments when a new spirit seemed to be abroad on the campuses of some English universities (Thompson & Bornat 1994). That period of possibilities saw developments for learning outside con-ventional settings with the growth of the adult literacy movement in inner city areas and the deliberate production of texts drawn directly from life history for use by adults and published for local audiences (Centerprise 1977). As a conscious departure from documentary conventions in historical research, and by attempting to find new methodologies in the space created by discussions initiated by Glaser and Strauss (1967), oral history set out to define a territory for itself in an area overlapping with sociology.

Oral history developed under the influence of a modernist belief in the possibility of future change and with commitment to a particular type of change. To give it the label 'socialist' today is to pronounce an academic exclusion order, however its leading protagonists clearly identified themselves with socialist traditions of explanation and change and most probably still do. This has had definite implications for oral history as a self aware project and, in my opinion, accounts for its particular instrumental qualities.

Instrumentality has recently been levelled as a criticism of feminist methodology by a leading ethnographer. His accusation is that this may encourage 'dogmatism' since both oppression and emancipation have a plurality of meanings (Hammersley 1992, p. 199-203). His attack, as feminists point out, is couched in terms which distract attention away from inequalities in research methodologies. The goal of oral history, to achieve a "shared *authority*" (my emphasis), to

> "redefine and redistribute intellectual authority, so that this might be shared
> more broadly in historical research and communication" (Frisch 1990, p. xx)

is, I argue, one which allows for differences both in terms of present understandings and past experience.

What I have been describing may be a generational effect. Perhaps future oral historians will tread different paths. Certainly in other parts of the world, oral historians have other preoccupations beyond those which we in England have developed. Nevertheless, all are likely to be instrumental in their own way. In the Ukraine, as in other parts of the former Soviet Union, oral history is developing partly in response to a need to write a new history of the past, but also as a way of bringing retribution against that other past and those who profited from it (Perks 1993). In the Sahel, oral historians work with local communities, particularly with women, to record perceptions of a changing environment – climatic, social and cultural – with a view to incorporating such knowledge into development projects and to evaluating them (Cross & Barker 1991). In India, oral historians working with rural health workers are helping to develop successful interventions in leprosy prevention and treatment programmes (Kakar forthcoming).

Oral history's involvement with instrumentality comes from an awareness of the way in which telling life experience can easily lead to some form of personal or social transformation. To be able to put a stamp on the past, to recognise it and claim it is a way of authenticating an account and the person who gives that account. Oral historians working with disadvantaged groups and individuals talk of 'empowerment' and, though this is an elusive and overworked term it clearly has some measurable meaning in these contexts, and elsewhere. To have a notion of empowerment requires theories of power and its distribution. Oral historians, from their work, whether elitist or populist, clearly work with notions of power inequalities. Where recognition of class and race led the way initially, gender, age, sexuality and disability have followed. Oral historians work with a view to restore, empower, reclaim, give back and revalue. The terms used vary, but they tend all to relate to people making changes in their lives.

Oral history as a set of practices includes many examples of instrumentality. I feel that this commitment to change distinguishes it from auto/biography. Where auto/biography uses the text as its boundary, oral history, with its focus on outputs, goes beyond the text to make connections with present situations and to seek remedies or explanation. Its membership and audience is therefore broadly based in a wide range of settings, traditions and ways of working. To be effectively utilitarian and instrumental its language needs to be understandable and its terms of reference meaningful, both to those who take part in it as an activity and to those who are its audience. Its origins as a dialogue give rise to a commitment to a theorising which is within the understanding of those whose lives are the data. This is a quality which I do not find so far in auto/biography. Looking back at the definitions which I quoted at the start I find a language which risks the transformation of ordinary lives and the common sense understandings which surround them into an unrecognisable and estranging code.

Conclusions

In seeking out the similarities and differences between auto/biography and oral history I am aware that I have ranged loosely across ways in which both terms are used and understood. This is inevitable. Both enjoy an immense popularity currently and encompass an enormous and, at points, overlapping literature. I have pointed out the areas of shared activity. I feel that this is important since oral history can only learn and develop from an awareness of commonality and helpful comparison. However, I do feel that there are important differences in our approaches to understanding the past through memory and reflection. In part these differences relate to our own particular histories and I have spent some time outlining where I think oral history comes from in order to make this point. In part I feel that this is because of the traditions which each has drawn on and the language that is a part of these. Oral history has a background in history and in sociology whereas I see auto/biography coming from an association between sociology and literary theory. There is an openness in oral history which I see as essential to its mission and its method, an inclusiveness which means that both the exotic and the mundane are both eligible and sought after. The interrogative nature of oral history opens up possibilities to extend reflection and interaction within the interview and afterwards. Finally, the focus on a text, as distinct from the voice on tape and the way this may be negotiated into an output, means that auto/biography has a narrower goal and speaks to a smaller and less differentiated audience compared with oral history. In part I see a difference in the way the two approaches deal with interactions, there is a fundamentally social nature to oral history which means that it is forced to consider divisions, inequalities and policy at all stages of its enterprise.

Perhaps because we gave ourselves a strongly instrumental, empowering tradition oral historians have found it more difficult to put our own selves into accounts. The urge has been to make space for others to talk and reflect. Even though oral historians are now more sensitive to the various ways in which an awareness of self affects the accounts given, this awareness tends to be reserved almost exclusively for an analysis of the subject or at most the interactions of selves in the interview. The self of the interviewer is only just coming into focus and so far the selves we are learning about are exclusively women's. It is the analysis of self which auto/biography encourages that I feel provides a link between the two endeavours. I began by indicating the common ground between us – our shared interest in process, our awareness of the way reality may be manufactured in remembering, the connection with existential issues and the acceptance of a reflexive understanding of the self. It is by building links in this last area that I feel oral history has most to gain and auto/biography has most to communicate to us. As oral historians we can only benefit from a deeper focus on the self and the personal. More about where we have come from, how we account for this, how we work, how our work changes us, how we relate to interviews and what the outcomes are for our future selves, can only improve our skills and make oral history more accessible and understandable to the world at large.

References

Adams, John (1993) "A fair hearing: life review in a hospital setting" in Bornat, Joanna (ed.) *Reminiscence Reviewed: perspectives, evaluations, achievements,* Open University Press, Buckingham.

Adams, John, Bornat, Joanna, Prickett, Mary (1993) "Life history interviewing with frail older women: 'You wouldn't be interested in my life, I've done nothing'". Paper presented to British Society of Gerontology Annual Conference, Norwich 1993.

Atkinson, Dorothy. (1993) "'I got put away': group-based reminiscence with people with learning difficulties", in Bornat, Joanna (ed.) *Reminiscence Reviewed,* Open University Press, Buckingham.

Baum, Willa K. (1972) "Oral history in the United States", *Oral History* 1:3, pp. 15-29.

Bornat, Joanna (1992) "The communities of community publishing", *Oral History* 20:2, pp. 23-31.

Bornat, Joanna (1993a) "Presenting" in Shakespeare, Pam, Atkinson, Dorothy & French, Sally (eds) *Reflecting on Research Practice: issues in Health and Social Welfare,* Open University Press, Buckingham.

Bornat, Joanna (ed.) (1993b) *Reminiscence Reviewed: perspectives, evaluations, achievements,* Open University Press, Buckingham.

Centerprise (1977) *Local publishing and local culture: an account of the work of the Centerprise publishing project, 1972-77,* Centerprise, London.

Chamberlain, Mary (1975) *Fenwomen: a portrait of women in an English village,* Virago, London.

Cross, Nigel & Barker, Rhiannon (eds) (1991) *At the Desert's Edge: oral histories of the Sahel,* Panos, London.

Davidoff, Leonore & Westover, Belinda (eds) (1986) *Our work, our lives, our words: women's history and women's work,* Macmillan, Basingstoke.

Evans, George Ewart (1972) "Approaches to Interviewing", *Oral History* 1: 4, pp. 56-71.

Frisch, Michael (1990) *A shared authority: essays on the craft and meaning of oral and public history,* SUNY, Albany.

Glaser, Barney & Strauss, Anselm (1967) *The discovery of grounded theory: strategies for qualitative research,* Aldine de Gruyter, New York.

Gluck, Sherner Berger & Patai, Daphne (1991) *Women's words: the feminist practice of oral history,* Routledge, London.

Grele, Ronald (1985) *Envelopes of Sound: the art of oral history,* 2nd ed., Precedent, Chicago.

Hammersley, Martin (1992) "On feminist methodology", *Sociology* 26: 2, pp. 187-206.

Humphries, Steve & Gordon, Pamela (1992) *Out of sight: the experience of disability 1900-1950,* Northcote House, Plymouth.

Kakar, Shanjiv (forthcoming *Oral History)* "Leprosy in India: the intervention of oral history".

Liddington, Jill & Norris, Jill (1978) *One hand tied behind us: the rise of the women's suffrage movement,* Virago, London.

Lummis, Trevor (1987) *Listening to history: the authenticity of oral evidence,* Hutchinson, London.

McCrindle, Jean & Rowbotham, Sheila (eds) (1975) *Dutiful Daughters: women talk about their lives,* Penguin, London.

Minister, Kristina (1991) "A feminist frame for the oral history interview" in Gluck, Sherner Berger & Patai, Daphne (eds) *Women's words: the feminist practice of oral history,* Routledge, London.

Passerini, Luisa (1989) "Women's Personal Narratives: Myths, Experiences and Emotions", in Personal Narratives Group (eds) *Interpreting Women's Lives: feminist theory and personal narratives,* Indiana University Press, Indiana.

Perks, Rob (1993) "Ukraine's forbidden history: memory and nationalism", *Oral History* 21:1, pp. 43-53.

Portelli, Alessandro (1988) "Uchronic dreams: working class memory and possible worlds" *Oral History* 16:2, pp. 46–56.

Portelli, Alessandro (1991) *The death of Luigi Trastulli: memory and other stories: form and meaning in oral history,* SUNY Press, New York.

Portelli, Alessandro (1993) "We're all on tape: voice recording and the electronic afterlife" in Bertaux, Daniel & Thompson, Paul (eds), *Between the Generations: Family models, myths and memories,* International Yearbook of Oral History and Life Stories, Volume II, Oxford University Press, Oxford.

Potts, Maggie & Fido, Rebecca (1991) *'A fit person to be removed': personal accounts of life in a Mental Deficiency Institution,* Northcote House, Plymouth.

Roberts, Elizabeth (1984) *A Woman's Place: an oral history of working-class women 1890–1940,* Blackwell, London.

Stanley, Liz (1994) "Sisters under the skin? Oral histories and auto/biographies", *Oral History* 22:2, pp. 88-89.

Stuart, Mary (1993) " 'And how was it for you Mary?' self, identity and meaning for oral historians", *Oral History* 21:2, pp. 80-83.

Thompson, Paul (1988) *The Voice of the Past,* 2nd edition, Oxford University Press, Oxford.

Thompson, Thea (1981) *Edwardian Childhoods,* Routledge & Kegan Paul, London.

Thompson, Paul & Bornat, Joanna (1994) "Myths and memories of an English rising: 1968 at Essex", *Oral History* 22:2, pp. 44-54.

Wilson, Amrit (1978) *Finding a Voice: Asian Women in Britain,* Virago, London.

Woodin, Tony (1992) "Recent British Community Histories", *Oral History* 20:2, pp. 76-70.

Zukas, Miriam (1993) "Friendship as oral history: a feminist psychologist's view", *Oral History* 21:2, pp. 73-79.

Section Five
Documents and The Field

34

Evidence and Proof in Documentary Research: 1. Some Specific Problems of Documentary Research

Jennifer Platt

'Documentary research' is not a clearcut and well-recognized category, like survey research or participant observation, in sociological method. It can hardly be regarded as constituting a method, since to say that one will use documents is to say nothing about *how* one will use them. It is possible, however, that the mere fact of using documents as a data source does pose distinctive problems; the extent to which this is so is one of the themes of this paper.

Discussions of the use of documents in the standard methodological literature are sparse and patchy. In 18 general textbooks on research methods[1] only 7 devote a significant amount of space to anything to do with the use of documents, and these often either conflate it with other points (e.g. under the general heading of 'unobtrusive measures' or 'available data') or concentrate on only one type of use. Where there are discussions, they tend to be about what types of document exist and what problems they bear on rather than about how to use them;[2] the tacit assumption is made that later chapters, with titles such as 'Analysis of Data' or 'Tests of Hypotheses', deal with that, although their contents usually imply survey-type quantitative data that would only be likely to be approximated by content analysis from the main types of documentary research. In the sociological literature there are also very few more specialized monographic discussions of problems of documentary research; indeed I have been unable to identify any since the classic but, I suspect, now largely unread work of the late thirties and forties on 'personal documents'[3] apart from the literature of content analysis[4] and

Source: *Sociological Review*, 1981, vol. 29, 1, pp. 31-52.

discussions of official or unofficial statistics and archives.[5] Valuable though such discussions are, they are far from covering all the problems and it seems highly desirable that, at a time of increasing scepticism about the methods with which the textbooks have been traditionally more centrally concerned, some more systematic work should be done in this area.[6] There is some danger that, as part of the reaction against survey methods, any careful concern with method and the justification of conclusions will be abandoned. Insofar as that happens, different research traditions are likely to become closed subcultures with no basis of communication with each other, and even the possible invocation of the concept of paradigm[7] would not make that a happy outcome. The participant-observation/fieldwork tradition has now produced some very valuable systematic accounts of method[8] to set beside those on survey method, and there is no reason why the same should not be done for other areas.

General knowledge suggests that there are some quite different but fairly clear intellectual traditions within sociology associated with reliance on documentary sources: (i) quantitative content analysis, (ii) historical study, (iii) sociology of literature, (iv) linguistic/ethnomethodological, (v) 'personal documents'. There are also more peripheral uses of documents in research that fit into none of these traditions. This discussion will attempt to concentrate on those aspects of the use of documents which are not specific to any one type of use or tradition; to do otherwise would be in effect either to exclude some major actual uses of documents or to create an ideal type of 'documentary research' which included features not logically linked to the use of documents *per se*. My personal interest in this topic arises from the accidental coming together of several different research topics and experiences, each raising questions intrinsically difficult to answer or not covered by the usual books on method. The main such experience has been work on the history of the antique trade and antique collecting, which entails some conventional historical research, as well as opening up the possibility of some systematic study of the large number of books that have been written about antiques; it also, given the connections of the topic with many aspects of social, economic and artistic history, gives rise to some acute problems in the use of secondary sources. Also relevant have been the problems of analysis in a study based on intensive unstructured interviewing[9] where the interview protocols become documents, and another study using journal articles and textbooks as its basic data. Examples from these research areas will be drawn on to illustrate points, although issues will be discussed in a more general way.

Although the distinction is somewhat arbitrary, for convenience of presentation this first paper will concentrate on those aspects of documentary research which are most directly related to the specific characteristics of documents, while the second will deal with those more obviously shared with other types of research. The precise definition of 'document' is not very important, but for the purposes of this discussion it is taken to include at least some of the representational features of pictures without words. (In principle some of the discussion is equally applicable to other kinds of artifacts, and archaeologists have considered some of the issues.) The specific characteristics of documents which raise the greatest problems are that the available stock normally exists already and cannot be created to order, and that contextual information needed to establish their meaning is often missing. For the purposes of this discussion, which concentrates on questions of evidence and proof, the issues arising are defined as being: (i) how to establish the authenticity of a document; (ii) whether the relevant documents are available; (iii) problems of sampling; (iv) how to establish the extent to which a document can be taken to tell the truth about what it describes; (v) how to decide what inferences can be made from a document about matters other than the truth of its factual assertions. Not all of these, of course, necessarily arise or constitute problems in relation to any given research topic or style.

Establishing Authenticity

There are many instances where a document is not an authentic member of the class to which it purports or appears to belong: wills, other legal documents and letters are forged or falsified, literary works are attributed to authors who did not write them, jokes and satires may inadvertently be taken at face value. An inauthentic document may still be of much interest, but it cannot be fully and correctly understood unless one knows that it is not authentic. Procedures are, therefore, needed for establishing authenticity. Criteria are also, in principle, needed for deciding when it's worth applying such procedures; in practice the normal criterion is only to look closely when there is felt to be some reason for suspicion in a particular case, or when inauthentic examples of the class are known to be common. Guidelines would still be desirable to indicate when there should be felt to be reason for suspicion; the simplest case is that where the sociologist does not need to decide because authenticity is already disputed among those studied, as in many legal cases.[10] I have not come across any systematic list of other suspicious circumstances, but among those referred to in passing are the following, almost all of which are equally relevant where the question is not whether the document as a whole is authentic but whether the version one has of it is correct or has errors arising from copying, reproduction[11] or other modes of transmission: (i) the document as it stands does not appear to make sense, or has obvious errors in it; (ii) different versions of the same original document are current; (iii) the document contains internal inconsistencies of literary style, content, typeface or handwriting, etc; (iv) the document is known to have been transmitted via many copyists; (v) the document is known to have been transmitted via someone with an intellectual or material interest in the version given passing as the correct one; (vi) the version available is derived from a secondary source suspected on other grounds of being unreliable; (vii) the style or content are in some way inconsistent with that of other instances of the same class – e.g. it contains anachronisms; (viii) it fits too neatly into a standard formula or literary form. It will be noted that most of these criteria can only be applied if one already has some other relevant knowledge of the class of document and/or its social context, and that this 'knowledge' in turn may be grounded on documentary sources which are in principle equally open to question.

Once the question of authenticity has been raised, an attempt must be made to answer it. This may be done either by an analysis of the document itself or by exploring other circumstances associated with it. Historians (and lawyers) have developed elaborate methods of detection[12] involving such matters as the types of paper and styles of handwriting typical of periods or individuals, the characteristic kinds of error made in careless copying of different kinds, and so on; art historians lay tremendous emphasis on known provenance of works of art as a guide to their authenticity – although provenances have in their turn been falsified. Sociologists seldom in practice seem to be faced with the problems to which these techniques can provide solutions, since they do not often work with primary sources which are handwritten or drawn and/or regarded as individually important by people in a position to tamper with them without immediate detection.

Availability of Documents

The next issue is that of the availability of suitable documents. Unless the documents used are generated by the sociologist, which is inappropriate or impossible in many fields, he must use what he can get. Some documents one might like to have will never have existed, others have been lost or destroyed, and others still exist but one cannot get access to them. The equivalent of the last case could arise with any type of data, so will not be considered here. The loss and destruction of documents gives rise to two kinds of difficulty: an inadequate quantity of data, and, where there is reason to believe that there are differential loss rates, a qualitatively unsatisfactory distribution of data. Where there are simply not enough data, one is tempted to over-interpret what is available, and to treat it as representative of the larger class that originally existed without any knowledge that it really is so. Without knowledge of other members of the class one cannot know what the conventions of the genre are, or indeed whether there is a defined genre and if so where its boundaries lie. A single reference to a phenomenon may indicate the start of a trend, or the existence of a pattern, but may be just historically idiosyncratic. Where there have been differential loss rates this makes what survives less representative, although the knowledge that it is so gives a firmer basis for interpreting what does survive. Often, however, one does not know whether the loss rate was differential or not; one may have reason to believe that it was, but this 'reason' may be to some extent speculative rather than grounded in specific data. For instance, it seems plausible that those few cases where the accounts of early antique dealers have survived to the present day should be unrepresentative of the whole body of dealers existing at the time, partly simply because so few have survived, and partly because one reason for survival of accounts is the survival of the business where others have not survived. Unless, however, one has other sets of accounts, or other sources of data on the typicality of the business, one cannot be sure. Even if one approaches the matter conservatively, and treats the accounts as those of an unusually solid and successful business, this does not tell one how a successful business at that time differed from an unsuccessful one – although it may refute some hypotheses about the necessary conditions for success. There are some cases where the surviving documents may be regarded, not as typical of the original population, but as more significant, because their survival indicates that they were more popular or more highly valued. Unsuccessful books printed in small editions are less likely to be found now than very popular ones. This is a great consolation to the frequenter of secondhand bookshops, but one of limited value, since it does not help if one is interested in what was originally produced rather than what became successful, or in ephemera on cheap paper as much as calfbound editions with prestigious illustrations.

The case of the documents that never did exist raises problems analogous to those of perspective in fieldwork. Very often only one set of parties to a relationship produces documents that bear on it, and such documents are obviously likely to be misleading about the total of what went on. One is tempted to make inferences on the basis of intuition, general knowledge, or theory about what the content of the 'missing' documents would have been, but this is clearly dangerous. It may also happen that those who write are, rather than representative of one set of parties to a relationship where the other side is unrepresented, simply an unrepresentative sub-set of the larger group. One might argue that sufficient senior politicians write their memoirs for these memoirs to be regarded as representative of senior politicians more generally, especially in view of the tendency for opponents each to try to justify their actions. But there seems every reason to believe that those antique dealers who write their memoirs are in that respect atypical of antique dealers more generally. What general meaning, then, can one attach to what they say? One can certainly go beyond just treating them as idiosyncratic. If most of the authors describe their background as middle class and explain how they were drawn to the trade by their interest in collecting beautiful things, it would be rash indeed to assume that this was the typical pattern, in particular because it seems likely that such characteristics would make dealers more prone to write books. But given that one knows that, say, size of business, character of town and clientele, period of specialization and type of goods dealt in are significant distinctions, one can check the distribution of the businesses reported on with respect to these variables; if one finds a wide variety, and/or if the same points are reported irrespective of such variations, one has greater confidence that what is described can be taken as representative.

However, there are certain types of anecdote that recur again and again; one cannot infer from this that such situations occurred in life more frequently than others which do not make such good anecdotes, although the fact that anecdotes of that type appear in many books may suggest that they describe common experiences of dealers. Another possible line of argument is that if most of the books express views that run counter to the norms of the wider community, or cover matters sufficiently technical for the wider community to have no norms on them, then they must be regarded as at least to some extent typical of antique dealers as opposed to the general population – though how typical is unclear. Again, if the books – as they do – take opposed stands on a controversial and professionally important matter such as auction rings, this evidently demonstrates that they are not reporting only one side of an argument, though it tells one nothing about the prevalence of the different viewpoints or the possible existence of yet other ones. If, however, among those who approve of rings a rather uniform set of justifications for them appears, this could demonstrate not so much a shared subculture as a shared understanding about what is likely to seem persuasive to the readers of such books; perhaps it makes the imputation of a subculture more plausible if the norms stated in overt argument are also demonstrated in action in anecdotes whose central point is a different one.

Convincing as these suggestions of criteria may seem, it must again be noted that they rest on commonsense assumptions on such matters as who writes books and how, and at best allow for greater confidence rather than secure inference.

Sampling Problems

These considerations are very much related to questions of sampling; indeed, they may be regarded as indicating where the problem is one of defining the sample one has got rather than of choosing what sample to select. But sometimes in documentary research there are large numbers of potentially relevant documents, and the possibility of sampling in the usual sense arises. An initial difficulty, when one cannot create more data (by further observation, conducting interviews, etc.) is that there will be no fresh data on which one's hypotheses can be tested; this suggests that, if one wishes to employ a hypothesis-testing model of the research process, one must be careful not to use all the data up in exploratory stages, and this might suggest some sampling procedure; but useful samples can only be taken if one knows something about the population and has a sampling frame. But unless other researchers have been there first one may well not know enough about the population, or have anything that could serve as a sampling frame.

G. R. Elton suggests that, where no lists exist, the historian should deal with the problem of abundance by 'controlled selection, that is to say by choosing on principles which have nothing to do with the real question asked or the ultimate product ... the first selection ... should arise from a total survey of the material and be systematic with reference to it, not to the historian's purpose'.[13] This suggestion is intended to prevent the bias that might arise from selecting only those documents that bore on, or even supported, a particular preconceived hypothesis; obviously it implies a preference for research where the questions asked arise from the data rather than from prior theoretical interests, and assumes that the historian has already decided enough about what he is substantively to study to select a particular archive on which to start. I take it that the arguments about the impossibility or undesirability of the approach are too familiar to need rehearsing here. In this case, as in others, a very strong emphasis on faithfulness to the specificity of the data entails a theoretically arbitrary delimitation of which data shall actually be collected, at least initially.[14] Contemporary social groups and organizations often have convenient physical boundaries, and it is noticable that fieldworkers normally choose such settings; the archive probably represents the nearest documentary equivalent. Since data are not always conveniently arranged into archives, even to accept Elton's principle would often leave one with little guidance.

Whether or not one follows a hypothesis-testing model, the problem of creating a sampling frame may still arise. For some categories of documents, comprehensive listings do exist, whether, like catalogues of Roman inscriptions or some bibliographies, they have been devised for research purposes or, like catalogues of books in print or lists of wills, they have not. Whatever the purpose for which they have been devised, it is highly probable that the categories of documents have been defined more narrowly or broadly than is suitable for a new researcher's purposes, or that the principles of classification crosscut those which he would wish to use. For instance, in relation to my research on antiques I was delighted to find a comprehensive bibliography on glass.[15] I became somewhat less delighted when it turned out to include every aspect of the technology of glass manufacture, and works on industrial and commercial uses of glass, as well as those aspects which interested me.

One may thus be driven, as I have been, to attempt to compile one's own comprehensive listing of documents in the relevant field; this is an enormously laborious task. Titles or descriptions can be misleading, so only if one inspects each document can one be quite sure that it is of the type one is interested in; *The China Hunters' Club,* by 'The Youngest Member'[16] turns out to be an amusing fiction rather than the true history of an early collectors' club. Many sources of information are careless, or follow unfamiliar conventions, which can lead to misunderstandings; I have often found that what appeared to be two separate books on antiques was actually the same book listed in different ways in different sources. The subject catalogue of the National Art Library at the Victoria and Albert Museum is splendidly comprehensive, indeed excessively so for some purposes; every entry in some parts of it has to be checked against the author catalogue to find whether it refers to a book or only to a brief article. Workers on other topics will certainly be able to add to these examples. A related problem is how to know when to stop; how many defunct journals' review sections, secondhand book catalogues or publishers' advertisements in the backs of old books must one read before being entitled to conclude that a further search is not likely to turn up anything new? After spending some weeks on this sort of work, one may wonder whether one's research time could not be better spent in other ways.

The question of when to stop is not a purely rhetorical one. The answer to it is easier if the research is mainly concerned with documents that have been influential, for these, by definition, will have left traces behind them; the search does not need to be extended beyond a reasonable cross-section of the documents in principle likely to have been influenced. (Note, however, the assumption here that the relevant influence is one that is primarily shown in documents; even when one is studying the intellectual history of an academic discipline, there may be reason to believe that there are components of the oral subculture not adequately represented in what is published.)[17] If, however, the research really is concerned with the whole range of documents which originally existed (highly desirable if Whig versions of history[18] are to be avoided) the answer to the question of when to stop must be something more like 'when all potential types of source have been thoroughly sampled and several further instances of each type do not bring anything new to light'. (This assumes good knowledge of available types of source, which is easier to come by in fields already worked over by others.) Pragmatic and/or principled judgments may also be made, when time or other resources are limited, about how far the likely return justifies further input on this rather than other aspects of the research. But can such tasks of enumeration be avoided? In practice one may suspect that they frequently are; in principle it is hard to see any alternative if one wishes in the end to make well-founded statements about, say, the number and character of books on antiques published at various times, or changes in the types of distinction among research methods made by sociologists, let alone to draw samples for more detailed study which can claim to be representative.

A quite different problem which arises in the sampling of documents is that of whether they are independent of each other. I was pleased to find two books by the same authors on much the same topic 35 years apart, thinking that this would give a good indication of changes over the period: on reading the second, however, I found that a considerable number of the chapters were identical![19] A commoner problem is that of plagiarism of the works of others. Antiques have come to be studied in an increasingly scholarly way, and there are many complex details involved in questions of attribution, identification and dating; there is also much popular interest of an unscholarly kind. In consequence there are many popularizing books which draw on the scholarly work, more or less competently. The line between plagiarism and popularization is hard to draw, depending to a considerable extent on the degree of acknowledgment given to the work of other authors; certainly the scholarly writers have sometimes seen the popular work as both plagiaristic and incompetent.[20] Where there is plagiarism, or for that matter acknowledged copying, the work may still be treated as an independent case for some purposes, but not for others. Whether or not there is any element of plagiarism, similar issues may arise where there are clearly-defined genres;

the writing of a 14-line poem with a certain kind of rhyme-scheme cannot be treated as a personal fact about the poet in the same way as the writing of a poem of non-standardized form can. (For further discussion of the question of genre, see the second part of this paper.)

Does it Tell the Truth?

The documentary researcher is often using the document as a source of information on that to which it refers – in effect as a surrogate researcher; it is vital, then, to know how far its account can be relied upon. This is a matter of how the document is used rather than of what it is in itself: a legal document may be studied as an example of legal forms, or as an account of a particular contract; a picture may be looked at as a work of art in its own right, or studied for the light it throws on costume and furniture when it was painted;[21] a work by another social scientist may be treated as a datum relevant to conventions on how to present social-scientific data, or as a source of data on the matters about which it writes. When a document is being used in the second way, the user must consider how far it can be taken to tell the truth about what it describes. What criteria can we apply to help us make such judgments?

Probably one of the first writers to deal with this subject systematically was John Craig. He starts from some simple assumptions: that 'All men have an equal right to be believed, unless the contrary has been established from elsewhere',[22] so 'great probability is composed of many testimonies of primary witnesses'; the probability of a report is decreased in proportion to the distance in time or place of the event and the number of people through whom it has been transmitted. By adding a few numerical assumptions he is enabled to conclude, by Newtonian method, that 'the present probability of the story of Christ is as great as that which a man (in the times of Christ himself) would have had who received the history by only word of mouth from '8 disciples of Christ'.[23] Q.E.D. This is an attractive approach, though unfortunately it has some serious difficulties both in the particular empirical assumptions that it makes and in its failure to consider the possibility that one may not know through how many people a story has been transmitted.

Craig's emphasis on the importance of direct witnesses, and the attempt to evaluate the degree of proximity of a report to them, have also been taken up by other, later writers. Naroll suggests a ranking of types of secondary source by degree of proximity, in this order: datum report, participant report, observer's report, derivative report, scholar's report, (citing primary sources), reader's report (not citing specific passages from primary sources).[24] He also suggests six factors relevant for data quality control where the data are reports on practices in alien societies: (i) collection of specific case reports, (ii) use of direct observation and participation, (iii) length of stay in the society, (iv) reporter's familiarity with the language, (v) the reporter's role in the society, (vi) the explicitness and generality of the report on the matter of interest

(p. 14). These factors are all concerned with either how full and detailed the information was to which the reporter had access, or with how much care and detail he reported on it. The list was compiled in the attempt to answer the problem of which author to believe when there were conflicting reports on the same society, but it could to some extent be used to judge how far to accept a single report. He suggests yet another list of possible criteria in relation to historical data: (i) the time lapse between the event and the report, (ii) the extent to which the author had a professional stake in the report, (iii) the extent of agreement between authors with opposing views, (iv) the proximity of the author to the event recorded, (v) the intensity of involvement of the author with the event, (vi) the degree of relevant technical experience of the author and (vii) the degree of explicitness of the report. It will be noted that this list for the first time raises the possibility of reporting distorted by personal interests rather than just by lack of full information about what happened, and so introduces a whole range of other questions.

These questions are addressed directly by Langlois & Seignobos, who list a variety of possible sources of distortion which might affect one's general or particular confidence in an author. Among those that add something to those quoted above are these: (i) that the author was seeking some practical advantage to himself; (ii) that he was in a situation where he was compelled to violate the truth, as when, for example, drawing up a formal document about a situation where practice was inconsistent with rule or custom; (iii) his vanity led to exaltation of himself or his group; (iv) he wanted to please his public, or to avoid shocking it; (v) he tried to please by literary artifice, introducing misleading elements of the picturesque, noble or dramatic; (vi) although in a position to observe the events reported, he was led by illusion or prejudice to observe incorrectly; (vii) he was badly situated for correct observation; (viii) he could observe, but did not record his observations immediately in a full and unambiguous system of notation; (ix) he did not actually observe the events, but gives an officially-correct or customary version of them; (x) the facts reported are such that they could not have been learnt by observation alone, because they were normally secret or private, or are generalizations about large numbers of people over long periods of time![25] As the authors point out, these apply where the statements are, or purport to be, based on firsthand observation; where they are secondhand, they should in principle be applied to the first observer as well.

It is evident that all these possible sources of distortion may indeed have led to biased reports. As one modern sociological textbook remarks, 'With answers to these questions, the investigator will usually be able to eliminate records that are in doubt and accept the rest as credible evidence'![26] None of the textbooks, however, provide much explicit guidance on *how* one is to get answers to such questions, which is the practical problem with which the documentary researcher is faced. Nor do they raise any questions about the existence of a simple, factual truth in relation to which accounts can be judged as biased, or tell the investigator what to do if all the available documents appear to be biased in one way or another. (Except that the implication of the quotation from Nachmias & Nachmias is that what he should do is give up; this may be true, but is not helpful.)

Some of the questions seem rather easier to answer than others, at least when the circumstances are favourable. If the author has made his own position and methods of data collection clear, one may judge their implications; if he has not, another contemporary source may provide the same sort of information about the author in person, or about general practice at the time. However, it is not always clear what one should do with such information; someone who was not in a very good position to see may nonetheless happen to have seen the key events correctly, and even a royalist author of literary bent may be reporting nothing but the truth, as even a cynical republican would recognize it, when he describes the chivalrous behaviour of the king. Besides, there is an obvious danger of circularity, inferring royalism from the favourable picture given of the king and then using the inference to devalue the account. Where more than one account of the same events is available, the matter becomes different: one may legitimately infer that the differences are attributable to difference of viewpoint, physical or intellectual, and attempt to construct from the sources a superior composite account. But such a composite account is not necessarily superior; one source may simply be accurate and the other not.[27] If, other things being equal, one source had better access than the other, a superior recording technique, or less personal involvement, one presumably accepts, or at any rate prefers, its account and rejects the other. But the circumstances are not always favourable; authors frequently do not describe their situation and methods, and other accounts of the same events are frequently not available.

If there is only one source, one may attempt to make adjustments for its biases, assuming that the king was probably not quite so consistently chivalrous, the speech not exactly in the words of the supposedly verbatim account, the role played by the author's group not quite so essential or conspicuous; this is inevitably a speculative and uncertain activity. It also takes for granted some commonsense theories about the processes involved. In principle these theories might themselves be tested, so that the typical errors of reporting could be identified as precisely as the typical errors made in copying from different types of handwriting have been. I do not know of work specifically directed to this aim, except perhaps some by psychologists on perception and memory; Bartlett's classic work is highly suggestive.[28] But it seems very likely that the typical specific errors made by different groups at various times and places are not the same, so modern research which provides the only way in which a privileged set of observations could be constructed with which to compare reports, might not be much help in relation to historical documents.

An alternative or supplementary approach to the single source is to consider the likelihood of distortion in relation to the subject matter. Langlois & Seignobos[29] suggest that there are some sorts of fact about which it is difficult to lie or to be mistaken, because they are such that they are very easy to observe (e.g. the existence of a city) or were widely known at the time among the audience to which the writing was directed. They also point out that one's confidence can reasonably be greater when the author was not particularly interested in a specific fact and mentions it only incidentally,[30] or when it runs counter to his expectations and habits of mind or the general impression he wished to produce. Once again the points are convincing, but they both assume the absence of subtle forms of bad faith which have anticipated the application of such criteria, and involve commonsense theories and the danger of circularity.

I do not wish to discuss here the senses in which there may be taken to be a simple, factual truth of which various reports give more or less satisfactory accounts. The absence of epistemological discussion from the writings of historians on these matters is indeed refreshing, if at times somewhat startling; how important such absence is depends on the nature of the accounts and of the information that is wanted from them. To treat all accounts as merely 'accounts' solves some problems but, like operationalism in relation to problems of validity, does so at the cost of ignoring the reason for being interested in the matter in the first place.

But if, on whatever grounds, all the available documents appear to some extent biased, what is one to do about it? It is not feasible, except possibly in very unusual circumstances, simply to subtract the erroneous parts and to proceed securely on the basis of the remainder, both because of the likelihood that there would be no remainder, and because even if probable error can be identified it is not always thereby evident what would be correct. It has been suggested in the literature that there are some occasions when independent but separately dubious sources can give mutual support[31] either by conveying the same general impression or by providing different factual items that fit together into a coherent picture of one event, and this is a valuable suggestion, despite the elements of judgment implied by the concepts of sameness and coherence. Beyond that, one is thrown back by some writers on such criteria as 'historical imagination'[32] or that 'answers must be probable; they must agree with what is known to be possible in human experience'[33] this means, in effect, the application of commonsense theories.

Todd has a much more satisfactory and more explicit approach, which he works out by examining instances of the way historians reason in practice. He quotes an example from Bullock's work, where he decides to believe a document from one participant in an episode rather than another: '... there are basically two Papens that fit the evidence, and ... they are such that we can understand either one ... (but) if we suppose that Schroder was lying and Papen was telling the truth we cannot see how to put ourselves in Schroder's shoes at all, at least without inventing circumstances for which there is no evidence. But on the hypothesis that Schroder was telling the truth and Papen lying we can imaginatively re-enact both their roles. Hence the latter hypothesis is to be preferred.'[34] This approach can be highly convincing in a context of rich data, where there is other evidence besides that of conflicting documents to help one interpret them and where there are many details which an interpretative hypothesis must fit and which therefore might refute it; where data were thin, it could be dangerously speculative. Even where there are not two documents with conflicting accounts of the same event, but one document and some contextual information, the same strategy may be used (and probably often is) to make judgments about the extent to which it can be trusted. As Todd points out, an alternative approach is to apply supposed psychological laws, e.g. 'Witnesses never distort the truth in a way unfavourable to themselves'. Even if true in general, such laws ought only to be applied if the hypothesis that they exist has been directly investigated, but it would scarcely be possible for the researcher on a particular topic to do such research himself as it turned out to be relevant. However, it might be more convincing, as well as more feasible, if it could be shown that there were customs and intellectual styles of this sort specific to the milieu producing the documents of interest.

What Inferences Can Be Made?

These considerations also bear on the next aspect of our topic: the making of inferences from documents about matters which they do not directly describe. The most minimal inference occurs when the existence of conventions about the form which documents of a certain kind should take is inferred from the presence of certain kinds of similarity among them. It is of the utmost importance for interpretation that such inferences be made, though in the absence of supporting information (e.g. textbooks which give instruction on the writing of correct sonnets, journal articles or legal contracts) it is not obvious how to distinguish between the effects of a convention and of the same causes independently producing the same effects. (A study was done in which respondents were asked to write convincing suicide notes, and the results were then compared with genuine suicide notes and found to have significant differences from them.[35] Such data suggest, on the assumption that the sample of respondents had equal access to the conventions on how to write suicide notes, that what the authentic notes had in common was not conventional. Data of this type are desirable, though seldom likely to be available.) Becker has argued, to me convincingly, that the conventions about how to write journal articles ensure that they are unrepresentative of all the sociology that is done[36] and other writers have made similar points.[37] It is curious, in the light of this, that in the large number of citation studies it is almost invariably assumed that frequency of citations can be taken as an indication of the influence or prestige of the work cited, and the possible influence of convention is not considered.

This inference is characteristic of the inferences that may be made from the content of documents to the beliefs, motives etc. of those producing them; the connecting link is a theory about the reasons why such beliefs etc. should be expected to produce documents with such content. The inference can be justified to the extent that the theory is known to be correct. My comment above about citation studies has two implications: (i) that independent evidence is needed to support such a theory, and to get such evidence one would need to investigate the theory itself, and (ii) the inference depending on such a theory is weakened further to the extent that there is an alternative theory which could also account for the form the document takes. It follows from this latter, however, that if no such alternative theory can be found the inference has some plausibility even in the absence of independent support for the theory.[38] Such inferences have been made both to the characteristics of groups and to those of authors as individuals. Whether such inferences seem plausible will depend not only on the support available for connecting theories, but also on sampling considerations: if only a few of Shakespeare's plays survived, one might draw conclusions from their characteristic imagery about his personality; given that many survive, and show different patterns of imagery, one is more likely to draw conclusions about his art.[39] Letters, diaries and autobiographies may give a graphic picture of the characters and attitudes of some individuals; whether they can be taken as representative of their class or time is another matter. (It could well be argued that when one is most tempted to make such an assumption, because of the absence of other data, it is most likely that those who have produced such documents are thereby unrepresentative. This too is, of course, a connecting theory, whose merits can be investigated.)

On other occasions the desired inference is not to the beliefs etc. of the author but to the real state of affairs lying behind the production of the document. There are numbers of examples of analyses of propaganda[40] where, for instance, the real state of German/Italian relations or of successes in battle on a particular front, is inferred from statements not overtly about these facts or even, perhaps, suggesting the opposite. Here what seems to be happening is that it is the motives of the authors that are taken as given, and the inference made is about the documentary content that such motives would lead to in varying objective situations. The inference might be grounded on previous data about what was said in various situations on which independent data are available, or might be speculative/commonsensical; whichever it is, the connecting theory is again necessary.

Another kind of inference commonly attempted is that from the document to the characteristics of its audience. What the document directly shows, more or less implicitly, is its author's *assumptions* about his audience – a point which one needs to bear in mind when interpreting it as evidence of his personal concerns; these must have some weight, since he is likely to have been more familiar with them than the researcher is. However, to address oneself to an audience is not the same as to be identified with it, although one may feel that in a field such as that of antique collecting, where the boundary between amateur and professional is vague and often crossed, or writing sociology, where writers and audience are to a large extent the same group, writers can more easily be assumed to be representative of their audience. Different kinds of work show varying degrees of consciousness of their audience – some seek popularity, others aim to manipulate, or are pure self-expression, and so on.

Once again evidence is needed to identify what is going on. Relevant types of evidence are either independent documentation (sales figures, reviews, comments by contemporaries on reception, audience surveys) or confirmations of the connecting theories needed to support inferences from content to audience.

Conclusion

A brief review of the main topics covered in this paper will consider how far each reveals problems distinctive of documentary research. Authenticity, in the sense where the alternative is forgery or mistaken authorship, can only apply to documents; as soon, however, as the sense is slightly broadened to cover other forms of incorrect identification or deliberate misrepresentation or use of false fronts the essential problems are clearly the same as when the data are observations or reports of other kinds.[41] The questions of existence and availability of desired documents have much in common with practical issues of access, perspective and social visibility in observational research. The status of different types of account and their recurring patterns, and how to evaluate it, is a quite general problem; the documentary researcher merely does not have the opportunity of the fieldworker to generate fresh data of the same or other kinds to get behind the original accounts,[42] unless those who produced the documents are still alive. The problems of lack of choice in sampling, and the need to construct one's own sampling frame, arise in many other types of research (even if they are not always confronted); documents have less propensity to move house or fail to co-operate than people, so may make the task easier. Methods of search for individuals in an unknown population of documents, and of deciding when to stop searching, seem closely analogous to issues raised by 'snowball' samples for interviewing. The making of inferences from documents is in essence much like the making of inferences from other forms of behaviour, with the practical limitation again that there is likely to be less possibility of laying hands on supplementary information desirable to assist inference.

We conclude, therefore, that there are important senses in which documentary research has problems which are not significantly different from those of research using other data sources. A more general moral might be suggested, which is that the distinctions commonly made among 'methods' of research in terms of their data sources may be analytically unhelpful. (It is hoped to pursue this point further elsewhere.) Nonetheless, each data source gives rise to its own special technical problems. If adequate 'connecting theories' are to be developed, the form which they will take must be one of specifying, firstly, general propositions about how people behave ('other things being equal, people act in ways they construe as being to the advantage of their families'); given such propositions, their application to the particular type of data to be used must be developed ('in societies where suicide is seen as shameful, the suicides of those with surviving close relatives will be under-reported'); ideally, they would then be elaborated into precise technical recipes for dealing with the immediate data ('in society x, the actual suicide rate should be estimated as y% higher than that given in the official statistics'). Such propositions are empirical ones exactly like those in sociology generally; method and methodology cannot be separated from substantive concerns – and it follows that substantive research is needed for them to progress.

Notes

The support of a Leverhulme Foundation Research Fellowship during the period when much of the work for this paper was done is gratefully acknowledged.

1. Those which do treat the subject are N. K. Denzin: *The Research Act in Sociology,* Butterworth, London, 1970. Peter H. Mann: *Methods of Sociological Enquiry,* Blackwell, Oxford, 1968. D. & C. Nachmias: *Research Methods in the Social Sciences,* St. Martin's Press, N.Y., 1976. Bernard S. Phillips: *Social Research: Strategy and Tactics,* Macmillan, N.Y., 1976 (3rd edition). Matilda White Riley: *Sociological Research: a Case Approach,* Harcourt, Brace and World, N. Y., 1963. Claire Selltiz *et al: Research Methods in Social Relations,* Methuen, 1965. Pauline V. Young: *Scientific Social Surveys and Research,* Prentice-Hall, Englewood Cliffs, N. J., 1964 (4th edition); the others are: Russell L. Ackoff: *The Design of Social Research,* University of Chicago Press, Chicago, 1953. Stephen Cole: *The Sociological Method,* Rand McNally, 1972. Julienne Ford: *Paradigms and Fairy-Tales,* Routledge & Kegan Paul, 1975. Johan Gaining: *Theory and Methods of Social Research,* Allen & Unwin, 1967. Franklin H. Giddings: *The Scientific Study of Human Society,* reprinted by Arno Press, N.Y., 1974 (Original edition 1924). William J. Goode & Paul K. Hatt: *Methods in Social Research,* McGraw-Hill, N.Y., 1952. John A. Hughes: *Sociological Analysis: Methods of Discovery,* Nelson, 1976. Sanford Labovitz & Robert Hagedorn: *Introduction to Social Research,* McGraw-Hill, N.Y., 1971. Robert Rosenthal & Ralph L. Rosnow: *Primer of Methods for the Behavioural Sciences,* Wiley, N.Y., 1975. Gideon Sjoberg & Roger Nett: *A Methodology for Social Research,* Harper & Row, N.Y., 1968. Margaret Stacey: *Methods of Social Research,* Pergamon Press, Oxford, 1969.

2. Peter Mann's *Methods of Sociological Inquiry* (Blackwell, Oxford, 1968) is an honourable exception to this generalization, although even it does not touch on analysis.

3. Gordon W. Allport: *The Use of Personal Documents in Psychological Science,* Bulletin 49, Social Science Research Council, N.Y., 1942. Herbert Blumer: *An Appraisal of Thomas & Znaniecki's 'The Polish Peasant in Europe and America',* Social Science Research Council, N.Y., 1939. Louis Gottschalk *et al.: The Use of Personal Documents in History, Anthropology and Sociology,* Social Science Research Council, N.Y., 1945.

4. e.g. Bernard Berelson: *Content Analysis in Communications Research,* Free Press, Illinois, 1952. Ithiel da Sola Pool, ed.: *Trends in Content Analysis,* University of Illinois Press, Urbana, 1959.

5. e.g. Jack D. Douglas: *The Social Meanings of Suicide,* Princeton University Press,

Princeton, N. J., 1967. Harold Garfinkel: *Studies in Ethnomethodology*, Prentice-Hall, Englewood Cliffs, NJ., 1967. Barry Hindess: *The Use of Official Statistics in Sociology*, Macmillan, 1973. Eugene J. Webb *et al: Unobtrusive Measures*, Rand McNally, Chicago, 1966.

6. There is a large literature on questions of method arising in the use of documents, but it is written by and for historians (e.g. G. Kitson Clark: *The Critical Historian*, Heinemann, 1967. G. Kitson Clark: *Guide for Research Students Working on Historical Subjects*, Cambridge U.P., 1969. G. R. Elton: *The Practice of History*, Sydney U.P., 1967. C. V. Langlois & C. Seignobos: *Introduction to the Study of History*, tr. G. G. Berry; Duckworth, 1898). Although this is very instructive, it leaves many issues of interest to sociologists uncovered, or dealt with very superficially.

7. Thomas S. Kuhn: *The Structure of Scientific Revolutions*, University of Chicago Press, 1962.

8. Howard S. Becker: 'Problems of inference and proof in participant observation', *American Sociological Review*, 23, 1958, pp. 652-660. Robert Bogdan & Steven J. Taylor: *Introduction to Qualitative Research Methods*, Wiley, N.Y., 1975. Severyn T. Bruyn: *The Human Perspective in Sociology*, Prentice-Hall, Englewood Cliffs, NJ., 1966. Barney G. Glaser & Anselm L. Strauss: *The Discovery of Grounded Theory*, Weidenfeld & Nicolson, 1968. Leonard Schatzman & Anselm L. Strauss: *Field Research: Strategies for a Natural Sociology*, Prentice-Hall, Englewood Cliffs, NJ., 1973. Jacqueline P. Wiseman: 'The research web', *Urban Life and Culture*, vol. 3, no. 3, Oct. 1974.

9. Jennifer Platt: *Realities of Social Research*, University of Sussex Press, 1976.

10. Albert S. Osborn: *Questioned Documents*, Lawyers' Cooperative Publishing Co., Rochester, N.Y., 1910.

11. A classic example of the problems that can arise for social science from poor reproduction is Freud's analysis of Leonardo da Vinci's sexual attitudes on the basis of an incorrect reproduction of a detail in one of his drawings.

12. Langlois & Seignobos, op. cit.; Osborn, op. cit.

13. Elton, op. cit., p. 70.

14. cf. Schatzman & Strauss, op. cit.

15. G. S. Duncan: *Bibliography of Glass*, Dawsons, 1960.

16. Mrs. Annie Slossom (pseud. 'The Youngest Member'): *The China Hunters' Club*, Harper, N.Y., 1878.

17. Jennifer Platt: 'The social construction of "positivism" and its significance in British sociology 1950–1980', paper given at B.S.A. Conference, April 1980. James D. Watson: *The Double Helix*, Penguin, Harmondsworth, Middx. 1970, p. 149.

18. Herbert Butterfleld: *The Whig Interpretation of History*, Bell, 1931.

19. Robert & Elizabeth Shackleton: *The Quest of the Antique*, John Milne, 1908. Robert & Elizabeth Shackleton: *The Book of Antiques*, Tudor Publishing Co., N.Y. 1943.

20. e.g. M. L. Solon: *Ceramic Literature*, Charles Griffin & Co., 1910.

21. e.g. Joseph Strutt: A *Complete View of the Dress and Habits of the People of England*, ed. J. R. Planché, 1842.

22. John Craig: *Craig's Rules of Historical Evidence 1600; History and Theory, Studies in the Philosophy of History*, Beiheft 4; Mouton, Hague, 1964, p. 5.

23. Craig, op. cit., p. 27.

24. Raoul Naroll: *Data Quality Control*, Free Press of Glencoe, N.Y. 1962, p. 31.

25. Langlois & Seignobos, op. cit., pp. 166-177.

26. Nachmias & Nachmias, op. cit., p. 131.

27. Langlois & Seignobos, op. cit., pp. 195-196.

28. Frederic C. Bartlett: 'Social factors in recall' in ed. Eleanor E. Maccoby *et al.*, *Readings in Social Psychology,* Methuen, 1966.

29. Langlois & Seignobos, op. cit, pp. 185-187.

30. It is one of the painful paradoxes of documentary research that such incidental mentions may be the best evidence for a general state of affairs, but are inevitably far harder to find without inordinate amounts of wasted work than direct discussions of the subject of interest.

31. Blumer, op. cit.; Langlois & Seignobos, op. cit.

32. Clark (1967), op. cit.

33. Elton, op. cit., p. 86.

34. William Todd: *History as Applied Science,* Wayne State University Press, Detroit, 1972, pp. 36-37.

35. E. S. Shneidman.& N. L. Farberow: 'Some comparisons between genuine and simulated suicide notes ...', *Journal of General Psychology* 56 pp. 251-256, 1957.

36. Howard S. Becker: 'Introduction' to Clifford R. Shaw, *The Jack Roller,* University of Chicago Press, 1966.

37. John Lofland: 'Styles of reporting qualitative field research', *American Sociologist,* Aug. 1974, vol. 9, pp. 101-111.

38. G. Polya: *Patterns of Plausible Inference,* Princeton University Press, Princeton NJ., 1968, pp. 31-32.

39. Caroline Spurgeon: *Shakespeare's Imagery and What it Tells Us,* Cambridge U.P., 1961. G. Wilson Knight: *The Wheel of Fire,* Methuen, 949.

40. Alexander L. George: 'Quantitative and qualitative approaches to content analysis', in ed. Pool, op. cit.

41. cf. Erving Goffman: *The Presentation of Self in Everyday Life,* Doubleday, Garden City N.Y., 1959.

42. Jack D. Douglas: *Investigative Social Research,* Sage Publications, 1976.

35

Mass-Observation's Fieldwork Methods

Liz Stanley

the subjectivity of the observer is one of the facts under observation ...
Collective habits and social behaviour are our field of enquiry, and individuals
are only of interest in so far as they are typical of groups ... Mass-Observation
intends to make use not only of the trained scientific observer, but of the
untrained observer, the man in the street. Ideally, it is the observation of
everyone by everyone, including ourselves. (Mass-Observation, 1937: 2, 30,
97)

surrealism is a science by virtue of its capacity for development and discovery
and by virtue of the anonymity of its researches. Like science it is an apparatus
which, in human hands, remains fallible. (Madge, 1933: 14)

My chapter is concerned with exploring some aspects of the history
of ethnographic fieldwork methods in the period immediately
before, during and then after the Second World War. This history
closely involves an independent research organization, Mass-Observation,
which had an extremely high public profile in Britain over this period.
Mass-Observation was a mass membership and politically radical alternative
social science research organization which was active between 1937 and 1949
(useful introductions are provided by Calder and Sheridan, 1984; Cross,
1990; Sheridan, 1990, 1994; Stanley, 1995b).[1] Mass-Observation overall, as
well as the three particular research projects I will be discussing later, has
an interesting relationship to the development of ethnographic methods.
Mass-Observation was active during the historical 'moment' in which, before
the 1939–45 world war, the academic disciplines in Britain were shifting
and changing, seeking new alliances or even reconfigurations, and then after
it, when new boundaries between the disciplines were being assembled and
they were jockeying for place in anticipation of the expansion of higher
education. In this context, Mass-Observation acted as a catalyst, a point of

Source: *Handbook of Ethnography*, 2001, Sage, pp. 92-108.

reference, and also a source of threat, for a number of the social sciences; and it was also, although more covertly, seen as a source of ideas as well.[2] The role of ethnographic fieldwork in Britain over this period was undergoing considerable development, developments which also occurred across the three Mass-Observation projects discussed later, as well as within academia. Indeed, fieldwork methods of investigation were of considerably wider academic interest at this time than just to sociology and anthropology. In particular, in Britain there was an enormous interest in developing an applied economic sociology as a 'synthetic social science' which would draw all the others under this umbrella within the expected expansion of higher education, and observational methods were seen as providing a potentially key approach within this. Beyond these historical significances, Mass-Observation is interesting in the history of fieldwork methods in another respect, because of the attempts made in a number of its research projects not only to use such methods but also to represent the results of this in innovative ways.

In the following discussion, I explore the complex and interesting relationship between Mass-Observation and the university-based social sciences in Britain, outlining what kind of 'alternative' to university-based social science Mass-Observation provided and also some of the divergent emphases within it. I then move on to examine some of the issues that arise in making generalizations about what 'it' as an organization was and did. Amongst its heteroglossia of methods, Mass-Observation used a range of fieldwork techniques, typically in distinctive ways in its different research projects. After outlining some of the non-obtrusive fieldwork methods it used, methodological aspects of three particular projects Mass-Observation carried out are discussed. These projects are known as *May the Twelfth,* the 'Economics of Everyday Life' and 'Little Kinsey'; they have been chosen for discussion here because, although they were carried out in different phases of the research 'life' of Mass-Observation between 1937 and 1949, they used related methodological strategies but had different degrees of success in bringing these to written and published conclusion.[3] The final section of the chapter looks at James Clifford's (1988) idea of 'surrealist ethnography' and considers to what extent and in what ways these three Mass-Observation projects exemplify the defining characteristics of this, and also why they experienced different degrees of success.

Mass-Observation and Social Science

The genesis of Mass-Observation as an organization was 'announced' in a variety of ways by its three founders, Tom Harrisson, Charles Madge and Humphrey Jennings, in newspaper letters and radio broadcasts, and in its earliest publications. Mass-Observation was variously portrayed by them as a new form of social science, an anthropology at home, a synthetic sociology, and as an alternative to the very different form that the university-based social sciences of the day had taken. Therefore, fundamental to the way that Mass-Observation was constructed and publicly presented were its apparently sharp differences from mainstream social science. However, outside of such public pronouncements, a much more complex relationship existed between Mass-Observation and social science. For instance, a number of well-known social scientists were associated with Mass-Observation; most notably, Malinowski was its treasurer during the earliest period of its existence, but the economists Philip Sargant Florence and John Jewkes, the sociologist Adolph Lowe, the psychologists T.H. Pear and Oscar Oeser and a good many others had a watching interest, sometimes supplied small sums of money for particular research projects and more often sent students to 'help out'. Malinowski's impact went further than this, and the continuing emphasis in Mass-Observation of the central necessity of practical fieldwork is in part due to the influence of Malinowski on Tom Harrisson and Charles Madge, although in part also due to two other influences on Harrisson: the work of Chicago School sociology, and the 'penetrational' fieldwork methods used by Oscar Oeser, which I discuss later.

Neither then nor now was ethnographic field-work in Britain exclusively associated with anthropology or with only qualitative ways of working. The work of 'Chicago School' sociology and its emphasis on observation and the conduct of fieldwork-based research was of interest to many British social scientists as well as to Mass-Observation. In addition, the Survey Movement of the late 1930s (Buhner et al., 1991) encompassed 'surveying' in the broad sense as well as the numerical one, and a number of people associated with it were on the fringes of Mass-Observation, including Alan Wells (1936) and Terence Young (1934). In addition to anthropology and sociology, applied psychology and economics in 1930s Britain were also interested in fieldwork methods, with members of these disciplines having a range of involvements with Mass-Observation. Oscar Oeser, a social psychologist at the University of St Andrews, for instance, took a considerable interest in Mass-Observation's research in Blackpool in the later 1930s and his methodological ideas about the uses of 'penetrational' fieldwork methods for community studies played an important part in underpinning Mass-Observation convictions about the importance of fieldwork for the work it was engaged in (Oeser, 1937, 1939; Stanley, 1992).

The idea of a complete separation between an 'oppositional' Mass-Observation and an 'institutionalized' social science was, then, more rhetorical than matched by strict practice. Instead, a wide variety of crossover points existed between Mass-Observation and social science, involving ideas about new topics and methodological innovations, as well as the movement of some researchers from Mass-Observation to academia or from academia to Mass-Observation (Stanley, 1990). Another indication of this complex interrelationship is provided by contemporary academic reviews of Mass-Observation publications, which expressed interest in it overall but commented on what were perceived as serious methodological problems (Bunn, 1943; Johoda, 1938, 1940; Malinowski, 1938; Marshall, 1937), although some discussions were more critical (Firth, 1938, 1939) or later even dismissive (Abrams, 1951).

Mass-Observation came into existence around the 'Abdication crisis' of 1936 as reacted to by three men, Harrisson, Madge and Jennings, who had rather different characters and interests. Consequently, at its inception the organization was not one but three rather different although related parts, focusing around, first, 'Worktown' (the covering term for Harrisson's various projects researching aspects of life 'from the inside' in the mill town of Bolton)' and also 'Seatown' (the working-class holiday resort of Blackpool, also in the North of England); secondly, modes of representation and particularly photography and film (Jennings' photographs and film-making of 'ordinary life' in Bolton and elsewhere, and his interest in using the techniques of documentary film-making in textual form); and, thirdly, involving 'ordinary people' in observing themselves as well as other people (Madge's interest in the observer as a 'subjective camera', with useful facts being seen as the result of many hundreds of such observations, and his organization of a 'National Panel' of mass observers to produce these). There were also shared concerns which drew Harrisson, Madge and Jennings together, including socialist politics and an engagement with surrealism; the practice as well as theory of Mass-Observation; and a political and ethical commitment to reworking the relationship between 'ordinary people' and science. The result was what Nick Hubble (1998: 10) has termed its 'politicizing of aesthetic techniques'.

Madge was a fairly well-known poet as well as a journalist, and during 1936 and 1937 he had experimented with both collective and found poetry. His discussions of this, both contemporaneously and with hindsight, emphasized the anti-elitist ideas about authorship and inspiration which underpinned both. In his found poetry in particular, Madge juxtaposed images and apparently discontinuous text to encourage the active involvement of readers, as Jennings was doing with photographic collages (Madge, 1933, 1937; Madge and Jennings, 1937). One of Harrisson's (1937) first publications was *Savage Civilisation*, an idiosyncractic account of the time he had spent in the New Hebrides (now Vanuatu) living with 'head hunters'. However, this text is more than idiosyncratic, for it is structured around discordancies of images and styles and uses a kind of 'montage' approach to writing an ethnographic account that demonstrates the extent to which Harrisson, sometimes depicted as uninterested in or even antipathetic to surrealism (McClancy, 1995), was in fact considerably influenced by its ideas about representation. Jennings, a friend of Andre Breton, a key figure in French surrealism, was co-organizer of the 1936 international surrealist exhibition which took place in London and closely involved in formulating styles of photography and documentary film-making which eschewed or undercut the realist claims more usually made for these representational means (M-L. Jennings, 1982; H. Jennings, 1986). By 1937, Jennings had carried out a number of photographic projects with Harrisson in 'Worktown', and had also worked with Madge on the production of one of

Mass-Observation's earliest publications, *May the Twelfth,* a book about the Coronation Day of George VI using a textual version of montage combined with collage, to which I shall return later.

The interest of Harrisson, Madge and Jennings in the practice and theory of Mass-Observation is connected through their shared albeit rather different interest in surrealism, more particularly the theory 'beneath' surrealism which reworks the Freudian idea of the unconscious by casting this as impersonal and shared and giving rise to collective forms of expression in the image (that is, its exteriorized form), rather than seeing it as operating through the symbol (which represents an interiorized, psychologized and depoliticized notion of the unconscious). Harrisson was always self-consciously concerned with the 'mass' in Mass-Observation, something expressed not least through his close association with the publisher Victor Golancz, who was to have published a planned series of books from its work (only one of which materialized), and who was the key promoter of the Left Book Club in Britain.

Stuart Laing (1980) has proposed that there were five key meanings to the notion of 'mass': the new social conditions of the 1930s, the 'common man', the mass as observers of society and each other, the collection and organization of large amounts of documentation, and the public. While these were all involved in Mass-Observation, particularly when the research eye moves away from the triumvirate of Jennings, Madge and Harrisson towards the large numbers of other people who very quickly became involved in its work, its activities included other meanings of 'mass' as well. In particular, as the quotation from *Mass-Observation* at the start of my discussion indicates, 'mass' included both a recognition of the individual nature of observation and also a principled rejection of an individualized idea of the individual. What the 'mass' in Mass-Observation was concerned with was a focus on habits or repeated behaviours and the observation of these, and not on opinions or thoughts. It was from this that its research genesis around the investigation of public reactions to the Abdication crisis and the Coronation had derived, for these were seen by Harrisson, Jennings and Madge as two related events of resonant social importance in revealing the collective unconscious around the interplay of 'surface and image'.

Jennings left Mass-Observation after the production of *May the Twelfth,* partly in reaction to Harrisson's overbearing approach but also to concentrate on documentary film-making and specifically the short on 'Spare Time', filmed in Manchester, Salford and Bolton. It has been claimed that the change in style of Mass-Observation writings thereafter resulted from Harrisson's suppression of Madge's surrealist concerns (McClancy, 1995), although in fact this was due to something much more mundane: the huge amount of very diverse research data that the National Panel quickly produced, with Madge as its organizer needing to find ways of responding to and dealing with this (personal interview, Charles Madge with Liz Stanley, 23 June 1990).

Sociology and anthropology, the disciplines most obviously challenged by Mass-Observation, responded to it with a fascinated gaze which was coupled with criticizing its approach as that of a failed realist 'documentary' project and also one which rejected scientific expertise (e.g. Firth, 1938, 1939; Johoda, 1938, 1940; Malinowski, 1938). Certainly one impulse in Mass-Observation promoted non-elitist notions of authorship, eschewed certainty and disputed the conventional authority of science; however, at the same time it also promoted its own (better) version of science, and notions of authority, hierarchy and expertise were still very much a part of its approach. For instance, it was Madge as the organizer, compiler and interpreter of the National Panel's monthly responses to 'directives', as well as Harrisson as the orchestrator of the diverse range of activities that took place in 'Worktown', who looked for not only the surface information in documents of different kinds, but also the hidden patterns that existed across them. Again, the quotation from *Mass-Observation* which opens my discussion suggests that these twin but, as it turned out, contradictory impulses were consciously and deliberately part of Mass-Observation from the outset. Thus, although Mass-Observation involved 'the observation of everyone by everyone, including ourselves', it also involved 'trained scientific observers' as well (Mass-Observation, 1937: 97). These 'trained observers' were the more permanent Mass-Observation personnel who soon joined Harrisson and Madge and then worked on or organized various of its projects, some funded via commercial sponsors, some from money given by Victor Golancz, Ernest Simon, Lord Leverhulme and other charitable sources of sponsorship, as well as through 'Worktown' and the National Panel.

In spite of considerable overlaps of people, interests and approaches between Mass-Observation and the university-based social science disciplines, important differences remained. First, howsoever embedded in ideas about science, the idea of 'us observing ourselves', with this being done by observers without academic training, went against the grain of the 1930s professionalizing approach in the ascendant in the academic disciplines. Secondly, the notion of mass observers as 'subjective cameras', with analytical interest being directed towards the complexities of *how* observers saw and interpreted as well as *what,* was one which proposed that 'subjectivity' was not an optional extra, a 'bias' that could be removed by rigour, method and training. Perhaps more than any other aspect of Mass-Observation's approach, this idea challenged the increasingly scientific notion of professional expertise in mainstream social science, and indeed, as I shall go on to suggest, the version of it also contradictorily present in Mass-Observation itself. Thirdly, Mass-Observation promoted use of a hetero-glossia of methods, particularly non-obtrusive methods such as counts, observations, follows and overheards, as well as day surveys and day diaries compiled by mass observers (Stanley, 1995a). For Mass-Observation, what made these methods effective was their use in a variety of different locations and then the analysis of the resultant data by examining the internal differences that resulted, rather than attempting to iron most of these out as irrelevant 'ends'. Very different ideas about method were being promoted in mainstream social science, with the result that, over time, Mass-Observation's approach to sampling came to be seen as deeply flawed, its methods as producing renegade data, and its analytic focus on differences within a data-set as illegitimate (as Stanley, 1995a discusses).

Organizational Complexities

So far, like many people who write about Mass-Observation, I have treated it as the product of three strands of intellectual and political interest which came together as a single organizational entity: 'it' stood for and did various things. Thus its objective was to study British life and find out what people really thought and did (Hubble, 1998); it conducted 'an anthropology at home' (Chaney and Pickering, 1985, 1986); it used a combination of straightforward reportage mixed with social science surveys, with the Worktown project being such a survey (Baxendale and Pawling, 1996); and I myself have characterized it as a mass radical alternative sociology (Stanley, 1990). Having worked on a wide range of the projects associated with Mass-Observation across its original period of active life (1937-49), however, I have become increasingly uncomfortable in making such generalizations, given the way the organization changed over time and the large number of internal fractures within and the loose structure of it. Mass-Observation was actually less of a unitary organization and more a set of interlinked practical, political and epistemological projects. Moving away from the level of public pro-nouncement and into the everyday conduct of the varied projects associated with Mass-Observation, what is revealed is an internally complex and highly differentiated kind of research organization, one marked by divergencies and internal fractures as well as some common features.

There was the simple and obvious distinction between the National Panel research organized from Blackheath in London initially by Charles Madge, and the 'Worktown' projects orchestrated in Bolton by Tom Harrisson working with a range of colleagues and volunteers. Thus the different approaches embedded within Worktown and the National Panel indicate the one line of internal separation and differentiation.

In addition, the relationship between Mass-Observation and university-based social science was not only complex but also changed markedly over the period of the original phase of Mass-Observation between 1937 and 1949 (Stanley, 1990, 1995b). Harrisson's approach was typically oppositional and combative, but also contradictorily combined with determinedly seeking academic support and academic contexts in which to promote Mass-Observation. Madge, however, was more conciliatory, more friendly with many academics, and more attracted to the apparatus of 'science' in imposing some kind of order on the mammoth amount of data that the National Panel had generated.[4] Indeed, the difference went further, for Harrisson was a keen proponent of the idea that Mass-Observation represented a new form of social science, inductively producing social laws concerning the workings of society which would be directly comparable to the laws which the Darwinian approach had produced for the natural sciences; while Madge's goals for its research activities were more modest and focused on small accretions of knowledge gained piecemeal. Consequently their different approaches to 'the mainstream' and to research and science constitutes a second line of internal difference.

Added to this, there was a distinction, first in Worktown and then in the activities which grew up around Mass-Observation's London headquarters, between those people who were volunteer mass observers whose involvement in Mass-Observation might consist only of sending written responses to National Panel directives, and the people who worked (often without much payment) over sometimes lengthy periods of time as 'hands on' researchers. Both mass observers and more involved volunteers might take part in various of the different activities of the organization, and a particular project could involve a distinct set of people who knew little or nothing about those who were involved on its other projects. Moreover, the various projects carried out proceeded from sometimes very different methodological bases, with some adopting entirely observational fieldwork-based methods and others using more direct methods of questioning, and with some focusing on behaviour while others were concerned more with opinion. And this was in spite of the very clear rhetorical insistence in its more public pronouncements that Mass-Observation eschewed direct methods, used only naturalistic observational methods, and was interested only in behaviour and not opinion.

Also over the period of its original 'life' between 1937 and 1949, all of these different internal differentiations and separations within Mass-Observation could and did change over time, the fourth line of internal difference. The most important disjunctures are represented by prewar, wartime and postwar phases in the 'life' of Mass-Observation, but other changes also brought about knock-on effects over time as well. A key example of this 'domino effect' concerns the organizational crossover between Harrisson and Madge which took place in November 1938. Madge felt increasingly swamped by the vast amount of material that came into Mass-Observation's headquarters from its National Panel members, and this, combined with interpersonal difficulties between him and Harrisson, resulted in them swapping organizational places, Harrisson taking charge of the National Panel and Madge moving to Bolton to conduct research on the 'Economics of Everyday Life'. This changeover seemed to the volunteers who had worked with Harrisson in Bolton as effectively the end of "Worktown". For them the Worktown project was composed by the activities established and flamboyantly managed by Harrisson, while Madge's approach was more methodical and conventional and concerned to carry out a specific piece of research. Harrisson indeed perceived the change as considerably more than one of emphasis; in an undated memo to Dennis Chapman, he explained the difference by criticizing the 'academic tendencies' of Madge and Gertrud Wagner, a sociologist Madge had recruited to the project (Mass-Observation Hist: TH to DC undated),[5] their painstaking conventionality in research terms at the expense of verve and innovation.

Some of the implications over time can be seen by looking briefly at the research careers of two members of Mass-Observation. One of the researchers working on the 'Economics of Everyday Life' project, Geoffrey Thomas, cut his research teeth on it; when war started he moved into the wartime Government Social Survey, then postwar he became the Director of the Government's Statistical Office and so in charge of the decennial Census. The career of Thomas thus represents an approach supposedly the antithesis of the observational and non-intrusive methods pioneered by Mass-Observation in the prewar period, although, as I have already noted, beneath the rhetorical surface methodological matters were always more complex. Similarly, Madge developed ideas about research very different from Harrisson's and, through contacts which he established with the economists Philip Sargant Florence and John Maynard Keynes around the 'Economics of Everyday Life' research, in 1940 he left Mass-Observation to carry out savings and spending research for the government; and this then underpinned his move into more institutionalized forms of social science, initially as director of Political and Economic Planning (PEP) and then, in 1950, as Professor of Sociology at the University of Birmingham.

I shall return to the Worktown 'Economics of Everyday Life' research later, and have introduced it here to point up the complexities aud changes masked by treating Mass-Observation in unitary terms, by showing how an apparently simple change could have consequential implications for a number of aspects of the organization. In what follows I explore some of the ways in which fieldwork methods were used in three particular Mass-Observation projects: *May the Twelfth,* a book resulting from an investigation of Coronation Day and published soon afterwards in 1937; the 'Economics of Everyday Life' project carried out between November 1938 and early 1942; and the 'Little Kinsey' project carried out in 1949 at the cusp of the change from the old-style Mass-Observation to its transition into a commercial survey organization. These projects span Mass-Observation's organizational life, involved different sets of people, and occasioned different methodological and indeed epistemological responses around the changing use of fieldwork methods within Mass-Observation.

Fieldwork Methods in Three Mass-Observation Projects

For many social scientists contemporaneously, and indeed until comparatively recently, Mass-Observation was known about mainly through swingeing criticisms made of it by Mark Abrams (1951), for it has been only from the 1980s on that archival research on Mass-Observation has been carried out. Abrams' critique derives from a very different kind of methodological position from Mass-Observation's; in part it reflects Abrams' role in a competitor market research organization, and anyway it also reduces the complexities of the research ideas and practices being used by Mass-Observation to some comforting and dismissable simplicities. In fact, at any one point in time between 1937 and 1949 Mass-Observation was dealing with a large number of research projects around the three main trajectories of its activities, in Worktown, through the National Panel, and in the commercially funded market research which was sometimes co-terminous with its other work, sometimes tangential, but always financially important. The research methods used across these projects were very diverse, although a fair degree of commonality was provided, first, by key researchers moving across projects, and, secondly, because much of the written output from Mass-Observation was produced by a small number of 'writers' who worked in its London headquarters and whose work imposed a common rhetorical style on its written outputs.

The National Panel research, coordinated initially by Charles Madge, included the regular use of day surveys and day diaries as well as asking its members to respond to the monthly 'directives' or interlinked sets of questions sent out from London (Stanley, 1995a). These data were written up in different ways, including as summary discussions in the regular 'Mass-Observation Bulletin' sent to Panel members, as reports to sponsors and funders where appropriate, and also within other kinds of Mass-Observation publications.[6] Research in Work-town under Tom Harrisson was equally diverse, and included paintings and poetry by friends of Harrisson, photographs from Humphrey Spender, as well as essays and reports which resulted from Harrisson's promotion of non-obtrusive methods and particularly observation. Harrisson had indeed, on occasion, suggested observers should put corks in their ears, the better to focus their observation on actual behaviour untrammelled by preconceptions derived from hearing talk (and 'observation' here also included 'counts' of behaviours and 'follows' of people whose behaviour was particularly interesting). Harrisson's central concern was with behaviour and not opinion, with what was public rather than private, although overall the Worktown research, including the 'Economics of Everyday Life' project which I discuss later, also included talk, particularly in the form of 'overheards' of naturally occurring conversation, within the social context in which it arose. The commercial research undertaken by Mass-Observation could be carried out via the National Panel, or through the Worktown project, or independently of these. It more often made use of formalized counts, or utilized Mass-Observation specific ideas about sampling populations, or involved formal interviews of 'key people' in relation to the topic investigated. In addition, all three sites of research used a form of covert or informal interviewing, in which a mass observer would engage someone in conversation and in effect carry out an interview, but without the 'respondent' being aware that this was the nature of the exchange,

Much of Mass-Observation's research was topic-based, including around, for instance, smoking behaviour, 'the suit' worn by men and its social significance, anti-semitic behaviour in connection with fascist marches in London, purchasing behaviour in shops, and sexual behaviour of different kinds of which the 'Little Kinsey' research was its apotheosis (Stanley, 1995b) and which I shall discuss later. The non-obtrusive methods associated with Worktown research under Harrisson were those also at the heart of the

'Economics of Everyday Life' project under Madge. These were well-established and distinctive methods promoted bullishly by Mass-Observation in its encounters with mainstream social science, although the original source was Harrisson's insistence on the importance of 'actual behaviour' rather than post-hoc formulated 'opinions' about behaviour. The key methods here were: first, 'counts' of behaviour of particular kinds, sometimes at a number of locations at exactly the same point in time (some of the research used in *May the Twelfth,* for instance, resulted from this); secondly, 'observations' of behaviour, focusing on exactly what was done how it was done and by whom (Mass-Observation's research on men's and women's smoking, for instance, derived from this); thirdly, 'overheards' of talk, often private conversations publicly engaged in, sometimes public talk of different kinds; and, fourthly, 'follows', situations in which mass observers followed people around, observing what they were doing, overhearing the talk they engaged in, sometimes also making counts of aspects of their behaviours. One early example of this is a report produced on a fascist 'Black Shirt' march in Bermondsey in London in 1937 by Herbert Howarth (Mass-Observation File Report 1937 A3), which contains a reported observation of people leaving a tube station, the group they formed and the position at different points in time of individuals within it noted graphically; their talk and conversation is recorded verbatim and assigned to particular people identified by age, sex and so on; and the reactions, including the spoken comments, of the crowds assembled to watch the march, are noted.

May the Twelfth: Day Surveys and an Ethnographic (Photo)montage[7]

Not long after Mass-Observation came into existence and its National Panel operational, a leaflet entitled 'Where were you on May 12th?' was widely distributed from February 1937 on, asking for people to respond to a set of questions about their behaviour on Coronation Day in May and to send these anonymously to Mass-Observation's London address, with seventy-seven such responses being received. In addition, National Panel responses were sought and were received from a further forty-three people; a 'Mobile Squad' of twelve Mass-Observation roving reporters in London and elsewhere were involved in reporting and commenting on the day's events around similar questions; and Humphrey Jennings took many photographs of Coronation Day, mainly of the crowds that assembled and the buildings they gathered outside of or occupied, as his photographic montages of the day show (e.g. M-L. Jennings, 1982: 16).

May the Twelfth: Mass-Observation Day Surveys 1937 by Jennings and Madge was published later in 1937. The structure of this book in one sense follows the course of Coronation Day and its events as these occurred in different parts of the country. Thus its opening chapter is concerned with preparations for the Coronation in the three months beforehand; the second and third chapters provide detailed accounts of the events as observed in London and elsewhere in Britain on the actual day of the Coronation; the fourth chapter provides many individual reactions to its events and emotions; and the fifth and last chapter provides the results of the 'normal' Mass-Observation day survey for May 12th 1937. Jennings and Madge describe themselves, and appear on the book's cover, as its editors rather than as authors, in fact two editors among seven, and they write that they had arranged the material they were dealing with 'in a simple documentary manner' (1937: 347). However, the 'documentary manner' involved is by no means simple and considerably departs from the 'record the facts = the truth' notion of documentary, as even a cursory reading of the book suggests.

May the Twelfth is in fact not concerned with 'the Coronation' at all in the sense in which other documentary media of the time was concerned with it. That is, it is not concerned with the ritual events surrounding kingship itself, the actual consecration and coronation of George VI. Its focus is not on the apparently main events of the day at all, but rather on the side shows, those mundane necessary events which had been carried out beforehand to make it 'work' on the day, and the minutiae of the activities that 'ordinary people' in London and elsewhere in Britain engaged in. These events and behaviours of 'ordinary people' are presented in the form of both montage, each chapter composed by numbered segments containing press cuttings placed cheek by jowl with personal statements with editorial interventions; and also collage, because a multiplicity of agreeing and disagreeing people, points of view and geographical locations are included. The effect is to turn the gaze of the reader away from kingship and onto the mass of people, something which ironicizes the ritualistic aspects of the Coronation, or rather democratizes it as actually an event in which the responses of ordinary people are central rather than ancillary.

At the same time, *May the Twelfth* is concerned with more than the surface of behaviours, events and locations; and Chapter Four in particular deals with the often perverse or unexpected nature of people's responses to the Coronation, occurring almost 'in spite of themselves', while in one section the responses of particular people are presented on the same page with the reactions of their neighbours. This chapter is preceded by a quotation from Freud's *Totem and Taboo,* and is primarily concerned with the personally unexpected nature of people's 'beneath the surface' emotional responses to the day's events, but the social expectedness of these in relation to the symbolic and 'primitive' ritual of the consecration of kingship. Thus Jennings and Madge, for instance, comment about a report of people exchanging clothing with each other that similar activities are also a feature of the responses of 'savages' to the totemic rituals surrounding kingship.

May the Twelfth centres people 'speaking for themselves', with the role of the editors in constructing this being only minimally signalled, typically by implication through the artifices by which material is included and arranged rather than by direct statement of their editorial activities. The result is very much to emphasize that there was no single 'May 12th', but rather a large number of occasions composed by the specific experiences of many groups of people in their particular locations and with their particular vantage-points and, once brought together and assembled within the text, by the multiplicity of differences between these people even though apparently engaged in the 'same event'. Indeed, the representation of these actually constitutes the organizing framework of not only this chapter, but also the whole of *May the Twelfth*.

As well as the text itself, there are five separate indexes at the end of the book. The 'General' index is a conventional topic-based one, but which once more focuses upon 'the people' and their experiences, rather than on kingship and the Coronation itself. The four other indexes are of London streets and other places, the cuttings from newspapers and periodicals used in the book, popular songs, and the reports received from mass observers. The effect is not merely to enable the reader to chart their own routes through the text, but also to enable them to construct their own distinctive version of the day through what is a kind of 1930s text version of the hypertext linkages that can be written into web-based electronic documents. The result of this innovative approach to indexing is to encourage, by providing the means for, an active and non-linear reading of the text, and by so doing to undercut editorial authority through its overt dispersal of control over how readers might use the text.

For the book's editors, there was a point to this research venture which went well beyond the investigation of Coronation Day itself:

> From a scientific point of view, this book so far has no doubt been of interest in showing the kind of behaviour which Mass-Observation can observe. But it has been arranged mainly in a simple documentary way, without much attempt to suggest further possibilities of analysing the material. The unity of the material on May 12 is due to all the social life of that day being hinged on a single ceremony of national importance. On any other day, this unity will tend to disappear, and it is for social science to discover the unity, or lack of it, which is typical of a normal day... But the purpose ... is to show another way in which the material ... can be analysed. (Jennings and Madge, 1937: 347)

This 'other way' was to analyse the day survey responses in relation to 'social areas', the term the editors use to indicate the three kinds of social networks a given observer is connected with: the people they know first-hand in all aspects of their lives; strangers and newcomers; and those public and/or mythical people and institutions that form the 'social horizon' known only abstractly and at third-hand. These were then used, in 'an experimental and try-out' way, to analyse reports from three different kinds of people with the possibility of reaching a 'scientific classification'; however, the editors also note that 'Other persons classifying the reports would almost certainly reach a different set of results' (pp. 370-1). This raises the twin but contradictory focuses on 'scientific classification' and 'different researchers, different results' that I noted earlier; and here they mark not only the same project, but also the same analytic strategy.

A Missing Voice: The 'Economics of Everyday Life' Project[8]

As noted earlier, in November 1938 Charles Madge and Tom Harrisson changed organizational places, with Harrisson taking charge of the National Panel in London and Madge's new involvement focusing on directing the 'Economics of Everyday Life' project in Worktown. Madge's particular interest was in its savings and spending component and his wider role in this project tailed off and then ended during 1940. However, the 'Economics of Everyday Life' project and the involvement of its other researchers remained active until early 1942, and it brought together Mass-Observation's concern with the minutiae of everyday life and the idea of using an applied economic sociology to investigate the dire economic straits daily experienced by many working-class people. An undated Worktown memo (Worktown/ 46, from other evidence probably written between late 1938 and late 1939) provides a list of the key researchers on the project (Charles Madge, Gertrud Wagner, Dennis Chapman, Geoffrey Thomas and Stanley Cramp), and also gives information about involvement from mainstream social scientists (Terence Young at the University of London was carrying out a shopping survey for Mass-Observation; Professors Ford at Southampton and Jewkes and others in the Economics Department at Manchester University were asking students to go to Worktown; and the importance of 'Dr Lowe' and his *Economics and Sociology* (Lowe, 1935) and the work of Bowley and Allen (Allen and Bowley, 1935) is commented on).[9]

Another internal memo (Worktown/46.B) describes the project as concerned with the 'factors influencing spending and saving at the income levels which include the great majority of the people of England'; and it states that Mass-Observation's planned fifth book on Bolton would be the 'Economics of Everyday Life', focusing on the actual observation of economic behaviour in everyday life. An important part of the planned research involved an investigation of savings and spending and was Madge's particular concern,[10] although much of the research was carried out by other 'Economics of Everyday Life' researchers as well as by him. This included what was at the time the unusual (both for Mass-Observation and for mainstream social science) method of carrying out detailed structured interviews with individual savers and also with representatives from savings organizations. Alongside this, a number of more specifically 'Mass-Observation' kinds of research took place, concerned with clothes, including the social function of the suit; the effects of Lent on retail sales; household budgets; the Worktown stomach, and the role of money; and also the role of work in Worktown. These different aspects of research were combined (again unusually both for Mass-Observation and for mainstream social science) with a 'special area study'.[11]

The idea of 'functional penetration', drawn from research concerned with unemployed Scottish jute workers in Dundee carried out by Oscar Oeser (1937, 1939) and colleagues, was an important influence on the 'Economics of Everyday Life' project. Oeser's research was an early kind of community study using ethnographic methods, in which members of the research team lived and in some cases worked in the area of study. Harrisson was particularly interested in Oeser's work; Oeser had visited Mass-Observation in Worktown and also Seatown, and the idea of 'functional penetration' influenced the 'Economics of Everyday Life' project, including through its researchers forming a team, members of which lived in Worktown and carried out a wide variety of linked research activities there.

Another innovative aspect of the research involved a 'special area study' which focused on a group of streets in the centre of working-class Bolton, a total of 630 adults (300 males and 330 females). As well as looking at the occupation, employment situation and household spending and saving patterns of these people, the special area study was also concerned with 'opinion forming'. The study was carried out using ethnographic and observational means, with Mass-Observation's researchers here too being influenced by the idea of 'functional penetration' of an area, with different members of the 'Economics of Everyday Life' research team becoming members of and investigating different aspects of the local community.

There are a number of differences between the research that was actually carried out and the contents of the planned book, first because various of the original features of the research were never completed, and secondly because some that were, and particularly here Madge's work on savings and spending, took on a trajectory of their own. There are also important continuities. First, the 'everyday' aspects of economic life remained central to the investigation, with the researchers looking at topics such as the social function of clothes and of food consumption. Secondly, the main method of carrying out the research was observation of public behaviour backed up by 'counts', 'over-heards' and 'follows', with direct questioning of people about their private behaviour and opinions being analytically secondary to the general patterns built up through non-intrusive methods. And thirdly, work was seen as fundamental to social life, with 'work' conceptualized so as to include domestic labour as well as paid employment within the labour force. Overall, economic and social life were conceptualized as one and the same, or, rather, the economic was seen as a definitional component of 'the social'.

A number of aspects of the 'Economics of Everyday Life' project were highly innovative. The project combined investigating the everyday with an inductive theoretical analysis of this, and in both respects differed from 1930s mainstream social science, apart from the kind of economic sociology being promoted by Jewkes, Lowe and others. It was aware of gender, as well as of age, class, region and temporality as structural variables. It took gender seriously throughout its composing pieces of research, including by arguing that women made the economic system 'work' while receiving only a small proportion of its resources. In addition, it emphasized that in Worktown women worked throughout the economy as well as within the domestic sphere of the household. The project centred the role of money as an anonymous system of exchange binding together production and consumption; and it recognized that the use of money, if not necessarily its generation or its control, was largely the prerogative of women. Here again the project was highly innovative in refusing to separate consumption from production, seeing both as symbiotic and as fundamental to any under-standing and theorization of everyday economics. And as well as these innovations with regard to method and theory, the 'Economics of Everyday Life' project was methodologically and epistemologically distinctive in some interesting ways.

Its particular utilization of the idea of 'functional penetration' was premised on the view that social life needed to be experienced in order to be understood, and that asking questions 'from the outside' was insufficient for proper understanding, which required actual participation in some kind of functional role in working and living in an area as the basis of fieldwork. It was for this reason that the project was based on its fieldwork researchers living in the area and knowing and observing it from the inside, and they participated in a wide range of activities in Worktown and took it as axiomatic that their research required this.

The work carried out within the 'Economics of Everyday Life' project shared with Mass-Observation more generally the view that the observer was central to research, not merely as a collector of information from other people, but rather as a 'subjective camera', someone who necessarily interpreted what was seen and heard and therefore what was recorded. Consequently, what was recorded was treated as contingent upon those who researched it as well as those who provided it. The 'Economics of Everyday Life' researchers worked closely together, gathered daily in the house Harrisson had rented and which was used communally. The specific research they were each engaged on was discussed by all members of the 'Economics of Everyday Life' team. Their broad approach was very different from the developing ideas of mainstream social science concerning objectivity and detachment, for they saw knowledge as collectively produced, necessarily interpretational and grounded in specific contexts, times and places, although related to more general themes and ideas.

The 'Economics of Everyday Life' project also put its particular spin on the more general Mass-Observation view of observation as its methodological cornerstone. The larger part of the project's research was based on a range of observational studies rather than direct questioning or other intrusive or semi-intrusive methods. Its concern was people's behaviour, what people actually did, rather than their post-hoc reports or interpretations of it. However, this is not to say that the project ignored interpretation and its role in mediating between the observation of behaviour and reporting this, as already indicated. It saw knowing about a community or an activity as an essentially collaborative activity, in the sense of bringing together and using different accounts from observations conducted from different viewpoints. In addition, it recognized that the informal aspects of research, gained by 'just living' in the area of study, were as important as those activities formerly defined as 'research' in the narrow sense.

The 'Economics of Everyday Life' project was not completed nor was any part of it published contemporaneously, although many fragments of writing and many recordings of data exist; and so it is impossible to say with any certainty how the completed research might have been presented in a published form. What remains are the large number of fragments, and the incomplete pieces of writing that would have formed the basis of a final text. These give a fascinating, indeed tantalizing, impression of what might have been, but in the form of a jigsaw puzzle for which at least half the pieces are missing. A number of factors were involved here.

First, Madge seems to have undertaken the project with a specific interest in savings and spending derived from his discussions with Maynard Keynes, and he left as soon as this took off. He was also more often than not absent from the 'Economics of Everyday Life' research, even during the period when he was its director, and certainly he failed to give it the kind of firm overall guidance that might have brought it to a successful published conclusion. Secondly, after Madge left, Harrisson and other full-time Mass-Observation researchers in its London headquarters were called up for wartime military service, and then, as money ran out and/or as the 'phoney war' gave way to real war, so the project's key researchers necessarily moved on too. Thirdly, without clear direction, the remaining research became more diverse, as the researchers 'followed their noses' and interests emerged 'on the ground'. And fourthly, unlike a number of other Mass-Observation projects, there was no experienced 'writer' involved who took or was assigned responsibility for writing up the research and so imposing some kind of textual order on its diversity. However, as the discussion of 'Little Kinsey' which follows will suggest, even if there had been a Mass-Observation 'writer' involved, a final published text might still not have resulted. The contradictory methodological and epistemological positions I noted earlier remained unresolved, indeed unarticulated, in this project, and led to the development of a positivist numerically based approach to savings and spending being carried out, but with this being hand in hand with the development of an observational and 'penetra-tional' approach to economic life more generally.

Who Says and What Counts? From 'Churchtown' to 'Little Kinsey'[12]

The research team that carried out the 'Economics of Everyday Life' project was one in which, initially at least, there was a clear chain of command from its director, Charles Madge, to the researchers who worked to his direction. Similarly, behind the proclaimed democracy of the mass observers' involvement in the National Panel there was a national headquarters and a chain of command in which other people, directed by first Madge and then by Harrisson, drew together the myriad of observational responses to directives. Thus a hierarchical organizational structure existed around the National Panel as well as the 'Economics of Everyday Life' project: embedded in Mass-Observation as an organization was a contradiction between its publicly pronounced principle of Mass-Observation and 'speaking for yourself', and its increasingly 'professional' group of specialists who produced analytical knowledge from the descriptions provided by 'their' mass observers and wrote its public documents. This contradiction became crucial with regard to the 'Little Kinsey' research carried out in 1949.

In March 1949 Mass-Observation produced an internal memo headed 'Directive for penetrative work on sex survey' (TC12: Box 2, File 15p; Box 3, File 15), which sets out a programme for three closely linked kinds of research within a special area study of 'Churchtown', the city of Worcester.[13] The first and most important was for observational research of public courting and sexual behaviour, to include at least three dance halls to be visited on a number of occasions over a seven-day period, the 'worst' public houses, and some pornographic bookshops. The second component was the provision of back-up statistics, including arrest figures for eighteen sexual offences. The third component was for two types of interview to be conducted: formal interviews with 'executives', including clergy from the main religious denominations, and 'representative' officials, such as a probation officer, police officer, doctor and bar keeper; and a larger number of 'informal' interviews, where the person concerned did not know they were being interviewed but instead thought they were having a casual conversation with a stranger. The formal interviews were to focus on people's views about changes in sexual morality, and the informal ones on courtship, picking up, and kissing, cuddling and other kinds of public sexual behaviour.

At the point that the March 1949 memo was composed, the whole of the proposed study was to consist of 'penetrational' work around the three planned components of the project in 'Churchtown', with this then being compared with another contrasting local area study, of 'Steeltown', the city of Middlesborough. The different components of the research were to enable the research team to 'compare and contrast' their observational and non-obtrusive measures internally *within* each area study against its statistical and interview data, as well as *between* 'Churchtown' and 'Steeltown'. However, the main focus of the research changed rapidly and markedly: the observational components became subordinated to three major national surveys which were carried out only a few weeks after the memo was written but which are not even mentioned in it. The first was a national random representative survey of 200 people – known as the 'Street sample'; the second was a randomly selected postal survey of 1,000 each of clergy, doctors and teachers – the 'Opinion Leaders' survey; and the third was a postal survey of Mass-Observation's 1,000 strong National Panel.

This research, known within Mass-Observation as 'Little Kinsey' because it was conceived against the backcloth of the recent publication of the first Kinsey report in the United States, was paid for by the *Sunday Pictorial* and was in part published in a series of articles that appeared in the newspaper on 3, 17, 24 and 31 July 1949. As well as these short articles, written by *Pictorial* journalists from materials supplied by Mass-Observation, it was also intended to publish a Mass-Observation book, and a manuscript was produced and sent to the intended publisher, Allen and Unwin. However, the book on 'Little Kinsey' was not published at the time,[14] and precisely why remains a puzzle which in the last resort is insoluble, not least because the writer on this project, Len England, in 1949 also the Office Manager of Mass-Observation, was unable to remember the details of why it failed to appear (personal interview, Len England with Liz Stanley, 22 August 1990). However, three overlapping factors seem to have been involved: organizational changes within Mass-Observation; external changes which affected what were seen as more and less acceptable research methods; and the ways in which the earlier observation material and the later survey material, when brought together within the draft manuscript, occasioned intellectual problematics which Len England as its writer was unable to solve.

In 1949, around a series of internal changes and in the wake of 'Little Kinsey' being carried out, the organization's old-guard and most importantly its remaining founder members surrendered their managerial and other interests in Mass-Observation, and a new guard took what then became 'Mass-Observation Ltd' into a new life dealing only with commercial market research. Behind these changes was the development and use of the computer and the postwar availability to research organizations not only of computer facilities but also of researchers skilled in their use. By 1949 Mass-Observation had its own computer and a number of research staff who were computer-experienced and, more importantly, had a very different attitude towards what was methodologically acceptable. For these newer members of staff, most of whom had been trained in the context of wartime research involving the quantified analysis of attitudinal research using representative sample data, 'scientific' styles of research were deemed to be the only acceptable ones. Pressure from them meant that what had been originally envisaged as a piece of qualitative research in the observational style pioneered by Mass-Observation, added to by the statistical and interview materials, instead became a large-scale national representative sample survey supported by two smaller surveys (see TC12: Box 2/A, letter 10 December 1938 from Len England to Brian Murtough, the Features Editor of the *Sunday Pictorial*). These and wider related developments about 'scientific' research in postwar Britain contributed to what became the 'Little Kinsey' emphasis on attitudes, and the move away from the originally planned observational and 'penetrational' studies of 'Churchtown' and 'Steeltown'. But other factors were involved as well, connected with the existence of both the 'new' survey data and the 'old' observational data and how these were brought together in the manuscript of 'Little Kinsey'.

The three related surveys are reported on in the text of 'Little Kinsey' in a tabular form (usually in whole percentage terms – 'out of every hundred X responded …'). These numerical statements are then embedded in arguments developed around the topic that each chapter focuses on, and they are surrounded by extensive qualitative material which had been written verbatim by the interviewers as they worked through the questionnaire with members of the 'Street sample'. However, cutting across the material derived from the three surveys, there is also an earlier Mass-Observation observational and ethnographic presence in the text. This is formed by extensive quotation from reports by the Mass-Observation researchers who had worked in the initial 'Churchtown' and 'Steeltown' phase of the research (in the chapters dealing with prostitution and with sexual morality in particular); by Mass-Observation researchers who had written about public sexual behaviour in Seatown (Blackpool) in an earlier prewar project (in the chapter concerned with sexual morality); and by a Mass-Observation investigator writing about his involvement in a 'homosexual group'.

This ethnographic presence is clearly articulated within the text, and in effect if not in intent it subordinates the quantitative survey data and its analysis to the qualitative observational material. The dominant note is the existence of differences of opinion and points of view between British people on sexual matters, with the result that these competing rhetorical and methodological presences speak past each other about different kinds of data and 'facts' about sexual behaviour and sexual opinion. Thus, for instance, the survey data in 'Little Kinsey' is itself used in a very particular way. Categorical conclusions are only infrequently drawn about any aspect of 'people and sex', and instead the numerical data are presented around comparisons and differences between the three different survey groups, and through statements about differences within each survey group by age, education, income, sex, by whether people lived in villages, towns or cities and whether they were churchgoers or not. The result is that almost every statement has alongside it an alternative one, with both being presented as factual and true for different groups and individuals. Certainly the text of 'Little Kinsey' at a number of points indicates that the facts must be allowed to 'speak for themselves', but then it goes on to provide *alternative* facts, depending on people's social location, their class, age, sex and so on, and also whether they were surveyed, interviewed or observed.

Such textual complexity was in fact characteristic of Mass-Observation writings, for these typically encompass a polyphonous set of textual strategies which, through their diversity, signal that no one of these is to be seen as bearing the stamp of 'authority' within the text, which is rather authorially or editorially dispersed (as I have already noted regarding *May the Twelfth*). However, in some of Mass-Observation's published writings, different stances and points of view are brought together by the 'voice' of the writer articulating one particular point of view, so that the authorial stance is made consonant with one of the points of view represented within the text. An interesting and successful example of this is Mass-Observation's study of Britain's falling birth-rate, *Britain and her Birth-Rate* (Mass-Observation, 1945), which centres on women's dissatisfactions and their refusal to live lives like their mothers, and which relates this to their changing perceptions of relationships. In *Britain and her Birth-Rate* textual closure is achieved through centring one particular point of view, that of 'women' as a category group, a collectivity; however, the writer of 'Little Kinsey' took on a more difficult task, that of both representing the multiplicity of competing 'voices' made apparent by its methodologically contrastive data, and also producing a scientific text that made clear what 'the facts' were. Although a manuscript in more or less final form was written, 'Little Kinsey' was not published contemporaneously. A number of attempts were made to wrestle with the dissatisfactions that were felt in-house about the draft manuscript, some of which were expressed to the external assessors of the project, who came from the voluntary bodies that Mass-Observation had consulted before the research began. However, precisely when and why, and by whom, the manuscript that reached Allen and Unwin was abandoned is not known. Certainly comparing the typescript with the earlier *Britain and her Birth-Rate*, some of the problems are clear. On the one hand, 'Little Kinsey' must have seemed sadly wanting in contemporary survey terms; and on the other, it offered neither precision in its numerical analysis nor even any clear statement as to 'what was going on' about sexual life in Britain. 'Little Kinsey' was written as a 'scientific' piece of work, rather than, as with *May the Twelfth*, a 'literary' one; and this produced constraints over the way its diverse facts could be represented, while the absence of either an internal ('the women') or an external ('science', 'surrealism') authorial point of view compounded these problems.

'Surrealist Ethnography' and the Fieldwork Methods of Mass-Observation

James Clifford (1988) has written on the idea of 'ethnographic surrealism' and in passing has invoked but not discussed the more radical possibility of 'surrealist ethnography'. Clifford's 'hypotheses' about surrealist ethnography are tantalizingly brief (1988: 146-7) and in fact focus on the notion of ethnographic surrealism, largely because in his view there are no pure types of surrealist ethnography to discuss, although for him Gregory Bateson's (1936) *Naven* comes perhaps closest. However, Clifford's brief comments suggest that surrealist ethnography should include five defining elements:

1. the central mechanism of the use of collage; that is, bringing things together that 'naturally' inhabit different times, places, contexts;
2. the use within this of 'moments' cut from their context of 'natural' occurrence and forced into a jarring proximity with each other;
3. the assumption both that there is a basis for comparison between these things at some deeper level, and also the sheer incongruity of such comparison on first sight;
4. the 'foreignness' of the elements assembled in the ethnographic collage in their context of presentation (and, although Clifford does not specifically note this, also of the means of their representation);
5. the resulting text leaves openly manifest the constructivist procedures involved in producing it.

Lying behind these is what seems to me an additional defining element of surrealist ethnography, which is that the text remains 'unfinished' in the sense of requiring an active engagement on the part of the reader to make sense of the collage of materials used, to make congruent, in diverse ways, what is incongruent or fractured within it, or indeed to resist doing so.

These ideas are interesting not least because of the resonance they have for thinking about Mass-Observation and its uses of fieldwork methods. And so in this conclusion I want to consider whether and to what extent these defining criteria of 'surrealist ethnography' are appropriate for thinking about the ways that Mass-Observation used fieldwork methods and attempted to produce written accounts of its research which reflected the complexities of everyday life thereby revealed. My discussion of *May the Twelfth*, the 'Economics of Everyday Life' and 'Little Kinsey' has focused on methodological aspects of these projects and how and in what ways these impacted upon the textual representation of the research. This provides a basis for thinking through the idea of surrealist ethnography.

Most obviously, of these projects, *May the Twelfth* consists of a collage of reports, sights and sounds assembled from different places which are represented and contained textually. In addition, the draft manuscript of 'Little Kinsey', both when examined through a close textual reading and also when this is compared against the many fragments of research records that survive from this project, demonstrates some of the same quality of collage and montage, for it assembles jarring elements in the co-presences brought together in its pages. In comparison with this, there is no certain way of knowing how the composing elements of the 'Economics of Everyday Life' project might have been brought together and what kind of text would have resulted. However, from the disparate fragments that remain, and the ways these 'come at' the notion of economic life from a wide variety of different vantage points, it might have taken a similar textual form, but whether successfully as with *May the Twelfth*, or unsuccessfully as with 'Little Kinsey', cannot even be guessed at. If *May the Twelfth* is a completed jigsaw, and 'Little Kinsey' one missing only a few pieces, the 'Economics of Everyday Life' project has only a small number of its pieces joined together.

May the Twelfth reads, if not as a harmonious whole, then certainly as a fully completed project, with its discordancies, shifts and jumps clearly being fully intentional ones. This style of reading (and of writing) may be unfamiliar to present-day readers raised on more conventional academic writing; however, for many of its contemporary readers, who were likely to have been self-styled intellectuals or fellow-travellers for whom the names of Jennings and Madge would be already known, its credentials as a piece of experimental or surrealist writing would have been 'announced' by its authorship. In discussing 'Little Kinsey', I pointed out that the writer of this manuscript faced a probably impossible task, that of assimilating research data from different epistemological discourses and wielding them into a whole which needed to be articulated in the 'voice' of science. The result here is in fact ultimately disruptive, rather than there being merely discordant co-presences within the text. Compared with these other two projects, what final form the planned text of the 'Economics of Everyday Life' project might have taken remains unknown, but clearly it would have had to have wielded together the more positivist savings and spending material and the more interpretivist observational material on the other aspects of the economics of everyday life that the project generated.

While there are points at which the comparisons that the editors of *May the Twelfth* want readers to make are introduced in forced ways (of the 'savages do this too, you know' kind, for instance), generally the text is left considerably more open than this. By comparison, the draft manuscript of 'Little Kinsey' seems a failure, in the sense that the reader is neither given the firm guidance in how to read it that 'science' would have provided, nor are they enabled to read it in any other way. The result is that it is very difficult for the reader of 'Little Kinsey' to move from the forced co-presences within it, of fact and interpretation and abstracted numbers and grounded observations, to think about the comparisons, similarities and differences between them. Interestingly, the research fragments of the 'Economics of Everyday Life' project do permit these kinds of deeper comparisons, but only because there is no 'account' of what these are meant to add up to as a whole.

The 'exoticism' of *May the Twelfth* was achieved by subverting the apparently central nature of the ritual of kingship, and instead assembling an 'elsewhere' of the ordinary streets and people of Britain, engaged upon those other, more mundane and, the implication is, more important events that composed Coronation Day 1937. The 'Economics of Everyday Life' project achieved a similar effect in at least some of its composing pieces of research the social significance of 'the suit' and the 'Worktown stomach', for instance – by exoticizing the quintessentially ordinary through focusing on it in detail and thereby assigning to it a significance not usually accorded. The text of 'Little Kinsey' could have achieved a similar effect to *May the Twelfth* by constraining the reader to note the comparisons between its more 'exotic' and potentially scandalous observational materials and the survey material it also contains; however, this did not happen and it is really only in the leftover observational material and the appendix containing an account of a 'homosexual group' (also leftover from earlier research) that this occurs.

May the Twelfth is an extremely 'open' piece of writing in the sense that there is little overt editorial control of the text. This begins, indeed, with the book's title, which does not include any reference to the Coronation; that it is 'about' this has to be read into the title by the reader. This is interestingly compared with the 'Economics of Everyday Life' materials, which exist in the form of research notes, drafts and fragments which are connected mainly through having been provided by researchers working on the same project rather than intellectual coherence or connectedness. Here there are *only* spaces around its fragments, which the reader necessarily fills to make any kind of sense of the project and what it was about, and no closure exists or can be made of these. In contrast with both, the draft manuscript of 'Little Kinsey' has a clear structure which derives from the apparent centrality of the survey material; and written drafts of chapters nearly all exist in what looks like final form and fit this structure closely. The degree of openness that exists here is provided in part by the unconventional emphasis on the 'ends' in its numerical data, and in part through the inclusion of observational materials from the earlier phase of the research. It is interesting to contemplate what the palimpsest text of the fieldwork studies of 'Churchtown' compared with 'Steeltown', only faintly observable in the text of 'Little Kinsey', might have been like if the earlier research strategy had not been superseded; given the memo outlining the earlier text and the fragments that remain, it might well have been a fully-realized observation- and fieldwork-based piece of writing.

May the Twelfth most certainly promotes, indeed in some respects requires, an active readership. I have noted its innovative use of indexing, which permits and indeed encourages the reader to move through the text in non-linear ways. In addition, the structure of the main text brings together through its use of collage and montage effects that are not fully realized, in the sense that it is the reader who has to make the links between these in order to make sense of its chapters and how these fit together. Again, the reader can approach the fragments of the 'Economics of Everyday Life' material in an open way because there is no encompassing text, no move towards any whole. The draft manuscript of 'Little Kinsey' has a relatively 'flat' way of using its different kinds of data, in which the reader is immersed in detail and provided with little indication of how to respond to what an analytical reading suggests are unresolvable tensions within it.

Overall, *May the Twelfth* was clearly an intentionally 'surrealist' project and one that exemplifies, indeed in some respects exceeds, the attributes attributed to 'surrealist ethnography'. It centrally uses collage and montage in the way the text is structured and presented, and these mechanisms represent in anti-referential ways the highly complex 'reality' of Coronation Day 1937. Clearly the two key editors structured the resultant text to be read on a number of different levels, the surface one of apparent description of the events on 12 May 1937, but also the 'beneath the surface' workings of the unconscious in underpinning people's often 'unexpected' and incongruently 'primitive' reactions. The text is a very 'rough' one that deliberately makes use of its 'report' character - paragraphs are numbered, reports are included and referenced to people by their age and sex, different kinds of text are brought together on the same page for the reader, rather than the editors, to unpack. Throughout the reader has to be an 'active reader' in working out the points of connection, the alluded to meanings, the intended conclusions to be drawn.

By contrast, the other two Mass-Observation projects I have discussed are not fully intentional examples of surrealist ethnography. Certainly they share some of its attributes, although sometimes these came into existence because problems that occurred prevented a more conventional kind of text from being produced, rather than having been deliberately chosen ways of writing and representing research materials. Also the 'Economics of Everyday life' project and 'Little Kinsey' both faced the same problematic as *May the Twelfth*, that of how best to represent the complexity of the research experience of everyday life, with its multiple points of view and shifting understandings and conclusions, within a single text. Indeed, as Clifford notes, this was the problem faced by Bateson's (1936) *Naven*. Here Bateson grappled with the interpretive hermeneutic issues involved by trying, and failing, to assimilate these within a functionalist, empiricist and realist generalized account, producing instead an ethnographic text which struggled to represent the epistemological issues, rather than the (failed) solution to these. But for these two Mass-Observation projects, the issues involved were compounded by trying to do this while also grappling with two sets of research data produced from different approaches and epistemological positions. Overall, the evidence here points in a different direction from that *of May the Twelfth*. This is that the complexity and the need to 'handle' the different kinds of research data was experienced as a problem, in the case of 'Little Kinsey' a largely insuperable problem, rather than as an opportunity. There is little sense that the researchers in the 'Economics of Everyday Life' project, and the writer of the text in the case of 'Little Kinsey', were able to call upon a well-articulated rationale and a set of intellectual principles for representing, even if not resolving, this which surrealist ideas provided and which, in my view, marks *May the Twelfth* as a fully realized surrealist ethnography.

What a discussion of these three projects brings into view is that the major contradiction embedded in the heart of Mass-Observation as a whole also impacted in consequential, although different, ways on these particular projects. Mass-Observation had a principled commitment to two equally founda-tional but mutually antagonistic principles: the idea of observers being 'subjective cameras' interpretively recording the world in their own ways; *and* the hierarchicalism of the 'new science' that Mass-Observation wanted to produce through the synthesizing role provided by its core researchers and writers, analysing and synthesizing the material that its mass observers merely collected. These produced not only different research approaches and different kinds of data, but also implied different ways of representing these, different styles of writing, different kinds of texts. It was only when one of these gained ascendancy over the other that a successful text resulted, in the way that surrealism enabled in the case of *May the Twelfth*. However, the 1949 changes which occurred in the wake of 'Little Kinsey' removed the contradiction thereby engendered by removing from the organization its commitment to observation and interpretation and firmly hitching 'Mass-Observation Limited' to the high positivism of contemporary market research. And here it was a clear commitment to conventional market re-search ways of operating that enabled another albeit very different resolution.

Although the use of fieldwork methods and approaches to research Britain survived and later flourished, what was lost sight of until fairly recently was this interesting and contentious past, in which political radicalism and methodological radicalism met through the activities and researches of Mass-Observation. The histories of the social sciences, market research, survey methods and fieldwork methods are closely intertwined in Britain over the period from 1937 to 1949. As I have endeavoured to show in the case of fieldwork methods, these complexities are shown in interesting ways through looking at Mass-Observation, its connections with and also separations from academia, and its attempts to use these methods in a number of its research projects.

Acknowledgements

This chapter was written while I was the Faculty of Arts Senior Research Fellow at the University of Auckland, New Zealand. During the period of the Fellowship I was based in Women's Studies, and I am grateful to Professor Maureen Molloy, Dr Heather Worth and Ms Hana Mata'u for making my time there so enjoyable, as well as to the Faculty of Arts for awarding me the Fellowship. I am as always extremely grateful to Dorothy Sheridan, Archivist at the Mass-Observation Archive at the University of Sussex, for help above and beyond the call of duty.

Notes

1. See here some of the original early Mass-Observation publications and particularly Mass-Observation, 1937, 1939; Madge and Harrisson, 1938.
2. These come together and can be glimpsed in the pages of Bartlett et al., 1939, one of the compilations from a series of social science conferences convened to consider aspects of the likely expansion of higher education.
3. Inevitably this also means that some original materials are available only in archival sources. However, as my discussion indicates, a good deal of the relevant materials are widely available in published form in books and journal articles and can be accessed by interested readers in the usual way through libraries.
4. See here, for instance, the widely available microform set of papers from 'The Tom Harrisson Mass-Observation Archive', published by Harvester Press, which is both voluminous and contains only one part of Mass-Observation's records, that concerned with its internal file reports.
5. In a few cases it is not possible to provide references to secondary sources for readers of this chapter, as some of Mass-Observation's activities have not yet been published on. In these cases, I provide a reference to an archive source, which in all cases refer to collections held in the Mass-Observation Archive at the University of Sussex, UK.
6. In the first two years of its activities, these included not only responses to the monthly directives but also pieces of research concerned with the use of Persil washing powder, smoking behaviour, a fascist march in Bermondsey, the blackout and other air raid precautions, the West Fulham by-election, social attitudes to margarine, reactions to advertising, newspaper reading, the non-voter, the US diamond market, clothes, washing cloths, bad dreams and nightmares, personal appearance, a 'square deal' for railways, propaganda, the impact of railway posters and sport in wartime.
7. In addition to Jennings and Madge's (1937) *May the Twelfth*, see also Laing, 1980;

M-L. Jennings, 1982; Chaney and Pickering, 1986; Hubble, 1998; and also Stanley, 1995a on Mass-Observation's day surveys more generally.

8. The 'Economics of Everyday Life' project not only has an extremely interesting topic of investigation, it is also interestingly bound up in this particularly crucial 'moment' in the development of fieldwork methods in Britain, and closely connected with a number of the 'methodological writings' that Mass-Observation staff were involved in producing at this time. See here Stanley, 1992 for a more detailed discussion.

9. The traffic between Mass-Observation and academia went in both directions. After the war Charles Madge moved into academia. Dennis Chapman joined the 'Economics of Everyday Life' project after working with Rowntree on his 1930s study of poverty in York; during and at the end of the war Chapman worked with David Glass and Ruth Glass on the reconstruction study of Middles-borough; while following the war he worked as an academic in the Business School at the University of Liverpool, as well as being involved in the formation of the Association of University Teachers (for an example of his sociological work, see Chapman, 1955). Similarly Gertrud Wagner had both a prewar, a wartime and a post war track record as an academic in addition to her involvement in the 'Economics of Everyday Life' project. Initially she had been involved on the periphery of the Marienthal study carried out by Paul Lazarsfeld and Marie Johoda; later she was involved in carrying out a Liverpool-based university study of the evacuation of children from Manchester (Wagner, 1939), while after the war she returned to Austria and to an academic career there.

10. See here Mass-Observation Archive Topic Collection, archival references TC6.A-I; TC7.A-J; WT24.A-D.

11. See here respectively Mass-Observation Archive Topic and Worktown collections, archival references TC1.C; TC6.E; WT24.B,C; WT24.D; WT33D; and WT36.C, F, I.

12. As the last project carried out by 'old' Mass-Observation before it became a conventional market research organization, the sex research known within the organization as 'Little Kinsey' is of particular interest in tracing its final methodological shifts and changes. See Stanley, 1995b and 1996 for detailed discussions of this project.

13. Mass-Observation's involvement with this new piece of research came about because of its headquarters' links with voluntary agencies concerned with 'sexual' matters, including divorce, 'motherhood', under-age sexual activity, venereal disease and so on. The impetus was in part the forthcoming publication of the first part of the Kinsey Report in the United States, in part Mass-Observation wanting to investigate 'public opinion' about such matters; and accordingly it consulted key figures within the community of voluntary agencies that it frequently worked with.

14. However, the version which exists in typescript in the Mass-Observation archive was published in full in Stanley, 1995b.

References

Abrams, Mark (1951) *Social Surveys and Social Action*. London: Heinemann.

Allen, Roy and Bowley, Arthur (1935) *Family Expenditure: A Study of its Variation.* London: Staples Press.

Bartlett, Frederick, Ginsberg, Morris, Lingren, Ethel and Thouless, Ralph (eds) (1939) *The Study of Society.* London: Routledge and Kegan Paul.

Bateson, Geoffrey (1936) *Naven: A Survey of the Problems Suggested by a Composite Picture of the Culture of a New Guinea Tribe Drawn from Three Points of View.* Cambridge: Cambridge University Press.

Baxendale, John and Pawling, Chris (1996) 'The documentary film and Mass-Observation', in *Narrating the Thirties: A Decade in the Making, 1930 to the Present.* Basingstoke: Macmillan. pp. 17–45.

Buhner, Martin, Bales, Kevin and Sklar, Kathryn Kish (eds) (1991) *The Social Survey in Historical Perspective, 1880–1940.* Cambridge: Cambridge University Press.

Bunn, Margaret (1943) 'Mass-Observation: A comment on *People in Production',* *Manchester School,* No, 31: 24–37.

Calder, Angus and Sheridan, Dorothy (eds) (1984) *Speak for Yourself: A Mass-Observation Anthology.* London: Jonathon Cape.

Chaney, David and Pickering, Michael (1985) 'Democracy and communication: Mass-Observation 1937–1943', *Journal of Communication,* 36: 41–56.

Chaney, David and Pickering, Michael (1986) 'Authorship in documentary: sociology as an art form in Mass-Observation', in John Corner (ed.), *Documentary and the Mass Media.* London: Edward Arnold. pp. 29–44.

Chapman, Dennis (1955) *The Home and Social Status.* London: Routledge and Kegan Paul.

Clifford, James (1988) 'On ethnographic surrealism', in *The Predicament of Culture: Twentieth-Century Ethnography, Literature, and Art.* Cambridge, MA: Harvard University Press, pp. 117–51.

Cross, Gary (ed.) (1990) *Worktowners at Blackpool: Mass-Observation and Popular Leisure in the 1930s.* London: Routledge.

Firth, Raymond (1938) 'An anthropologist's view of Mass-Observation', *Sociological Review,* No. 31: 166–93.

Firth, Raymond (1939) 'Critique of Mass-Observation', unpublished lecture, Newcastle Literary and Philosophical Society, 30 January 1939.

Harrisson, Tom (1937) *Savage Civilisation.* London: Gollancz.

Hubble, Nick (1998) 'Walter Benjamin and the theory of Mass-Observation: surveillance contra surveillance at the first media coronation', unpublished paper, Surveillance Conference, Liverpool John Moores University, June 1998.

Jennings, Humphrey (1986) *Pandemonium.* Glencoe, IL: The Free Press.

Jennings, Humphrey and Madge, Charles (eds) (1937) *May the Twelfth: Mass-Observation Day Surveys 1937.* London: Faber and Faber.

Jennings, Mary-Lou (ed.) (1982) *Humphrey Jennings, Film-Maker/Painter/Poet.* London: British Film Institute in Association with Riverside Studios.

Johoda, Marie (1938) 'Review of *Mass-Observation* and of *May 12',* *Sociological Review,* No. 30: 208–9.

Johoda, Marie (1940) 'Review of *War Begins at Home',* *Sociological Review, No.* 32: 129–31.

Laing, Stuart (1980) 'Presenting "Things as They Are": John Summerfield's *May Day* and Mass-Observation', in Frank Glovership (ed.), *Class, Culture and Social Change.* Brighton: Harvester Press, pp. 142–60.

Lowe, Adolph (1935) *Economics and Sociology.* London: Allen and Unwin.

McClancy, Jeremy (1995) 'Brief encounter: the meeting, in Mass-Observation, of

British surrealism and popular anthropology', *Journal of the Royal Anthropological Institute,* 1: 495–07.

Madge, Charles (1933) 'Surrealism for the English', *New Verse,* 6: 14–18.

Madge, Charles (1937) *The Disappearing Castle.* London: Faber and Faber.

Madge, Charles and Harrisson, Tom (1938) *First Year's Work, 1937–1938, by Mass-Observation.* London: Lindsay Drummond.

Madge, Charles and Jennings, Humphrey (1937) 'Poetic description and Mass-Observation', *New Verse,* No. 24.

Malinowski, Bronislaw (1938) 'A nation-wide intelligence service', in Charles Madge and Tom Harrisson (eds), *First Year's Work, 1937–1938, by Mass-Observation.* London: Lindsay Drummond. pp. 81–121.

Marshall, Thomas T.H. (1937) 'Is Mass-Observation moonshine?', *The Highway,* No. 30: 48–50.

Mass-Observation (1937) *Mass-Observation.* London: Muller.

Mass-Observation (1939) *Britain by Mass-Observation.* Harmordsworth: Penguin.

Mass-Observation (1945 *Britain and her Birth-Rate.* London: Advertising Standards Guild.

Oeser, Oscar (1937) 'Methods and assumptions of field work in social psychology', *British Journal of Psychology,* No. 27: 343–63.

Oeser, Oscar (1939) 'The value of team work and functional penetration as methods in social investigation', in Frederick Bartlett, Morris Ginsberg, Ethel Lindgren and Ralph Thouless (eds), *The Study of Society.* London: Routledge and Kegan Paul. pp. 402–17.

Sheridan, Dorothy (ed.) (1990) *Wartime Women: A Mass-Observation Anthology.* London: Heinemann.

Sheridan, Dorothy (1994) 'Using the Mass-Observation archive as a source for women's studies', *Women's History Review,* 3: 101–13.

Stanley, Liz (1990) 'The archaeology of a 1930 Mass-Observation project', Sociology Occasional Paper No. 27.

Stanley, Liz (1992) 'The "Economics of Everyday Life": A Mass-Observation project in Bolton', *North West Labour History Journal,* No. 17: 95–102.

Stanley, Liz (1995a) 'Women have servants and men never eat: Mass-Observation day diaries 1937', *Women's History Review* 4: 85–102.

Stanley, Liz (1995b) *Sex Surveyed 1949–1994: From Mass-Observation's 'Little Kinsey' to the National Survey and the Hite Reports.* London: Taylor and Francis.

Stanley, Liz (1996) 'Mass-Observation's "Little Kinsey" and the British sex survey tradition', in Jeffrey Weeks and Janet Holland (eds), *Sexual Cultures: Communities, Values and Intimacy.* London: Macmillan. pp. 97–114.

Wagner, Gertrud (1939) *Preliminary Report on the Problem of Evacuation.* Liverpool: University of Liverpool Department of Social Sciences in association with the University Settlement.

Wells, Alan (1936) 'Social surveys and sociology', *Sociological Review,* No. 28: 274 –94.

Young, Terence (1934) *Becontree and Dagenham: A Report for the Pilgrim Trust.* London: Becontree Social Survey Committee.

36

"Déjà Entendu": The Liminal Qualities of Anthropological Fieldnotes

Jean E. Jackson

During the past three years I have been interviewing fieldworkers, almost all of them anthropologists, about their fieldnotes. I became interested in this topic while exploring my own relationship to my fieldnotes for a symposium on the topic (see Jackson 1990). However, chats with fellow anthropologists proved so fascinating that I decided on an interview format and began looking for "natives" in a more systematic fashion. The rather nonrandom sample of seventy that has resulted is mostly from the East Coast, with a bias toward the Boston area. With the exceptions of one archaeologist, one psychologist, two sociologists, two political scientists, and one linguist (all of whom do research "in the field"), all are card-carrying anthropologists in terms of training and employment.[1] The only representativeness I have attempted to maintain is a reasonably balanced sex ratio and a range of ages.[2] Although the data come from anthropologists,[3] I suspect that any fieldworker will respond to and identify with most of the themes this chapter addresses.

Virtually all respondents expressed strong and ambivalent feelings about their notes. The subject of fieldnotes is clearly complex, touchy, and disturbing for most of us. Probing into why this is so tells us some things about social science – particularly anthropology – and its discontents.

A productive approach for understanding these unruly feelings is to analyze all the ways in which fieldnotes are liminal – possessing the characteristic of being betwixt and between, "neither fish nor fowl." Twilight is a temporal liminality, swamps a geographical one, lungfish a zoological example, hermaphrodites a sexual liminality. Liminality necessarily occurs when we impose classification systems upon the natural world; what is

Source: *Representation in Ethnography*, 1995, Sage, pp. 36-78.

interesting is that it is a conspicuous feature in the symbol system of every culture, often accompanied by marked affect.

Why liminality is highlighted in ritual and symbol and associated with high affect is debated in the literature. A functionalist social-structural explanation would suggest that since liminality reveals gaps and confusions in rules and classifications, to highlight liminality in symbol and ritual is to appropriate threatening ambiguity to illustrate just how important clarity and unambiguity are.[4] A functionalist psychological explanation would deal with the ways in which "betwixt and between" phenomena disturb one's sense of order and purpose and are hence emphasized and paid attention to because the resulting sense of order and control relieves anxiety.[5] This chapter suggests that a clue to the source of the strong feelings that interviewees revealed about the topic of fieldnotes lies in their striking liminality.

How are anthropological fieldwork and fieldnote-taking liminal? To give a sense of my argument, let's imagine me watching a ritual during my field research in the Northwest Amazon. The ritual itself, a male initiation rite, has all of the features associated with ritual liminality: ambiguity, a dissolution of most or all categories and classifications, role reversals, a suspension of numerous rules, periods of seclusion, and a stress on the absolute authority of the elders (Turner 1967, also 1974). The other ritual I am engaged in, fieldwork and fieldnote-taking, involves similar liminalities. To begin with, I am only marginally participating in the Tukanoan ritual: for one thing, I am not a native, and furthermore, the work I am engaged in requires that I not participate fully. My continual movement back and forth between participant and observer roles, between incorporation into the community and dissociation from it[6] is a quintessentially betwixt and between status. My behavior, especially my fieldnote-taking, serves to remind me, and them, that I am in the field but not of the field.

I am also betwixt and between in that in this particular fieldwork I am in between student and professional status. I am also geographically and culturally floating in a kind of limbo,[7] because although I am indeed far from home in any number of respects I will not remain with the Tukanoans I now live with.[8] Like the male initiands, I am also, in a sense, in a period of seclusion, during which many familiar categories and classifications are dissolved. Moreover, role reversals have occurred insofar as I have gone from being a graduate student to an ignorant, rude, snooping child (see Jackson 1986). And although I have the status of relatively wealthy, authoritative, and high-prestige outsider, I am also extremely dependent on the people I live with for "emotional gratification, food, information, shelter" (Kondo 1982, 4).

Fieldwork is clearly liminal in many respects; in the following section I systematically outline how fieldnotes reflect and contribute to this state.

Types of Liminality in Fieldnotes

I have organized the kinds of liminality revealed in the interview material into three overarching categories: (1) betwixt and between worlds, (2) betwixt and between selves, and (3) betwixt and between words. The first discusses the kinds of liminality found in the generic fieldwork enterprise. The second refers to the ways in which fieldnotes mediate between the fieldworker's different roles, stressing his or her personal relationship to fieldnotes. And the third refers to the liminalities found in the relationship between fieldnotes and other genres of writing. It should be noted that these categorizations are somewhat arbitrary and hence some topics are inevitably mentioned in more than one section of the article – for example, the issue of privacy.

Between Worlds

Between Home and Field. While in the field, fieldnotes connect the anthropologist to home, to the anthropological profession, and, upon return to base, to the field. For example, several interviewees noted that fieldnotes served to remind them (and the natives) that they were doing a project, not just "sitting on a mountain in Pakistan drinking tea." One interviewee said, "My field notebook was always a small notebook that would fit into my pocket. As a result it was a kind of badge." Several also mentioned that, at first, they generated fieldnotes to reassure themselves and their advisors that they were "doing their job."

For many respondents, fieldnote-taking often seems to reflect a more general tension, both geographical and temporal, between being there, immersed, trying to "go native" to some extent, and simultaneously thinking about the subsequent analysis and write-up. One respondent stated, "As Lévi-Strauss says about the Nambicuara, with me in Paris and them in Brazil, then it works. From a distance. While there, you and they are one, and it doesn't work."

Upon return, except for a few artifacts, the fieldnotes are the only physical link between the anthropologist and this powerful experience. Fieldnotes are the means through which the significance of this experience becomes transformed from an engrossing period, in which everything in one's life is radically altered, to a period of being engrossed in a writing project, one that will establish or maintain one's professional career:

> Looking at them, when I see this dirt,[9] blood, and spit, it's an external tangible sign of my legitimacy as an anthropologist.[10]

> Yes, the only physical stuff you have from fieldwork. It made you an anthropologist ... and the only evidence was the stuff you brought back.

One might want to claim that, in a certain sense, anthropologists are always in a liminal state between the two cultures, regardless of which one they're in at a given point in time, and that fieldnotes continually remind them of this. The links that fieldnotes create to both cultures sometimes seem alienating and wrong; as we shall see, interviewees express this with comments about resenting their fieldnotes.

The field is also a liminal state between two very different stages in graduate training. It is commonplace that fieldwork is a coming-of-age process. Several interviewees offered pithy and often sophisticated remarks:

> Fieldnotes is an extension of that rite of passage called fieldwork. That says it. One of the Palladiums of fieldwork as a kind of holy ritual process … fieldnotes becomes one of those objects that bring good out of this rite of passage.

> When I was a student, the fact that you had come back from the field … you could call full professors by their first name. The more esoteric, exotic [your fieldwork site was], the more you had passed your serious rite of passage.

Doing fieldnotes a certain way (or, for some, doing them at all) is often associated with one's mentor and graduate department philosophy. As graduate students mature and increasingly choose to "do it my way," changes in their approach to fieldnotes can be a part of this maturing (see Jackson 1990). For some anthropologists, fieldnotes are a diploma, and the continued production of fieldnotes is a sign that one is a member in good standing in the anthropological club. However, for a few interviewees fieldnotes are less tools of the trade and more crutches of the apprentice. In either case, how one writes and uses fieldnotes can represent one's training, graduate school persona, *and* one's liberation from graduate school and dependent, cadet status. Traditionally, anthropological fieldwork has implied research involving isolation, a lengthy stay, and layers of difficulty in obtaining information.[11] Overcoming these difficulties is seen as demanding a near-total marshalling of one's talents and resources. Fieldnotes are precious for many reasons: because of the labor of getting them, because they are one's ticket to a dissertation, subsequent publishing and a job, because the information is unique, and so forth. While hard work in any research creates value for the resulting documents, the irreplaceability of many sets of fieldnotes and the special circumstances under which they are obtained make their value unique, different from notes taken in a library, for instance, or during a laboratory experiment. As respondents affirm, you "sweat blood" for them. Yet many interviewees also commented on how worthless their fieldnotes were in some ways – because they were indecipherable, incomplete, dis-ordered, and so on. The very factors that make them valuable upon return home (they were gathered in an exotic, isolated, "primitive" setting) make them deficient in terms of other "home" criteria (one does not have time to order fieldnotes, one writes them by hand – sometimes clandestinely – and so they are messy, etc.). Once again we see contradictory and ambivalent opinions expressed about fieldnotes.

The boundaries of the field can be fuzzy or can shift over time. Many fieldworkers enter and leave the field several times, and if one takes one's fieldnotes to a hotel room in a city, for example, for interim analysis, both the anthropologist and fieldnotes will occupy a geographically liminal state. One interviewee stated, "You should get away and go over them, talk to them."

Or the boundaries of "the field" can shift in other ways. One respondent said, "For example, in Nicaragua, it's such an ongoing event, and I can't say, 'Something's happening but it's not of relevance.' "

Fieldnote-taking can be a crucial defining feature of just what the field is. An anthropologist who studies recombinant DNA laboratories commented, "Sometimes I don't take notes on purpose. ... I use it as a protective device. My way of turning off."

Between Fieldworker and Native. Anthropologists often claim that a special relationship occurs between themselves and the native. This idea was present in some interviewees' definitions of fieldnotes:

> I don't think the *fact* of notes is unique, but the type of notes is ... special. We try so hard to get close to the people we're working on. Most anthropologists are not really satisfied until they've seen them, seen the country, smelt them. So there's a somewhat immediate quality to our notes.

It is commonplace that anthropology depends on this "going native" aspect of information gathering far more than sociology or, even more so, psychology. A clinical psychologist wants to acquire understanding and empathy but hardly feels pulled to "go native." Anthropologists say that "your measure of success is how comfortable you feel ... and to what degree you become socialized to the culture." But a conflict exists in any fieldwork situation, first, because as we have seen, the natives do not ever permit one to "go native" entirely and, second, the anthropological enterprise depends on a precarious, liminal balance between being an insider and an outsider:

> Anthropology is a combination of this interaction with people and writing. Fieldnotes is an intermediate step between the immediate experience of interaction and the written outcome ... no matter how much one may understand the other, it doesn't have a certain kind of reality until it's put into fieldnotes.[12]

Fieldnotes can thus be seen to mediate between anthropologist and native. In the following quote, a certain sense, *both* anthropologist and fieldnotes play this role: "Oneself is the instrument. In relationship with the other. And fieldnotes is a record of that."

One respondent answered the question about anthropologists creating their documents thus: "But the 'create' part is somewhat accurate because it is being filtered through the person one is talking to, who's creating the document." Often, the anthropologist's nonnative status, his or her being neither fish nor fowl, can aid the research. The element of geographical liminality was noted by one respondent: "Most people had confidence that I wasn't a witch, for instance, and they could tell me things that wouldn't have consequences down the road because I'd just take it away with me." Many interviewees felt that fieldnotes set up barriers between themselves and the natives. One must gain confidence and intimacy to get good fieldnotes, and this can be aided by the natives' "not knowing" or "forgetting." One interviewee stated, "The main thing is that they didn't realize I was taking notes." Another interviewee said, "The people being observed forget you're there. There is something unethical about that, they go on about their business, and you're still observing." The moral unease this engenders comes out in statements such as "I always feel as though I have a dual identity, it makes me feel sneaky and dishonest" and "Oftentimes a conversation the other person thinks is spontaneous, I begin to turn it into an interview, and I think that's highly questionable." This ambivalence about the anthropologist/native relationship often comes out in concern about ownership of fieldnotes. One anthropologist agonized over this issue for a long time:

> My issue has always been, what right do I have to divulge this information that's been given to me? The Bakaga are very jealous of their songs. So it's an issue of confidentiality, but within the local context. I eventually decided, resolved it. Yes, I do, and, furthermore, I have an obligation.

He made his decision in part by considering these fieldnotes as *not* his. He said, "Several older Bakaga decided to turn their knowledge over to me. So I'm a caretaker. It's not mine. I feel I can't make decisions about it." This individual first speaks of making a decision and then says he feels he cannot make decisions.

Anthropologists and their fieldnotes are in a liminal situation insofar as many speak of the notes being neither entirely the private property of the anthropologist nor of anyone else. In some cases, others' use of fieldnotes can potentially harm the native community; an example given below of fieldnotes being subpoenaed illustrates this quite well. Many interviewees mused about whether their notes were strictly private property or somehow belonged to the native community. One interviewee stated, "It is an issue with the Jakanda, but I feel I sweat blood for them so when a young Jakanda anthropologist who hasn't done anything says the notes belong to them I don't feel too conflicted." But he later said,

> After I die they ought to be available to others, although I don't want to think about it – then my paranoia comes back. But enough scarce resources have been spent on me by funding agencies, and the Jakanda gave me so much, and so they should be available.

A further complicating factor is natives' claims to fieldnotes because of confidentiality. One respondent said, "On the other hand, my question is that taking fieldnotes … we're reporting on the public and private lives of the natives. To what extent are the documents our own? And for either side, the observer and observed. I don't think there's an easy solution."

Fieldnotes' mediating between anthropologist and native can be further complicated by natives' feelings about notebooks, cameras, and tape recorders. Suspicion, dislike, and misunderstanding abound in the interview materials. Geographical, temporal, occupational, and perhaps motivational liminality infuse the following example of interaction between anthropologist and informant. An interviewee stated,

> I couldn't take out the notebook, it was disruptive. She knew I was writing it down, but it changed her storytelling. The next day she'd clarify. So the first chance I got, I'd go into the next room and type it up. She wasn't resentful [of my note-taking], but it interrupted the flow. At some level she'd forget she was telling things to [me] who was "working," and the next day she'd remember.[13]

Fieldnotes figure in interviewees' attempts to deal with negative feelings about informants. Many anthropologists use fieldnotes, especially a diary,[14] for what we can call the "garbage-can function" – a private place to vent spleen, to have control, to speak in a civilized language for a while:

> Fieldnotes allow you to keep a grip on your sanity.

> I learned that an anthropologist never becomes a member of the society one is studying, and one has to accept it. This journal gave me a release, I could express this, if only to myself.

Finally, fieldnotes' role as a link between anthropologist and native conflicts with the notion of fieldnotes as emotionally detached, scientific materials:

> After he died I couldn't play the tapes. ... I couldn't even look at them. It has a lot, I suppose, to do with your relationship to the people. They never were "subjects" of my research. So I've always had a hard time seeing this as "data."

The question of whether anthropology is humanities or science is the focus of a great deal of debate in the literature. Grappling with this issue led interviewees to disclose contradictory feelings about their fieldnotes because the notes themselves possess this "neither fish nor fowl" epistemological status:

> I know a lot of people will be antagonistic, but the more the anthropologist can stand outside the fieldwork process emotionally, the better off the document will be. This is always a problem because on the one hand to get the data you have to be emotionally involved, but to write the document you have to be emotionally distant.

I'm a Boasian and fully believe in asking people what's on their minds, but I try to write down what they say as literally as possible ... and what they say is the fieldnotes.

How I listen to an interview ... what I have to do to be able to hear ... trying to enter their consciousness and their reality.[15]

Between Experience and Representation: Fieldwork versus Fieldnotes. Despite the fact that fieldnote-taking is ostensibly a part of fieldwork, many anthropologists say they feel a tension between doing fieldwork and writing fieldnotes. As Thoreau noted, we cannot both live our lives and write them, and many interviewees commented on how frustrating it is to try to live the life of the natives as fully as possible and yet find time to write up the information gathered:

I had the same obsession with completeness everyone else does. Except ... you end up not doing fieldwork. Ten minutes can take 4 hours' write-up ... an anthropological dilemma.

Many interviewees described how fieldnotes can disrupt the flow of fieldwork:

I slowed down. More concerned with the hour to hour. You forget to take notes because you feel this is your life.

Many fieldworkers clearly feel that writing and processing fieldnotes is a lonely activity, a burden, and sometimes an ordeal. Simple exhaustion and time crunches account for some of this, as well as other material difficulties such as lack of light or space. A few interviewees spoke of longing to be liberated from the fieldnotes and what they represent, and a very few actually took this step, justifying it in terms of time constraints. One respondent stated, "Fieldnotes get in the way. They interfere with what fieldwork is all about." Yet for many the two are inextricably linked:

So I think there was something about the typing of the notes that was very important ... a ritual. That part of the day when you felt you were accomplishing something.

[I had] to write something down every day. To not accept everything as normal.

Several anthropologists spoke of a need to be concerned about being too much "in the field." One respondent said, "So I feel better taking notes ... because it's clear that we're interviewing." Some commented that fieldnotes help preserve a necessary, although at times painful and disturbing, marginal status with regard to going native.[16] One interviewee said that "your wife and kids will probably go more native than you" because the fieldwork enterprise *requires* that you not live like the natives.

Fieldnotes are thus in several respects both an aid and a hindrance to fieldwork – another ambiguous, liminal status.

Between Selves

This section explores the anthropologist's personal relationship to his or her notes. It could also be titled "between roles." As we have already seen, fieldnotes both mediate between and serve as symbols of the roles the anthropologist plays, at times highlighting the contradictions between them. Furthermore, many anthropologists identify with, yet also feel alienated from their notes. I term this the "me/not me" liminality.

Fieldnotes and Self. Quite a number of interviewees' definitions of fieldnotes involved the self in some fashion.

To one respondent, fieldnotes are "the description of the situation that the anthropologist is in with respect to the intellectual problem – the reason for being there in the first place. Archival stuff is field *data*. Notes are the documents *you* create."

For some anthropologists, fieldnotes are an assistant, an aide-memoir, in a fairly uncomplicated, straightforward manner. In these instances the boundaries between fieldnotes and self are fairly clear-cut. A respondent said that fieldnotes "fix in my memory the incident I'm describing so that when I later read them, a flood of detail comes back into conscious memory, and the subsequent analysis I do is not of the fieldnotes but of the memory."

For some interviewees, fieldnotes fall far short of memory. For these anthropologists, memories contain graphic or aural qualities that conventional fieldnotes cannot compete with.

> I was disappointed that they weren't as magical as my memory. My memory is a recreated memory, and there are a lot of visual features to my memory, whereas fieldnotes were much more sort of mere rendering. They jog my much more real memories of the events.

For some interviewees, fieldnotes are "not me" in an almost competitive way. While fieldnotes' superior recall is acknowledged as an aid, they are nonetheless resented and sometimes envied for being more accurate. They remind one of one's faulty memory, or they cramp one's style:

> In a way when doing my thesis I in a certain sense wanted to lose them because then I would write it up out of whole cloth, my understanding of them and my knowledge of other lowland South American societies. My fieldnotes were constantly contradicting this. Challenging my constructions of Bamipa culture and social life, so in that sense I wanted to just be rid of them. So they've

always been a good corrective to oversimplification. They've been a constant critic, a critic who knows the Bamipa better than I do in certain regards.

[It's like] saying Leach's book is brilliant *because* he lost his fieldnotes. ... He could sort of invent, or create, embroider, rather than be tied down to the messiness of daily data.

Anxiety about loss of fieldnotes has come up so many times and so dramatically – images of burning appear quite often – that I have concluded that for some interviewees fear about loss is accompanied by an unexamined attraction to the idea. The many legends, apocryphal or not, about lost fieldnotes probably fits into this category of horrorific and yet delicious, forbidden fantasy. One interviewee said, "So maybe the people who lost their notes are better off."

Other interviewees spoke of an unclear relationship between memory – "headnotes" (Ottenberg 1990) – and written notes. Here the boundary between self and fieldnotes becomes fuzzier:

So they [other people] think I'm not using them. I *am,* though. But people look at that [unopened packages of fieldnotes] as a kind of laziness. [But] *I* am the best field notebook I have. I know the information.

Various quotes revealed a fear of fieldnotes dominating or at least having too much power or too much presence, such as "They can be a kind of albatross around your neck" and "They seem like they take up a lot of room. ... They take up too much room."

Fieldnotes can represent a requirement to justify or judge oneself, as they did for the interviewee who stated, "Only when doing this are you constantly asked to evaluate yourself, are you asking yourself, you're asking, 'What am I doing?' " And the evaluation might not be favorable, as in the following responses:

It's partially a fear. Part is that it's your personal property, people can see you in a state of intellectual undress. People don't like to have to defend themselves. Why don't I have quantitative data for sheep? I don't *know* why!

Rereading them, some of them look pretty lame. How could you be so stupid or puerile?

Or they can be an affirmation:

[There's] a feeling of confidence that if one could manage this one could manage almost anything.

I do get pleasure in working with them again, particularly my notes from my first work. A feeling of sort of, that is where I came in, and I can sometimes recapture some of the intellectual and physical excitement of being there.

Many interviewees spoke of how fieldnotes reveal what kind of person one is: messy, responsible, procrastinating, exploitative, tidy, compulsive, generous. Because of all the ways in which fieldnotes are linked to important issues in interviewees' life and work, fieldnotes themselves become a sign and symbol of who the individual is, as a professional and, to some degree, in a comprehensive sense:

> When I think of activities I do, that's a lot closer to the core of my identity than most things.

> I have a lot of affection for my notes in a funny way ... their role here – in the U.S., my study, in terms of my professional self. Something about my academic identity. I'm not proud of everything about them but I am proud of some things about them ... that they represent. Probably in a less conscious way some motive for my not wanting to make them too public.

> My primary identity is someone who writes things down and writes about them. Not just hanging out.

Thus fieldnotes provide an ongoing opportunity to examine oneself, at times are seen as an extension of self, and, for many, they can be a validation or betrayal of self. An interviewee said, "Fieldnotes can reveal how worthless your work was, the lacunae, your linguistic incompetence, your not being made a blood brother, your childish temper." An interesting illustration of this is one anthropologist's account of how her subpoenaed fieldnotes were discredited, as a way of discrediting her expertise and authority:

> "They're dog's breakfast!" they [the opposition lawyers] would say. "How can you expect anything from this?" ... It had been written on a [piece of paper on] the back of a Toyota and [was] totally incomprehensible to anyone but me. But it was an attack on my credibility. ... I said, "This is a genealogy." *"This* is a genealogy?" Our lawyer would jump in, "Yes, of course."

Malinowski's (1967) diary was mentioned by many interviewees regarding this issue. With regard to whether they will validate or discredit the self, fieldnotes are most definitely betwixt and between.

For many interviewees, the unique qualities of the field make fieldnotes a far more unique and personal document than other kinds of note-taking. As already noted, creating fieldnotes – and subsequently working with one's creation – evokes powerful feelings for many anthropologists. While the strength and nature of such feelings vary with the anthropologist, the project, and the actual field situation, fieldnotes' ability to elicit strong feelings is due, in part, because one is disoriented, challenged, confused, or over-stressed *and* euphoric, energized, and engaged when creating them. This results in their creators feeling attached to them and identifying with them apparently far more than how most lawyers, journalists, or psychologists feel about their notes – which is not to say that these professionals do not have strong feelings about some of their notes; it is a question of degree. An interviewee stated, "One feels possessive towards fieldnotes because they are so linked to oneself. ... It's like they're part of me. To turn them over to a university archive is one of the most difficult things to do." Another interviewee commented on the link between fieldnotes and self, with reference to Boas's diary: "[They] reveal a lot and for that reason they are valuable documents. Does the anthropologist see the culture, or see himself in the culture ... see the social context from which he comes as somehow replicated in the culture?" Interestingly, this interviewee thinks she will destroy her fieldnotes before she dies.

The existence of a set of fieldnotes can, as we have seen, be an affirmation or represent accomplishment or the meeting and overcoming of a stiff challenge. But fieldnotes, once created, can represent potential alienation and unintentional hurt to oneself and the natives. Of course, this issue of potential alienation is a major difference between fieldnotes and headnotes. The written notes become far more separated from one's control, even taking into consideration the lack of control associated with memory's tendency to fade and distort. For most anthropologists, fieldnotes demand serious attention with regard to confidentiality, privacy versus sharing, and obligations to the profession and posterity. For example, one anthropologist felt torn by his obligations to the pro-Indian organization that facilitated his gaining access to his fieldwork community. He stated, "They applied considerable moral pressure [to have access to his fieldnotes]. The danger is that when I'm speaking I can be polite, but the fieldnotes are in black and white." Whereas memory and cognition are eternally changing, or at least are potentially doing so, fieldnotes, once written, become fixed – although, of course, the mind can work with them at different times and reinterpret them. As we have seen, memories are not fixed and can paradoxically appear to be more useful for this reason. An interviewee said that "it reifies certain things, to get it into boxes. For me ... a lot gets lost when they're translated onto these cards." Hence headnotes can appear to be both truer to and more congruent with one's sense of self. But since memories can fade and become distorted, we have some compelling reasons why the anthropologist's relationship to fieldnotes typifies a liminal, ambiguous state. Fieldnotes are both better and worse than headnotes; they evoke a high degree of both negative and positive affect, and the rules for how to think about and write them are confused, leading one to doubt oneself.

One interviewee differentiated fieldnotes from other written materials connected with fieldwork precisely in terms of the connections between written record, mind, and memory:

> That might be closer to a definition of a fieldnote: something that can't be readily comprehended by another person. ... A newspaper clipping can be a fieldnote if it needs to be read by me. ... It's what I remember; the notes mediate the memory and the interaction.

For many anthropologists, fieldnotes' ability to trigger memory and occasion new analysis greatly increases their value. However, this is complicated because of the issue of reliability of one's memory, as illustrated by the following:

> I don't mean to sound too Proustian about it, but suddenly an event years later causes you to rethink, reconceptualize your field experience, but also will trigger off memories you may not have recorded. What is the status of that material?

> So I didn't take notes, I would rely on my memory. ... I didn't realize before fieldwork the incredible selectivity of one's mind. A source of great anxiety. I felt I shouldn't be filtering as I was. I eventually concluded that I couldn't do anything about it, and so became reconciled.

> Are memories fieldnotes? I use them that way, even though they aren't the same kind of evidence. It took a while for me to be able to rely on my memory. But I had to, since the idea of what I was doing had changed, and I had memories but no notes. I had to say, "Well, I *saw* that happen." I am a fieldnote.

An interviewee commented on other consequences of the close link between fieldnotes, mind, and self by stating, "Unlike the historian, or literary scholar, where the text is independent to some extent, he approaches it with a kind of freshness. The anthropologist spends so much time going over the same material, there's a quality of *déjà entendu.*" Another interviewee spoke of the act of creating fieldnotes as depleting self: "I'd get only one chance to write it down, because every time you do you use up your quota of freshness of insight. You run out your string on that." For some, mind and fieldnotes are completely interdependent; as one interviewee stated, "It's not a random sample, it's much better designed. But because the design and values are in my head, it's dead data without me." Another noted that as understanding increases, fieldnotes decrease – the notion that comprehensive fieldnotes are produced only at the apprentice stage:

> He [my advisor] said he could make sense of early notes but less sense of them later, even though I understood more. I was making telegraphed notes by then ... a dramatic dropoff. ... So I wrote less and less as I was learning more and more.

For some, fieldnotes interferes with the dynamic interaction between mind and fieldwork. An interviewee stated, "The record is in my head, not on paper. The record on paper, it, because it's static, interferes with fieldwork. ... Keeping fieldnotes interferes with what's really important." A complex interdependence involving mutual support and mutual impediment clearly exists between fieldnotes and mind. This mutual dependence involves order, comprehensiveness, and veracity and both negative and positive value –

potential benefit to the fieldworker and his or her intended audience[17] and potential danger to the fieldworker and the native.

Sometimes, the interviewee, working with the fieldnotes, feels different in some way from the person he or she was when creating the fieldnotes, as shown by the following quotes:

> Later I can see people's intentions more clearly. So there is more value in the notes, in hindsight. In some ways, it's like looking at another me.

> They're useful as a document for what happened and as a device for triggering new analysis, to go back as a different person or with different theoretical interpretations, at a different stage in life.

Sometimes, anthropologists work with these earlier selves as well as the information fieldnotes contain. One anthropologist stated,

> Especially after time has passed, and you go back and it's as if they're written by someone else. I find myself interpreting and scrutinizing them. Wouldn't change them. I write commentaries and date the commentary. Poking fun at myself, usually, I guess, with posterity in mind.

Many interviewees speak of the consequences of fieldnotes' separation from self. For example, one interviewee said, "A separate body of work, now, and sometimes I don't recognize what I've written, so now reviewing my fieldnotes is sometimes like doing fieldwork all over again."

Even though fieldnotes have a separate existence, for many interviewees their notes and their selves are spliced in a kind of organic, mystical way. Other factors contribute to respondents' confusion about this matter, of course, such as worries about compromising informants, the possibility of misinterpretation, or the possibility of personal material being read or even published without permission. As noted above, the specter of Malinowski's diary made an appearance in many of the interviews, as it did when an interviewee said, "What fieldnotes are good for is revealing something about the fieldworker. We now see Malinowski as a colonialist, racist, male chauvinist pig."

Many commented on the problematic status of their fieldnotes being used without them there to interpret:

> Whereas my notes are a mnemonic for me ... and therefore more information will come out of the notes than is there, but I have to be there. I don't know how to deal with this. For example, I have a number of different genealogies. I make a comment in the notes that it's wrong. But I don't explain why this guy would say he was this kind of cousin. I know it, though.

> All my notes are mine. In some ways because I'm the only one to decipher them. It is a certain amount of protection.

In sum, it is clear that fieldnotes are both "me" and "not me" in many ways, and this quality poses problems for many ethnographers.

The link between the potential value of fieldnotes for others and the me/not-me theme comes up again and again in the interviews: "Fieldnotes are rubbish, garbage, and will be even more so upon my death"; "They are incredibly important documents and I have to organize them, send them to an archive"; "They are valuable, yes, but only so long as I am alive to give them life and meaning." Clearly, the complex and ambivalent attachment many anthropologists feel toward their fieldnotes confers an equally ambivalent value on them; in some ways, how anthropologists talk about the value of their fieldnotes best conveys the quintessential me/not-me essence of fieldnotes. For some interviewees, the attachment is connected to the amount of time invested in them:

> I'm sure the attitude towards the notes themselves has a sort of fetishistic quality – I don't go stroke them, but I spent so much time getting, guarding and protecting them ... if the house were burning down I'd go to the notes first.

> I busted my ass to get them. ... I packed that [tape recorder] all over. It linked me to the product, a real sacrifice to get it.

Other interviewees are attached because fieldnotes are connected to important experiences in their lives:

> I do have that protectionist feeling. The first batch – it's like the first child is different from the second. You love them both, but the first is special. I wouldn't want them saved for posterity, yet I feel personally invested, too close.

> I do have a feeling that they're an important part of my self there. ... In some ways they are associated with the experiences I had in Afghanistan, in particular the relatively powerful experiences, those incredible religious ceremonies.

For some, this attachment, along with other negative or positive emotions, is triggered by the physical manifestation of the notes. One interviewee stated, "I don't have the physical associations with the tapes I once had ... feeling a kind of connection, an inability to separate from them. I experience this still when I listen to them: a horror, shock, disorientation." This quote reflects, somewhat extremely, the complex feelings of connection and separation many interviewees remarked on. Attachment, in all of its meanings, was expressed by one interviewee who said, "I read through a chunk of them and then put them away. I write and I can't bear to look at them." For some, the attachment to the physical notes takes on an almost fetishistic quality. Although the speaker's comments might be full of irony or sarcasm, the feelings expressed are nonetheless fervently felt, perhaps enhanced, because of this self-awareness:

It's like they're part of me. To put them in a box and mail them Federal Express ... I want to travel out there and put them on the shelf myself, at least. Yes, they'll make copies. But it's not copies, it's the originals that have the power.

One can make the argument that if fieldnotes are liminal, secret, sacred, or somehow associated with these qualities, powerful feelings will arise because of this alone:

It's – there's some power, it's like shutting it out, not repression, the equivalent of that in physical things. I haven't thought about this before but, yes, I have strong feelings. If I look in them, all this emotion comes out, so it's like hiding something away so it won't remind you, it won't be so powerful.

Looking back at the notes ... I relive the emotions and have to process it all over again. ... I wrote this piece about bureaucracies and every time I reread about the incidents I had to reprocess it, and I think I exorcised some of that negative affect, so that this time when I had to face a bureaucrat I didn't feel the anxiety and apprehension I had felt earlier ... paranoia, uncertainty.

The typed notes, also, a sense of, often, aversion. I can sympathize with that feeling of not wanting to go too close to that part of the room.

Self and Other. The many expressions of anxiety and guilt in my interviews stem, in part, from the me/not-me liminality because of fieldnotes' ability to become separated from oneself and what one stands for. Doing fieldnotes, in some situations at least, creates the proverbial double bind. Writing fieldnotes constantly reminds many anthropologists that they are, in fact, not in the field just to be friends or just to help the natives, but to do research; as a consequence, interviewees reported experiencing feelings of being exploitative, of being a colonialist, and so forth. Hence their overall feelings, especially their ambivalence toward their fieldnotes, are heightened. We are reminded that a prime characteristic of liminal situations is high affect.

According to some interviewees, whether one is or is not creating documents – and what "documents" *means* – is problematic because of the role of the (native) other:

Maybe I just view my task not so much as creating but transmitting, being a broker, an intermediary, a partner. It's their words.

Well, it's not *we* who create our documents. It's funny, since I'm into the interpretive side of anthropology. But I really do believe that the events, the relationships, etc., are the primary documents that are comparable to the documents that historians deal with, and our fieldnotes are reflections, just like historians reflect.

I never think of my fieldnotes as a document. I feel the people are sort of a document. I did not create these people.

Anthropologists create documents not *ex nihilo*. My people's behavior is the document. I see them lived as documents, and as second order I write them as documents, and as third order publish them. The historian is cut off, the documents are bloodless. But I am not free, I'm also constrained. I can be corrected by my people as a historian cannot be. They're [historians] actually freer with the document. I can be corrected. ... They [the natives] won't laugh at a joke. Or [I can be] physically stood up.

Because fieldnotes are a preparatory phase to writing ethnography, in this function they can be seen as helping to distance the anthropologist from an identification with the (native) other – the fieldworker moves away from the doing toward the writing part of the research. Yet many interviewees comment on how fieldnotes keep the connection to the field, thus helping continue the dialogue and identification with the other and the "collapse of identity" (Kondo 1982) felt by some anthropologists as necessary to successful fieldwork.

Quite a number of fieldworkers carry around with them images of additional others who are involved in their fieldnote-making. One anthropologist said, "My notes always assumed someone was looking over my shoulder, asking me to validate."

As noted above, many interviewees commented on how one's fieldnotes can be used to make *others'* points and test *others'* hypotheses. Hence there are two kinds of others interacting with self: the native other and the other who might read or otherwise use one's fieldnotes – once again, an example of fieldnotes' liminal status.

Thus fieldnotes are liminal because interviewees see them in terms of identification with and alienation from the self and in terms of both increasing and decreasing mutual understanding between self and other.

Between Words

This section continues the discussion of fieldnotes as an object that exists apart from their creator. Fieldnotes are separate objects that exhibit certain characteristics: they are written or taped words, ciphers, or other symbols that are recorded under certain conditions. They are a kind of literary genre, capable of being compared to other kinds of writing. These characteristics influence and constrain the relationship between fieldnotes and the fieldworker. Whether fieldnotes are understood or misunderstood, used productively or misused, depends in part on these characteristics. In short, this section asks, what *kinds* of words comprise a set of fieldnotes? Expectably, the answer is not at all clear.

Although all kinds of writing are the authors' creations, fieldnotes differ from other kinds of writings in that they are not for public consumption. Furthermore, the literary canon (if we can speak thus) defining their form and content is extremely vague. Furthermore, they are way stations rather than the end point.

Quite a number of interviewees commented on how field-notes occupy an interstitial place between observed "reality" and a finished piece of writing:[18]

> When you're writing for a book you are writing for an outside audience. The fieldnotes are an intermediate stage. One fear is that they're subject to a lot of misinterpretation, a fear, one, that they are wrong and someone will use them, or, two, they're subject to manipulation the author doesn't want. In that sense they're a text, cut off from their roots, different from social reality.

Fieldnotes are betwixt and between in that they are midway between reality and a published document *and* midway between the anthropologist and the reader of any resulting publication.[19] "Raw" fieldnotes may make no sense to either the native or the Western reading public; most often they need the anthropologist as mediator, to explain and further transform them. One anthropologist stated, "They come in chronological order for most people, not neatly classified the moment you get it. ... Half the work is sifting through those notes and creating something out of it." For this reason, one anthropologist located the personal, inviolable aspect of fieldwork in the creative process *after* fieldnotes were taken:

> I wouldn't mind sharing or reading someone else's, because what I'm doing with my fieldnotes no one else is going to do. You could write a paper that I wouldn't write on my fieldnotes.

Another noted the incongruence between the public nature of the final product and the private nature of this stage of the process of getting there: "It's curious that we make highly public published statements based on highly private materials."[20]

Questions about who has a claim to these words, who can do what things with them, came up in the interviews again and again:

> I gave 100 myths to a Yugoslavian who published them without citation. He sent me the book. I don't think he felt to blame. It was unethical, but it was descriptions, he didn't distinguish between his work and mine. But if it had been done in English I would have been extremely angry. ... I felt it was appropriate to give them to him. He probably felt the myths didn't belong to me and they don't. But it's a lot of work.

One interviewee spoke of rights that changed over time: "I want first crack, I haven't even written my thesis. But there's a time limit as to how long I could sit on them without working on them." Another spoke longingly of the possibility of sharing: "It would be such an advantage ... to enter a place with some of that background." Reluctance to share derives in part from the above-discussed link between field-notes and self:

I haven't, and I'd be of two minds … who they are and what they'd want it for.
Fieldnotes are – it's strange how intimate they become and how possessive we
are.

For many interviewees, fieldnotes are betwixt and between a personal
diary and a scientific document. One area of disagreement among interviewees with respect to defining fieldnotes is the degree to which they are
seen as objective or subjective. Of course, a lot of this has to do with the
individual's notions of how anthropology contrasts with other social sciences,
anthropology's weaknesses and strengths, and how they, as individuals, fit
with or rebel against the profession's canons and epistemological position:

A peculiar mixture of personal and hard data, and you always have to contend
with this.

Because we do fall in between, we allow the personal … not sociologists, who
can pull out 20,000 questionnaires. I don't think this is the way to get insight,
but we do have a problem with our methods of being able to judge the
competence.

But the highly personal, uncategorizable ones, they are much more meaningful.

Fieldnotes can represent the tension between controlled, "scientific" research
and the osmotic, spontaneous, flexible kind. One interviewee reported on
feeling disturbed at another anthropologist's highly systemized ways of
acquiring and processing data: "It fits his compulsiveness. … I don't think he
had room in that system for a fascinating spontaneous conversation with
someone." The difference and distance between "objective" reality and
subjective experience can change during the research; in the following case,
field-notes were allied with the objective side:

What happened was the more I got into fieldwork the less I did [the fewer
fieldnotes I took] … partly because my personal private experience or reaction
to things and what was the more objective reality out there got less – the
difference between them.

The ambiguous status of fieldnotes as a written record of both objective and
subjective experience became apparent in anthropologists' critiques of other
anthropologists:

Anthropologists have tended to fetishize their notes, they quote their notes as
text.

Some anthropologists have never had a hunch and if they did, they'd be scared
by it. The category "hunch" is something anthropologists don't bring to the
field. This is why you should take a journal. I get tired of reflexive anthropology: "me, me, me." But hunches do come out in a journal.

A nice example of how subjective experience interconnects with "data" is the following: "That journal, of course, is also a kind of data, because it indicates how to learn about, yes, myself, but also how to be a person in this environment. Subsequently I see it as part of the fieldnotes." Many interviewees mention a trade-off between fieldnotes functioning as scientific documents that should be accessible to others and as a private journal. One interviewee said, "A bit of contradiction – the sort of private diary aspect is very important, but to the degree you censor them because someone else may have access, you inhibit this function."

However, the vast majority of anthropologists contrast fieldnotes with harder data; that is, however these interviewees defined fieldnotes, they managed to indicate in some form that a crucial component of fieldwork and note-taking involves attention to subjectivity:

> Something about the identity of anthropology, first of all, concerns the subjectivity of the observer ... and ... the definition of fieldnotes is a personally bounded – in the field – and personally referential thing.

The majority not only consider this unique to anthropology but also see it as a strength. One anthropologist said, "In anthropology we don't see it only as an extension of someone's self, but also a methodology of the discipline." A political scientist noted, "Anthropologists are self-conscious about this process called the creation and use of personal fieldnotes. I think it's dangerous that political scientists aren't." However, unease, ambivalence, and defensiveness on this subject also came across in many of the interviews:

> If I felt that ethnography just reflected internal states I wouldn't be in this game.

> I tend to believe my notes reflect reality as closely as possible.

Because, regardless of one's stance with respect to positivism or phenomenology, one worries about the effect of what is "in here" on what one observes "out there":

> [Fieldnotes are about] everything I saw and observed that I thought was relevant to what I saw as interesting. I realized I was imposing a structure that might be losing me things, but one has to do that.

Many anthropologists expressed the tension between the advantage of having a receptive, tabula rasa mind versus being informed, systematic, and selective. This emerged in discussions of the value and/or worthlessness of their initial note-taking as compared to later periods of fieldwork:

> Well, [the beginning of fieldwork is] a very useful and significant time. They [fieldnotes] are harder, because you feel you have to write everything down and you don't know what "everything" is.

One interviewee commented on a possible covert reason behind his department's not providing adequate training for fieldwork:

> I had to ask obliquely for fear of revealing my inadequacy. [The reply was]
> "Well, you know, just do it … and don't do anything stupid, but work it out." It
> was like parents telling their children about sex. When pushed past this they'd
> say, "Well, we don't want to constrain you, anthropology is changing, the
> boundaries are being constantly defined." It was deliberate that we were not
> inducted into the methods.

Finally, many anthropologists, predictably, expressed conflicting,
ambivalent feelings about future value:

> I don't know, I have moods of thinking I'd burn the whole lot before I die, and
> then moods of thinking that that would be quite irresponsible, and then moods
> of thinking "What makes you think they're so important, anyway?"

We have seen that the question about disposition of fieldnotes at death
elicited many statements showing the ambiguous nature of fieldnotes as
something intimately linked to the anthropologist and yet having an existence
apart. Interviewees differed; for some, fieldnotes totally depend on the
fieldworker to give them meaning, while for others, what changes after death
is that the anthropologist, as well as the natives, becomes an object of study
via the fieldnotes. One anthropologist stated, "After you die, your fieldnotes
become someone's historical documents." Here the creation becomes the
vehicle for a new creation about the creator. Despite most interviewees joking
about the unlikely event of someone considering their work so important that
they would merit such attention, the ambiguous relationship of fieldnotes to
their creator came out clearly.

Fieldnotes are created documents[21] that share some features with novels,
paintings, and musical compositions: they are new, and yet they affirm
already existing truths, sometimes extremely powerfully. Yet fieldnotes *are*
different. An interviewee said, "It *is* creating something, not creating it in the
imagination sense, but creating it in terms of bringing it out as a fact."
Fieldnotes are closest, perhaps, to nonfiction creations such as biographies
and documentary films:

> You have to be very careful and sure and honest with yourself that what you're
> recording has to be objectively true, and along with the personal satisfaction
> you have to have a responsibility to the environment you're treating, … to be
> aware of a kind of hubris that would lead you to impose yourself on the
> material.

Yet interviewees seemed to feel that ethnography has an additional problem,
one not encountered by conventional documentary filmmakers in their
attempts to translate observed and felt reality into a film to be comprehended
by an other: the problem of translation from another culture and language.

Fieldnotes, at least stereotypical anthropological ones, are supposed to aid in the revelation of truths that emerge out of quite foreign contexts, even though a given truth might be felt to be universal. Fieldnotes are supposed to reveal an other that is not the other created by a novelist or portrait painter, for the former is incomprehensible without the translation and interpretation which the ethnographer must provide. It is the ethnographer who quintessentially creates this kind of representation:[22]

> Malinowski ... says [when] he's coming into Kiriwina, "It's me who's going to create them for the world."

> We do more than historians ... we create a world.

Although many kinds of human creations may be initially viewed by their intended audience only through a glass darkly, traditional ethnography is, perhaps, a different kind of creation because its translation tasks precede and dominate its other goals.[23]

Conclusions

Many of my interviewees were all too aware of their mixed feelings about fieldnotes, indicating their unease by using familiar words from the anthropological lexicon of ritual, such as *sacred, exorcism, fetish,* and *taboo.* They also commented on our tendency to *avoid* talking about fieldnotes or to *only joke* about them.[24] Fieldwork *is* a kind of ritual, a rite of passage. In Turner's (1985) terms, fieldwork has some of the qualities of *comunitas,* a period during which people negate, affirm, and create meaning[25] and (at times mystically) participate in native life. Fieldnotes can be seen to assume a heavy emotional valence and sacredness because they are objects crucial to the performance of the rite.[26]

Furthermore, if fieldwork is a coming-of-age process, then writing fieldnotes would seem to be a remarkably well-designed and effective ordeal that tests the anthropologist's mettle. One can rely on advisors only so much in these trials, for it is eventually necessary to forge ahead into unchartered territory, if a genuine transformation in the initiand is to be achieved. One's first fieldnotes are a link to one's advisor, and for some interviewees these fieldnotes are both a sign of this link and a sign of having successfully broken it. The confusion and resentment many anthropologists express about their training regarding fieldnotes and about professional canons perhaps is necessary, given the socialization function that fieldnote-taking performs. Perhaps this is why anthropologists delight in jokes about "rules" for doing fieldwork, complaining on the one hand about a lack of rules and yet on the other how inadequate, if not downright stupid, are the rules that they were told to follow.[27]

Indeed, the overall confusion noted by the vast majority of interviewees surrounding the doing and meaning of fieldnotes suggests the feature found in ritually liminal situations of a suspension of rules.

Fieldnotes are intimately tied up, then, with the fieldworker's transition to a new state; returning from fieldwork, fieldnotes in hand, is a kind of graduation. Fieldnotes can be seen as a diploma and a license to continue to practice anthropology:

> I remember reading a novel by Barbara Pym of an anthropologist burning his fieldnotes in a ritualistic bonfire in the back yard. It was inconceivable of someone doing that and remaining an anthropologist. I found this passage to be fascinating and very provocative.

One source of provocation undoubtedly is the nagging doubt that many anthropologists have regarding whether or not the ethnographer would have the *right* to burn fieldnotes: if a larger community helped produce them (e.g., funding agencies, native informants), shouldn't this community have some say in their disposition?

Another way that fieldnotes are chameleonlike for some interviewees involves fieldnotes' ability to take on the romance and the exotic, grubby character of the field and yet also represent the colonialist, statist, litero-centrism of the West from which the fieldworker must flee[28] in order to do successful research.

Fieldnotes are not only liminal in the sense of "betwixt and between," they are a mediator. They accompany the fieldworker home and provide the means to be symbolically transported back to the field during write-up. They are materially of the field, with their "dirt, blood, and spit." They also index the field. Yet they serve to remind the researcher while in the field that he or she stands apart, and they often remind the native of this as well. They are betwixt and between perceived reality and the final version intended for the public. They are a translation from one meaning system to another, and they provide the means (and often the incentive) to continually re-translate.

Hence fieldnotes mediate between worlds and between the personas that the anthropologist assumes in different places and at different times. Field-notes also straddle the fence between sacred and profane, being seen by some interviewees as holy and taboo, with associations made between fieldnotes and rituals ("writing them up every night"), involving fetishes, ordeals, and high affect, and yet also seen as a matter-of-fact, nuts-and-bolts task that must be attended to every day.

For some anthropologists, field notes symbolized the crucial period of seclusion in this particular initiation rite's bush school. Other anthropologists spoke of fieldwork as a chance to leave school behind and to go out into the wide world and live. For some interviewees, fieldnotes signaled their adult, scientist, and professional status. For most, fieldnotes represented a problem between research via living and doing and research via writing.

In sum, many characteristics associated with liminality emerged in these interviews: the theme of embarking on a quest; the notion of undergoing an ordeal which, if done correctly, will bring about a transformation in the individual; a suspension of rules; high affect; and, at times, an association with the sacred. Fieldnotes, in short, are both *déjà entendre* because they are so linked to the anthropologist who created them and evidence of just how mysterious and *jamais entendu* "the field" can be.

Notes

1. To protect the confidentiality of my interviewees, any potentially identifying details in the quotations that follow have been altered.
2. Given the sample's lack of systematic representation, this chapter should be seen in qualitative terms. The reasonably large sample size guards against bias in only the crudest fashion because so many complex variables are present. Although I cannot *claim* to represent any group, I do feel the sample represents practicing anthropologists living in the United States. Some are famous, others obscure; some have reflected about fieldwork and fieldnotes extensively (a few have written on these topics), whereas others describe themselves as having been fairly unconscious (or even hostile) to such matters. My sample is thus more representative of the profession than if I had written a chapter based on published comments about fieldnotes – the last thing many of my interviewees contemplate undertaking is writing on this topic.

   I should comment that although this chapter is inspired by the current interest in "ethnographies as text" (see Marcus and Cushman 1982; Clifford 1988) my methodology necessarily produces findings differing from these and similar work in two crucial respects. One is the fact that most of the anthropologists I interviewed are not enamored of the "anthropology as cultural critique" (Marcus and Fischer 1986) trend, even though all of them had very interesting comments to make about fieldnotes. The other is that, given the frankness and strong feelings – especially the ambivalence and negativity – that emerged in the interviews, I doubt if my interviewees, even those who might be inclined to write about fieldnotes some day, would ever say in print some of what they said to me. For all I know, some interviewees might later have regretted being so frank with me (something that often surprised me at the time), although this does not necessarily make what they said any less true. While I certainly do not think I got the *entire* truth from anyone, given that a confidential interview setting can elicit ideas and feelings people might not come up with by themselves, I believe that the material I obtained from my interviews is different – complementary – to material acquired from the literature on fieldnotes.
3. My interview procedure was the following: I first asked interviewees to tell me whatever they have to say about the subject of fieldnotes. Almost all were willing to do this. Then I asked about the following topics: (1) their definition of fieldnotes, (2) training – preparation and mentoring, formal and informal, (3) sharing fieldnotes, (4) confidentiality, (5) disposition of fieldnotes at death, (6) feelings about fieldnotes, particularly the actual, physical notes, and (7) whether "unlike historians, anthropologists create their own documents." I also tried to query those who had more than one field experience about any changes in their approach to fieldnotes.

Interviews lasted at least an hour. Lacking funds for transcription, I did not use a tape recorder, but I did try to record verbatim as much as possible.

Along the way, of course, I discovered other issues I wish I had been covering systematically – for example, the interdependence of "headnotes" (remembered observations) and written materials. In later interviews I asked about the mystique of fieldnotes and whether fieldnotes are connected to anthropologists' – or anthropology's – identity.

Several people initially asked why I chose such a nuts-and-bolts topic, but they all seemed interested in the subject (no one declined to be interviewed). In fact, fieldnotes seems to be a remarkably good entry point for obtaining opinions and feelings about bigger issues, probably better than asking point-blank questions about them.

4. Why liminality exists as a concept has been explained with reference to the presumed need a society has to order experience by classifying the universe – both to allow its members to think and interpret and to use such classifications for society's own ends. Such a system of classification allows a society's members to not only "make sense" of the myriad of stimuli assaulting the five senses but to be able to judge some as more beautiful or better than others. Since this is achieved by highlighting some attributes of certain phenomena and ignoring others, so the argument goes, possible confusion and conflict threaten when instances of boundary-straddling become apparent. Gluckman (1963) argues that ritual, and formal behavior in general, serve to keep potentially confused, ambiguous, and conflictive roles distinct by highlighting their differences. Also see Babcock (1978).

5. See Crocker (1973) and Morris (1987) for discussions of various social, cognitive, and affective/emotional theories explaining why, under certain circumstances, liminality is highlighted and exaggerated.

6. In a sense moving between two different social systems; see Weidman (1970, 262).

7. Sojourners of all kinds are in a geographically liminal state and are often liminal in other respects, especially those undertaking pilgrimages. Fieldwork can be likened to pilgrimages and quests.

8. See Rabinow (1977):

> Fieldwork, then, is a process of intersubjective construction of liminal modes of communication. Intersubjective means literally more than one subject, but being situated neither quite here nor quite there, the subjects involved do not share a common set of assumptions, experiences or traditions. (p. 155)

He also refers to fieldnotes as liminal since a process of mutual construction of a hybrid world by both ethnographer and informant takes place (p. 153). Kondo (1982) speaks of this hybrid world as "the conspiracy my informants and I had perpetrated" (p. 6).

9. I have vast amounts of statements linking fieldnotes with dirt and mess. One possible interpretation comes from Crocker who points out that liminal social roles are associated with liminal symbols. Hence, just as prophets or boys undergoing initiation are expected to be dirty, so would fieldnotes. Dirt is liminal because it is matter out of place (Crocker 1973, 70; see Douglas 1966).

10. Compare:

> When I look back at them, the 500 or so pages or notes are clearly my own. I see here where I spilled my coffee and there where my pen was running out of ink. My mind goes back to the sounds and smells of a New Guinea morning, and insights surface from somewhere in the cobwebbed depths of my memory. Certainly it was necessary to sift and sort through the data, but the intimate relationship which had developed between the fieldnotes and myself made it a very different phenomenon from the research I was to take on next. (Podolefsky 1987, 15)

11. Which, of course, can be found in any long-term, intense participant-observation fieldwork even though not undertaken by an anthropologist. See Van Maanen (1988).
12. See Pratt (1986):

> To convert fieldwork, via fieldnotes, into formal ethnography requires a tremendously difficult shift from the latter discursive position (face to face with the other) to the former. Much must be left behind in the process. Johannes Fabian characterizes the temporal aspect of this contradiction when he speaks of "an aporetic split between recognition of coevalness in some ethnographic research and denial of coevalness in most anthropological theorizing and writing." (p. 32)

13. Of course, the opposite situation can obtain when informants *demand* that their words be written or taped: "Write this down! Isn't what I'm telling you important enough?"
14. Some interviewees, however, contrasted fieldnotes with diary in their definitions.
15. This quote from a female interviewee is a very "emphatic" and "interpretive" kind of statement. See Kirschner (1987) concerning "subjectivist" and "interpretive" approaches to fieldwork and how these correlate with the gender of the ethnographer. An interpretive view of such attempts at empathy, according to Kirschner, would see them as leading to a "false sense of mystical communion with the inner life of the Other, and therefore a projective illusion" (p. 217).
16. Goffman (1989), the patron saint of many fieldworking sociologists, says the test of penetrating the society you're supposed to be studying involves getting to the point where "the sights and sounds around you should get to be normal. You should be able to play with people, and make jokes back and forth. ... You should feel you could settle down and forget about being a sociologist" (p. 129). But sociologists cannot "go native" either, for the same reasons my interviewees gave.
17. Some interviewees spoke of potential value to the natives, especially if the fieldwork had applied to activist aspects.
18. The fieldnotes themselves vary in this regard, of course; informants commented on how fieldnotes contain material that represents several stages of the transformation of observed interaction to written, public communication: "raw" data, ideas that are marinating, and fairly done-to-a-turn diagrams and genealogical charts to be used in appendices in a thesis or book.

19. Crapanzano (1977) might agree that because fieldnotes are between the "reality" perceived in the field and a published ethnography they are also a mediator between the ethnographer as deconstituted self in the field and reconstituted self acquired through writing an ethnography, which will "'free' him to be a professional again" (p. 71): "The writing of ethnography is an attempt to put a full-stop to the ethnographic confrontation" (p. 70).

20. Freilich (1990) notes that

> the sparsity of writings on anthropological field methods and field experiences is explained by ... the "rewards" field workers receive for keeping their errors and their personalities hidden and for maintaining a romantic attachment to the fieldwork mystique, (p. 36)

Note that this statement preceded the explosion of writings about fieldwork beginning in the mid-1970s. Also see Geertz (1988) on "the oddity of constructing texts ostensibly scientific out of experiences broadly biographical" (p. 10).

21. A reminder: The meaning of some of these statements depends on a specific definition of fieldnotes; definitions varied substantially among the interviewees.

22. "Even experimental ethnographies which are self-conscious accounts of the evolving process of understanding in the field, must also in some sense BE an understanding of another cultural form, to qualify as ethnography" (Kondo, 1982, 6).

23. I would argue that this is a crucial distinction between what stereotypical sociology and stereotypical anthropology would bring to the same fieldwork situation – regardless of where it occurs and the social scientific goals of the research.

24. Joking and avoidance behavior are frequently encountered ways of dealing with conflicting, difficult relationships and subjects of conversation.

25. Compare Crapanzano's (1977) comment that "indeed, the 'movement' of fieldwork can be seen as a movement of self-dissolution and reconstitution" (p. 70).

26. See Crapanzano (1987): "For Kondo, as for many anthropologists, fieldwork becomes a sort of Faustian voyage of discovery, of descent and return" (p. 181). Also see Jackson (1990).

27. See Bowen (1964, 4) on advice about cheap tennis shoes.

28. We are talking about the stereotypical fieldwork situation, which has not represented the majority of fieldwork situations for quite some time (see Pelto and Pelto 1973) and is much less representative today.

References

Babcock, B. A., ed. 1978. *The reversible world: Symbolic inversion in art and society.* Ithaca, NY: Cornell University Press.

Bowen, E. S. 1964. *Return to laughter: An anthropological novel.* New York: Doubleday.

Clifford, J. 1988. *The predicament of culture: Twentieth-century ethnography, literature, and art.* Cambridge, MA: Harvard University Press.

Crapanzano, V. 1977. On the writing of ethnography. *Dialectical Anthropology* 2 (1): 69-73.

Crocker, J. C. 1973. Ritual and the development of social structure: Liminality and inversion. In *The roots of ritual,* edited by J. D. Shaughnessy, 47-86. Grand Rapids, MI: William Eerdmans.

Douglas, M. 1966. *Purity and danger.* Harmondsworth, England: Penguin.

Freilich, M., ed. 1970. *Marginal natives: Anthropologists at work.* New York: Harper & Row.

Geertz, C. 1988. *Works and lives: The anthropologist as author.* Stanford, CA: Stanford University Press.

Gluckman, M. 1963. Rituals of rebellion in south east Africa. In *Order and rebellion in tribal Africa,* edited by M. Gluckman, 110-37. London: Cohen & West.

Goffman, E. 1989. On fieldwork. Transcribed and edited by Lyn H. Lofland. *Journal of Contemporary Ethnography* 18 (2): 123-32.

Jackson, J. E. 1986. On trying to be an Amazon. In *Self, sex, and gender in cross-cultural fieldwork,* edited by T. L. Whitehead and M. E. Conaway. Urbana: University of Illinois Press.

Jackson, J. E. 1990. "I am a fieldnote": Fieldnotes as symbol of professional identity. *In Fieldnotes: The makings of anthropology,* edited by R. Sanjek, 3-33. Ithaca, NY: Cornell University Press.

Kirshner, S. R. 1987. "Then what have I to do with thee": On identity, fieldwork, and ethnographic knowledge. *Cultural Anthropology* 1 (2): 211-34.

Kondo, D. K. 1982. Inside and outside: The fieldworker as conceptual anomaly. Paper presented at the annual meeting of the American Anthropological Association, Washington, DC.

Malinowski, B. 1967. *A diary in the strict sense of the term.* London: Routledge & Kegan Paul.

Marcus, G., and R. Cushman. 1982. Ethnographies as texts. *Annual Review of Anthropology* 11:25-69.

Marcus, G., and M. Fischer. 1986. *Anthropology as cultural critique: An experimental moment in the human sciences.* Chicago: Chicago University Press.

Morris, B. 1987. *Anthropological studies of religion: An introductory text.* Cambridge: Cambridge University Press.

Ottenberg, S. 1990. Thirty years of fieldnotes: Changing relationships to the text. In *Fieldnotes: The makings of anthropology,* edited by R. Sanjek, 139-60. Ithaca, NY: Cornell University Press.

Pelto, P., and G. H. Pelto. 1973. Ethnography: The fieldwork enterprise. In *Handbook of social and cultural anthropology,* edited by J. J. Honigmann. Chicago: Rand McNally.

Podolefsky, A. 1987. New tools for old jobs: Computers in the analysis of fieldnotes. *Anthropology Today* 3 (5): 14-16.

Pratt, M. L. 1986. Fieldwork in common places. In *Writing culture: The poetics and politics of ethnography,* edited by J. Clifford and G. Marcus, 27-50. Berkeley: University of California Press.

Rabinow, P. 1977. *Reflections of fieldwork in Morocco.* Berkeley: University of California Press.

Turner, V. 1967. Betwixt and between. In *The forest of symbols: Aspects of Ndembu ritual,* edited by V. Turner, 93-111. Ithaca, NY: Cornell University Press.

Turner, V. 1974. *The ritual process.* Harmondsworth, England: Penguin.

Turner, V. 1985. *On the edge of the bush: Anthropology as experience.* Edited by E. L. B. Turner. Tucson: University of Arizona Press.

Van Maanen, J. 1988. *Tales of the field: On writing ethnography.* Chicago: University of
    Chicago Press.
Weidman, H. H. 1970. On ambivalence in the field. In *Women in the field,* edited by
    P. Golde. Chicago: Aldine.

Section Six
Viewing the Field: Visual Methods

37

Visual Anthropology: Image, Object and Interpretation[1]

Marcus Banks

Abstract

Until recently, the subdiscipline known as visual anthropology was largely identified with ethnographic film production. In recent years, however, visual anthropology has come to be seen as the study of visual forms and visual systems in their cultural context. While the subject matter encompasses a wide range of visual forms – film, photography, 'tribal' or 'primitive' art, television and cinema, computer media – all are united by their material presence in the physical world. This chapter outlines a variety of issues in the study of visual forms and argues for rigorous anthropological approaches in their analysis.

Anthropology and Visual Systems

In recent years there has been an apparent shift in anthropology away from the study of abstract systems (kinship, economic systems and so forth) and towards a consideration of human experience. This has resulted in a focus on the body, the emotions, and the senses. Human beings live in sensory worlds as well as cognitive ones, and while constrained and bounded by the systems that anthropology previously made its focus, we not only think our way through these systems, we experience them. For anthropology, this has involved a shift away from formalist analytical positions – functionalism, structuralism and so forth – towards more phenomenological perspectives. Correspondingly, under the much misapplied banner of postmodernism,

Source: *Image-based Research: A Sourcebook for Qualitative Researchers,* 1998. Falmer Press, pp. 9-23.

there has been an increased focus on ethnography and representation, on the modes by which the lives of others are represented. At worst, this has been manifest in a depoliticization of anthropology, an extreme cultural relativism that concentrates on minutiae or revels in exoticism, and a de-intellectualization of anthropology where all representations are considered equally valid, where analysis is subordinate to (writing) style, and where injustice, inequality and suffering are overlooked. At best, the new ethnographic approaches are historically grounded and politically aware, recognizing the frequent colonial or neo-colonial underpinnings of the relationship between anthropologist and anthropological subject, recognizing the agency of the anthropological subject and their right as well as their ability to enter into a discourse about the construction of their lives (see Figure 1.1).

Until recently, visual anthropology was understood by many anthropologists to have a near-exclusive concern with the production and use of ethnographic film. In the first half of the century it was film's recording and documentary qualities that were chiefly (but not exclusively) valued by anthropologists. But while film could document concrete and small-scale areas of human activity that could subsequently be incorporated into formalist modes of analysis by anthropologists – the production and use of material culture, for example – it quickly became apparent that it could add little to our understanding of more abstract formal systems – in kinship analysis, for example. From the mid- to late-1960s onwards attention turned instead towards the pseudo-experiential representational quality of film, anticipating

Figure 1.1. Gabriel Reko Notan discusses his experience as a telegrapher for the Dutch East India government with anthropologist R.H. Barnes, in Witihama, Adonara, Indonesia.

the appreciation of a phenomenological emphasis in written ethnography by a decade or two. Now film was to be valued for giving some insight into the experience of being a participant in another culture, permitting largely Euro-American audiences to see life through the eyes of non-European others.

While in some ways very different positions – film as science, film as experience – there is an underlying commonality between them. Both positions hold film to be a tool, something that allows 'us' to understand more about 'them'. More specifically, film was something 'we' did to 'them'. We can hypothesize that this is one of the reasons why ethnographic film came to dominate what became known as visual anthropology.[2] Ethnographic film produced using 16mm film cameras renders the anthropologist/filmmaker entirely active, the film subject almost entirely passive. Beyond altering their behaviour in front of the camera (or indeed, refusing to 'behave' at all) the film subjects have little or no control over the process. Partly for technical reasons they rarely if ever get to see the product before it is complete and they typically have no access to 16mm equipment to effect their own representations. Ethnographic still photography, probably more commonly produced than ethnographic film for much of the century, has been very much a poor second cousin to film in the traditional understanding of visual anthropology, perhaps because the active-passive relationship between anthropologist and subject is less secure: 'the natives' can have and have had more access to the means of production and consumption.

What was missed until recently was that film was one representational strategy among many. A particular division lies between written and filmed ethnography (see Crawford and Turton, 1992), but within the realm of the visual alone there are clearly differences between forms. For example, ethnographic monographs are frequently illustrated with photographs, very often illustrated with diagrams, plans, maps and tables, far less frequently illustrated with sketches and line drawings. Yet even this range of representations – some full members of what is traditionally understood to be the category of visual anthropology, some far less so – consists largely of visual forms produced by the anthropologist. Traditionally, the study of visual forms produced by the anthropological subject had been conducted under the label of the anthropology of art. Only very recently have anthropologists begun to appreciate that indigenous art, Euro-American film and photography, local TV broadcast output and so forth are all 'visual systems' – culturally embedded technologies and visual representational strategies that are amenable to anthropological analysis.[3] Visual anthropology is coming to be understood as the study of visible cultural forms, regardless of who produced them or why. In one sense this throws open the floodgates – visual anthropologists are those who create film, photography, maps, drawings, diagrams, and those who study film, photography, cinema, television, the plastic arts – and could threaten to swamp the (sub)discipline.

But there are constraints; firstly, the study of visible cultural forms is only visual *anthropology* if it is informed by the concerns and understandings of anthropology more generally. If anthropology, defined very crudely, is an

exercise in cross-cultural translation and interpretation that seeks to understand other cultural thought and action in its own terms before going on to
render these in terms accessible to a (largely) Euro-American audience, if
anthropology seeks to mediate the gap between the 'big picture' (global
capitalism, say) and local forms (small-town market trading, say), if anthropology takes long-term participant observation and local language proficiency
as axiomatic prerequisites for ethnographic investigation, then visual studies
must engage with this if they wish to be taken seriously as visual anthropology.[4] Not all image use in anthropology can or should be considered as
visual anthropology simply because visual images are involved. It is perfectly
possible for an anthropologist to take a set of photographs in the field, and
to use some of these to illustrate her subsequent written monograph, without claiming to be a visual anthropologist. The photographs are 'merely'
illustrations, showing the readers what her friends and neighbours looked like,
or how they decorated their fishing canoes. The photographs are not subject
to any particular analysis in the written text, nor does the author claim to have
gained any particular insights as a result of taking or viewing the images. It is
also possible for another anthropologist to come along later and subject the
same images to analysis, either in relation to the first author's work or in
relation to some other project, and to claim quite legitimately that the exercise
constitutes a visual anthropological project.[5]
    A second constraint returns us to a point I made in the opening paragraph.
One of the reasons for the decline of formal or systems analysis in anthropology – particularly any kind of analysis that took a natural sciences model[6]
– was the realization that formal analytical categories devised by the
anthropologist (the economy, the kinship system) were not always that easy to
observe in the field, being largely abstract. To be sure, earlier generations of
anthropologists were confident both of the existence of abstract, systematized
knowledge in the heads of their informants, and of their ability to extract
that knowledge and present it systematically, even if the informants were
unconscious of the systematic structuring. However, as these essentially
Durkheimian approaches lost ground in the discipline, and as anthropologists
concentrated more on what people actually did and actually thought about
what they were doing, so doubts began to set in about how far any
systematicity in abstract bodies of knowledge was the product of the anthropologists' own rationality and desire for order.[7] This does not, however,
invalidate the current trend in anthropology towards seeing visual and visible
forms as visual systems. The crucial difference between the visual system(s)
that underlie Australian Aboriginal dot paintings and a particular Aboriginal
kinship system is that the former is/are concrete, made manifest, where the
other is not and cannot be except in a second-order account by an
anthropologist. It is the materiality of the visual that allows us to group
together a diverse range of human activities and representational strategies
under the banner of visual anthropology and to treat them as visual systems.
With some important exceptions, the things that visual anthropologists study
have a concrete, temporally and spatially limited existence and hence a

specificity that a 'kinship system' or an 'economic system' does not and cannot.[8]

In what follows, I shall unpack some of the ideas above, relating them more specifically to the history of visual anthropology, and some specific examples.

The Visual in Anthropology

The history of the visual in anthropology cannot be properly told or understood outside of an account of the history of anthropology itself, for it is intimately related to changes in what is understood to be the proper subject matter of anthropology, what methodology should be used to investigate that subject matter, and what theories and analyses should be brought to bear on the findings. Clearly this is not the place to rehearse the entire history of the discipline and the reader with less familiarity with anthropology's origins and subsequent development should turn to another account.[9] There have been one or two pieces by anthropologists, however, that have explicitly linked the parallel histories of anthropology and either photography (for example, Pinney, 1992c) or cinema (for example, Grimshaw, 1997).

Nonetheless, for much of anthropology's history the emphasis was on the study of indigenous visual systems (usually under the label of 'primitive art') and comments on the uses of film and photography by anthropologists were confined to methodological footnotes and the like until the last two decades or so. By and large, studies in the anthropology of art have mirrored wider theoretical concerns in the discipline as a whole, although, as Coote and Shelton note, the subdiscipline has 'hardly – if ever – taken the [theoretical] lead ... [and] it is yet to significantly influence the mainstream' (1992, p. 3). Typically, from the early days of anthropology, we find works such as Haddon's *Evolution in Art* (1895) which attempts to trace the 'evolution' of stylistic devices by applying then-standard but now discredited social evolutionary theory developed in the second half of the nineteenth century (see Figure 1.2).

Yet despite the influence of 'Primitivism' on artists such as Picasso and the Cubists earlier generations of anthropologists resolutely confined themselves to the study of 'primitive art' in its own cultural setting and failed to set an agenda that would concern itself with 'art' as a broad category. This has not only led to an absence of anthropological studies of European 'fine art' and artists (and those elsewhere working within a European-influenced tradition) until recently, it has also led to an absence of anthropological studies of art in societies where anthropologists have long worked (such as China, Japan and India) but where the high culture of those societies, including their art forms, has been the preserve of other scholars.[10] Yet while these earlier studies insulated themselves from the traditions of art history and connoisseurship, they were nonetheless influenced (if unconsciously) by Euro-American categories of 'art' and the art object. It is only recently that the issue of

		ART.				INFORMATION.			WEALTH.		RELIGION.
	DECAY	Degeneration of Pictorial Art through incompetent Copying.	Conventional Treatment for Decorative Purposes.	Simplification through repeated Copying.	Degradation resulting from the Monstrous in Art.	Alphabetical Signs.	Arithmetical Signs.	Personal and Tribal Signs or Symbols.	Personal Ornaments and Objects emblematic of Power or Status.	Money.	Auspicious and Magical Signs.
STAGES OF DEVELOPMENT.	**EVOLUTION.**	Pictures.	Groups.	Series or Patterns.	Combinations or Heteromorphs.	Phonograms.	Conventionalised or Abbreviated Pictographs.	Emblems.	Ornamented Useful Objects.	More or less Conventionalised Models of Useful Ornaments.	Symbolism and Conventionalism.
	ORIGIN.	Solitary Decorative Figures.				Pictographs.			Useful Objects.		Realism.

REALISM.

Figure 1.2.
(above) Synoptic table of stylistic evolution and decay from Haddon's *Evolution in art* (1895: 8); (left) 'Skeuomorphs of Basketry' (Haddon 1895, Plate III) showing hypothetical origins of scroll designs (top) and examples of bronzework and pottery designs supposedly derived from these.

aesthetics has been examined by anthropologists of art. Alfred Gell has urged the adoption of 'methodological philistinism', akin to the 'methodological atheism' adopted by sociologists of religion, in studies of art (1992). That is, anthropologists should abandon notions of aesthetics which are formed by the ethnocentric assumptions of the Euro-American 'art cult' (Gell, 1992, p. 42) and should consider art instead as a technical system. Conversely, Jeremy Coote cites philosopher Nick Zangwill who says 'one could do aesthetics without mentioning works of art! Sometimes I think it would be safer to do so.' (cited in Coote, 1992, p. 246). In other words, it is not only possible but perhaps also desirable to separate analytically the visual systems we term 'art' from the value systems (aesthetics) within which we normally understand 'art'.

In contrast, the anthropological approach to film and photography has been largely anti-aesthetic and focused upon the technological and methodological. While studies of non-western art were at least conducted within the framework of broader anthropological analysis, film – and to a lesser extent photography – has occupied a much more narrow and marginal place within the discipline. As an object of study, photography has received by far the more attention, with several studies devoted to a reading of historical photographs produced by others both as an insight into past (and present) ethnographic contexts (for example Geary, 1988; Ruby, 1995) and as an insight into the history of anthropology itself (for example Scherer, 1990; Edwards, 1992). There is also a literature on photography as an object of practice – that is, how can photographs be used in anthropological fieldwork and data collection? (See, for example, Collier and Collier, 1986.)

An anti-aestheticism is seen much more sharply at work in the anthropological writing on film, however. Here, there are almost no studies of non-ethnographic film, and very few of non-ethnographic film practice (though see Powdermaker, 1951 on the Hollywood film industry, and Dickey, 1993 and R. Thomas, 1985 on the Indian film industry). There are several studies, however, of ethnographic film practice. While some of these are insightful and relate the production of ethnographic film to the production of ethnographic knowledge more widely (for example, Loizos, 1993; MacDougall, 1978, 1992), others fall more into the 'how I made my movie' vein – or, as Loizos put it succinctly 'Look, Ma, I made a movie!' (Loizos, 1989, p. 25).

In general, visual anthropologists have been more concerned with the content of ethnographic film than with film as a medium. That is to say, there is little explicit anthropological consideration given to the properties of film as a medium of visual representation, beyond early endorsements of its powers as a medium of record (see, for example, most of the contributions to Hockings, 1995 – a re-issue of a volume that was first issued as a result of a conference held in the 1960s). Instead, there is a plethora of mostly short reviews of the content of particular ethnographic films (the journals *American Anthropologist* and *Visual Anthropology* both incorporate specific film review sections along with their book review sections), and some longer review pieces also exist. Many of these deal with a predefined corpus of film, whether the output of individual filmmakers, or the output of television.[11]

Issues

With a variety of initial positions established, and a brief assessment of some of the work that has been done on the visual in anthropology, it is now possible to address a number of issues that the study of the visual has raised.

First and foremost is the issue of veracity, of the visual as a medium of record. For earlier generations of anthropologists, operating within a more positivistic frame of analysis, the division between the visual forms of 'the informants' and their own visual forms – art vs. mechanical reproduction – seemed largely self-evident. Indigenous art was often non-representational (by the naturalistic conventions of post-Renaissance and pre-twentieth century European art) and needed to be interpreted, while photography and film apparently captured 'reality' unproblematically. There are however objections to such a simplistic dichotomy, some of which were noted at the time. For example, A.C. Haddon, a British anthropologist who shot the first ever fieldwork film footage in 1898 in the Torres Strait Islands (Australia), conducted his ethnography partially within a salvage or reconstruction paradigm – trying to gather data on the life of the Torres Strait Islanders as it was before European contact. In order to film a short section of a ritual dance, connected with an initiation cult that had already died out under missionary influence, he directed the Islanders to create cardboard replicas of the masks

Figure 1.3. Frame still of Torres Strait Islanders performing part of the Malu-Bomai ceremony for A.C. Haddon, 1998.

worn in the ceremony (see Figure 1.3). Thus the film is in one sense a record of what happened – men wore masks and danced – but in another sense is a fiction, an account of something that could not (or could no longer) be seen.[12]

Claims to veracity – or image as evidence – presume complete and authoritative control and intention lying with those who produce the image, and who have faith in their ability to record reality or their vision of reality convincingly. Yet the intention lying behind early (and later) uses of photography cannot be assumed to be unproblematic. Joanna Scherer has shown, for example, that studio portrait photographs of Sarah Winnemucca, a Northern Paiute (Colorado) woman, taken in the period 1879–84 cannot simply be read as representations of Native American women by (presumably) white, male, European photographers (Scherer, 1988). Indeed, Scherer demonstrates that Winnemucca seems to have exercised some control over her representations, by adopting certain poses, manner of dress, and so forth. But then as now the photographs – and the representations they embodied – formed part of a wider economy of photographic images, some of which were inserted into a still wider economy of discourse concerning the place of Indians in nineteenth century American society. Scherer assesses that Winnemucca seems to have mismeasured these economies, and that by conforming to a generalized 'Indian Princess' stereotype in her appearance and representations her photographs appear to have hindered her in her attempt to be taken seriously as a spokesperson for Indian rights. The formal studio portraits therefore reveal multiple levels of intentionality and meaning.

Figure 1.4. Photograph of Aranda boy, Central Australia, taken by Baldwin Spencer aroundc 1901

Similarly, Howard Morphy has pointed out that while the early anthropologist of Australia, Baldwin Spencer, tended to work within the 'scientific' social evolutionary paradigm of late nineteenth and early twentieth century anthropology, his use of the camera can at times reveal a far more humanistic and subjective engagement with his supposed 'objects' of study (see Figure 1.4) (Morphy and Banks, 1997, p. 8).

A further issue of particular relevance to the anthropology of visual systems lies in the analytical separation of form and meaning. Although some earlier work in visual anthropology assumed the socio-cultural neutrality of photographic reproduction, at least in some circumstances, this idea now holds little currency.[13] A good example of cross-culturally variable linkages of form and meaning is provided by Chris Pinney's work on Indian photography (Pinney, 1992b). Pinney notes that certain formal or stylistic techniques, identified as montage and doubling, can be observed in a wide variety of visual media in India – popular bazaar prints, studio photographs and home video (see Figure 1.5). He also notes that these bear a superficial or formal similarity to uses of photomontage American traditions of art photography, such as Dadaist uses.

However, Pinney warns that images from the two traditions should not be read in the same way. At least one of the intentions underlying photomontage

Figure 1.5. 'Doubled' portrait of a bride taken from a Central Indian wedding album, ca. 1983

doubling in the Euro-American tradition is to 'disrupt the unity of time and space ... on which Western [narrative] realism depends' (Pinney, 1992b, p. 95); fracture and dissonance in the image subvert culturally specific notions of single-viewpoint perceptions of reality and attendant notions of narrative (how reality is represented and 'read'). By contrast, Pinney argues that Indian representational strategies rest, at least in part, on local notions of the person: divisible persons, in fact, whose inner core of personality cannot be directly perceived but is made visible through action. As actions (manifest through the body) are multiple, so multiple viewpoints of the body in photography are unproblematic. Montage and doubling in the Indian tradition are essentially conservative representational strategies, reinforcing rather than subverting a culturally specific view of reality.

Discussions such as these on how best to represent reality lie at the heart of the final issue to be discussed here – the fallacy of the so-called invisible camera. From the 1960s onwards ethnographic film production and documentary film production more generally sought to explore ways in which 'natural' and spontaneous human behaviour and interaction could best be observed by the motion picture camera. In some ways these endeavours, and the attendant debates, were direct descendants of the 'natural science' paradigm in pre-war anthropology and its (misplaced) enthusiasm for photographic media as neutral recording devices. However, with the paradigm shift to more interpretative anthropology, discussed above, styles of filmmaking were developed that sought to be sympathetic, even empathetic, with the rhythm of life as it is lived, and to be as reactive as possible to actual events in people's lives – the camera following, rather than dictating action.[14] Hence the observational cinema movement was born, appearing in recent years (albeit with some modifications) on British and other televisions as the 'fly-on-the-wall' documentary. At the heart of some, though not all, thinking in this area were attempts to get around some kind of Heisenberg observer-effect principle; if the film subjects could be persuaded to ignore or forget the presence of the camera, then their speech and actions thus recorded would be normal, unconscious, quotidian.

The classic view on this, and one closest to the old 'natural science of society' paradigm, was articulated by Margaret Mead who, apparently unconscious to the sociological embedding of technological development, predicted a brave new dawn for anthropology with 360 degree cameras 'preserv[ing] materials... long after the last isolated valley in the world is receiving images by satellite' and when 'large batches of material can be collected without the intervention of the filmmaker or ethnographer and without the continuous self-consciousness of those who are being observed' (to be achieved by self-loading, self-focusing cameras) (Mead, 1995, p. 9 – but first published in 1975).[15] The fallacy of course lies not in assuming that the camera can become invisible to those it films but in assuming that a socially, temporally and historical viewpoint can be overcome in what it sees. Even the classic 'invisible cameras' of modern industrial societies – high street bank security cameras, roadside traffic cameras, 'eye in the sky' surveillance cameras on helicopters – are socially located and 'see' from a particular, socially constructed viewpoint. The camera, whether strapped with a brace to the ethnographer's shoulder for permanent wearing (so that the subjects never know if they are being filmed or not), or positioned in a high corner of a building society ceiling, is a social actor and is inevitably involved in the social drama that unfolds before it. Its very presence confers importance and significance on the scene it reveals, to the viewer if not to the participants.

Material Visions

Finally, let us conclude by returning to the issue of the materiality of the visual form. A photograph, to take one example, is a material object with form as well as content. Once developed and printed it may be pasted by its owner into an album, shown to known and unknown others, sent to kin and friends, placed on display in a gallery, filed away in an archive, treasured by loved ones after the death of its owner, and so on. Once manifest in the world it begins a career and accumulates a series of linkages and social embeddings (cf. Appadurai, 1986). Part of its history is revealed by the object itself – traces of glue and paper on the reverse where it has been peeled from an album page, creases where it has been folded and tucked in a wallet, the name of the studio or photographer that created the image, and so forth. Another part of its history is revealed by its formal similarity or connection to other such objects – studio portraits, prison mugshots, family snapshots, anthropometric illustrations – and the social context within which such objects exist. 'History' here does not necessarily imply any particularly great time depth – a photograph taken by an anthropologist in the field and published within months to illustrate a journal article already has a history involving several persons and is embedded in a particular set of social, cultural and economic relations between those persons.

Take another example, this time of ethnographic film. In a review of several ethnographic films broadcast on British television in the 1970s, Peter Loizos notes that several anthropologists who reviewed individual films shortly after broadcast were rather critical of them, demanding in particular more information (Loizos, 1980). Loizos notes that these reviewers, who were often specialists in the ethnography of the societies portrayed, seemed to be reviewing the films as though they were reviewing an academic monograph. In effect, they were making a material category error; by focusing on the content of the films, they failed to appreciate the form and the historical trajectory of the object (a television programme created for, and broadcast to, a non-specialist mass audience) and thereby failed to read it correctly.

While the materiality of the visual object is important, so too are the technologies for the production, dissemination and viewing of the object. Anthropologists are well aware that there are no socially neutral technologies – all are embedded in complex historical, social and ideological frameworks (hence the fallacy of the 'invisible camera' mentioned above). For example, the film historian Jean-Louis Baudry, has pointed out that there is nothing 'natural' about the dimensions of a cinematic image, its framing or its composition, all of which derive from a western Renaissance aesthetic (Baudry, 1985, p. 534 – first published 1970), and the same is obviously true for all other visual media.

What all this points to is that visual anthropology is a subdiscipline of great complexity, a complexity that is generated not by spurious theorizing on the part of its practitioners, but by the very complexity of human social relations. Visual anthropology is not merely making and watching ethnographic movies, nor a pedagogic strategy, nor a tool to be employed in certain fieldwork contexts. Rather, it is an exploration by the visual, through the visual, of human sociality, a field of social action which is enacted in planes of time and space through objects and bodies, landscapes and emotions, as well as thought.

Notes

1. My thinking in this article has been strongly influenced by a number of colleagues, but most specifically by Howard Morphy and Elizabeth Edwards, to both of whom 1 am very grateful. Most of the ideas were developed while I was working on an ESRC-funded project to compile an online catalogue of early ethnographic film (award number R000235891), during the course of which I developed a much stronger appreciation of the use of visual media in anthropological research, but also of the materiality of visual media and their social location.

2. There are other reasons too for ethnographic film's dominance, especially in recent years. See Banks, 1988, 1990.

3. Recent collections of essays in visual anthropology that embody this approach include Banks and Morphy, 1997; Devereaux and Hillman, 1995; Taylor, 1994. Compare these with Hockings, 1995, the second edition of a work that appeared first in 1975; both editions are dominated by articles on ethnographic film – largely emphasizing the documentary, recording aspect – and almost no articles consider the possibility that visual anthropology might concern itself with visual forms produced by anyone other than the anthropologist.

4. My right to speak for sociology is far less grounded than my self-claimed but challengable right to speak for anthropology; nonetheless, I would assume that with appropriate changes to the definition this statement would hold true for visual sociology.

5. Indeed, Evans-Pritchard's photographs of the Nuer of the southern Sudan, published in his various ethnographies, have been subject to just such re-analysis, and although neither Farnell (1994, p. 929) nor Hutnyk (1990) to my knowledge claim to be visual anthropologists I find both, but particularly Farnell, to offer some highly relevant comments.

6. A classic starting point for this kind of approach is Radcliffe-Brown's book *A natural science of society* (1957).

7. The classic case for anthropologists – whether they agree with it or not – is Rodney Needham's claim that 'there is no such thing as kinship' (Needham,

1971, p. 5). I should perhaps stress that Durkheim is nonetheless alive and well in some branches of anthropology, and that the exploration of systematic bodies of knowledge is still highly relevant in some areas – ethnobotanical classification, for example.

8. The exceptions all broadly group together under the heading of performances – be they of dance, ritual, music, theatre, etc. – which often have an important visual aspect, as well of course as their other sensory and emotional aspects. Also somewhat transiently concrete are visual forms that are very quickly effaced – body decoration, for example. However, while the idea of such forms is clearly abstract, the performances themselves nonetheless exhibit temporal and spatial specificity. The relationship between the idea of ritual and the specificity of its performances has been explored in part by Humphrey and Laidlaw (1994), and although they do not make it explicit, there is a visual anthropological subtext to their analysis.

9. A wide variety of texts exist which aim to present an overview or history of anthropology, though few of them make specific mention of the visual. For a general account of the specifically British approach Kuper (1996) is probably the most straightforward, while Langham (1981) is a more detailed account of the early period. Two recent encyclopedias probably offer the most wide-ranging overviews – Ingold (1994) and Barnard and Spencer (1996). Other works which specifically address the place of the visual in anthropology will be mentioned elsewhere in the main text of this chapter.

10. Recent writing in the anthropology of art has moved in two related directions – a study of the place of non-western art in the contemporary art markets and galleries of Europe and America, leading to an anthropological evaluation of 'western' aesthetics, and a study of the place of non-western art in the ethnographic museums of the nineteenth century, contributing to the anthropological evaluation of 'the primitive' in European society. For the former, see recent work by Dussart (1997), Morphy (1995), and N. Thomas (1997), while MacClancy (1988) provides an insightful account of London auction house practice. For the latter, see Stocking (1985). Anthropological approaches to the 'high' art of India, China and Japan are thin on the ground, though significant insights are to be found in a recent series of essays on Indian Jain art (Pal, 1994), while Chris Pinney has done more than most to address the popular arts of India in an anthropological framework (for example, 1992a, 1992b).

11. Peter Loizos considers a number of filmmakers in his 1993 book, while Mick Eaton (1979) concentrates on Jean Rouch as does Paul Stoller (1992). A variety of articles have concerned themselves with corpuses of television ethnographic film, particularly concentrating on Granada Television's (UK) 'Disappearing World' series – see Banks (1994), Ginsburg (1988), Henley (1985), and Loizos (1980).

12. I am very grateful to Paul Henley for making me see this point (in the 1996 Paul Spencer Lecture at the University of Kent). See also Balikci (1995) on reconstruction in ethnographic film.

13. There are several examples of this assumption, but two well-known ones are the position adopted by Margaret Mead and the actual work conducted by Sol Worth and John Adair. Mead's position (1995, p. 9, but first published in 1975) regarding the static surveillance camera is discussed below. Worth and Adair (1972) attempted to translate the Sapir-Whorf hypothesis concerning the cognitive determinism of language to the realm of the visual by training cinematographically illiterate Navaho to use 16mm film cameras, under the

initial impression – later modified – that the cameras would, as it were, see in Navaho. See also the discussion of Jean-Louis Baudry (1985) on the historically cultural bias of the cinematic image, below.

14. In some formulations of the history of documentary and ethnographic cinema, a certain technological determinism can be detected, arguing that the development of lightweight film cameras (and later, video cameras) and crystal synchronization between film camera and sound recorder, obviating the need for a cumbersome cable linking camera operator and sound recordist, brought about the development of observational cinema. Such arguments of course rest on the assumption that technological development is essentially asocial, that technology is developed independently of social need or social construction, something for which sociologists of science have failed to find evidence (e.g., Latour, 1996).

15. The irony is that while the empiricist positivism of Mead's position, not to say its hints of laboratory behaviourism, is wildly out of fashion today, most fieldworking anthropologists would welcome several hours of relatively unmediated footage of this kind if it came from a period before that for which adequate written ethnography and other texts exist. It is for this reason that I began the HADDON Project in Oxford to compile an online computerized catalogue of archival film footage of ethnographic interest. HADDON can be reached at the following URL: http://www.rsl.ox.ac.uk/isca/haddon/HADD_home.html

References

Appadurai, A. (1986) (ed.) *The Social Life of Things: Commodities in Cultural Perspective,* Cambridge: Cambridge University Press.

Balikci, A. (1995 [1975]) 'Reconstructing cultures on film', in Hockings, P. (ed.) *Principles of Visual Anthropology,* Berlin and New York: Mouton de Gruyter.

Banks, M. (1988) 'The non-transparency of ethnographic film (Editorial)', *Anthropology Today,* 4, 5, pp. 2-3.

Banks, M. (1990) 'Experience and reality in ethnographic film', *Visual Sociology Review,* 5, 2, pp. 30-3.

Banks, M. (1994) 'Television and anthropology: An unhappy marriage?', *Visual Anthropology,* 7, 1, pp. 21-45.

Banks, M. and Morphy, H. (1997) (eds) *Rethinking Visual Anthropology,* London and New Haven: Yale University Press.

Barnard, A. and Spencer, J. (1996) (eds) *Encyclopedic Dictionary of Social and Cultural Anthropology,* London: Routledge.

Baudry, J.-L. (1985 [1970]) 'Ideological effects of the basic cinematographic apparatus', in Nichols, B. (ed.) *Movies and Methods Volume II,* Berkeley and Los Angeles: University of California Press.

Collier, J. Jn and Collier, H. (1986) *Visual Anthropology: Photography As a Research Method,* Albuquerque: University of New Mexico Press.

Coote, J. (1992) '"Marvels of everyday vision": The anthropology of aesthetics and the cattle-keeping Nilotes', in Coote, J. and Shelton, A. (eds) *Anthropology, Art and Aesthetics,* Oxford: Clarendon Press.

Coote, J. and Shelton, A. (1992) 'Introduction', in Coote, J. and Shelton, A. (eds) *Anthropology, Art and Aesthetics,* Oxford: Clarendon Press.

Crawford, P. and Turton, D. (1992) (eds) *Film As Ethnography,* Manchester: Manchester

University Press in association with the Granada Centre for Visual Anthropology.

Devereaux, L. and Hillman, R. (1995) (eds) *Fields of Vision: Essays in Film Studies, Visual Anthropology and Photography,* Berkeley: University of California Press.

Dickey, S. (1993) *Cinema and the Urban Poor in South India,* Cambridge: Cambridge University Press.

Dussart, F. (1997) 'A body painting in translation', in Banks, M. and Morphy, H. (eds) *Rethinking Visual Anthropology,* London and New Haven: Yale University Press.

Eaton, M. (1979) (ed.) *Anthropology-Reality-Cinema: The Films of Jean Rouch,* London: British Film Institute.

Edwards, E. (1992) (ed.) *Anthropology and Photography 1860-1920,* New Haven: Yale University Press in association with The Royal Anthropological Institute, London.

Farnell, B.M. (1994) 'Ethno-graphics and the moving body', *Man,* 29, 4, pp. 929-74.

Geary, C. (1988) *Images from Bamum: German Colonial Photography at the Court of King Njoya, Cameroon, West Africa, 1902-15,* Washington: Smithsonian Institution Press.

Gell, A. (1992) 'The technology of enchantment and the enchantment of technology', in Coote, J. and Shelton, A. (eds) *Anthropology, Art and Aesthetics,* Oxford: Clarendon Press.

Ginsburg, F. (1988) 'Ethnographies on the airwaves: The presentation of anthropology on American, British and Japanese television', in Hockings, P. and Omori, Y. (eds) *Senri Ethnological Studies No. 24: Cinematographic Theory and New Dimensions in Ethnographic Film,* Osaka: National Museum of Ethnology.

Grimshaw, A. (1997) 'The eye in the door: Anthropology, film and the exploration of interior space', in Banks, M. and Morphy, H. (eds) *Rethinking Visual Anthropology,* London and New Haven: Yale University Press.

Haddon, A.C. (1895) *Evolution in Art: As Illustrated by the Life-histories of Designs,* London: Walter Scott.

Henley, P. (1985) 'British ethnographic film: Recent developments', *Anthropology Today,* 1, 1, pp. 5-17.

Hockings, P. (1995) (ed.) *Principles of Visual Anthropology* (2nd ed.), The Hague: Mouton.

Humphrey, C. and Laidlaw, J. (1994) *The Archetypal Actions of Ritual: A Theory of Ritual Illustrated by the Jain Rite of Worship,* Oxford: Clarendon Press.

Hutnyk, J. (1990) 'Comparative anthropology and Evans-Pritchard's Nuer photography', *Critique of Anthropology,* 10, 1.

Ingold, T. (1994) (ed.) *Companion Encyclopedia of Anthropology,* London: Routledge.

Kuper, A. (1996 [1973]) *Anthropology and Anthropologists: The Modern British School* (3rd revised edition), London: Routledge and Kegan Paul.

Langham, I. (1981) *The Building of British Social Anthropology: W.H.R. Rivers and His Cambridge Disciples in the Development of Kinship Studies,* Dordrecht: D. Reidel.

Latour, B. (1996) *Aramis, or the Love of Technology,* Cambridge, Mass.: Harvard University Press.

Loizos, P. (1980) 'Granada television's disappearing world series: An appraisal', *American Anthropologist,* 82, pp. 573-94.

Loizos, P. (1989) 'Film and fidelity', *Anthropology Today,* 5, 3, pp. 25-6.

Loizos, P. (1993) *Innovation in Ethnographic Film: From Innocence to Self-consciousness, 1955-85,* Manchester: Manchester University Press.

MacClancy, J. (1988) 'A natural curiosity: The British market in primitive art', *Res,* 15, pp. 163-76.

MacDougall, D. (1978) 'Ethnographic film: Failure and promise', *Annual Review of Anthropology,* 7, pp. 405-25.

MacDougall, D. (1992) 'Complicities of style', in Crawford, P. and Turton, D. (eds) *Film As Ethnography,* Manchester: Manchester University Press in association with the Granada Centre for Visual Anthropology.

Mead, M. (1995 [1975J]) 'Visual anthropology in a discipline of words', in Hockings, P. (ed.) *Principles of Visual Anthropology,* Berlin and New York: Mouton de Gruyter.

Morphy, H. (1995) 'Aboriginal art in a global context', in Miller, D. (ed.) *Worlds Apart: Modernity through the Prism of the Local,* London: Routledge.

Morphy, H. and Banks, M. (1997) 'Introduction: rethinking visual anthropology', in Banks, M. and Morphy, H. (eds) *Rethinking Visual Anthropology,* London and New Haven: Yale University Press.

Needham, R. (1971) 'Remarks on the analysis of kinship and marriage', in Needham, R. (ed.) *Rethinking Kinship and Marriage,* London: Tavistock.

Pal, P. (1994) (ed.) *The Peaceful Liberators: Jain Art from India,* Los Angeles/New York: Los Angeles County Museum of Art/Thames and Hudson Inc.

Pinney, C. (1992a) 'The iconology of Hindu oleographs: Linear and mythic narrative in popular Indian art', *Anthropology and Aesthetics,* 22, pp. 33-61.

Pinney, C. (1992b) 'Montage, doubling and the mouth of god', in Crawford, P.I. and Simonsen, J.K. (eds) *Ethnographic Film Aesthetics and Narrative Traditions: Proceedings from NAFA 2,* Aarhus: Intervention Press.

Pinney, C. (1992c) 'The parallel histories of anthropology and photography', in Edwards, E. (ed.) *Anthropology and Photography, 1869–1920,* New Haven and London: Yale University Press in association with The Royal Anthropological Institute, London.

Powdermaker, H. (1951) *Hollywood, the Dream Factory: An Anthropologist Looks at the Moviemakers,* Secker and Warburg.

Radcliffe-Brown, A.R. (1957) *A Natural Science of Society,* Glencoe, Ill: Free Press.

Ruby, J. (1995) *Secure the Shadow: Death and Photography in America,* Cambridge, Mass.: MIT Press.

Scherer, J. (1988) 'The public faces of Sarah Winnemucca', *Cultural Anthropology,* 3, 2, pp. 178-204.

Scherer, J. (1990) (ed.) *Picturing Cultures: Historical Photographs in Anthropological Inquiry* (a special edition of *Visual Anthropology,* 3, pp. 2-3), Harwood Academic Publishers.

Stocking, G. (1985) (ed.) *Objects and Others: Essays on Museums and Material Culture,* Madison: University of Wisconsin Press.

Stoller, P. (1992) *The Cinematic Griot: The Ethnography of Jean Rouch,* Chicago: University of Chicago Press.

Taylor, L. (1994) (ed.) *Vizualizing Theory: Selected Essays from V.A.R. 1990–4,* New York: Routledge.

Thomas, N. (1997) 'Collectivity and nationality in the anthropology of art', in Banks, M. and Morphy, H. (eds) *Rethinking Visual Anthropology,* London and New Haven: Yale University Press.

Thomas, R. (1985) 'Indian cinema – pleasures and popularity', *Screen,* 26, 3-4, pp. 116-32.

Worth, S. and Adair, J. (1972) *Through Navajo Eyes: An Exploration in Film Communication and Anthropology,* Bloomington: Indiana University Press.

38

Picture This: Researching Child Workers

Angela Bolton, Christopher Pole and Phillip Mizen

V isual methods such as photography are under-used in the active process of sociological research. As rare as visual methods are, it is even rarer for the resultant images to be made by rather than of research participants. Primarily, the paper explores the challenges and contradictions of using photography within a multi-method approach. We consider processes for analysing visual data, different ways of utilising visual methods in sociological research, and the use of primary and secondary data, or, simple illustration versus active visual exploration of the social. The question of triangulation of visual data against text and testimony versus a stand-alone approach is explored in depth.

A set of photographs shows the various sites and scenes of activity in a small branch of a burger bar. We see: a group of children having a party, shots of the counter, a teenage employee serving a drink, the stock-room, the kitchen, the staff-room.

Other pictures in the same set of prints show a seaside caravan site: a welcome sign at the gate; keys laid out on a desk; stacks of sheets in a linen cupboard; a 'milkfloat' with 'Housekeeping Department' emblazoned across it. Back in the burger bar two teenagers dressed in uniform oversee the children's party, a group of younger children are looking at and apparently listening to a teenage boy who stands at the front. He appears to be in charge. The technical quality of these photographs is variable, some are blurred, others obscured by thumbs, none come anywhere near a professional standard but this is hardly surprising given that the photographer has viewed and recorded aspects of her working life through a cheap, single-use, disposable camera with a fixed focus lens. Lindsey, the photographer, is 14. She attends a British secondary school full-time but also holds down two part-time jobs. One, in the 'Housekeeping Department' at a caravan site, she has held since she was 12. More recently she has worked at the burger chain

Source: *Sociology*, 2001, vol. 35, 2, pp. 501-518.

alongside Nathan, a 15-year-old boy from the same school, the boy who
appears to be in charge in the party photo. In his photo diary, in which he has
chosen and written about six of his own photographs Nathan tells us 'I am
now head of parties'. As Lindsey's photograph seemed to indicate, Nathan
was indeed in charge.

These photographs serve as a useful introduction to this paper, the focus of
which is to engage with debates about the role of photography in sociological
research. Increased interest in the use of the visual in sociology raises

important questions about the capacity of photography and other visual media, to act as more than mere illustrations of sociological endeavour. Arguments that Visual Sociology has a capacity to go beyond representation, attribute to it a role in broader sociological enquiry, where it can create rather than merely collect distinctive data. As such, we argue that this conceptual differentiation between visual sociology and Visual Sociology imbues the latter with analytical value not present in other research methods. Moreover, it offers the sociologist an opportunity to gain not just more but different insights into social phenomena, which research methods relying on oral, aural or written data cannot provide.

Using examples from our research into the working and economic lives of 11 to 16 year olds (Mizen, Bolton and Pole 1999), which involved research participants taking, or perhaps more accurately making, photographs of the part-time jobs alongside more conventional research methods of interview, focus groups and written diaries (Pole, Mizen and Bolton 1999), the intention of this paper is to explore the possibilities and constraints which inform the capacity of Visual Sociology to make a distinctive contribution to under-standing aspects of social life.

Recent trends and debates about Visual Sociology raise important methodological questions about the status and treatment of different sources of data relative to one another and highlight debates about power and the conduct of research, about ethics and the generation and nature of knowledge. Throughout this paper we draw upon our own research with working children to engage with these and other issues. In the first section we consider very different ways in which visual approaches to sociological research have been used to open up some of the possibilities of this under-used medium. Next, we reflect upon the use of photographic methods in pursuit of an understanding of child employment and in conducting research with children as active participants, not passive subjects. To situate the broad themes of the paper within our own research practice we look at issues of power, selectivity, making sense of data and macro versus micro or 'the big picture', considering both content and form of the visual data. In the final section we explore both accord and disjunction between visual and other forms of data and assess the use of photography as a tool in the development of our own sociological understanding of child employment.

Visual Sociology: discipline or method?

Visual images imbue modern society with potent and persuasive means to convey information, evoke mood or sell products. Rarely do we get what we see, so much so that, as viewers, we approach visual imagery with something of a jaundiced eye. Are we seeing a fair representation of reality in the visual image, indeed in the photographs described above? We know that photographers can be highly selective in constructing their subject and so as sociologists, as consumers, as viewers we rarely respond to images as simple truth. We are used to visual material being shot through with a hidden or not-so-hidden agenda – having an ulterior purpose.

Within sociology and social research the separation of talk or text and visual image remains striking. Most sociological texts or monographs will contain only one visual image. We are exhorted not to judge a book by its cover, and yet here it is that we generally find the only use of visual material! Paradoxically it may be the very power and ready accessibility of visual images, the apparent transparency of their message, which leads us to dismiss their value as a serious source of data and sociological understanding. Increasingly well-versed in reading and de-coding pictures or photographs, in stepping back from this apparently simple route to understanding, we may suspect the veracity of the academic message or claim to knowledge which comes in this medium, we look for conventional, textual confirmation. At best in sociological research we tend to 'read' visual material as ancillary to the text, supportive or illustrative of the real message, at worst we dismiss it as a suspect or lazy representation of reality. Rarely is it used in such a way as to 'speak for itself or in a way which recognises its capacity to bring a distinctive contribution to sociological enquiry.

Despite this, the use of visual methods in sociological research is growing with dedicated publications and increasing interest in the potential for visual methods not only to unlock access to elusive data but also to contribute to sociological understanding through the use of visual techniques (Harper 1998). That more sociologists seem happy to include visual methods in their research design suggests that visual sociology maybe moving away from its traditional supporting role to one in which Visual Sociology is recognised as for its own heuristic and analytical merit.

The visual exploration and representation of sociological problems and issues is posed here and by others as an under-used approach, largely appropriated by semiotics yet with a much broader application, and, we would argue having a potential affinity with a more realist-materialist perspective. The analysis of popular visual culture now underpins some strands of sociology as a discipline. Feldman (1995) claims semiotics, the divining of social meanings through the signification of cultural symbols and artefacts, as an epistemological approach in and of itself. This strand of sociology often has the visual iconography of the everyday at its centre. However, our argument, which accords with that of Collier (1967) might be dismissed by post-modern thinkers and semioticians as a naïve realist approach, in its claim that the collection and analysis of extant visual material is to be differentiated from the research-active doing or making of sociology through visual means. Methodologically we wish to look further at Harper's (1998) claim of a natural marriage between ethnography and visual methods.

In response to these divergent aspects of the visual in sociology two key questions arise for us. First, is it to be the case that the *doing* of visual sociology will continue to be limited largely as Becker (1974) and later Banks (1998) have noted to the making of ethnographic films or can it be drawn into mainstream sociological praxis? Secondly, can visual sociology be rescued from the semioticians to take a place in a critical but realist or materialist approach to the exploration of social problems, in our case the shape and meaning of child employment in social, economic and family context?

The first issue to consider is whether all forms of visual material can be viewed as sociological data. Are we to think of collections of family photographs in the sense of 'documents of life' (Plummer 1983), another form of secondary data to add to the bigger picture, one more component of a thorough approach to documentary research? Or should we become more alert to the potential of visual methods, specifically photography, as a potent means to access neglected forms of primary data? Most simply the sociological analysis of visual material can be divided along these lines into the analysis and interrogation of existing visual material and the creation of new primary data. Collier (1967, p. x, cited in Harper, 1998:27) makes a finer distinction within the latter to stress the role of visual techniques in the active process of investigation. He distinguishes between the use of visual material to merely represent, illuminate or document known social processes, events and meanings through the familiar devices of the front-cover illustration or sporadic in-text photograph on the one hand and on the other, the active research process whose *raison d'être* is the development of sociological understanding *through* visual techniques and the generation of primary visual data sources.

Those who seek to delineate Visual Sociology as a discipline tend to accord with the latter to see their distinctive contribution as the *a priori use* of visual techniques for the development of sociological understanding. Although the resultant images may subsequently be compared with archival material for a 'then and now' approach or set alongside other data sources, the important distinction is that the images have been created as part of a sociological investigation; the visual element has been part of an active process of seeking and hopefully reaching understanding, rather than merely illustrating findings arrived at by other means. Consequently, the sociologist who takes a few photographs at the end of their research to illustrate and support what they have learned by non-visual methods is generally to be disqualified. They have not by this definition engaged in Visual Sociology.

Records of Culture or Records About Culture?

The focus on an active process does not generally extend as far as the participants, it is not they who are to be active. The emphasis on writing for and about the researcher as image-maker rather than image-gatherer tends simultaneously to relegate the participant to the other side of the lens bringing into play Worth's (1980) distinction between visual records *of* culture and records *about* culture. Those made by participants detailing their own lives are records of culture. Therefore much of what is presented as visual sociology becomes a record *about* culture.

Visual records *of* culture are to be found in open-access television, and the BBC's Video Nation series. In these short video diaries some of which are akin to poems, reminiscences, lectures or moral exhortations, the visual element privileges the 'talking head' with the rest of the visual world, the visual detritus and detail of everyday life which may confirm, contradict, expand or situate the spoken accounts squeezed to the sides. The moving picture is not the same as the frozen still, though arguably more 'real' and with the rapid development and decreasing cost of multimedia technology enabling the transfer and transformation of one media into another perhaps soon to be no less accessible to the sociologist. Video lends itself to diary work in private time and space or by empowered individuals in public. Hubbard's (1991) powerful project 'Shooting Back: A Photographic View of Life by Homeless Children', attempts both, working with a marginalised group and using empowering methods. Homeless children, dispossessed and powerless are allowed for once to describe their environment rather than their environment defining them. But in most visual sociology the researcher remains the central, powerful, defining presence.

In inviting the participants in our study of working children to take photographs of their part-time jobs and their working lives more generally, our intention was to gain access to a visual record *of* their culture rather than *about* their culture. In this sense, the fact that they were behind the lens becomes at least as significant, if not more significant, as what is in front of it.

Their choice of what to include in the frame and what to leave out provides us as the researchers not merely with data as illustration, but with a form of data which has been selected and subject to a process of analysis for its significance to the culture of the research participants. With this reading of our photographs, the distinction between those who are researching and those who are being researched becomes blurred.

Ways of Seeing: different strands of Visual Sociology

What then are the implications of the distinction between the collection of visual data for the purposes of sociological *analysis* (Visual Sociology) rather than the *illustration* of established or even emergent findings (visual sociology)? By this definition, Visual Sociology has something like a 25-year history, linked to a body of work drawn together by key figures such as Howard Becker. The links with anthropology, of course, root visual sociology in a long established research tradition most popularly exemplified in *Balinese Character,* Mead and Bateson's extensive and partly-visual cataloguing of a culture unfamiliar to Western eyes (see Harper 1998). Visual Sociology has since developed in several directions. Becker (1998) has explored the blurred boundaries between art photography, photo-journalism and social investigation, challenging us to discern where one melds into the other. But the artistry of the image is not generally the primary concern of the sociologist. What then is the usual role of the visual in sociological research? Some augments community or topographical surveys with visual material, whilst Harper (1998) argues that there exists a natural marriage between visual sociology and ethnography. A third strand records social change over time, as distinct from the one-off recording of social phenomena. Again this maybe at a community, topographical or biographical level (see Davis 1993 and Rieger 1996 for two review articles).

If Visual Sociology, as an active and arguably distinct discipline, has a relatively short history, a longer-lived approach has been the sociological analysis of the genesis and role of the visual arts and aesthetic movements and the relationship between aesthetic values, epistemology and the evolution of philosophical thought. Berger's 'Ways of Seeing' (1972) is the classic in the discipline. Elizabeth Chaplin's (1994) work both continues and goes beyond this tradition to catalogue her own artistic endeavour. She reaches beyond the conventional boundary of art history to update us on the visual metaphors of our times; both those embedded in contemporary artistic outpourings and those created through visual material, which has been newly and explicitly made for sociological purposes.

Looking at the different strands in greater detail, Harper's claim of an affinity between the aims of ethnography and the data which may be gathered by visual methods is tempered by recognition that its application has been limited to date outside of ethnographic film (Worth and Adair 1972). Payne (1993) also identifies this limitation of the visual in ethnographic community studies, most classic community studies failing to explore the visual in their urban topography, allowing their attempts to be constrained by language when photographs or diagrams (see Cohen 1997 for use of the latter) of the community setting under study would have set the context, located the social interaction in the surroundings which shape, constrain or enable everyday life (Payne 1993). Amongst those who have crossed over into visual methods, ethnography's traditional preoccupation with the marginalised and powerless would seem to continue. Some have used photography to enter into and work amongst what is arguably a community of interest, though often a community characterised by the disinterest of mainstream society: homeless men on the move in the United States, the 'hoboes' of the 1930s rediscovered for the 1980s (Harper 1982).

A further strand is the overtly campaign-oriented photography, which has grown out of political protest or action, using the methods of the photo-journalism of the 1930s or repeating earlier photographic social and topographical surveys. In the work of the 'serious photojournalists' of the early twentieth century Becker acknowledges a collective and sociological debt to those who 'made it their business to record the poverty and hard times of Depression America, their work very much informed by social science theories of various kinds' (1974:3). Most famously the Farm Security Administration organised the visual documentation of migration during the Great Depression and the dogged survival of those who remained in the dustbowl of the American Midwest (Rieger 1996). Later collectives of the 1970s and 1980s in the United States include 'The Atomic Photographers Guild' and 'The New Topographers', the eponymous titles conveying their shared 'common framework of revisionist principles' (Davis 1993:57).

Both photo-journalistic exposes and topographical surveys in the United States inspired later photographers to revisit earlier sites and subjects (Rieger 1982; Klett et al. 1984). Arguably re-photography is a methodological approach rather than a strand of Visual Sociology, but one worth recounting for its elongated use of time-series photography. This approach is more usually associated with the breaking down of change or movement into its constituent parts - the process of walking, rendered as a series of stills; the speeding up of still or filmic images of infinitesimal processes or constant movement until patterns, ebbs and flows emerge from the detail, for example, the passage of human and vehicular traffic through a city (see Reggio's film *Koyaanasquatsi,* made in 1983). In the process of photographing social change the time lapse may be a century or more, or half a life-time as photographers return to the scene or subject of an earlier photographer's work to record and analyse the impact of social processes on towns, land, buildings or individuals during the time which has lapsed. In Rieger's (1996) case the time-lapse is less. He returns fifteen years on to repeat his original community studies of 1970, seeking out the same position from which to record social or community change in its minutiae, change of building use, physical decay, the closure of businesses, increase in traffic. In one of the most striking (perhaps because it is biographical) examples of the re-photography approach, Ganzel

(1984) traced the subject of Dorothea Lange's iconic Depression portrait of a 'migrant mother' and her children in a labourers' camp taken in 1936. Florence Thompson and family abandoned her native Midwest and travelled to the fields of California, where they eked out a survival as casual farm labourers. Thompson came to represent the impact of the Great Depression as a result of Lange's portrait, becoming 'probably the single most famous image' (Rieger 1996:28). Her prematurely aged face looks off to the side of the camera, two of her daughters hide their faces in her neck. Forty years later in Ganzel's 1979 portrait, the former migrant mother, now nearly 80, sits in the garden of her California home, surrounded by her grown-up daughters who smile out at the camera. Superficially, it can be read, misinterpreted perhaps, as a photograph of success, of stability against the odds but her story testifies to the endurance of casual low-paid work and poverty throughout her adult years (Rieger 1996). To equate these examples of re-photography and photo-journalism with issues of culture discussed earlier, then these photographs clearly represent examples *about* culture rather than *of* culture.

In some photo-journalism the blurring of the boundary between art and documentary or social commentary is evident. For Davis (1993) Misrach's boundary-crossing images, chosen for their elegiac qualities, document the poisoning and physical destruction of the American Midwest by the Cold War activities of nuclear and bio-chemical testing and conventional bombing practice in the ancient spaces of the Nevada and Utah deserts. Davis (1993:53) describes Misrach's (1992) work as a 'huge mural of forbidden visions ... which dissolves the boundary between documentary and allegory'. In this work an artist's eye and professional photographer's technical pro-ficiency combine to compose the subject matter of ruined landscape, military detritus and the corpses of malformed animals. Few sociologists working through visual means blur the boundaries between art and sociology as fully as Elizabeth Chaplin (1994), who not only sets art history in social context, detailing the transformative possibilities of politically motivated art movements, but who in her own photography takes up the Gramscian challenge of building a counter-culture, counter-pointing in exhibition her own 'feminist' (close-up, intimate, detailed) images against what she charac-terises as man-made, masculinist images.

More recently, sociological research which employs visual methods seems less challenged by the pressure to produce contextualised, objective, empirical sociological research than exercised by the abandonment of this goal. Harper (1998) critiques the increasing pull in the direction of a post-modern or new ethnography. Here the representational image is no longer measured in terms of objectivity, instead the researcher-photographer is recognised as shaping visual data from their world-view, credited with little more than this. Essentially the post-modern challenge to the visual sociologist has been to abandon the pretence of objectivity, to surrender the panopticon gaze and put down the camera. The implication is that visual sociology has merely aped the erstwhile gold-standard of the anthropological approach to document with a cool detachment every aspect of the 'foreign' culture under study. The camera is posed as just one more objectifying tool of colonialist enterprise – now brought home to bear down on the marginalised at close hand.

Whilst the implicit challenge to an unthinking positivism and concealed power relations between observer and observed is to be welcomed, a post-modern ethnographic approach goes much further. Ethnographic standards of both immersion in subject and striving towards wholeness of account are abandoned in recognition of inescapable partiality and partisanship. The danger in our view is that this can lead inexorably back to an introverted celebration of the researcher's view in which participants are largely side-lined, interpretive and analytical attempts halted and a paradoxically empiricist outcome results, where mere surface representation is all.

Shooting the Present: young people and work

Reflecting on the different strands of sociology conducted through visual methods we accepted the challenge to avoid photographic surveillance of the young people with its corollary of paternalistic intervention (Hebdige 1988), but simultaneously we have resisted the relativism of the account and the over-privileging of the text or story implicit in a post-modern reading. Instead, we ask whether photography can play a role in a critical but realist or materialist approach to the exploration of social problems – in this particular instance, the working lives of children. Although we value the emphasis upon context process and multi-method working that emerges clearly in Rieger's work, our aim was not to record social change but to explore a social phenomenon in context, in our case the shape and meaning of child employment in Britain today for the children themselves. To do this we offered a group of seventy young workers an opportunity to make a photographic account of their part-time jobs. As part of a wider, year-long research programme which included interviews, written diary work and focus groups we provided the same young people with disposable cameras and gave a commitment to develop two sets of prints, one for us and one which they could keep.

Our first viewing as a research team of the young people's photographs brought forth an initial disappointment about the tremendous selectivity with which some had approached their subject. There were few action shots. There were few people. We saw workplaces rather than work in action. Several of those who had spent the first half of the year talking in interviews and writing in diaries about busy working environments duly presented us with photo-graphs of empty shops and hairdressing salons at the beginning or end of the working day.

However, in the context of Visual Sociology rather than visual sociology the absence of action and people has significance in the depiction of culture which goes beyond mere representation of the workplace and the experience

of work. The photographs, which the young people had produced, brought to life their working environments. They showed in detail not only their workplaces but also their role within them. For example, photographs were taken of stockrooms, of rubbish skips and of toilets. Goffman's notion of front and back stage is evident in these and many of the photographs. The bundles of towels accumulated in the back room of a hairdresser's contrast with the row of neat hair dryers and styling tables. It is with the dirty towels that the photographer spends much of her working day. The decision to photograph a jumble of chairs taken by a part-time glass collector and general

dogsbody at a social club conveys very clearly the reality of the tasks to be carried out as part of the cleaning regime at the club. The pictures convey the reality of the culture of young people's work in a way which the children's written and spoken words do not. They are representations *of* their work culture, rather than an external researcher/photographers representation *about* their culture.

Beyond Content to Form

At an early stage in the research process issues relating to the form of data as well its content began to emerge, from the absences as well as the positive images recorded. Several aspects are worth exploring. The first is that data generated by this alternative means tended to confirm written and spoken accounts of the content of jobs and the nature of workplaces, showing visual evidence of what we had begun to gather through other means of the social positioning of young people within the workplace. However, through the photographs we have seen places normally unseen by customers and hitherto by ourselves. Some of these elements were clearly new data for us: the material settings of the young people's workplaces: tools; implements; colleagues and the physical plant of their daily or weekly working lives. In addition the form of the pictures indicates relative powerlessness at work. Many photographs were snatched, not only in the inevitable sense of a snapshot or freeze-frame of an active scene but also in the making of a secretive record. Of these a significant amount were taken at times when workplaces were not busy, empty even, perhaps when the visual endeavour was safest (in terms of keeping a job) or when it was least disruptive for the young person to take photographs.

Moreover, several young people had earlier decided to opt out of the photographic stage of the research for this very reason, fearing that taking photographs might jeopardise their employment. Others who wanted to do the photography and initially anticipated no problems in taking a camera into work returned cameras with only one or two shots taken, having been asked to stop taking photographs by their employers. In these situations it is the absence of photographs that begins to tell us something about the work experiences of the children by providing an insight into the power relations that govern their employment. It also stimulates a set of questions relating to their employers as to why they might object to the young people taking photographs.

Some Analytical Strategies

Prosser and Schwartz approach the analytical processing of visual material through the issue of 'the fallibility and selectivity of the picture maker' (1998:125). The researcher's beliefs and standpoint underpin the making of the images and therefore shape the data and must be rendered visible in the analysis. In our case the picture makers are the young people themselves so we can, to an extent, side-step the issue of our own critical distance and are faced instead with their fallibility and selectivity.

In one sense, the young people were our field researchers, working to our research remit as technicians (Finch 1986) in the wider research process. However, to marginalise their role in such a way is to misunderstand both the role and the significance of the photography in our research. Our only instructions to the young people were to take photographs of their work, which showed what it was like to work and what the work meant to them. The photographs were, therefore, composed and selected by the young workers as research participants rather than research objects. They are their interpretation of what is significant to our research focus and in this sense represent initial data analysis. However, issues of significance and analysis do not end with merely selecting or composing and taking the photographs. As the research progressed, issues of the relationship between the photographs and other forms of data became important. As did the way in which the photographs were read and interpreted by us and by the young people. The work of Rieger (1996) and Becker (1998) may help in explaining issues of significance, or meaning, and processes of data analysis here.

Rieger (1996) has advocated the use of visual material in relation to other evidence and as a theoretically situated activity, the researcher having decided the appropriate meanings, signs and symbols to collect as visual evidence of their theoretical target or concern – a purposeful and selective data collection. He takes a somewhat deductive approach, perhaps anathema to the ethnographer but with the caveat that 'the conscientious researcher will document any and all aspects of the phenomenon that could contribute to it sociologically' (1996:42). The researcher/photographer's understanding of images and captured details will develop with the elicitation of other accounts – spoken, written, statistical, demographic – which are then set alongside the visual account.

Becker (1998) argues that visual sociology is '(almost) all a matter of context', the viewer's response to the work as much as a key to whether a work is deemed sociological or not as the processes undertaken by the researcher/photographer. He advises a methodical approach to the analysis of images, a literal poring over of an image, a naming of everything that is seen with the object of making the taken-for-granted rise to the surface, breaking down the privileging of the central image or object of focus. Context may be spelled-out, or not. Where provided it may be through a written, analytical account of the social phenomenon and processes depicted, the researcher setting the images in theoretical context, spelling out how they have made meaning from the images. Alternatively, a simple presentation of the images allows saturation of the reader/viewer's eye with image after image, allowing meaning to filter through and the reader/viewer to extract their own meanings.

Neither Rieger nor Becker falls into the trap of treating images as short-hand or easy-to-read versions of other data sources. For us the starting point of analysis was necessarily the acknowledgement of what was missing alongside that which was present and only then the exploration of what was presented. Arguably some of our analytical strategies derived from our decision to explore the photographs in relation to individual biographies of the young people and from accounts that they wrote of their photographs. However, these have to be seen against our naïve readings of the photographs as stand alone documents and the emerging themes as we looked to understand individual accounts more fully and to understand the patterns and forms which emerged as the project progressed with various sources of data.

Missing the Bigger Picture?

Many of the tasks and duties described in interviews with the young people and in the diaries which they kept appeared in photographs: cleaning; carrying and serving refreshments for a sports team; washing up; neutralising perms; feeding animals; serving customers. However, comparison of different data sources also suggested to us that there were significant omissions from the photographs. Reading what was and what was not in the photographs in the context of what we knew, or thought we knew from other sources, became important.

For example, John, 12, works on his father's sheep farm. He selected six of his photographs to write about, including one of himself on a quad bike. It could have been a photograph of any boy showing off a treasured possession with no relation to working practice. But he wrote, '*(T)his is when I go out on my quad to check all the sheep to see if they are all right*'. In interview John had talked about riding around the large farm to perform his regular task of checking on the animals, '*I go on my quad then around the fields to check like if there is anything wrong with anything, or if anything has been killed like or died*', and now he wrote

the same about this photograph, simple confirmation. Without alternative data sources we risked interpretations which missed, concealed or skewed the nature of John's work, prior knowledge was important in this case.

In another, further clarification was also needed. At first sight, few pictures showed sheep farming in action, or even sheep, although in interview John had used a vivid visual metaphor, describing the huge numbers of sheep as looking like 'a *white blanket across the farm*' when they are all gathered up together. The point was to understand why the primary work of the farm seemed missing in John's photograph. Talking with him about this he pointed to the tiny, far-off dots on the pictures. A huge flock of sheep was not the point of his photograph or his analysis of his work. The sheep are not usually gathered together, but are scattered across the huge farm. Their tiny dots on the hillsides showed us the farm's extent for the first time. It also put into context and demonstrated the significance of the earlier photograph of the quad bike. Seeing the fields and hillsides of the farm, its size, the distances John needed to cover and the size of machinery, whose use had been meticulously detailed in John's work diaries, conveyed scale. Active processes were difficult for him to capture whilst he was engaged in them, but were represented in the shots of machinery, sheds, dogs and hills. This is arguably triangulation plus something extra, the all-important topographical context, the scale of the setting that John, who at 12 years of age was already an experienced farmworker, took for granted. One reading of this example was that John had merely attempted to photograph the farm where he worked. However, this does not do justice to John as a researcher or to the capacity of Visual Sociology to convey more than just a simple visual representation. As context was added to the data by viewing the photographs alongside other data sources the significance of his representation in relation to the scale of his work became clear. Moreover, whilst John had been uniquely positioned as both photographer and subject, issues about the nature and experience of his work did not become explicit until the viewer's response had been added.

Illustration or Analysis?

Although the close fit of different forms of data confirmed some accounts in a straightforward manner other more serious disjunctions required written or verbal exploration. On balance we are left with greater confirmation than challenge to earlier conventional data through the accumulation of images which closely accord with spoken and written accounts. In which case we might ask was visual research really needed? Have we used photography as a method for doing Visual Sociology or merely an expensive add-on to conventional qualitative sociological methods? Over time, elements of difference and the potential for analysis at a deeper level became apparent. In many cases the same account was repeated, augmented through the different media. In others our understanding was extended or changed by a further aspect of form, that of the young people's response to their own photography. In itself this is another data source.

Finally, a broader social process became evident. In the gradual accumulation of photographs from young people in different parts of the country, doing similar jobs, employed at a similar (low) level of the service sector, photographing the same tasks and processes, similar details came through the different media throughout the year, repeated, cumulative, even showing similar interiors to similar-sized modest houses, possibly indicating a similar social positioning. We see little evidence of affluence, more the mainstream, the economic middle-ground – not Middle England – but something more akin to the majority experience of fluctuating fortunes, service sector work, some financial insecurity, but most come from homes with one or more adults in work and live in small semi-detached houses on housing estates or inner-city and urban terraces. In the backgrounds, potent images of surrounding environs: the terraced houses of a small Welsh former coal and steel town hit by industrial shut-down in both industries on a massive scale; razor wire atop the boundary fences of an inner-city school: another near neat well-kept estates of modern semidetached houses. As fieldworkers we knew the environs of the schools but not outlying catchment areas, nor house type nor size nor decor, nor the young people's own rooms, which some photographed to show us, often with possessions bought from their wages. The photography gave us access to broader data, perhaps beginning to take us beyond the specific cases of our research participants.

Conclusion

Our use and discussion of visual methods in sociological research so far, pose a challenge on two levels, first to sociological neglect of the meanings of visual signs and signals within society and second to the use of visual means to convey understanding to the reader who in everyday life is used to interpreting visual signals. The reader is also a viewer (Harper 1998). It is our belief that some approaches to sociology have set up and defended a false denial of our visual sense and sensibility which arguably delineates Visual Sociology as a subdiscipline. Our research advocates the role not of just photography but of Visual Sociology more generally, as an element of a broader methodology for sociological enquiry. Our argument has been that it has the capacity to produce unique datasets and to facilitate analysis which may tell us more about social phenomena than analysis of textual, verbal or observational data. However, we do not automatically wish to privilege visual over other forms of data and we have argued that visual methods can complement, augment, confirm and enlarge on other methods. Nevertheless, we do wish to emphasize that visual methods and visual data do have a distinctive contribution to make.

For us visual research has proved thus far most valuable in taking us beyond the taken-for-granted level and into areas which were not always clearly revealed by the young people, who could be too entangled in their own experiences of work to see the need for verbal explanation. In this context, their photographs acted as another way of 'making the familiar strange' to them and the strange familiar to us. This has particular potency when research participants take the photographs, the researcher does not know how the data will shape up, and is not therefore the final arbiter of form or content. The researcher works not only with what has been captured but also with what has not been captured. For us, the absence of people and 'action' in some of the photographs became as significant as what was captured by the photographer. By placing photography alongside other forms and sources of data and by contrasting the snapshot effect of photography with a longitudinal time-scale, we were able to include what lay beyond the frame in our analysis. The photographs worked at a number of levels, in what they depicted, in promoting questions either about what was depicted or what was absent even where this was an absence of photographs themselves and as a form of triangulation with other research methods.

Careful multi-strategy research and the creation of situated accounts, which challenge the dismissal of the photograph as only a surface representation, could add to many forms of and approaches to research. We reject the proposition that only relative or 'fictional' judgements can be made. When research participants are the sociological photographers and relationships with alternative data sources are carefully explored both of these propositions can be challenged. All the indications are that the 'phenomenon' of child employment makes more sense when explored *with* children within a socio-economic context, taking account of the materialist conditions which shape their lives. In this sense, we would argue that the photographs, which they produced, and the Visual Sociology which they have facilitated have resulted in accounts *of* rather than merely *about* their working lives.

Acknowledgement

The research outlined here came from the Work, Labour and Economic Life in Late Childhood Project funded by the Economic and Social Research Council, as part of 'Children 5-16 Growing into the Twenty First Century', award number L129251035.

References

Banks, M. 1998. 'Visual Anthropology: Image, Object and Interpretation', in J. Prosser, (ed.), *Image-based Research: A Sourcebook for Qualitative Researchers*. London: Falmer Press.

Becker, H. S. 1974. 'Photography and Sociology'. *Studies in the Anthropology of Visual Communication* 1:3-26.

Becker, H. S. 1998. 'Visual Sociology, Documentary Photography, and Photo-journalism: It's (Almost) All a Matter of Context', in J. Prosser (ed.), *Image-based Research: A Sourcebook for Qualitative Researchers*. London: Falmer.

Berger, J. 1972. *Ways of Seeing*. Harmondsworth: Penguin.

Chaplin, E. 1994. *Sociology and Visual Representation*. London: Routledge.

Cohen, P. 1997. *Rethinking the Youth Question*. Basingstoke: Macmillan.

Collier Jr, J. 1967. *Visual Anthropology: Photographs as a Research Method*. New York: Holt, Reinhart, Winston.

Davis, M. 1993. 'The Dead West: Ecocide in Marlboro Country'. *New Left Review* 200:49-73.

Feldman, M. 1995. *Analysing Qualitative Research*. London: Sage.

Finch, J. 1986. *Research and Policy: The Use of Qualitative Methods in Social and Educational Research*. London: Falmer Press.

Ganzel, B. 1984. *Dustbowl Descent*. Lincoln: University of Nebraska Press.

Harper, D. 1982. *Good Company*. Chicago: University of Chicago Press.

Harper, D. 1998. 'An Argument for Visual Sociology', in J. Prosser (ed.), *Image-based Research: A Sourcebook for Qualitative Researchers*. London: Falmer.

Hebdige, D. 1988 *Hiding in the Light*. London: Routledge.

Hubbard, J. 1991. *Shooting Back: A Photographic View of Life by Homeless Children*. San Francisco: Chronicle Books.

Klett, M., Manchester, E. *et al.* 1984. *Second View: The Rephotographic Survey Project*. Albuquerque: University of New Mexico Press.

Misrach, R. 1992. *Violent Legacies: Three Cantos*. New York: Aperture Foundation.

Mizen, P., Bolton, A., and Pole, C. 1999. 'School Age Workers: The Paid Employment of Children in Britain'. *Work, Employment and Society* 13: 423-38.

Mizen, P. and Pole, C. 1997. *Work, Labour and Economic Life in Late Childhood*. ESRC Children 5-16 Programme Pack. Swindon: Economic and Social Research Council.

Payne, G. 1993. 'The Community Revisited: Some Reflections on the Community Study as a Method'. Unpublished conference paper, British Sociological Association Annual Conference, University of Essex.

Plummer, K. 1983. *Documents of life*. London: Allen and Unwin.

Pole, C, Mizen, P., and Bolton, A. 1999. 'Realizing Children's Agency in Research: Partners and Participants?' *International Journal of Social Research Methodology* 2:39-54.

Prosser, J. and Schwartz, D. 1998. 'Photographs within the Sociological Research Process', in J. Prosser (ed.), *Image-based Research: A Sourcebook for Qualitative Researchers*. London: Falmer.

Rieger, J. H. 1982. 'Rural Nonfarm Residence in the Midwest'. *Rural Sociologist* 2:215-32.

Rieger, J. H. 1996. 'Photographing social change'. *Visual Sociology* 11:5-49.

Worth, S. 1980. 'Margaret Mead and the Shift from Visual Anthropology to the Anthropology of Visual Communication'. *Studies in Visual Communication* 6:15-22.

Worth, S. and Adair, J. 1972. *Through Navajo Eyes: An Exploration in Film Communication and Anthropology*, Bloomington : Indiana University Press.

Biographical note: Angela Bolton is senior policy officer at Barnardos. Christopher Pole is Senior Lecturer in Sociology at the University of Leicester. Phillip Mizen is Lecturer in Sociology at the University of Warwick.

Address: Christopher Pole, Department of Sociology, University of Leicester, University Road, Leicester, LE1 7RH.

Section Seven
Reflecting on Fieldwork Experience

39

Method of Study

Ken Pryce

The main method adopted for the research on which this study is based was participant observation. Participant observation, because it deposits one inside the culture of the group studied and forces on one the role of involved actor and participant, affords the academic researcher a unique opportunity of getting the right leads and following through situations whereby he can replace superficial impressions with more accurate insights. By combining his outsider's perception with an insider's view of the way of life under consideration, the researcher can thus get behind the statistical shapes and patterns and explore at first hand the wide variety of adaptive responses he encounters, studying them from the value position of the people themselves, in their own terms and on their own ground. All the time he does this through prolonged, intensive direct exposure to actual life-conditions over a relatively long period of time. Not only can the findings of this intensive approach supplement and add significance to data gathered by more quanti- tative techniques, they can generate fruitful hypotheses which quantitative research can later refine and test.

The St Paul's Area in Bristol – problems of orientation

When I started my research in Bristol, not only the coloured community, but the entire city of Bristol was totally unfamiliar to me. Getting to know the St Paul's area was especially difficult, because initially I was living outside it in trendy middle-class Clifton, the university area.

My entrance into St Paul's and environs was gained concurrently at three separate points. The first point of entry was through Shanty Town – the domain of the hustler and the teenybopper. My introduction to Shanty Town

Source: *Endless Pressure: A Study of West Indian Lifestyles in Bristol*, 1979, Bristol Classic Press, pp. 283-301.

took place on my first night in Bristol while I was prowling around on my own in the city centre. As I was boarding a No. 11 bus going into the St Paul's district, a very friendly and garrulous Jamaican – a man in his early thirties – saw me and asked me if I was new in Bristol. He had heard me ask the conductor if the bus would take me to the section of the city where black people lived. Without revealing my true identity as a researcher, I told him I was a Jamaican like himself and that I was a student, but that I was new in Bristol and was interested in finding the Panorama Club (which already I had heard so much about from my new acquaintances in Clifton). My concealment of my role as a researcher was not intended to deceive, but merely to sustain the rapport which I was developing with the stranger. The man asked me my name, I told him, and he said his name was Segie. It turned out Segie was an ex-hustler who wanted to keep as far away from St Paul's as possible, because, to use his own words, he didn't want to get 'mixed up'. Segie said he was lucky always to meet West Indians on their first day in Bristol and told me of similar instances of meeting newcomers to Bristol in pubs and in the streets. I paid my first visit to the Panorama Club that night with Segie, though he said he hated going there. After the club I accompanied him to Grosvenor Road, where he bought 'johnny cakes' in the Sea-Island Cafe and hung around until he was able to find a friend from whom he could buy a 'smoke'. Segie hated the hustling scene, but he still visited the cafe regularly to buy 'drugs'. After that he took me to his flat in Montpelier, where we ate and drank together, and of course, smoked. Segie, who was a painter and decorator by trade, was out of work at the time. However, he worked when he felt like it, and this was usually in summer. Segie said he had just stopped working and would not work again until next summer; his woman would support him through the winter. She was away at the time as she had just got a job on a passenger ship as a stewardess. When we parted that night we agreed to meet again.

My second introduction to West Indians in Bristol was through a law-abiding West Indian working man. I was given his name by my head of department, who told me it would help my acquaintance with the West Indian community if I could meet this man, who could then arrange further contacts for me. The man turned out to be a mainliner and our first meeting took place at a commemoration service in honour of the then recently deceased Norman Washington Manley, ex-Prime Minister of Jamaica. At this service, which was held at an Anglican church in St Paul's, I met several other mainliners, including Prescott and Harry Saunders, who was then well in with that crowd, but who later rejected the mainline orientation to become an in-betweener. All the individuals I later came to regard as the principal West Indian mainliners were there. My main contact introduced me to the others and I found I was warmly welcomed and instantly accepted as one of them, despite the fact that we were meeting for the first time. In this group it was not necessary to be guarded about my true identity as a researcher. That very same night I received more than one invitation from people in the group to have dinner with them. I was also introduced to several English people, mostly women in the teaching profession who helped to make up the social circle of mainliners.

My third contact with the West Indian community was through saints and their churches, and it took place at around the same time as I was beginning to multiply my friendships with West Indians in other sections of the West Indian community. The three completely different ways in which I was gaining entrance to the field situation were helpful in that they exposed me almost simultaneously to three sections of the black community which were socially dissimilar both in their style and quality of life. They afforded me a kind of panoramic view of the West Indian scene.

Having gained entry into the St Paul's area, the second major problem was to work out a focus for the research. This was a difficulty inasmuch as I did not enter the field with any preconceived idea of what I would find. I only knew that I wanted to study life-styles and that I would go about it in a way that would make full use of my identity as a West Indian. I had no worked-out theory or hypothesis I was going to develop, no blueprint for action apart from my undergraduate training in sociology, and my only knowledge of life-style was limited to a single reading of Ulf Hannerz's book, *Soulside*.[1] I didn't even know then that my method of investigation would be purely observation and participation. Participant observation became more and more necessary the more qualitative the investigation became. My first hunch came only after weeks in the field, when it was agreed with one of my thesis advisors that I would start my research with an investigation into West Indian church people as a clearly identifiable group in the black community. Even then the situation was pretty vague as I still did not know exactly what I would study when I got into the church. The findings on the church, as well as all the other insights and hypotheses that later were to form the substance of the thesis, were developed in the actual process of investigation.

Saints

As I did not myself know of any West Indian church in Bristol at the time, I had to rely on some of my mainliner friends for advice and information about the religious life of West Indians in the city. Through discussions with mainliners I was able to discover the whereabouts of several of the churches, and I chose two to start with. These I visited on alternate Sundays and on some nights during the week as well. This first exposure to West Indian church life provided a focus and a starting point for my first serious exploration of the organization of West Indian social life in Bristol.

Ideally I would have liked to be able to move as freely as possible between the membership of all the West Indian churches in the city or, at least, to be able to maintain my membership in the two churches I started out with. Practical necessity, however, forced me to concentrate on just one. Firstly, I found that there were many doctrinal as well as sectional differences between the congregations, and that by continuing to be a member of more than one congregation at a time I was running the risk of being regarded as a 'spy' by all. Secondly, I found the precariousness of being a floating member of more than one congregation at the same time too worrying to sustain. To win the allegiance and support of the newcomer, each church tries to take the newcomer into its confidence by portraying the other congregation in the worst possible light. It is not difficult to visualize the embarrassment when it becomes known that you are sharing the secrets of more than one church at a time. Once I asked a middle-aged couple in the first West Indian church I visited in Bristol what they thought of Calvary United Brotherhood. The couple told me that they could not see themselves becoming members of that church because they were too 'loud' and the people making up the congregation were 'uncivilized'. They also thought that doctrinally the members in Calvary United were going astray. Subsequently, after having been received into Calvary, it happened that the pastor of Calvary made the very same uncomplimentary remarks to me about the style of worship in the church these two people were members of. Soon after that the middle-aged couple turned up at Calvary at the wedding ceremony of a man who was a relative of theirs as well as a baptized member of Calvary. After the ceremony, I went to see the pastor of Calvary in his study in his home, which adjoins the church. When the pastor opened the door to let me in, I suddenly became tense with surprise and confusion, for the middle-aged couple were in the pastor's room, sitting and having tea with him. I was then still a regular visitor to the Church of God sect, of which the man and his wife were leading members. As the pastor did not know of my involvement with them, he introduced us, saying that I was his latest convert and that he was delighted to have a person like me in his church. Wide-eyed with astonishment, the couple looked at me hard and questioningly as if to say. 'But I don't understand it, only last week you were at our church!' However, neither they nor I made the pastor any wiser or said anything about my connections with their church. We merely shook hands as I joined them at tea. We tended to avoid each other's eyes as much as possible. But the discomfiture and embarrassment of the situation was so upsetting for me that there was nothing I could do but cry excuse and leave. After this I stuck to Calvary and ceased attending the Church of God services altogether.

Despite my initial acceptance into the Calvary congregation and my successful adjustment to the demands it made on me both doctrinally and socially, there was still some curiosity as to my real motive for being in the church. The reason I always gave was that I was from a very religious background, but that my struggle to receive an education had drawn me away from the church somewhat, and that now that I was in Bristol, where there was a church, I just felt like going to church again. In supporting this line – which was only partly true – I was able to quote episodes from my own past relating to the religious situation in Jamaica, which we all shared in varying degrees as Jamaicans. This not only helped to make me appear plausible in the eyes of saints, it allayed any fear they might have had that somehow I was socially above them and their religion. In this respect, our common identity as

Jamaicans played a significant part in establishing a rapport. However, I was still highly conscious of the ethical implications of my approach and was on the look-out for the most appropriate opportunity to reveal my true role. This opportunity came one day when the pastor invited me to his home for dinner and told me about his background as a political organizer in Jamaica, and about the part he played in the Bristol bus dispute. Then, by way of informing him of my own political interests, I let him know of my role in Bristol as a researcher into West Indian social problems, explaining how this tied in with my studies at the university. This the pastor accepted, and he responded by by saying he would do everything he could to help. I was soon to discover, however, that he wanted something in return – my baptism and permanent membership of the church. The pastor went about this by carefully concealing my research interests from rank and file members in the church and by – to use his own words – taking me 'under his wings'. He would often invite me to dinner in his home, where we would talk about a wide range of topics, and then he would beseech me at the end of it to give myself up to the Lord. On such occasions I would answer that I had no objection to doing so, but that I was still trying to make up my mind. Sometimes the pastor would make special mention of me in sermons and publicly declare that the Lord had sent me, a talented man, to their church, and that this was further evidence of the Lord working in mysterious ways. He, and other members of the congregation, sometimes made me very generous gifts of shirts, hand-kerchiefs, combs, etc, which I dared not refuse for fear that my actions would be interpreted as impolite or insincere. Church brethren would drop in regularly – and unexpectedly – to visit me at my student hostel in Clifton. A special effort was always made to get me to accompany the brethren in their weekly visits to sister congregations in other parts of the South-west area. Whenever the pastor was present he would insist I sit beside him in his car, which was always driven by someone else. On such occasions he would hint to me that I could be an asset to the church if only I would get baptized and surrender myself to the Holy Ghost. The situation became increasingly tense as I tried to stall for as much time as possible. But this phase of my stay in the church was beneficial in one very important sense. Spending so much time 'under the wings' of the pastor brought me in contact with the bishops and many of the ministers from the other churches in the network, and taught me a lot about the top layer of the sect and its organization on a national level. However, it had the effect of cutting me off from the grass-roots membership, and worked against my getting to know ordinary members in the congregation on a personal level. When I tried to correct this situation by seeking out individual members of the congregation to talk with, and by inviting myself to their homes, I found that I was held somewhat at a distance by them. In their eyes I was still an 'unsaved' person, untutored in the ways of the church. To be accepted into their fold and treated as one of them, I needed to be 'saved', and I could only achieve this through baptism. What I was discovering was that to learn more about the church from the standpoint of ordinary members, I needed to be on the inside as a fully fledged believer. I had no choice therefore but to give in one Sunday morning when I and other unsaved persons like myself were called to the altar and asked if we were ready to be baptized. With hands laid on our heads, we were prayed for and cajoled into accepting baptism, which we all did. After my baptism, there was great rejoicing, and it was thought that the Holy Ghost was at work that day, and that a promise to the church had been fulfilled.

Baptism did make a difference to my status among saints. I was now treated with a new candour. Individual members would now compete to have me in their homes for dinner. Some even suggested that I move from Clifton and come to live nearer the saints. Others wanted me to come and meet their children. In their homes it was easier to chat casually. Saints would respond by playing religious records for me, by giving me religious tracts, by discussing their domestic problems and their general approach to life, and by encouraging me to remain steadfast in the Spirit. By establishing links such as these with rank and file members in the congregation I was able to rectify gaps in my observation of church life, and to achieve a fuller understanding of the sectarianism and ideology of saints.

Work with saints took up most of the time spent on the field-work stage of the research. Out of a total of twenty-four months in the field, twelve were spent singing, praying, eating, feasting, travelling, talking, discussing, visiting and attending services with saints. Though possibly the most interesting from a personal point of view, my investigation into the church was the most difficult, the most demanding, the most intricate, and certainly the most time-consuming. At least six of the twelve months spent in the church were used up just trying to stay on good terms with saints and trying to get accepted into the fold. The situation was made even more awkward by the fact that there was no way in which I could take notes on the spot without giving rise to anxiety and suspicion on their part. I found I needed to take notes most in my first encounters with saints, when I was getting to know them, yet this was the time when I was most closely watched by sect members. One man, after finding a notebook I had lost, even went as far as to search in it for anything that could indicate the kind of life I was leading outside the church. In addition to these strains, I found the services – which were generally whole day affairs – too wearisome and physically exhausting. Each service always left me groggy and, temporarily, somewhat mentally incapacitated, and this further interfered with my note-taking.

By far the greatest quantity of data collected were gathered from tape-recordings of services and functions of various kinds made by saints themselves. At first – after about three months -when I first used my own cassette tape-recorder to record services, I was not successful, as I found I could not easily concentrate on the sermons and rituals and manipulate the recording machine at the same time. Also, because I was always sitting at the back or some distance away from the pulpit, the quality of the reproduction I got on my recorder was always quite poor, as a result of background disturbances of various kinds which on tape drowned out what the speakers were saying. This made my efforts at data-collecting most frustrating and unrewarding, as after nine months, just when I was thinking of leaving the church, I found I had precious little to show for it in the way of hard data, which I badly needed to support my observational findings. I had, therefore, to rely on individual saints who were fond of making their own recordings to get the necessary taped data. But the sheer practical difficulties involved in getting taped material from saints made it a most time-consuming business for, in addition to borrowing tapes and re-recording the material on them, it meant staying on longer at the church to avoid giving the impression I was diving in for some kind of 'scoop', only to disappear completely from the scene. All told, the whole of the last six months spent in the church were used up simply amassing data and, more or less, slowly winding up relationships. However, despite the amount of time spent amassing data from tapes, it should be clear from reading the section on saints that tape-recorded data were not necessarily the most important of the materials used to study their life-style. Tape-recorded data were merely used to supplement and give weight and substance to richer, subtler information based on insight and observation, which could only be gathered by long, arduous months of repetition and routine.

The Other Life-styles in the St Paul's Area

Despite my deep involvement with saints and the totalizing effect of the church on my own personal life-style during the first twelve months of the field-work, I was careful not to neglect early contacts made in other sections of the community, notably among mainliners, hustlers, and some in-betweeners whose acquaintance I had made after I had already formed my attachments in the church. Therefore, by the time my stay at Calvary was over, I was already a familiar figure in the St Paul's area. Indeed, what actually happened was that after about three months of being in the church, my personal network consisted of two sets of friends only – the brethren at Calvary on the one hand, and mainliners, hustlers, in-betweeners, teeny-boppers and proletarian respectables on the other. As these were all West Indians living in or around St Paul's, it meant my involvement with the university in Clifton was considerably lessened. Clifton was simply a place I retired to, to change, to rest, to reflect and, most important of all, to assemble my notes.

My closest associates in the St Paul's area were all in-betweeners. As many of the in-betweeners I came to know were either full-time students or people desirous of studying something to further their careers, I was able to get to know them very quickly. My closest in-betweener friend was Sonny. Some benefits did accrue to the research as a result of having in-betweeners as close friends. For instance, because their in-betweener attitudes caused their circle of friends and acquaintances to be more varied than that of most other West Indians, by following the natural links in their personal networks I was able to meet a much wider cross-section of West Indians in a much shorter space of time than I would have been able to do otherwise.

Association with in-betweeners also brought me into closer contact with hustlers and teenyboppers, the reason for this being that most in-betweener sociability took place at night and revolved around such places as the Panorama Club, the Sea-Island Cafe, the blues dance and the Dive.

My familiarity with the street-corner crowd showed itself in different ways. Sometimes hustlers I was on speaking terms with would refer to me as 'the guy who goes around with Sonny'. Sometimes individual hustlers like Strode and Bang-Belly would joke that they saw me only at night. But I knew I was in when occasionally a hustler would turn to me and ask, 'What are you drinking, Ken?' when he was buying drinks for everyone in a group in which I was present; or when at 2 or 3 a.m. one of the regulars would come up to me and offer to drive me home to my hostel in Clifton.

Teenyboppers tended to relate to me through their interests and everyday concerns. For example, after a while some of the boys would come up to me at a blues dance and quite spontaneously discuss a new reggae tune that was newly released. From time to time I would be approached by an individual teenybopper and asked if I had seen so and so; and occasionally I would be assailed by a group of them loitering outside the Panorama Club and persuasively told to hand over anything I could afford as they were broke and needed money to go into the club.

In 'sparring' with in-betweeners, I also came to know several working families who were connected with my in-betweener friends either through kinship or through ties of friendship. These West Indians I tended to meet in their homes, in pubs, in the barber shop, at dances at the Mecca and, very occasionally, at meetings organized by mainliners. Through informal association with in-betweeners, then, I increased my knowledge of the different groups making up the West Indian community, and was able at the same time to find for myself a personal anchorage in the community at large.

Interestingly enough, this absorption in the life-style of in-betweeners spelt the end of my friendship with Segie, who wanted to keep me as his 'personal spar' and who, after his first rounds of showing me about, was doing everything in his power to keep me away from Grosvenor Road. He would warn me that I should stay away from Shanty Town, as it was too easy to get mixed up down there. This was for my own good, he would tell me, adding that his advice was based on his own experience. When Segie discovered my association with Sonny, whom he knew to be a friend of hustlers, and of my growing familiarity with the Shanty Town scene, he became very angry and in the end suggested we go our separate ways, as a continuation of our friendship would cause him to get mixed up with the guys again and that was exactly what he was running away from. Though I was to bump into Segie several times after that, our friendship stopped there, and in my published notes he does not appear at all, despite the fact that he was my very first informant in Bristol.

Living in St Paul's

I soon discovered that the view I was getting of the people of St Paul's was still mainly of their night-time activities, and that this bias showed up prominently in my notes. I decided to correct this one-sided view by moving from Clifton and taking up residence in St Paul's itself.

One day I saw a hustler friend of mine eating in the Sea-Island Café in Grosvenor Road. When I told him of my intention to move into Shanty Town, instantly he looked up at me, puzzled, then got up and walked off, shouting over his shoulder that I must be 'some sort of detective or something'. This man never spoke to me again. Strode too found it odd when I told him of my plan to move into St Paul's. He said I was a fool for wanting to leave Clifton, and that he knew many people who would give anything to change places with me. He advised me not to get 'hung up' on this place down here. My in-betweener friends, on the other hand, were most pleased with my decision to take up residence in the 'ghetto', as they were so fond of terming St Paul's.

Ignoring Strode's admonition and encouraged by the response of my in-betweener mates, I rented a room in St Paul's. I managed to find accommodation in a house owned and occupied by students – all English – from the university. The house was only a stone's-throw from the Grosvenor Road shopping street.

Living in St Paul's had obvious advantages. First of all my status in the eyes of the local inhabitants changed rapidly from that of an outsider (albeit an accepted one) to that of a bona fide insider. As I did not have the usual nine-to-five routine and was always seen drifting around with Sonny, who was always out of work, other non-workers tended to see me as one of them. They would talk to me about work, 'slave labour' and white employers, as if I was exactly like them and shared their point of view. Gambling, the police, music, 'white people', 'black people' and their own personal life-histories were other topics the men freely discussed with me as if there was no difference whatsoever between them and me.

Through closeness with hustlers, I got to know some of their women rather well – a possibility I had completely ruled out at the beginning of the project. Much of the information I gathered on the women, however, came to me only indirectly through quarrels and fights and slanging matches between the girls and their men which took place in my presence. Hustlers and prostitutes live out their lives as if they have nothing to hide, and public defamation of each other's character is a common form of personal retaliation whenever there is a clash of any kind. One sign of my insider status was that quite often a girl or a hustler would come up to me and divulge the details of a disagreement he or she was having with a mate. Without any prompting from me, they would divulge how the disagreement started, examples of previous clashes, why the transgressor was like he was, a whole list of past wrong-doings he was guilty of, and how he or she proposed to handle the situation caused by the present disagreement. Sometimes too, I would be asked my opinion, or even why I was so obviously different from most of the people around. Information divulged in this way could be on any matter, ranging all the way from jealousy or double-crossing to criminality or sex. For me such slanging matches and casting of aspersions always proved a windfall of information, although many of the personal details divulged in this way were often already common knowledge in Shanty Town.

Living in Shanty Town was, however, not without its difficulties. The difficulties I felt most were strains arising out of social and educational differences between myself and my informants; and role strain generated by my double role in which I was being a *real* participant at the same time as I was a *research* participant.

In matters of speech and clothing styles, etc, I managed to adapt quite successfully to the style of the particular group I was interacting with at any given time, but I found that whenever my education manifested itself, it functioned as a barrier between my informants and me. As I was never at ease with the obvious educational advantages I had over other West Indians in Shanty Town, this was one aspect of myself I was constantly under-communicating about. Of course, my university background was never a hindrance when I was interacting with mainliners. They all accepted that I was a sociologist and even showed an active interest in my research. With saints and proletarian respectables, the situation was somewhat different. They accepted the educational differences between myself and them and were not embarrassed in showing their pride in having me as a member of their church or as a visitor in their homes. What puzzled them no end, however, was why I had chosen to be a sociologist and not a doctor or a lawyer. They did not understand what sociology was all about, and were not interested in finding out. Although this indifference to my profession helped me in the sense that I was seldom required to explain my research role even when people were told I was engaged in research in the area, I could not from time to time help but feel alienated and depressed from a sense of somehow failing to measure up in the eyes of some saints and proletarian respectables.

On the whole, I was just simply regarded as a 'spar' among hustlers and teenyboppers. Occasionally, though, one of them would get to know from my in-betweener friends that I was 'from the university'. When this happened the particular hustler or teenybopper's attitude to me would suddenly change, and change for the worse. They would cease to be natural with me. Either they would remain silent and just listen, or they would show an exaggerated respect for me by avoiding me altogether, or they would be over-cautious in whatever they said in front of me, the assumption being that as an 'educated man' I was 'studying' them. I discovered later, too, near the end of my stay in Shanty Town, that many thought it odd that I kept so quiet about my educational attainments and did not use them to exploit the situation with women, or flaunt them with a view to being singled out for special treatment. These subjective reactions to me as an individual did not muddle my perception in any way. Instead, they deepened my understanding of the behaviour of the participants and opened my eyes to some of the underlying pressures that motivated them.

Paradoxically, the most troubling situations were in my reltions with my own in-betweener friendship group. The problem here was not one of precarious rapport; rather it was one of over-acceptance and a too-total identification with the behaviour and ideology of the group. For instance, in-betweeners never questioned my role as sociologist and researcher; rather it was applauded and was seen as a means through which I could draw attention to the grievances of black people. The problem was that it was impossible to remain a mere observer among in-betweeners. Increasingly, I had no choice but to abdicate my role as researcher and become a real participant. As I shared many similar interests with in-betweeners, I found real participation with them most enjoyable. Very often, too, I was the principal actor in interaction with them. The trouble was that this kind of involved participation was time-consuming, as I found it difficult in in-betweener gatherings to steer conversations along the lines of my research interests. In order not to spoil the rapport I would always submit to the pressures of the group. Consequently when I sat down to write my notes I would find that I was the main speaker and the principal actor. It was tedious taking down notes which were all about oneself. This over-absorption in the peer-group life of in-betweeners was more typical of my first months in Shanty Town, when I was first getting to know in-betweeners. I had not yet come to see them as different from myself (in some ways). Indeed, I was not even aware yet that they constituted a separate life-style in the community.

I first became conscious of my relationship with in-betweeners, and the separateness of their life-style in relation to other groupings in the community, when people began to refer to the in-betweener men I went around with as 'my Black Power friends'. My private reaction was one of shock and panic when I realized the situation I was caught up in. Shock, because I quite honestly did not have any idea that we had this image in the community, and panic, because as an investigator of life-styles I wanted to remain on good terms with people from as many life-styles as possible, and was afraid my Black Power image would alienate me from those sections of the community hostile to such manifestations. I then began to look at myself afresh in relation to in-betweeners, and it was in this re-examination that I discovered the in-betweener role pattern, and how it was related to the marginality of my own position in the community as a researcher. After this discovery I became a much sharper observer of in-betweener activities. But the price I paid for eternal vigilance was that I was never so completely at ease with them again, as I could never again completely shed my observer role. I was just as much an analyst of my own behaviour with them as I was of theirs. This does not mean that my earlier experiences with in-betweeners were too subjective to be of any research value; on the contrary, by being able to compare the deep subjectivity of the first phase with my now more analytical perceptions – now that I was conscious of our influence on each other – I was able to arrive at a richer and more thorough understanding of the in-betweener subgroup. This was just one example of the many ways in which I was able to make objective use of my subjective experiences in the field.

Other Data-gathering Techniques Used

Although participant observation was my main method of approach in this study, other data-gathering techniques were used to supplement and reinforce it. For instance, a very limited use was made of data published in books, of parliamentary papers and monographs, to orient the study historically and in particular to demonstrate that West Indians face a double problem of poverty and identity-confusion due to imperialism, and that their slave heritage was of paramount importance in determining the variations in their reactions to discrimination in Britain.

In addition, quite a lot of factual information was gleaned from back-dated copies of the *Bristol Evening Post* and official documents published by the Bristol city corporation, which were useful in providing background information on the local situation. Articles published in the *Evening Post* also yielded valuable information on the Bristol omnibus dispute of 1963.

To fill in gaps in the data gathered through pure observation, as well as to augment the biographical details of some of my informants – especially teenyboppers – it was necessary also to pay several visits to the offices of local probation officers, who allowed me access to their files. I also used a tape-recorder to good effect. Formally and informally I interviewed a wide range of people including hustlers, teenyboppers, social workers, one headmaster and one teacher, and some West Indian parents.

During the field-work one of my informants – a hustler – was an inmate of Horfield prison, serving a six-month prison sentence for shoplifting. I listened to his case in court, and also visited him at Horfield, with Sonny, during his term of imprisonment.

Understanding of local problems was greatly increased by participation in many social and political organizations in the St Paul's area, as well as by sitting on official committees set up by liberal welfare agencies functioning on a community level. Several happy weekends were also spent at week-end camps with mixed groups of youngsters from the St Paul's area, and while studying the church I paid several visits to more than one white Pentecostalist church in the St Paul's district.

A word about note-taking. As stated already, a vast amount of the data used in the study was obtained through the use of a tape-recorder. However, for most of the documentary and descriptive material, including verbatim remarks and speeches made by people in different situations, I had to rely heavily on memory. My method was to write down these observations as soon as possible after hearing or observing them. The rule of thumb I constantly exercised was to record them while they were still fresh in my mind, generally the same day. It was my practice never to record anything, especially conversations, after three days. I believe most of the information I recorded in this way was fairly accurate, if not accurate word for word, accurate in tone, flavour and in the emotions expressed. In the technique of writing down conversations and descriptions of scenes afterwards, it is surprising how efficient one's memory can become with practice, though in fact the task is a very arduous one. This is a technique that has been used by anthropologists such as Herbert Gans and Ulf Hannerz in their study of low-income communities in America.

In sum, this thesis can be regarded as an ethnography of the variable pattern of working-class responses that typify a black West Indian community reacting to its disadvantaged position in a white capitalist society, with some attempt to give a structural analysis and an interpretation based on the motives, emotions and understandings of the actors involved.

I have not, however, abandoned myself to a wanton and purely empiricist phenomenology. Against the backdrop of a broad macro-analysis, I have tried to impose order on the complexity of the data by formulating the key concept of the two 'life-orientations' which circumscribe the limits of a micro-analytical model in terms of which the life-styles may be adequately and meaningfully understood. As an ethnography, the study reports on the everyday interests and evaluations of West Indians, freely expressed in real-life situations and conversations. Furthermore, it presents this information impressionistically rather than in the form of precise, controlled, quantitative data easily amenable to statistical analysis.

A study such as this one has its drawbacks from the point of view of hard science. To name some: the selection of the hypotheses explored was guided by my own biases; I freely use quasi-statistical terms such as 'most', 'many', 'the majority of', when in fact the actual number of people on which these generalizations are based is a mere fraction compared with the total number[2] making up the community; and the evidence presented is plausible and illustrative rather than documentary or systematic.

A further problem arising out of the built-in limitations of the participant observation technique is that as a male researcher I had only limited access to the women in the West Indian community for research purposes. This is a problem that should be easily appreciated. Moreover, as in any working-class community there is a tendency for males and females in all age groups to associate in single-sex peer groups. I encountered these problems, to some extent, in researching in-betweeners, saints, proletarian respectables and mainliners. To correct the masculine bias of the research, then, what is needed is a female researcher investigating issues that involve the West Indian female population *per se*.

To these deficiencies in the work I readily admit. Yet I would still stand firmly behind the method and the main findings. Limitations they are, but such limitations are unavoidable in any qualitative study using the participant observation method. Participant observation permits the researcher to understand the problems of a group in a way that no other method will.

As far as the validity of the findings is concerned, any misgivings should be allayed by the fact that the study in its present form is no more than a very general and exploratory analysis, providing a view of broad patterns of behaviour not hitherto touched on in race relations studies in Britain. What I think I have achieved is a preliminary study of low-level empirical generalizations which, because they are framed analytically in ideal-typical terms, can be subjected to verification or proof by more rigorous methods of analysis and which provide a foundation for more systematic theorizing on race relations.

Notes

1. Ulf Hannerz, *Soulside – Inquiries into Ghetto Culture and Community*, N.Y. and London, Columbus University Press, 1969.
2. The West Indian population of Bristol was estimated at 8,000 in 1963. See John Morgan, 'Colour bar, Bristol fashion', *New Statesman*, 10 May 1963.

40

'Like that Desmond Morris?'

Gary Armstrong

In an attempt to redress gaps in our knowledge this study attempted a specific anthropological case study of a group of football hooligans. These were supporters of Sheffield United FC, nicknamed 'The Blades' due to their being founded by cutlers of the city's renowned steel industry. Borrowing this nickname all supporters of the club and also the Hooligan Element call themselves and each other Blades. For clarity I used this title when referring to the hooligans, and 'Unitedites' when referring to club supporters. Blades know they are hooligans, but do not refer to themselves or others by this term except in jest and ridicule. Instead they are into 'It' and their opponents are 'them' – better known as 'their boys' if from another town or city and 'the Pigs' when they are supporters of city rival Sheffield Wednesday, whose fans adopted the nickname of 'the Owls'. Against both opposition teams the Blades play an elaborate 'game'. Each week can bring a win, loss, or a draw. Blades are forever in pursuit of 'a good result'; this, however, can change with the opposition and the time of day. Whilst when facing Their Boys the match day provides the venue, when the opposition are fans of Sheffield Wednesday the venue is more flexible. When discussing them Blades prefer the term 'Pigs' to Owls, who in turn prefer 'Pigs' to Blades. This hostility extends beyond words and has resulted in violence since the mid-1960s, and reached an unprecedented level of frequency on the streets of the city centre at weekend nights from 1986 onwards. Two streets in particular, London Road, and West Street, each with a dozen pubs, were claimed as their 'patch' by Blades and Owls respectively.

The events which took place a few days before Christmas 1990 provided the Blades with a dishonourable defeat and a mutually recognized draw. Friday night had seen a late-night trespass by twenty Owls onto the Blades' 'patch'. However, only five Blades were around at the time; their spirited resistance left one, Bobby, concussed in hospital minus a front tooth and

Source: *Interpreting the Field: Accounts of Ethnography*, 1993, Clarendon Press, pp. 3-43.

Blades accusing the Pigs of despicable bullying. The following day United's visitors, Nottingham Forest, brought forty lads who managed to avoid the police and 'front' a few Blades after the game. Police arrived and prevented a battle as Blades ran to join their colleagues. Peacefully accompanying the Forest fans to their transport, two Blades received an admission that Forest were not claiming a 'result' because of the police. A suggestion was made that Blades arrive at a certain place in Nottingham when they played the return fixture four months later. Aware they were being followed by plain-clothes 'undercover' police (only they wore ear-muffs with collars up to conceal the ear-piece and radio wire), thirty Blades decided to have some fun. Walking in silence with definite purpose, the group took a dead-end route in the bus station then turned around and walked back. The three police continued their walk and moments later faced the brick wall, to the amusement of the group now watching and sniggering. Later, Blades were pushed and abused by police as they walked to pubs and the anthropologist was told by one of the two policemen who had followed the group at home and away for three years: 'Fuck off, Armstrong ... hangin' about wi this bleedin' shower.' The weekend events had made fascinating ethnography, had sown the seeds of retribution in two arenas, and had provided the most unequivocal advice in the six-year research period.

The question of how to research a phenomenon such as football hooliganism concerns the question of the status of fieldwork data once it is accepted that scientific enquiry does not proceed by any simple process of induction from 'facts' (Armstrong and Harris 1991). This problem is not a new one, but it seems to be in urgent need of serious discussion since it appears that some academics are convinced that analysis of any social situation is dependent on a 'correct' understanding of the macro, social structure. Consequently, data are relevant only as a source of 'apt illustration' of basic theoretical positions. Such an approach may lead to serious misunderstandings of the nature of the issue under consideration; it inevitably involves stereotyping (*ibid.*). However, if it is to be accepted that research data provide a yardstick against which hypotheses must be measured, then clearly we have to be very sure that these data are indeed not just apt illustrations; that they are collected and presented with as much objectivity as possible and in such a way as to represent as many facets as possible of the situation that is under study. This is a task that inevitably presents very severe difficulties in situations where, for whatever reason, it is hard to get satisfactory answers to all the questions that need to be asked. It is because any attempt to study the football hooligan raises all these issues that it is a task that involves a real intellectual as well as a practical challenge.

A study of football hooligans, based on 'ethnographic' information (the basis of this research), must meet three major criteria. Most crucially, it must answer a Structural-Marxist challenge that says that the British football hooligan is essentially to be understood as linked to the response of Capital to a crisis in the 'capitalist hegemony' in Britain (Taylor 1982); from this viewpoint the main significance of hooligan behaviour is political: it is both a manifestation of fascist thuggery and a means of frightening people into taking right-wing positions (see also Robins and Cohen 1978; Robins 1984). Simultaneously, the research must convince mainstream sociologists that its approach to the problem and the quality of the information it will collect will be such as to add a new dimension to those studies of football fans that do seek to base themselves primarily on empirical evidence (see Harrington 1968; Trivizas 1980; Critcher 1979; and the Leicester University research team of Dunning *et al.* 1984, 1987, 1989,1990). Thirdly, it must answer the constructs of the media and police (Phillips 1987; Appleby 1990, 1991; Home Affairs Committee 1991), not helped by pathetic claims of sociologists (see Dunning *et al.* 1990) which impose hierarchical structures and a high level of organization and conspiracy on the various hooligan gatherings. (For a challenge to this view see Armstrong and Harris 1991 and Armstrong *et al.* 1991). Research has to look beyond what some would see as common-sense assumptions.

Bearing the above in mind, I hereby declare my interests, which are in 'meaning' and 'motivation' located within a neo-Weberian perspective of *Verstehende* sociology–trying to think oneself into the situations of the people one is interested in, remembering how Evans-Pritchard (1951) stated that the anthropologist's fundamental aim was to investigate classifications, in this case the 'Hooligan'. This combined approach involves recognizing social and historical phenomena as beyond any single or simple identifying cause and trying to make sense from the social actors' viewpoint. As an end-product I attempted what Van Maanen (1988, p. 103) terms the 'impressionistic' style of ethnography, whereby the unfamiliar is presented to an audience 'seated ringside', whilst concomitantly trying to ascertain what are the actors' intentions and conscious choices within the class structure they are part of. This has been acknowledged by Leach (1954), Bordieu (1977), and Abrams, who suggests that the relationship of action and structure is 'a matter of process in time' and that such research must show the actor making decisions in complex circumstances (1982, pp. xiv–xv).

The starting-point for the analysis was what Goffman (1974, p. 564) described as ordinary, actual behaviour. Similarly Mary Douglas (1970, p. 12) stated that the only valid evidence comes from systematic observation of everyday life. Added to this was the approach Malinowski (1922, p. 18) evocatively described for researchers, who ideally should seek the 'imponderabilities of everyday life' which require detailed accounts of people over long time-periods in a variety of settings. This was for him the only way to illustrate how people handle the choices they face, and ties in with Turner's idea of 'optation' (1957, pp. 142-3), whereby an individual selects from a variety of possibilities. That said, however, the immediate problems was that Blades rarely sat round being highly articulate about the motives for their behaviour and the meanings of incidents they were involved in. Human motivation is not always easy to ascertain. We cannot always rely on the actors' explanations in these cases, so that the only course for the investigator is to try to present a 'rounded' picture of those involved so that the person may be seen in a proper context. This was the purpose of the study. It will, therefore, be asked how I got at their meanings. The answer is, by the standard techniques of good ethnographies – by watching and listening to Blades interacting with one another and with me, and by striving to make explicit to myself the common understandings which Blades as a group shared.

Social-science work on Britain is remarkably poor in good ethnography. The excellent works of Patrick (1973), Parker (1974), Gill (1977), Willis (1977), Corrigan (1979), Pryce (1979), Fielding (1981), and Hobbs (1989) stand out as unusual amidst surveys, questionnaires, interviews, and superficial impressionistic analysis. While often spoken of, participant-observation is, as Parker (1974) noted, 'rarely attempted and even less frequently successfully completed' (p. 15). This has been true particularly in the case of research into football hooliganism. Just as significant is the fact that the term has come to be a cliché without definition (cf. McCall and Simmonds 1969 and Bulmer 1982). There have been a number of studies that purport to be based on detailed observations of hooligans, but on closer inspection are not all they claim to be. So many claim to be 'doing participant-observation' when all they are doing is standing at a distance pretending to be 'with the Lads' and therefore sociologically 'Right On'.

Most previous researchers have had comparatively restricted contacts with the individual actors; indeed, some had none at all. The earliest attempt at going out amongst the research subjects came from social psychologist Peter Marsh and his team (1978a, b), who observed events on the terraces at matches, usually from the distance of the stand, at times using a video recorder to reproduce the dynamics of incidents. They also spoke to young supporters at matches and at school. However, details on the time-scale and possible problems the research may have encountered are omitted, as is any attempt to present the social background of the participants or to tell the reader how they spend most of their time when not acting as football hooligans. The book was an important work but was not followed in style by later researchers. Writing both before and after Marsh, criminologist Ian Taylor makes no mention of ever having attended a football match. His early (1971) theory is clearly not of the kind that could be based on empirical data drawn from such a milieu; his stance did not require empirical research, or for that matter historical validity. We gain the impression that Taylor attended a few games of Sheffield Wednesday, watched a few more on television, and from this research produced his theory. Researchers Pratt and Salter (1984) disappeared from the debate after one paper, which on close scrutiny did not live up to its claims of participant-observation.

Another author, heavily involved in 'Youth and Community' studies, is Dave Robins (1984; see also Robins and Cohen 1978). His attitudes, and the kind of relationships he made with the fans, are revealed in his description of a time when, in his words: 'Some eleven year old "kamikaze" Chelsea fans attacked West Ham supporters, who retaliated' (p. 15). He says he cried out, presumably in the middle of this mayhem: 'This is crazy ... over there' (p. 16), and pointed to the 'posh' seats of the director's box. Apart from raising the moral question of whether a researcher ought to try to urge violence against a particular group, what was Robins's competence in understanding his fans if he thought such words at such a time would have had the slightest effect? His own evidence showed that the teenagers he talked to seem to have been unimpressed by his attempts to get them interested in 'heroic, armed workers taking over key points in the city in the struggle for socialism' (p. 126). Again, he writes: 'I started a discussion group around the issue of "Why Football Violence?" Sitting around the tape recorder the mood was usually relaxed and sophisticated' (p. 13). Later he says: 'For the most part I avoided interviews with a more disturbed and psychopathic element in the ends. This is not for reasons of personal safety, but because I was concerned with locating the rise of soccer aggro within the experience of the main stream of working class youth' (p. 16). In saying this he is assuming what he should have set out to prove. He does not tell us how he decided who was a psychopath, or disturbed. Moreover, in using the word 'mainstream' he implies that the majority of the working class are an undifferentiated mass. Also, I would argue that, no matter how 'sophisticated' the audience, a tape-recorder is no substitute for direct observation of the actual behaviour of 'hooligans'.

The most prolific writers on the subject, and those with most funding from various concerned bodies, are the Leicester University researchers under the leadership of Eric Dunning, a sociologist. Significantly the most detailed material evidence so far presented by these sociologists is, as they note themselves, journalistic, being derived from a television documentary. This evidence was then used by them to support their position that the fans are of the lower working class—but this is surely not really an adequate basis for the construction of a theory (a fact acknowledged to me privately by the producer, but not by the sociologists). If ever there was an example of what the anthropologist Edmund Leach (1961, pp. 2-5) classified as academic 'Butterfly collecting', this was it.

Because their whole theory (see Dunning *et al.,* 1984 and 1987) is apparently based on observations at only *six* football matches, one might ask why, when they already had set out their theory on the phenomenon in earlier writings (cf. Dunning and Elias (1986)), they needed to send a researcher to any games at all. They note (1989) that a 'trained participant observer' can provide rich information of a 'more realistic kind than that to which we have been accustomed hitherto ...' (p. xiii), and that the task in regard to football hooliganism is eased considerably because of the small number of fans who fit that label, helped by knowledge of the context and situation and the sorts of fans likely to take part in such events – so far so good. Their researcher, Williams, from the accounts given in the books (1984 and 1989) went nowhere near the hooligans, while his undercover research was amongst fans whom he had never met before (or was ever to meet again), in three different countries. Whilst travelling 'undercover' with Aston Villa fans on an official supporters' club coach, stewarded by two policemen, Williams tells of 4,000 others who travelled independently to avoid such control. What 'trouble' occurred was blamed on 600 youths accused of being outsiders masquerading as Villa fans. The sociologist cannot enlighten us as to the identity of a single one of them. Later (1986) Williams attempts a more detailed analysis of these people, who are characterized by 'Rambo-like xenophobia ... anti-intellectualism and page three sexism' (p. 17), council-estate dwellers dressed like 'clones', who consider 'Paki-bashing' a sport. It is ironical that the researcher later (Dunning *et al.*, 1988) criticizes the impressionistic and sensational descriptions of the tabloid press, Later, (1990), we are presented with brief ethnography published, strangely enough, ten years after the research, which once again tells us nothing, yet conveniently fits their theories. Further afield, European researchers have not explored the participants deeply. In Belgium Waldergrave and Van Limbergen (1987) supplemented their observation with paid informants, and the Dutch academics Vanderbrug and Miejs (1988) paid fans to complete question-naires. This, then, is the state of 'participant' academic research by *the* 'experts' on the subject. In fact, in over twenty-five years of debate (and hysteria) on the subject, we have only two very good descriptive accounts of hooligan events, one by Allan (1989), a self-confessed hooligan, the other by Ward (1989) who, whilst admitting to writing a 'hooligan's-eye view' study, adds 'though I have never been a hooligan in the true sense of the word' (p. 190). However, he is being coy; the book is full of Ward-as-hooligan; all the same, his book remains a very important, informative (and good), if slightly sensational description of London hooligans and England fans travelling abroad. The only academic research which I consider com-plementary to mine are the recent (1989a, b, and 1991) Scottish studies by Richard Giulianotti. One other academic, O'Brien (unpublished thesis, 1986), has touched the fringes of the hooligans in a study which did not pretend to be a hooligan analysis, but is praiseworthy all the same.

So in total, what do we have? Marsh's thesis rests ultimately on the assumption that punches are pulled; Taylor's thesis falls unless the hooligans are fascist thugs; Robins's thesis suggests the fans are fascist fodder, dangerous unless led by the intelligentsia, but are meanwhile led by psychopaths. All that Dunning *et al.* have to say of theoretical relevance is that the lower working class (LWC) is significantly implicated in hooligan behaviour, at least as providing role models, while the media and police attribute a military structure to the groups. They all agree that the hooligans personify everything that is wrong in our society.

I had, while reading the above accounts, sufficient experience of fans to suspect that many of the ideas presented as the results of research, or at least as consistent with research, really stemmed from the assumptions and stereotypes of the writers. Because of these doubts therefore, I believed it necessary to go back to look at 'the facts' in order to decide the nature of the phenomena about which theories needed to be constructed. I proposed, before proceeding to analysis of the reasons for hooligan violence, to try to discover, in relation to a particular group, who was violent and when – and equally important, who was not violent and when. Clearly, the phenomena to be explained ought to influence the theory – and we did not know if the violence was perpetrated always by the same or different people on different occasions. We did not know whether those charged and convicted were or were not those most guilty. We knew virtually nothing about these people in other contexts.

While this is the aim of the full research (see Armstrong and Harris 1991), the specific aim of this paper is to present the conditions of possibility which produced the end-product. This aspect of research has already been debated, but little has been seen to arise from it. As Bordieu (1984) says, researchers should question the basis of their authority and the positions from which they write what they do. Others have described the omission of details about the researcher and researched as '... one of the great silences in the midst of ethnographic description itself (Pratt 1986, p. 42). These criticisms are valid. I believe, as Rabinow (1986, p. 253) has written, that the 'conditions of production of anthropology should be moved from the domain of gossip to that of knowledge'.

The purpose of my study was to look beyond mere appearances by taking Whyte's (1955) advice: 'The individual must be put back into his social setting and observed in his daily activities. In order to understand the spectacular event, it is necessary to see it in relation to the everyday pattern of life' (p. xvi). The research treated the football hooligans studied (that is, the Blades) as individuals who made their own choices within the constraints of the environment they shared. The hooligan and his activities are addressed but, at other times, the hooligan is workmate, boyfriend, brother, son, and neighbour. These relationships we knew nothing about, yet they involved basically what the fans did for the greater part of their time, when not confronting rival fans. The omission of all this presents an appalling lacunae.

While doing the study I did not feel I had to advocate any particular policy. Research was not established to look for a 'cure' for football hooliganism; it is not an illness to be cured. Besides, it is naive to believe that something as complex as the human ability to be hostile is something curable. This raises also an ethical point of academic research; as Becker (1967) asked: 'Whose side are we on?' I did not consider it my job to work as a control agent of the State. On this point I agree with Polsky (1969) when he says that he has nothing against social workers, probation officers, policemen, or anyone else trying to stop people from breaking the law: 'If a man wants to make that sort of thing his life work, I have no objection; that is his privilege. I suggest merely that he not do so in the name of sociology, criminology, or any other social science' (p. 140). Other relevant advice to researchers came from Gill (1977, p. 196), who writes how research amongst deviants must also encompass the 'normality, dignity and integrity' of the research subjects. Further, he adds that the researcher, when returned to academe, should regard the subjects as looking over his shoulder. On this issue I will be at variance with the Leicester researchers who, acting as what Baritz (1965) would call 'servants of power' and funded by both the Football Trust and government departments, have taken on the role of government (and therefore policy) advisors. Their 1989 book claims that they are the 'experts' working to 'cure' hooliganism. The implications about their role as sociologists and the debate around the privatization of law and order has, to my knowledge, not been discussed.

It would seem for the Leicester researchers that the hooligans are implicity beyond what Fichter and Kolb (1953) would call their 'moral community'. As such, the consequences of research need not worry the sociologist. I disagree; I regard the Blade 'community' as consisting of individuals who have as much right to fair representation as anyone. It may be asked, then, what use is my study.

Whether I would contribute to a greater understanding of an important social phenomenon I always doubted, but I could offer some interesting descriptions. This is significant, because as Murdock (1972) noted, colossal ethnography was anthropology's main contribution to knowledge. Even this, I considered, was more useful than theory without evidence. While describing events I pursued a Ph.D. thesis which began with my wanting to 'do something about football hooliganism'. When asked what was my 'approach' or indeed my aim in my early years, I honestly had no good idea. I took comfort in Barley's (1986) words when he stated: 'After all, most research starts off with a vague apprehension of interest in a certain area of study and rare indeed is the man who knows what his thesis is about before he has written it' (p. 12). As a result I began without a focus, yet to counteract the vagueness I decided to record everything. As Barley (1986, p. 55) correctly observed: 'When in doubt collect facts'. An 'average' Saturday would result in thirty sides of notes hand-written on A4 paper. But the vagueness was an advantage because new opportunities arose over the years – areas which I had to exploit to the full alongside the original proposals. Without a doubt the new elements – the changes in hooligan manifestations, police charges and tactics, the 'Hillsborough Tragedy', and the pronouncements of various politicians took on more significance than many of the ideas I originally had.

Publicly the personal element of a research project has usually been totally submerged by claims that the main concern is to develop theory, yet here I was beginning a study on an area of which I knew a little, but sensed that there was a lot more to know. The origins of this research may be found in the words of Corrigan (1979), who wrote, 'people's work has an effect upon the way in which they choose a research problem; but the main set of reasons for choice is to be found in the biography of the researcher' (p. 94). This is not always so; for many the subject is the 'OK' thing to comment upon (witness the dozens of so-called 'hooligan' experts who were heard in the media during the 1988 European Championships and more recently the World Cup, 1990). For this study, though, it is an applicable statement; this was a subject I had grown up with, and took place in an environment with which I was familiar. So, for this study biography is synonymous with subjectivity; this acknowledged, I hoped it could be put to creative use.

Quite when the research began is difficult to say. My earliest memories of hooliganism go back to 1968, to the local recreation ground where, in between some of the greatest games of football ever played and some of the greatest goals ever scored, I, along with dozens of others, would sit around and talk to some of the 'older lads', daunting as they were at 14 and even 16 years of age, who would tell us about fights at football matches and what it was like to be a 'skinhead' or a 'suede-head' (the youth fashions at the time). Then, a year later when I first started attending matches at Bramall Lane, I was to see at close quarters the fights on the Kop. I was terrified and remained that way until around 1973 when, realizing I was not the target for these rivals, I thought that maybe I should not worry so much.

Throughout the 1970s, the era I consider to be the peak of football hooliganism, I, together with hundreds my age, would stand at the back of the Kop thinking I was extremely 'hard', chanting. In hindsight, I must have looked ridiculous wearing a scarf tied about the wrist or hanging from the waist, complete with Doc Marten boots bought by parents who did not understand the symbolic significance of what they considered 'sensible' footwear. As soon as the fights started, most of my age-group would run like hell, watch events from a safe distance, chant, then return when the fight was over, and afterwards talk about it at school on Monday. Football and violence were synonymous. Later in the 1970s, some of my age-group actually joined in (I continued to run away). For some the excitement lasted only for one match; others stayed around for years.

Even when this adolescent excitement had passed I continued to follow 'our team', and over the years got to know many lads who were also football hooligans. Thus my association with the supporters of Sheffield United goes back over twenty years. I ran on the pitch some ten years on, to congratulate my heroes, walked three miles in snow 4.30 one Boxing Day morning to join coaches travelling to a match in London, and still harbour a desire to play for United and personally humiliate Sheffield Wednesday in a Wembley Final in front of a world-wide audience. Through following the Blades to seventy-five out of ninety-two League grounds I saw England and Wales, met hundreds of other fans, and had some of the saddest and most joyful times of my life. The team was everything, the camaraderie of the fans I have never been able to replace. Still Saturday brings one of the most anxious moments of the week: United's result first, followed by Wednesday's. A victory and defeat respectively makes my day.

In 1982, as part of an undergraduate dissertation, I combined my support for the club with research on the Blades. The research continued in 1983. Then, in early 1984 I began to immerse myself more in the personalities and events surrounding them; this continued until December 1990. From autumn 1988 I decided to reduce the previous level of intensive research based on and around the match-day, but continued to interview various individuals and tried to build up my understanding of personal backgrounds and the network of groups of mates that constituted the Blades, as well as attending matches. To help the writing-up process, for one period of four months in 1988/9 I did not attend a United match and spent my time in Holland and then London. My own reaction to this provided a kind of evidence as to fan motivation. As an unmarried postgraduate doing a thesis I found Saturdays empty; they needed occupying. I began by watching non-League football but found that was no substitute, I had to leave the whole scene alone. I began playing myself, but then got injured. Eventually I took a Saturday job; that cured my addiction somewhat but I still hung on the Radio 2 *Sports Report,* and I thought continually of the team and the lads. Saturdays will never be the same somehow.

Obviously, my own involvement had become particularly intense since 'the hooligans' had become not only 'mates' but the 'tribe' I was trying to analyse. I was involved, in a sense, even more than keen fans. I was also, of course, in a very different position from most of those, whether academic or not, who comment on 'hooligans'. Although I was never involved in football violence, studying hooligans involved me in none of the culture-shock experience by middle-class hooligan-watchers. After all, I was from the age-group of fans who did not know a football match without the possibility of a fight. Over the years I had seen many incidents at matches between fans, and football-related brawls in pubs and nightclubs between Blades and Owls. Moreover, I had walked the beat with the police during previous academic research so I had seen fights and violence in many other contexts, including fights and anti-social behaviour from students while at university. Violence understandably shocks and frightens, but you can get accustomed to seeing it. I began, because of my experiences, by being blasé about events around matches and, in the course of the research I sensed that I became more so. I was then 'at home' in the field. Because of this people may look down on the research, because as Barley (1990) noted of anthropology, one of its curious paradoxes is that to be classified as an 'expert' on a specific culture one has first to be completely ignorant of it, or what he calls 'a total foreigner' (p. 3). Yet, to have a-priori knowledge of a situation can lead to accusations of being a prior participant.

I was never a football hooligan by anybody's definition. Raised by a 'good' working-class family with parents who would like to have seen hooligans locked away for good, and preferably their son using his education to better purposes, my background is not far removed from many a Sheffield football hooligan. I grew up with hooligans, both Blades and Owls, and in the course of the study researched people I had been to school with and had known for years. Hence what I have done relates to the debate on the role of participant-observation (P.O.), and in this paper I have to confront my special position as someone of a similar culture to those under study, and one who, having some of the same advantages and disadvantages, was particularly well placed to become a participant in the phenomena observed, but instead chose Higher Education (an option a few football hooligans take, but not many), and later returned to study the events and people.

In the Field

The life of the anthropologist is full of incongruities: one day a seminar in academe, next day a mud hut in Africa or, in my case, a pub full of hooligans. Obviously I was to 'hang-out' with the Blades, go where they went and, to a considerable degree, do what they did. The presence of a researcher can be an enormous problem in itself, and how to behave in such a milieu certainly is. Quite simply, how does one conduct oneself when being a participant-observer with football hooligans? The previous research on football violence was of no help whatsoever. I was to be an observer, but as Punch (1979) has written: 'The complete observer role is a fiction, because he or she is always part of the situation and because distancing oneself may destroy precisely what one wishes to observe. Ineluctably, the researcher is drawn into some participation and must decide for himself where the border of legitimacy lies' (p. 6). From the beginning I decided to make myself and the nature of my research known, like Bulmer (1982, p. 219), believing that covert participation was a violation of the rights of the individuals being recorded. I did not 'infiltrate' therefore, and was not covert in my research. Had I taken this latter course I would, over time, have been found out, 'sussed', and possibly questioned or challenged as to my commitment to the Blades; or had I avoided that, I would have been the subject of ridicule and gossip as a member who went to matches and never got involved in confrontations, someone who thinks he's 'one of the boys' but isn't.

The Blades, like probably any social group which is the object of a social inquiry, found my position curious and at times difficult to comprehend. In the early part of the research a couple of the younger Blades, when I explained my position, thought it a wonderful excuse to 'steam into' people and then, if arrested, a great alibi as a way out of being charged. One of the older Blades, meeting me in a pub on Christmas Eve dinner-time, introduced me to his mate as 'a psychoanalyst' who was writing a book about the Blades. Others saw my role as completely humorous, cracking jokes about how I was a 'social worker' and how if they were arrested and put on probation, they could call and have a chat with me. Those who knew me well would describe me to more peripheral Blades as 'him whose doin t'book'. Blades and others aware of the study, having watched television and read popular daily newspapers, asked if my role was '... like that Desmond Morris?' It was difficult to reply yes or no to this.

Being open, then, gave me an honorary status as an acknowledged observer. This made it acceptable for me to move easily from one group to another at matches and on board coaches and, when in pubs, to join in many conversations with many groups. I also wanted to find out what their jobs were, their backgrounds, and to listen to words said in one context which could have a very different meaning in others. I was to learn how Blades changed their jobs, and how a job-title can often mean little with regard to the individual personality. Blades would suffer me going among several groups, realizing that I had a job to do, and would laugh as I 'popped up everywhere' asking questions. The fact that 'new faces' were always appearing meant that I had to be ever alert for new formations and networks and try to locate individuals I had never seen before. I tried to talk to newcomers, at times sacrificing time I could have used with Blades I had known a long time and whose company I would have enjoyed more. Had I not been open, such behaviour could have been seen as extremely insulting and ignorant.

While enjoying research I also valued full health, so that as a participant-observer when the 'action' came along the pressures on me were twofold. First, I was not to let Blades down – I decided to run away only if they did. Blades did not tell me to do this, it just had to be done. Conversely, if they 'stood' or chased rivals, so would I. Fortunately, the ephemeral nature of confrontations did not make for, or even allow, many crucial decisions. If I chased rivals I never caught one. When chased myself, no one caught me. On another level I did not want my presence to be one which encouraged further confrontation with rival fans in a 'stand-off. So I adopted a policy that when there were encounters, I would stay as near to the middle of the group as possible. At the same time I would try to keep my hands in my pockets, but if rivals came towards me I would pull out my hands as a gesture of willingness to confront them. Over the years I had cause to make physical contact only twice. Both were rather feeble attempts at punching, and totally in character with my ability as a fighter. In turn, only once was I assaulted – this was nothing to do with a football match but was part of the Blade-Owl vendetta. A thick lip for Christmas 1985 was punishment for being caught in the wrong place – a night-club in the wrong company, that is, with a 'wanted man' Blade by three Owls. Such research is not for everybody. When bottles were thrown in pubs and forty rivals ran towards me and five Blades, I saw for the first time the advantages of armchair sociology.

Back Home

Being Sheffield-born and a United fan, this was never going to be the wondrous journey of a middle-class student researching into the exotic (and violent) working class. I sought to be detached, but I was able to bring to the research a degree of reflexivity. The task of a reseacher must always be to 'fit in' and act as naturally as possible.

This I found no problem in doing. I had what Bordieu (1984, p. 2) has called 'cultural competence' to participate with this gathering. It is, perhaps, 'not done' in academia to say so, but when researching with groups of people, the primary aim is to be both known and popular. When these two elements are combined, people talk to you. The researcher need not as a consequence 'go native' or achieve 'over-rapport'. The research subject knows that the researcher is different, recognizes that distinction, and reacts accordingly. The Blades knew the nature of the study and, I think, recognized its significance and realized what things would have interested me. When I missed something many would tell me: 'You'd have loved it ...' or: 'It'd 'ave been reyt interesting for t'book'. At the same time I experienced emotions that had I not done such research I would never have known: being chased by a hundred rivals in a strange city; dodging bottles and glasses in pubs; the exhilaration of a successful 'stand' in the face of the 'enemy'; the chasing of numerically larger rivals; and the pride in 'posing', complete with police escort, in some city-centre 150 miles from home. Being 'there', though, could pose problems.

The most crucial element of the observations was the ability to locate myself near violence without participating in it. I needed to see what was happening, believing that if we want to understand violent behaviour we must be prepared to get close to incidents. As Coser (1956, p. 52) has stated, in studying conflict the researcher must be able to look at the 'exclusive values as divergent interests which the contenders pursue'. I felt it was important to know if some led the violence, if some were always or never violent, and whether perhaps it was a subject for boasts and lies. The most important quality, after the ability to locate oneself without imposing, is quite simply the ability to mix and mingle with a variety of people. As Whyte (1984) noted, 'a great deal of what is important to observe is unspoken' (p. 83). Perhaps like Parker (1974), my acceptance was due to a combination of similar character attributes: I too was 'amongst other things, boozy, suitably dressed and ungroomed, playing football well enough to survive and badly enough to be funny. "Knowing the score" about theft behaviour and sexual exploits' (p. 11). Being of similar age and appearance to many Blades, in Sheffield terms I 'looked the part', not that there was any risk of ostracism based on fashion. What to wear was not as important as what not to do when socializing in the pub and nightclub. I knew how to drink, when and what to talk about, when to say the appropriate thing and, more importantly, when to say nothing. I could converse on the same level as those being observed, the banter was second nature. I could interact without calling attention to myself, thus remaining an unobtrusive part of the scene. If Blades did something which offended my personal morality I did not show disapproval but could, if disagreeing with actions, make statements implying my point of view or joke about events and, in a sense, 'laugh it off'–the typical way amongst the Blades; at other times, as Hobbs (1988) noted, judgement has to be suspended.

For the vast majority of the time I was simply part of the scenery or just one of the Blades, a situation which brought with it the problems of familiarity and detachment. As Whyte (1955) has written: 'Whenever life flowed so smoothly that I was taking it for granted, I had to try to get outside of my participating self and struggle again to explain the things that seemed obvious' (p. 357). Like many other researchers on other projects I enjoyed the company of those researched so much that at times I felt guilty that I was not being more academic in approach. At time I laughed so much I almost cried; I was more than once the worse for drink; and spent one match acting as one of the match sponsors after a slightly drunken confidence trick with Andy, who bluffed his way past the commissionaire and we thus enjoyed free stand tickets and buffet and bar. At times I enjoyed the company I was in endlessly; at other times I was very frightened, and wondered why I was doing such a study. As Leach (1961) truthfully stated, field-work is 'an extremely personal and traumatic kind of experience'. Research into football hooliganism became more than a job; for years it was almost a way of life.

Alongside these feelings came questions which could not be answered: how could I like lads who threw glasses and kicked and punched rivals, who (once) made and carried petrol bombs to throw at the Owls? How could I cope with them as, in one context, violent people, yet at other times offering to put me up at their homes and arguing for my credibility and reliability to those suspicious in my absence? How could I not be the expert defence witness for all the lads I worked alongside? Frequently I knew police evidence to be incorrect, at times pure fabrication, yet what could I do? The answer was to take notes in court or avoid the court-room. On one level this aspect of the research proved the biggest dilemma: was I to become the Blades' regular most-credible defence witness, or was I never to help anyone so as to avoid this stigma. I chose the latter course, but felt very guilty that I was not returning some help for all that they had given me.

That the Blades accepted me despite this makes me grateful to them; perhaps they respected my 'difference'. I did not actively join in the fights; I did not spend much of my time when out with Blades in saying how much I disliked individual Owls. I did not boast about Owls whom I intended to punch. Like Whyte (1951, p. 304), I found those researched did not expect me to be like them. The very fact that I was doing such a study meant that I was different, and they knew it and reflected this in various statements which ranged from the serious: 'As an outsider what do you reckon to this Blade-Owl thing?', to the more joking: 'He's like us ... he just has more "deepo's" [inner thought] than we do!' My role as I saw it was to 'be there', watch, and listen carefully. If Blades considered I was one of them, or only slightly different, that was fair enough by me. In return I tried to be natural, remembering Polsky (1969) who, when writing about criminals, suggested that in studying them sociologists should neither spy nor become one of them. As Whyte (1984, p. 67) has written, the researcher has to live with himself more than worry about what other people think. I do not feel guilty about what I did. But taking Polsky's statements further, it must be stressed that within the Blades were such diverse groups and individuals that to have tried to be One of Them as defined by any standard of behaviour would have been futile, and would probably have resulted in both alienating them and receiving hostility or contempt from various factions. The task is to become accepted, while making it clear that there is a distinction between oneself and those studied. This has been better stated by Powdermaker (1966): 'The ethnographer must be intellectually poised between familiarity and strange-ness, while socially, he or she is poised between "stranger" and "friend".' Following this advice, Freilich (1970, p. 100), called himself a 'marginal native'. I saw myself in the same role, taking comfort in the words of Agar (1980, p. 456), who wrote: 'to be knowledgeable is to be capable of understanding what is going on on the basis of minimal cues', and be sensitive enough to look beyond words for what Geertz (1975) called the intentionality which distinguishes the wink from the twitch. Not all researchers are capable of this, and I suspect that some will accuse me of 'going native'. This is a problematic concept, with its anthropological origins and imperialistic overtones. I would argue that one can sympathize with the activities of those researched without becoming a practitioner of their aims and values. Also the term indicates that there are two worlds, research and reality, and that there is no overlap, obviously nonsense in this case.

Note-Pad and Pints

During six years of participant observation I was constantly involved in informal interviews with various individuals, and achieved around seventy semi-structured interviews with various Blades, all of whom I had known for at least two years. The aim was twofold: to try to locate individuals within the group networks that constituted the Blades; and to ask individuals about themselves and their backgrounds and, of course, attempt to ascertain motivation. This was the hardest and, at times, most embarrassing part of the research; some of the Blades whom I had known for years and even attended school with thought some of my questions 'daft'. One asked me why I questioned him about earlier happenings when I could answer them just as well, having been around as long as he had. I used note-pad and pen but found at times this inhibited conservation. When I put them away the conversation, (and the beer) flowed. I would then write the recollections into the early hours.

Unfortunately the week in 1987 when I began interviewing was the week when ten Chelsea fans stood trial at the Old Bailey, surrounded by massive media coverage about a 'brilliant undercover police infiltration' of their group – named appropriately, considering the later acquittal of the fans, 'Operation Own Goal'. The police operation had not really involved infiltration, but the media and police failed to see the inadequacies in their collective self-congratulations; this and further police activities posed problems. However, over the next year I continued interviewing Blades from different areas of South Yorkshire and met them wherever they chose. Some interviews were conducted in their homes, others in a café; the majority, however, were held in the evenings in a city-centre pub which had a relaxing atmosphere that allowed for private discussions and, incidentally, provided amusement for the two pub bouncers who knew what I was doing. On occasions when I was interviewing Blades in their local pubs, other drinkers (their mates) found the situation exploitable. A shout across the pub of 'Tell him I had six Chelsea fans in t'chip pan t'other night' remains in my memory.

The formal interviews I conducted proved a fascinating insight into personality clashes. Before being interviewed many asked who I had already spoken with; on hearing the different names many would single out individuals, saying: 'They'll tell you a load of crap' or suchlike. Every Blade warned me to be wary of what other people said, for each seemed to believe that if others were placed in the position of interviewee they would make nonsensical claims! For the most part I trusted the Blades' replies, although anything remotely controversial I checked (discreetly) with others. After seventy interviews I did not believe that any of them had 'sold a load of bullshit'. When Blades learned I had also spoken to a few Owls their attitude was always one of disdain. To a man, Blades told me the Owls were all total liars!

Informal occasions proved to provide for more interesting and significant ethnography than anything prearranged. As Whyte (1951, p. 510) has said, learning when in the field comes in flashes when we least expect it, and such flashes came variously in meetings with Blades while swimming, eating kebabs, sheltering from rain in the city-centre at 2.00 a.m., and attending engagement 'do's' and weddings. Other information on other hooligans came from my living for four years between three of London's rail terminals. Saturday mornings and evenings would see the movement of various northern groups of lads, sometimes pursued by or pursuing their London counterparts. My estate was a favourite haunt of many fans, providing many pubs and the odd fight. By hanging about I was able to talk with many different groups and learn a lot. Even shopping on Oxford Street in Central London one August Friday afternoon in 1990 saw my interest in shoes lost in pursuit of hooligans: why were a hundred lads sitting outside a pub outside of the football season? The answer was they were from Edinburgh, following Hibs to Millwall for a pre-season friendly. Two hours later I had a good idea of the hooligan scene in Scotland, details on how they had travelled and what they were intending to do. Only a work commitment that night prevented my taking up their invitation to go with them to the match.

At times I was to be found seeking information in the most potentially fraught of situations. One Sunday morning, when standing in a park chatting with a Blade whilst watching a local-league match, I was joined by the then-Lord Mayor of Sheffield whom I had known since childhood. On his leaving I told the Blade of his local fame; the Blade told me he had recently burgled his house (the Blade was to begin a nine-month prison sentence two months later).

'Is he o'reyt?'

The personal relationships the researcher develops are far more important than explanations of intent. As Whyte (1955, p. 300) found: 'If I was alright, then my project was alright; if I was no good, then no amount of explanation could convince them that the book was a good idea.'

This issue is related to that of the role of 'gatekeepers' of the research. Were there people whom I had to know in order to penetrate deeper into the group and its various activities? If there were, I was not fully aware of their importance but throughout just fell upon the 'right' people. In the beginning it was important that I knew Blades and had Blade mates. When the research began in 1984 I sought out two individuals, Ray and Andy, and told them about the proposed study and that I needed their help. During the previous year I had noticed that these two seemed to know Blades everywhere and would entertain all by that mimicry and wit. Both were extremely talented in these fields, in fact they were two of the funniest lads I had (and still have) ever met. They in turn had seen me at matches over the years and, both there and in city-centre pubs, would exchange, in Sheffield terms, the friendly and familiar greetings 'How do' and 'O'reyt?' They proved invaluable in the first two years of the research; both enjoyed talking for hours about 'the scene' and the personalities involved, both Blades and Owls. Being of a similar age, we had a lot in common. I learned a lot from them, as I did from many other Blades; we spoke on many subjects. If I were short of money they helped me out and I did the same when the boot was on the other foot. Both agreed that I had made the right choice in them, as individuals who knew what was happening and as 'people to be seen with'. The two were quite different personalities. Ray initially advised me on how to 'get in' with the core of the group. In September 1984, seeing me in a city-centre pub, he came over and said 'We're all gonna' Leeds in a couple o' weeks … four coaches, Pond Street, 10.00 o'clock, two hundred of us and we're gonna have 'em in their town centre. If you're serious about this study you'll be down there on one of 'em.' I often travelled on the same coach as Ray; he would then sit with me at matches and in pubs and point out Blades, giving me background information. Sometimes he would start conversations with Blades about incidents which he knew I wanted to know about, and afterwards would ask 'Did you get all that down then?' He also warned me about certain groups with whom I should 'take things slowly', and whom to be 'wary' of. During the 1985/6 season I wondered, at one point, whether Ray and I had a competition going, to see who had the latest information. On meeting he would say: 'Go on then', and we would then exchange details about the Blades which invariably corresponded. Ray finished his involvement with the Blades in the middle of 1986. He continued to attend matches though, and when I saw him he would ask me about the situation and the personalities, in effect an acknowledgement that I was 'in' and knew the score with the lads as much as he did.

Andy, although a great mate of Ray's, was very different in character. His extroverted character often had the whole pub or coach rolling about laughing at his impersonations, jokes, and impromptu singing. Opinionated and at times political in his discussions, he had a very serious side which manifested itself in his initial suspicion of me. Whereas Ray thought I was 'o'reyt' (alright), Andy thought I could be a 'copper's nark' and disliked the idea of studying people. When out drinking, away from the football crowd, he would often ask questions such as 'Are you studying us now?' – a difficult question to answer. I was picking up information, yet enjoying a social outing. At another time Andy commented: 'It's a bit spooky all this participant observation bit … we don't know how to 'tek yu.' There was no good explanation I could give. Later, after realizing that I was getting to know a lot of people, Andy made a very significant point, saying: 'It must be a big ego trip writing articles which all t'lads like to read. You love it as much as I do, you know, going to these pubs on a Saturday and everybody knowing you.' Ceasing his Blade involvement in 1986, Andy criticized me, accusing me of glorifying the subject and not addressing what he considered the correct issue, that is, the class system of Britain. Declaring he was ashamed of his past involvement, he said he did not want to be in the end-product and he later accused me of 'using' him and all the Blades. In 1986, after an incident in Cambridge town-centre, I was asked loudly in the pub the following Saturday by a Blade if I was there. Before I could answer Andy heard and jumped in, saying: 'you can guarantee he was there, standing in a shop doorway with his notebook.' A recognition, perhaps, that as Humphreys (1970) has said, the role of voyeur 'is a role superbly suited for sociologists' (p. 28). Andy's accusation is valid; participant-observation will always mean the researchers 'using' their contacts. In return, it is hoped that the end-product will in some sense be my gift: to present the reality of the Blades in contrast to the uninformed opinions surrounding them. I hope this is compensation for my 'using' them.

I continued the research for another four years, and while the relationship with Ray remained the same, that with Andy suffered; however, other individuals took their places. There was never one particular informant; rather, there were many Blades I could ring up and meet at any time, who were part of the core and would always welcome a beer and a chat about 'It', or tell me who I 'ought to 'ave a word wi' '. In the later years five Blades, Taff, Nick, Gordon, Joss, and Jim, all 'core' members, became close confidants and argued my position with those suspicious of me when I was not present. My biggest regret of the study was not being able to have Ray and Andy as great mates. They were research subjects, and to this day I regret we could not surmount that barrier.

Perhaps alone amongst researchers on this subject, I do not mind admitting that some of my 'hooligan subjects' became and remain good and valued friends. Parker (1974) achieved similar familiarity with his 'boys' and I totally support his sentiments when he writes: 'To some, talking about friendship in relation to social research may seem misplaced. Perhaps to those who have attempted a depth-participant observation study such sentiments will seem less irrelevant. All I can say is that *this* study would not have survived without that reciprocity' (p. 16). The journalistic technique of 'Hit and Run' is not confined to the tabloids, but exists too in sociology departments of academe; defenders of it might call it 'objectivity'.

Hanging About

A Sheffield background was vital for taking part in the chat and gossip which took up a major part of the time when Blades met together. Since the late

1970s I had become familiar with the city-centre night-clubs and pub 'scene' and the personalities who frequented them. When I was out with Blades I could add my anecdotes and observations to the chat. This is important, as Marcus and Fisher (1976, p. 31) noted: 'Empathy can be a useful aid, but communication depends upon an exchange.' Such knowledge was particularly crucial when Blades got on their favourite subject, the Owls. I knew and had known many Owls for years, some personally, others by sight or name—hence listening to the gossip I knew who was being spoken about and the places where they were seen. Simply by 'hanging around' the city-centre, I was also able to recognize Blades away from the match and compare an individual's behaviour in different contexts: the hooligans around the match versus the same lads out with girl-friends buying Christmas presents, and later when they were watching the match with their toddlers on their knees. To enhance this aspect of the research, I trained with a football team consisting of Blades and spent winter Sunday mornings watching another similar team. Sheffield has an amazing information network based on 'the lads'. Frequently I had information about fights the previous night given to me while watching Sunday matches. Another time of note was one Christmas Day in the pub at lunch-time, as a Blade and Owl argued over which side had run away the previous lunch-time in the annual city-centre Blade-Owl 'set-to'. This was rather an unfestive subject and probably un-Christian, considering that all of us had just left 11.00 a.m. Mass.

From these arenas and from the city-centre pubs and night-clubs I made many contacts and picked up as much, if not more, information than I would on a match day. At times, with prior knowledge based on experience, I visited city-centre pubs with the specific intention of meeting groups of Blades. At other times I was with other mates from Sheffield who were not part of the football 'scene'. Only later in the research did I appreciate the value of the latter when rumours abounded about me as undercover policeman. At this point some non-football mates 'put a word in' about my legitimacy to Blades they knew either from work, playing football with them, or from living in the same neighbourhood. The references I received from them would, of course, be taken back, told to other Blades, and the suspicion would then end. How anyone from outside Sheffield, considerably older than myself or speaking with what would be considered, a 'posh' accent, would have managed I do not know. I think the research would have been impossible or, at best, superficial. While a few Blades might well have agreed to give interviews, these would not even have scratched the surface of events.

Because the culture, surroundings, and people researched were not alien or exotic to me, my work cannot be everyone's idea of a classical anthropological ethnography. It could be said that, being familiar with the scene and the participants, I may have been insensitive to some aspects of the research which might well have struck, perhaps shocked, a stranger or a complete outsider. This I have to accept as a possible weakness, yet I have been fastidious in recording the most violent incidents to show readers that I am not 'covering up' for anyone. All the same, I believe that while I have

never been 'in' the hooligan element I had, in a sense, left the Blade scene
that I knew years previously only to return somewhat changed, and with the
ability to see things objectively. A year abroad in 1979/80 followed by three
years at university in London opened new horizons. A combination of seeing
things differently and the knowledge provided by a university education gave
me a general disenchantment with accounts of football hooliganism, and
convinced me that I should put my previous knowledge on this topic to better
use. Like any social researcher, I had to distance myself in order to look at the
events and people I was studying. For two years this was facilitated by my
working and living outside of Sheffield. Over the years an average of three
days a week were spent in the city, but living away allowed me to give the
subject a sense of proportion and a chance to evaluate the material I was
working with more objectively. Like Hobbs (1989, p. 15), I avoided going
native by going academic.

One aspect of this involved a constant exercise in self-denial. Stolen goods
were not uncommon and at times I was considered an ideal market. I was
offered football boots, T-shirts, and wrist-watches. 'I've got a lovely watch for
you Gary ... just something you'd need in your line o' work ... fifteen
pounds.' It was a bargain. I refused all 'bargains' with a joke. Travelling to
away matches on a coach I took the newspapers I always read, the *Guardian*
or the *Independent*. None of the Blades laughed, none of them cared, a few had
their own copies, others asked to read. I wore what clothes I felt the season
required, choice was not made to gain acceptance, nor to achieve anonymity
for covert participation (for more discussion on research and clothing, see
Liebow 1967; Patrick 1973; Parker 1974; Hobbs 1989). However, a conscious
decision to dress differently *was* made for a couple of 'big' matches when I
knew that trouble was likely and I would probably be in the thick of it. This
was more to keep the police at bay rather than rival fans, and it worked.
Once, after a confrontation between rival fans, two mounted police galloped
into the Blades, lashing out with large truncheons. Trapped against a wall I
saw the officer raise his truncheon, only to stop short of hitting me. I sensed
he found my sports jacket and the rolled-up copy of the *Guardian* not quite
the 'stuff' that hooligans were made of, and probably thought me an innocent,
liberal bystander caught up in events, and I was told to walk away. This
could, however, work the other way. Before another match, after a fight
outside a pub in a town-centre, twenty officers arrived and escorted the thirty
Blades to the ground. A PC decided that I was 'shifty looking' wearing a
sports jacket and a long trench coat. He warned me: 'If there's any trouble
today, I'm holding you responsible and you're nicked.' The PC stayed on my
shoulder, staring continuously at me. If I turned towards him he accused me
of being the 'ringleader', threatening me with: 'Don't pillock me', and adding:
'I'll fucking pull you and hammer you.' I was allowed to enter the ground on
condition I did not go into the visiting fans' enclosure. I had to conform and
spent the whole match alone, still receiving occasional glances from the
officer.

The Research Tools

The only research items I ever carried when with the Blades were a small note-pad and a small 'bookmaker's'-type pen, which could fit in the pocket of any garment. A camera was out of the question, and when interviewing only a note-pad and pen were used. A tape-recorder would inhibit some, while others were horrified by the idea of what could be seen as self-incrimination in the light of police activity at the time the interviews were conducted. Hence the most essential elements of this research, as in all research, is the researcher himself and his ability to be at the centre of events and see what is happening. To me this involved thinking ahead to what might possibly happen, and then deciding on a strategic position to listen and observe – the pub, the coach, the ground, or on the streets. For years I was a presence amongst the Blades and, throughout those years, I do not consider my presence affected a single incident nor any views held; mainly because I never saw it as my job to be a missionary against types of behaviour or to act as a moral example to others. In this field the method complemented that of Hobbs (1989), who explains: 'When contentious issues were being discussed, a compromise was reached and I often kept my mouth shut in favour of acquiring information that I considered to be more important than the sound of my own voice' (p. 11). The question that some will ask is, why did I take this stance? The answer is twofold: there was nothing to be gained from such a display of personal arrogance, and P.O. is pervaded by pragmatism.

In such a milieu personal values may have to be submerged. In effect, I had to agree with Hobbs (1988), who found that research: 'necessitated total flexibility on by behalf, and a willingness to abide by the ethics of the research culture and not the normal ethical constraints of sociological research'. (p. 7). Or to quote Bruyn (1966), the participant-observer should be 'interested in people as they are, not as he thinks they ought to be according to some standard of his own'. At the same time I do not take the position that each field-worker should be his or her own moralist. There is more to dilemmas than just the individual psyche, and research is fraught with guilts.

Because I had been around for many years with the Blades my face was familiar. Most of the time when a confrontation was likely, I was considered part of the Blades and counted in when various individuals were assessing the relative strengths of the group, with comments such as: 'Come on, we've got a good twenty here, a few old lads, we can have a go.' I counted fifteen occasions when, in confrontations, Blades at my side said to me: 'Come on Gary, let's "steam" these over 'ere', or 'let's get together and run in'. One match day in a rival town-centre talking to two local girls, one of the Blades I was with, whom I had known for three years, said to them, 'I'm a hooligan', and then pointing to me said, 'and he used to be one'. Others would laugh about how they remembered me years earlier 'whacking kids' at matches. I had no knowledge of such incidents. Normally, however, there was no pressure on me either to 'steam' or thump anybody, mainly because there was no one with the authority to demand or enforce such behaviour. Besides, over the years perhaps 50 per cent of the Blades who travelled on the coaches never got round to assaulting anyone. Significantly, though, while sitting in a pub late at night after Blades had chased Owl's all around the city-centre after a benefit match between the teams, one of the core looked at me and said: 'You'd have been as sick as any of us here if t'Pigs had 'ave run t'Blades tonight.' He was correct. From this a reader may question my violent predilections, but why? Is it not obvious that any outlook one has, violent or pacific, will affect research?

There was certainly some ambiguity in my role. Because I was often out and about with the 'core' Blades confusion over my true role could arise; one would joke when I was talking to him: 'Are we talking Blade to Blade? Which head have you got on, your journalist's or your hooligan's?' Other Blades were quite curious as to why I had chosen them and not what they considered a 'big club' like West Ham, Chelsea or Leeds. Many showed great interest in the study and asked a lot of intelligent questions about my role, the aim of the research, and the end publication. They were derisive about newspaper accounts of hooliganism and, I sensed, pleased that someone was taking the trouble to study the phenomenon at close hand. In the course of the research I published two articles; these were widely passed round and read and, if nothing else, helped clarify my position as to what exactly I was up to. On the day of the first publication in May 1985, more than a hundred Blades were gathered together in a benefit night for a colleague who had died. Two copies of the article were passed round that evening. Many, having read it, expressed surprise that I was the author, telling me that they had seen me around and did not realize that I was doing the study. Two years later, while sitting in a pub, another Blade showed me this article and asked me if I had seen it. When I told him I wrote it he too was surprised, because he had known me for six months and had not realized. Blades were also my critics. Some criticized a second article, published in February 1986, because it 'made us look daft', and while some said that I should not write anything bad about the Blades, others criticized me for glorifying football violence, saying that it was through people like me and the media that football violence existed. One, a core member, was extremely perceptive and said: 'You can't win, no matter what you write. You try to be impartial and present the truth, but no matter what you do there'll always be someone who'll complain.'

When together the Blades liked nothing more than a laugh, and frequently I was the object of their humour. Some would laugh about how I 'popped up everywhere', not only on the streets but before and after matches and incidents, listening in on their conversations. Because of this, throughout the research there were endless comments from the Blades of: 'Do you want a quote from me?'; 'Have you got that down in your little book?' and: 'That's another chapter for you.' The strange thing was, they had never seen me write anything in a book. Assuming that I carried a book, when they needed paper and pencil for a card score or for writing addresses or telephone numbers, I would frequently be asked to supply them. They would then be returned with thanks.

The Copper's Nark

Throughout the course of the research opinions about me were not uniform within groups. I was neither sought after nor disliked by any one particular group; rather, opinions about me were dependent on the individual: within the same group some believed I was a police informer, or in Sheffield terms a 'coppers' nark', while at the same time mates of the same group would openly meet me and discuss in detail events both recent and from years before.

A few Blades over the years did, of course, resent my presence. A few made comments on my lack of activity when it came to trouble. For example, at a match one complained: 'You come with us, you never get into a feyt and all you do is write about it. You're just riding on our backs.' Fortunately at that point events overtook the situation: the teams came out on to the pitch and the subject was left alone. Thankfully, criticism about my lack of activity was not frequent. What was frequent and more serious, though, was the fear that I could be a police informer. The original rumour that I was one was spread by a former Blade in his early thirties and an acquaintance whom I had regularly met in London while an undergraduate. We would drink together and travel north at the weekends. In 1984 when he learned of my further research with the Blades, for reasons known only to himself he decided to tell a few of his Blade friends that I was an informer. He persisted in this until 1986. Fortunately nobody really wanted his opinion, but the belief struck a chord with one of the well-known older Blades who, after allowing me to travel to away matches on his coach for a year, decided after reading the articles I wrote to ban me on suspicion of being a coppers' nark and, even worse, a Tory. In August 1985, after the first article, he said to me: 'It's people like you have made it impossible for all of us to have a drink and a day out–everywhere we go coppers are on to us. Also it's stuff like that which winds the young lads up.' More criticism from him came shortly after another article in February 1986, when, on seeing me at a match, he said: 'I don't know why you don't change your life-style. You've fucked it with us, you're not comin' on t'coach anymore, I don't know what you're telling them, "Johnny Law" on Monday. You're just a coppers' nark.' My arguments for the study did not make much impression, being summed up as: 'It's all middle-class crap. I hope you make a lot o'money out of it.' When I told other Blades what he had said they laughed, told me not to worry about it, and dropped the subject. The Blade also forgave me over time and would drink and chat with me.

Blades told me (as people in other walks of life had) that part of the problem was that I looked like a plain-clothes policeman. For this reason the suspicion that I was a police informer stayed with me throughout the research. It was not helped, of course, by the fact that in 1984–5 I was employed by a university and later by a polytechnic conducting studies on different aspects of policing, one in Derby the other in London. I decided not to keep this aspect of my life secret from Blades even if I did not wish to expand on precise details of my work. The first accusation came in November 1984 from Ray, after a local newspaper report stated that the police had detailed knowledge of the Blades' activities. At various other times throughout the next three years I continued to come under suspicion from a number of Blades. Significantly, though, none approached, confronted, or challenged me directly to prove my credentials, but always discussed the possibility with Blades they thought knew me well. These Blades would then tell me who feared me and why, and would give advice. In late 1986 Ray told me that two Blades, whom I had known for years, had asked about me before a match in a pub, and said: 'I told them you're a Sheffield lad who's knocked about wi' t'Blades for years, and knows he'd get killed if he "narked" on anyone.' He advised me to make sure that I explained myself and the research fully when speaking to people, and then added for confidence: 'I just fall about laughing when people say that', but told me that I had to remember that not everybody knew me as well as he did. Similar advice was given to me by one of the core members in 1987, who said that one youth I approached for an interview wasn't quite sure who I was. He said: 'I told him you're sound, but you have got to learn Gary that some lads you've got to take it slowly with and maybe you should come out wi' us a bit more, have a few more drinks, then approach him.' Duly reprimanded, I did as I was told and got an interview with the lad. My questions continued but became more subtle with strangers; at the same time, to those I knew well they became more straightforward.

There was a definite correlation between media publicity of police infiltration of football groups and the Blades' suspicion of me. Ironically, though, I was always amongst groups of Blades when news of the infiltrations and arrests resulting from them broke in the papers. In August 1987, I stood with seventy Blades on the sea-front on the south coast, waiting to go to a match nearby, while all read the headlines of the popular daily papers shouting that two Chelsea fans had been sentenced to ten years' imprisonment after a successful police undercover operation. I guessed that a few had suspicions about me as we stood in the sun.

In 1987 I was told that the question of whether I was an undercover policeman or not was debated by the core of the Blades on three separate occasions over a nine-month period, while they were out drinking on Friday nights when I wasn't there. Fortunately there were only two out of the approximately twenty-five present on each occasion who decided I was not to be trusted. Later one of these said to me, in effect voicing his suspicions in front of everybody else: 'You're the only one out of us who's sensible; all t'rest of us feyt.' The other said, referring to the possibility of the group having been infiltrated by an informer: 'It couldn't be one of us, we've known each other for a long time, we've been to school together.' Despite their suspicions, it did not stop them from talking to me or drinking with me throughout the rest of the research. While I was not there to defend myself in the debates, others were, and would mysteriously cite examples of me getting into fights in the past as proof that I couldn't really be a copper. Others considered the period of my involvement to be too long to be that of a police operation; after all, they had read in the papers that other operations had only lasted for between nine and eighteen months. Others could simply say they had known me for years and knew my mates away from football.

Problems still arose though. Withdrawal from the field made some suspicious about my absence. 'Leave t'door on a jar, set alarms for six, Armstrong's gone, "Dawn Raids" comin'" was once said in jest, but I sensed there was an element of fear about it. Eventually two of the core hatched a plan to have me checked out. Both had given me interviews and had been forthcoming with details of numerous incidents. Six months later they went to elaborate lengths to check their suspicions that I was also writing for the *Sunday Times* under a false name of Bill Buford, citing an article in March 1987 and saying it was my style of writing. Knowing I had written for *New Society,* one rang the editor's secretary and, using a false name borrowed from a weekly football magazine, pretended to be a journalist who liked my work and wanted to contact me with a view to asking me to write for them. The secretary gave three addresses, none of which I lived at anymore. Later that month, on the occasion of a Blade's engagement party, the two asked the DJ to announce a message, which specified the name of the journalist who they believed I was, asking him to meet a Mr David Lipsey, (then editor of *New Society)*, outside. The two, along with others, watched my reactions; perhaps fortunately for me I did not hear the request. Later in the night, after asking me to give various addresses where I had lived in London, the two told me of their plot and, along with five others, sat and had a debate about me. Though all the worse for alcohol, they decided I was not a policeman or journalist but, they asked, could I see how worried they were? Significant here is the fact that, when doing research, 'access' and 'information' is negotiated every time the researcher meets the subjects; it never remains in suspended animation.

All were wary and, in interviews, always specified I was not to use real names. Others were worried about what would happen if the police raided my flat and stole all the information. Later in the research Blades stayed with me in London, and others I was to show around the university. Months after I finished active research amongst the Blades, two core Blades told me that if it had not been for my presence they and, they believed, dozens of others would have been arrested and charged in a dawn raid by police. They said that what other Blades failed to see at the time, but not realized, was that my presence amongst them was probably the biggest deterrent to a police raid in the whole country, since I would have been a perfect defence witness – a fact which the higher echelons of the police must have been considering when, in 1988, Scotland Yard (Territorial Operations and Policy) made a discreet enquiry to a former academic employer as to whether they thought I would act as a defence witness at a trial of football hooligans.

One of the ironies of the research was that, in the course of it, I was never actually assaulted by a rival fan at or around a match. Apart from a solitary punch from an Owl, the only other punches I received came from the police. In total I received four thumps – two by the South Yorkshire police when I had been thrown on the floor and kicked by two others. Another time I received a punch in the face as a police officer ran past me; and once again by a mounted policeman outside the grounds of a match in West Yorkshire from whom I learned that the height of a toe-cap of a police boot when in stirrups was roughly equal to my neck! I was pushed by police dozens of times and called every expletive possible by various police forces. I was arrested on one occasion in March 1987, along with thirty other Blades on board the same coach. Initially told by the police that the charge was manslaughter (a youth was unconscious in hospital, and they probably genuinely feared he might be seriously hurt, although it turned out to be nothing of the kind) and, having been photographed, forced to give personal details, and interviewed, I, along with all the others, was released without charge. The police now knew of me and the research, and this was to have repercussions in Sheffield.

For the most part of the Sheffield police, once they knew of the study, left me alone. In part this was due to my supervisor explaining to the Assistant Chief Constable and two Chief Superintendents my activities at a special meeting held at their request in 1987. For the next three years various police officers gave me knowing stares when at matches in Sheffield; two, who were to follow the fans home and away for the next three seasons, went a step further and would occasionally stand nearby looking at me, making quiet comments to one another and any other officer with them. I sensed these words were not complimentary and had my suspicions confirmed when, as explained in the opening paragraph, one advised me on both the next step of the research and his general attitude to what I was doing. Disliked by police, suspected by some of the Blades, the researcher's life can indeed seem lonely!

Why Bother?

When all is said and done, what did the study show? The old argument in social anthropology is above whether it is ideographic or nomothetic. Sometimes, however, the researcher must wonder whether it is even ideographic; that is, can we even account for the behaviour of small groups we know intimately? By 'account' I mean, explain to others the reasons for behaviour that is apparently anomalous. One of the aims of the research was to try to seek motives. This was a massive problem, not least because the amount of motivation for individuals varied over time. This results in the problem of what is the correct way to understand motivation. From a theoretical viewpoint, constructing a model of what motivates people is actually impossible, because meaning only has value in its interpretation. So what fans do and the way they act is subect to interpretation; the way you as a researcher interpret depends upon your outlook, and this should never be forgotten.

It is as well to raise the limitations of the study. First, it is about the supporters of one club only and therefore cannot be presented as a general theory of football hooliganism. Secondly, it is a specific case-study with a specific research period of six years. In years to come the Blades will contain totally different faces; perhaps they will also have totally different standards of acceptable behaviour. But at the same time I believe that prolonged study with one group had its benefits, because research continued on 'quiet days' when rivals were not perceived as worthwhile opposition, as well as on 'big days' when hundreds would look for the confrontation. By seeing the quiet moments and the busy moments, any violence could be put into context. At the same time, continuing research outside the football season, I could address the question completely neglected by previous research – what do football hooligans do in the summer months when there are no match days and, more important, the rest of the week away from football matches? Perhaps the greatest asset of ethnography is the way in which the work can challenge those studies which use statistics as 'facts'. The study was able to examine both the level and frequency of violence, the extent of organization and leadership, the degree of racist and fascist involvement, and the back-grounds of the participants. Previous research, in most respects, will not be supported by it. The Blades were in no way influenced by 'outside' fascist groups, had no 'general' or hierarchical structure, and, unlike some sociologists, could differentiate amongst their ranks and could speak of 'rough' lads both in a football and non-football context. The composition of the 'core' hooligans was not the lower working class of Sheffield. The level of violence was also far lower than observers would have us believe. Blades recognize the diversity of their membership, even if the media, police, and researchers lump them together and label them. One Blade, a year older than me, well educated, successful in his business, and one of the main hooligans said: 'You've got a difficult job trying to make sense of all this. There's so many different groups and different views. All you can do is say this is how you saw it as an outsider and this is your interpretation.' He was right, that is all I can do, and at this point it is as well to state that I do not know why some men are more violent than others and I have no grand structural theory to explain hooliganism. My role was to investigate, try to interpret, and then ask how and why. What results in the analysis is a combination of me as an individual and me as an anthropologist acting with anthropological knowledge.

I am not a mirror of the Blades; I cannot claim to represent them. I recognize that I am what Parker (1974, p. 63) calls the 'third man'. I both reconstruct the action and interpret in my writing-up my version of events. There was a reality to be represented, but there was no set mode of representing the reality I saw. It must also be remembered, as Clifford and Marcus (1986) stated, that there is no such thing as a culture which is finite; someone else doing the same job could write about different aspects of the Blades. Individuals within the Blades might see matters differently, either because they were more involved or saw events from another perspective. Every ethnography, then, is incomplete; it is only a partial truth and is no more than a statement of the rules of the study of the discourse: work has always to be done. Meanwhile I can only aim through description to present myself as what Atkinson (1990, p. 27) would call a 'credible witness', remembering, as Humphreys (1970, p. 170) has said of ethnography, that it 'is always a matter of greater or lesser misrepresentation'.

I do not condone what the Blades did, hence I have no apologies for them. The aim was to show the facts (as I saw them); the intention is that the reader will find the accounts enlightening and thought-provoking. Perhaps then, when compared with the 90 per cent of time when their behaviour is considered 'normal' and socially acceptable, the Blades' violence and occasional antisocial behaviour can be put into its correct context. In a wider framework, one could look at and examine violence such as state-controlled torture, mass murder, inter-ethnic and religious violence, genocide, and war in a world-wide context, then look at football hooliganism and see that it is just a drop in the ocean. This is my point of view, in an area where there are thousands.

While analysis will draw in references to violence and antisocial behaviour cross-culturally, perhaps the greatest help to my research was my years spent working in factories, on building-sites, teaching, and doing various other occupations in Sheffield and London while financing both the Ph.D and years of study and, not least, being a student at university and living for three years in university halls of residence. Through a combination of all these experiences and the people I met on the way, I found that football hooligans were not so greatly different from many other people in other walks of life. Far from Williams's (1986) claim of their 'anti-intellectualism' Blades had a high regard for education (but not students). Many were curious about university and polytechnic, some had ambitions to study. They were not stupid, neither were they, to borrow from Giddens (1979, p. 71), 'cultural dopes'.

I do not expect the research will change attitudes towards the phenomenon in general and the hooligans in particular. One of the more fascinating aspects of the research was the reaction it provoked. I have met hundreds of people who knew what to do with 'Them': the ex-naval captain who refused point-blank to believe his Falkland heroes could be and were, at times, football hooligans, and the Italian literature lecturer who, five feet tall, middle aged and middle class, was convinced that she was a prime target for hooligans. For this reason neither she 'nor all my friends' ever travelled in London on a Saturday afternoon. Years of research could not convince them that the hooligans were not out to get them; I had obviously got it wrong. Academics often reacted with hostility or amusement. Well, wasn't it funny? Here was someone writing about hooligans; what did I have to do on Saturdays, get drunk and beat people up? Ho ho. Previous studies I had conducted on the police (see Chatterton 1987 and Edwards and Armstrong 1988) had never received this response; the researcher is 'good' and credible and the research similar if conducted on the forces of Good in society. Study the 'baddies' and you either become one too or at least compromise yourself.

The hostility I occasionally received was a symptom of the complexity of this issue. While every good-thinking citizen disliked 'Them' and 'It' – the hooligan and hooliganism – the fact that I had been given a grant to study the phenomenon was, to many people, a waste of public money. If I were a television war reporter than I would be doing a great job. That I was reporting on events which few people knew about did not make people think it worthwhile. I did not start events, yet everybody assumed that my job and duty was to stop them happening. When my response to questions on hooligans was not either retributive or totally condemnatory, people did not seem to understand. Rather like Pavlov's dog, the very mention of the term 'football hooligan' seemed to produce in many a dribble at the mouth.

A study of what Fielding (1982) would call an 'unloved' group whose collective activities invite total condemnation from all sections of society will raise controversial matters; perhaps the most significant one being the fact that I was in the company, and enjoyed the friendship, of a group of young men who were collectively abhorred by all; this will (and has) irritated people; arising out of this, judgement will be passed on the research and the researcher. This, though, is a by-product of the study; my main aim was to seek an 'understanding' of the fans and their behaviour, which is not necessarily to forgive but which may moderate condemnation. My task is to explain, not justify; or, to borrow from Kuper (1983, p. 204): 'the proof of our progress is that we can explain more.' For me, that justifies the research.

References

Abrams, M. (1982). *Historical Sociology* (Shepton Mallet: Open Books).

Agar, M. (1980). *Professional Stranger* (New York: Academic Press).

Allan, J. (1989). *Bloody Casuals: Diary of a Football Hooligan* (Aberdeen: Famedram).

Appleby, A. (1990). Independent Television News, 10.00 p.m., 13 March.

Appleby, A. (1991). Talk given to conference 'New Times for Football', Birkbeck College, 10 March 1991.

Armstrong, G. and Harris, R. (1991). 'Football Hooliganism: Theory and Evidence', *Sociological Review* (August).

–. Hobbs, D., and Maguire, M. (1991). 'The Professional Foul: Covert Policing in Britain the Case of Soccer', Paper given at Law and Society Annual Meeting, University of Amsterdam.

Atkinson, P. (1990). *The Ethnographic Imagination: Textual Constructions of Reality* (London: Routledge).

Baritz, L. (1965). *The Servants of Power* (New York: Wiley).

Barley, N. (1986). *The Innocent Anthropologist* (Harmondsworth: Penguin).

–. (1990). *This Native Land* (Harmondsworth: Penguin).

Becker, M. S. (1967). 'Whose Side Are We On?', 14 *Social Problems,* 239-47.

Bourdieu, P. (1977). *Outline of a Theory of Practice* (Cambridge: Cambridge University Press).

–. (1984). *Distinction: A Social Critique of the Judgement of Taste* (London: Routledge & Kegan Paul).

Bruyn, S. (1966). *The Human Perspective: The Methodology of Participant-Observation* (Englewood Cliffs, NJ: Prentice-Hall).

Bulmer, M. (1982) (ed.). *Social Research Ethics* (London: Macmillan).

Chatterton, M. (1987). 'Front Line Supervision in the British Police Service', in G. Gaskell and R. Benewick (eds.), *The Crowd in Contemporary Britain* (London: Sage).

Clifford, J. and Marcus, E. E. (1986) (eds.). *Writing Culture: The Poetics and Politics of Ethnography* (Berkeley: University of California Press).

Corrigan, P. (1979). *Schooling the Smash Street Kids* (London: Macmillan).

Coser, L. (1956). *The Function of Social Conflict* (New York: The Free Press).

Critcher, C. (1979). 'Football Since the War', in J. Clarke *et al., Working Class Culture: Studies in History and Theory* (London: Hutchinson).

Douglas, M. (1970). *Natural Symbols* (London: Crescent Press).

Dunning, E. and Elias, N. (1986). *Quest for Excitement* (Oxford: Basil Blackwell).

Dunning, E., Williams, J., and Murphy, P. (1984). *Hooligans Abroad: The Behaviour and Control of English Fans in Continental Europe* (London: Routledge & Kegan Paul).

–. (1987). *The Social Roots of Football Hooliganism* (London: Routledge & Kegan Paul).

–. (1988) 'Soccer Crowd Disorder and the Press: Processes of Amplification and Deamplification in Historical Perspective' in *Theory, Culture and Society,* Vol. 5.

–. (1989). *Hooligans Abroad* (second edn. with new introduction).

–. (1990). *Football on Trial: Spectator Violence and Development in the Football World* (London: Routledge).

Edwards, S. and Armstrong, G. (1988). 'The Game and the Job: The Street Offences Squad', *The Police Journal* (June).

Evans-Pritchard, E. E. (1951). *Social Anthropology* (London: Routledge & Kegan Paul).

Fichter, J. H. and Kolb, W. L. (1953). 'Ethical Limitations on Sociological Reporting', 18 *American Sociological Review,* 544–50.

Fielding, N. (1981). *The National Front* (London: Routledge & Kegan Paul).

–. (1982). 'Observational Research on the National Front' (in Bulmer 1982).

Freilich, M. (1970) *Marginal Natives: Anthropologists at Work* (New York: Harper and Row).

Geertz, C. (1975). 'Thick Descriptions: Towards an Interpretive Theory of Culture', in *The Interpretation of Cultures* (London: Hutchinson).

Giddens, A. (1979). *Central Problems in Social Theory: Action, Structure and Contradiction in Social Analysis* (London: Macmillan).

Gill, O. (1977). *Luke Street: Housing Policy, Conflict and the Creation of the Delinquent Area* (London: Macmillan).

Giulianotti, R. (1989*a*). *A Critical Overview of British Sociological Investigations into Soccer Hooliganism in Scotland and Britain,* Working Papers on Football Violence No. I (University of Aberdeen, Dept. of Sociology).

–. (1989*b*). *A Participant-Observation Study of Aberdeen Fans at Home and Away,* Working Papers on Football Violence No. 2 (University of Aberdeen, Dept. of Sociology).

–. (1991) 'Scotland's Tartan Army in Italy: the Case for the Carnivalesque', *Sociological Review* vol. 39, no. 3, August, pp. 503-530.

Goffman, E. (1974). *Frame Analysis* (Harmondsworth: Penguin).

Harrington, J. A. (1968). *Soccer Hooligans* (Bristol: John Wright).

Hobbs, D. (1988). *Doing the Business: Entrepreneurship, the Working Class, and Detectives in the East End of London* (Oxford: Oxford University Press).

Home Affairs Committee (1991). *Policing Football Hooliganism* (London: HMSO).

Humphreys, L. (1970). *Tearoom Trade: Impersonal Sex in Public Places* (Chicago: Aldine).

Ingham, R. (1978) (ed.). *Football Hooliganism: The Wider Context* (London: Inter-Action Inprint).

Kuper, A. (1983). *Anthropology and Anthropologists: The Modern British School* (London: Routledge & Kegan Paul).

Leach, E. (1954). *Political Systems of Highland Burma* (London: Bell).

–. (1961). *Rethinking Anthropology*, LSE Monographs on Social Anthropology No. 22 (London).

Liebow, E. (1967). *Tally's Corner* (London: Routledge & Kegan Paul).

Malinowski, B. (1922). *Argonauts of the Western Pacific* (London: Routledge & Kegan Paul).

Marcus, C. and Fisher, M. (1976). *Anthropology, a Cultural Critique* (Chicago: University of Chicago Press).

Marsh, P. (1978a). *Aggro–The Illusion of Violence* (London: Dent).

–. (1978b). 'Life and Careers on the Soccer Terraces' (in Ingham 1978).

McCall, G. J. and Simmons, J. L. (1969) (eds.). *Issues in Participant-Observation: A Text and Reader* (Reading, Mass.: Addison-Wesley).

Murdock, G. P. (1972). 'Anthropology's Mythology', *Proceedings of the Royal Anthropological Institute* (1971), 17-24.

O'Brien, T. (1986). 'Football, Violence, and Working-Class Culture', unpublished Ph.D. Thesis, Dept. of Communication Studies, Lancashire Polytechnic.

Parker, H. J. (1974). *View From the Boys: A Sociology of Downtown Adolescents* (London: David & Charles).

Patrick, J. (1973). *A Glasgow Gang Observed* (London: Eyre Methuen).

Phillips, D. (1987). 'Football Fans and The Police', in T. O'Brien (ed.), *Proceedings of the European Conference on Football Violence, Preston, Lancs.* (School of Community Studies, Faculty of Social Studies, Lancashire Polytechnic).

Polsky, N. (1969). *Hustlers, Beats and Others* (Harmondsworth: Penguin).

Powdermaker, H. (1966). *Stranger and Friend: The Way of an Anthropologist* (New York: Norton).

Pratt, J. and Salter, M. (1984). 'A Fresh Look at Football Hooliganism', 3 *Leisure Studies*, 201-30.

Pratt, M. L. (1986). 'Fieldwork in Common Places' (in Clifford and Marcus 1986).

Pryce, K. (1979). *Endless Pressure: A Study of West Indian Lifestyles in Britain* (Harmondsworth: Penguin).

Punch, M. (1979). *Policing the Inner City* (London: Macmillan).

Rabinow, P. (1986). 'Representations are Social Facts: Modernity and Post-Modernity in Anthropology' (in Clifford and Marcus 1986).

Robins, D. (1984). *We Hate Humans* (Harmondsworth: Penguin).

–. and Cohen, P. (1978). *Knuckle Sandwich: Growing up in the Working Class City* (Harmondsworth: Penguin).

Taylor, I. (1971) 'Soccer Consciousness and Soccer Hooliganism', in S. Cohen (ed), *Images of Deviance.* (Harmondsworth: Penguin).

–. (1982). 'Soccer Hooliganism Revisited', in J. Hargreaves (ed.), *Sport, Culture and Ideology* (London: Routledge & Kegan Paul).

Trivizas, E, (1980). 'Offences and Offenders in Football Crowd Disorders', 20 *British Journal of Criminology*, 276-88.

Turner, V. W. (1957). *Schism and Continuity in an African Society* (Manchester: Manchester University Press).

Vanderbrug, M. M. and Miejs, J. (1988). 'Dutch Supporters at the European

Championships in Germany', unpublished paper (Dept. of Communication Studies, University of Amsterdam).

Van Limbergen *et al.* (1987). 'Research on the Societal and Psycho-Sociological Background of Football Hooliganism', Unpublished Summary (Catholic University of Leuven, Belgium).

Van Maanen, J. (1988). *Tales of the Field: On Writing Ethnography* (Chicago: University of Chicago Press).

Ward, C. (1989). *Steaming In: Journal of a Football Fan* (London: Simon and Schuster).

Whyte, W. F. (1951). 'Observational Field Methods', in M. Jahoda, M. Deutsch, and S. Cook (eds.), *Research Methods in Social Relations,* Vol. II (New York, Holt).

–. (1955). *Street Comer Society* (Chicago: University of Chicago Press).

–. (1984). *Learning From the Field: A Guide From Experience* (Beverly Hills, Calif.: Sage).

Williams, J. (1986). 'White Riots: The English Football Fan Abroad', in A, Tomlinson and G. Whannel (eds.), *Off The Ball* (London: Pluto Press).

Willis, P. (1977). *Leaning to Labour: How Working Class Kids Get Working Class Jobs* (Farnborough: Saxon House).